# CASSIS DE DIJON

In 1979 the Court of Justice gave judgment in its now famous decision in *Cassis de Dijon*. Much loved by generations of law students and highly significant in shaping the evolution of the EU single market, this decision is a landmark case. As the judgment approaches middle age, this book revisits this decision with the benefit of hindsight: why did the Court of Justice decide *Cassis de Dijon* as it did? How has the decision been developed by the EU? And, looking forward, how has the decision been used to develop international trade? This book brings together some of the leading writers in the field of EU trade law, constitutional law and European history for a fresh examination of this ground-breaking judgment, looking at it from the perspective of its past (who, what and why); its present (is it making a difference?); and its future (how does it fit in international trade agreements, including any future UK-EU FTA?).

# Cassis de Dijon

*40 Years On*

Edited by
Albertina Albors-Llorens,
Catherine Barnard
and
Brigitte Leucht

·HART·
OXFORD · LONDON · NEW YORK · NEW DELHI · SYDNEY

HART PUBLISHING

Bloomsbury Publishing Plc

Kemp House, Chawley Park, Cumnor Hill, Oxford, OX2 9PH, UK

1385 Broadway, New York, NY 10018, USA

29 Earlsfort Terrace, Dublin 2, Ireland

HART PUBLISHING, the Hart/Stag logo, BLOOMSBURY and the Diana logo are
trademarks of Bloomsbury Publishing Plc

First published in Great Britain 2021

First published in hardback, 2021

Paperback edition, 2022

A catalogue record for this book is available from the British Library.

Library of Congress Cataloging-in-Publication data

Names: Albors-Llorens, Albertina, editor.  |  Barnard, Catherine, editor.  |  Leucht, Brigitte, editor.

Title: Cassis de Dijon : 40 years on / edited by Albertina Albors-Llorens, Catherine Barnard and Brigitte Leucht.

Description: Oxford, UK ; New York, NY : Hart Publishing, an imprint of Bloomsbury Publishing, 2021.  |
Includes bibliographical references and index.

Identifiers: LCCN 2020047642 (print)  |  LCCN 2020047643 (ebook)  |
ISBN 9781509936632 (hardback)  |  ISBN 9781509945795 (paperback)  |
ISBN 9781509936656 (pdf)  |  ISBN 9781509936649 (Epub)

Subjects: LCSH: Free trade—European Union countries.  |  Non-tariff trade barriers—Law and legislation—
European Union countries.  |  Antitrust law—European Union countries.  |  Customs administration—
Law and legislation—European Union countries.  |  Foreign trade regulation—European Union
countries.  |  European Court of Justice.  |  Treaty Establishing the European
Economic Community (1957 March 25)

Classification: LCC KJE5177 .C37 2021 (print)  |  LCC KJE5177 (ebook)  |  DDC 343.2408/7—dc23

LC record available at https://lccn.loc.gov/2020047642

LC ebook record available at https://lccn.loc.gov/2020047643

ISBN:   PB:      978-1-50994-579-5
        ePDF:    978-1-50993-665-6
        ePub:    978-1-50993-664-9

Typeset by Compuscript Ltd, Shannon

To find out more about our authors and books visit www.hartpublishing.co.uk.
Here you will find extracts, author information, details of forthcoming events
and the option to sign up for our newsletters.

# PREFACE

The decision in *Cassis de Dijon* holds a special place in the heart of any professor of EU law. The decision has the benefit of simple and appealing facts, and a (reasonably) clear judgment. It concerns a product that most of the audience know about and enjoy. It gives the professor a chance to teach about trade, constitutional law, federalism, litigation tactics, EU institutional dynamics and gastronomic appreciation. What's not to like? By any standard it is a landmark case of EU law whose effects have been felt well beyond the borders of the EU. For example, the Trans-Tasman Mutual Recognition Agreement contains a definition of mutual recognition that is 'directly derived from the EU judicial approach in *Cassis de Dijon* formulating the origin principle: "a good that may be sold in the jurisdiction of any Australian party, may be sold in New Zealand …".[1]

So the 40th birthday of *Cassis de Dijon* needed a celebration, and this we did in April 2019 when the Centre for European Legal Studies (CELS) hosted an inter-disciplinary (law/history/political science) seminar. Essentially the participants addressed three questions: First, why did the Court of Justice decide *Cassis de Dijon* as it did? Second, how has the decision been developed by the EU? Third, how has the decision been used to develop international trade? The fruitful discussions, facilitated by regular servings of *Cassis*, eventually came together in this volume.

The editors are very grateful to the participants for giving their time, their expertise and their memories. Special mention should be made of Marcus Gehring and Estelle Wolfers, both of Cambridge, who allowed us to draw on their contributions in the Introduction to this text. We are also grateful to CELS for funding the seminar and for subsequent interest in the discussions in the context of the development of mutual recognition regarding the UK's own internal market. We are particularly grateful to Hart Publishing for agreeing to publish this volume, especially Sasha Jawed, Tom Adams and Catherine Minahan, and to do so with their usual professionalism and expertise.

Albertina Albors-Llorens
Catherine Barnard
Brigitte Leucht
*June 2020*

---

[1] Available at www.oecd.org/regreform/WP2_Contribution-of-mutual-recognition-to-IRC.pdf.

# CONTENTS

# LIST OF CONTRIBUTORS

**Albertina Albors-Llorens**, Professor of EU Law, Fellow of St John's College, University of Cambridge

**Karen J Alter**, Professor of Political Science and Law, Northwestern University

**Catherine Barnard**, Professor of EU Law and Employment Law, Fellow of Trinity College, Cambridge

**Georges Baur**, Research Fellow, Dr iur, with the Liechtenstein-Institut, Bendern/Liechtenstein; former Assistant Secretary General of EFTA

**Inge Govaere**, Director of the Ghent European Law Institute (GELI), Ghent University, and Director of the European Legal Studies Department, College of Europe, Bruges

**Emilija Leinarte**, British Academy Postdoctoral Fellow, University of Cambridge

**Brigitte Leucht**, Senior Lecturer in European Studies, School of Area Studies, History, Politics & Literature at the University of Portsmouth

**Peter Oliver**, Visiting Professor at the Université Libre de Bruxelles

**Robert Schütze**, Professor of European and Comparative Law at Durham University and LUISS (Rome)

**Stephen Weatherill**, Jacques Delors Professor of European Law, Fellow of Sommerville College, Oxford

# 1

# Introduction: Why Revisit *Cassis de Dijon*?

ALBERTINA ALBORS-LLORENS, CATHERINE BARNARD
AND BRIGITTE LEUCHT

## I. Introduction

Identifying a suitable image for a book on a landmark case by the Court of Justice is challenging. The law is about rules, about principles, about the development, interpretation and contestation of ideas and concepts. The approach of the law does not lend itself to easy visualisation. But this is not quite true when it comes to *Cassis de Dijon*.[1] As generations of lawyers, political scientists and even contemporary historians can testify, this is the landmark case[2] associated with the image of a bottle: a bottle of the French blackcurrant liqueur, Cassis de Dijon.

Identifying a suitable image for *this* book, which examines the origins and legacy of the *Cassis de Dijon* case over 40 years, has nevertheless been challenging, particularly when seeking to avoid the clichéd depiction of a bottle of the French liqueur. The result of this effort is the nineteenth-century postcard on the cover of our book. The focus of this image is a map of the Département de la Côte d'or in eastern France, part of Burgundy, now the Bourgogne-Franche-Comté region, with the city of Dijon at its centre. The map is framed by local produce, including vegetables, fruit and, next to a couple of wine barrels, a bottle of Cassis. A boy on the left of the map, dressed in local attire and carrying a basket containing what looks like freshly picked grapes, further adds to the regional character of the

---

[1] Case C-120/78 *Rewe Zentral AG v Bundesmonopolverwaltung für Branntwein (Cassis de Dijon)*, ECLI:EU:C:1979:42.

[2] To support the claim that it is a landmark case, see, eg, M Maduro and L Azoulai, *The Past and Future of EU Law: The Classics of EU Law Revisited on the 50th Anniversary of the Rome Treaty* (Oxford, Hart Publishing, 2010); F Nicola and B Davies (eds), *EU Law Stories: Contextual and Critical Histories of European Jurisprudence* (Cambridge, Cambridge University Press, 2017), doi:10.1017/9781316340479; L Aran, *Landmark Cases on European Law*, available at https://eulaws.eu/?p=171; F Tarissan, Y Panagis, U Sadl, 'Selecting the cases that defined Europe: complementary metrics for a network analysis', *IEEE/ACM International Conference on Advances in Social Networks Analysis and Mining*, August 2016, San Francisco, CA, https://hal.archives-ouvertes.fr/hal-01366475/document.

image. At the same time, there is a red line around the Côte d'or, separating it from the surrounding *départements* on the map. Undoubtedly the demarcation line accentuates that the boy depicted here is part of and *belongs* to the Côte d'or area. While promoting the produce of this specific region, the image thus also addresses the issue of the boundaries of local and regional identity.[3] Indeed, French wine has long served as an expression of social relations, and as a space for negotiating changing relationships between national and regional identities.[4]

Fast forward to 1979, when our landmark case was decided. Cassis de Dijon has an alcohol content of only 15 per cent. This meant that until the Court of Justice's *Cassis de Dijon* decision, finding a breach of Article 34 of the Treaty on the Functioning of the European Union (TFEU), that beverage could not be sold in Germany, which insisted that fruit liqueurs had to have a minimum alcohol content of 25 per cent. The German Government was forced to defend its legislation on the grounds of public health – the purpose of the fixing of a minimum alcohol content was to avoid the proliferation of alcoholic beverages with a low alcohol content, which might 'more easily induce a tolerance towards alcohol than more highly alcoholic beverages'. It was a dreadful argument and one that was rightly rejected by a sceptical Court; the Court was not much more enthusiastic about the other argument raised by the German government based on the fairness of commercial transactions.

## II. What the Institutions did Next

*Cassis de Dijon* is famous for more than just this, however. The European Union (EU) law orthodoxy is that the Court created the principle of mutual recognition in *Cassis de Dijon*, but the full implications of the principle were tamed by the simultaneous development of the doctrine of mandatory requirements, now more commonly referred to as public interest requirements. Thus, with *Cassis de Dijon*, the basis for a non-absolute principle of mutual recognition was born, and this proved to be a turning point in the development of the single market.[5] This is because the decision was rapidly seized upon by the Commission, frustrated by the slow realisation of free movement of goods, in its Communication on *Cassis de Dijon*.[6] The principle of mutual recognition became the cornerstone for the EU's

---

[3] The postcard was probably produced by the Département de la Côte d'or to promote its local produce. The illustrator is unknown.

[4] M Demossier, 'Consuming wine in France: The "wandering" drinker and the *vin-anomie*' in TM Wilson (ed), *Drinking Cultures* (Oxford and New York, Berg, 2005) 129–54.

[5] See K Armstrong, 'Mutual Recognition' in C Barnard and J Scott (eds), *The Law of the Single European Market* (Oxford, Oxford University Press, 2002) 225; S Weatherill, *The Internal Market as a Legal Concept* (Oxford, Oxford University Press, 2017) 54–55.

[6] Commission Communication concerning the consequences of the judgment given by the Court of Justice on 20 February 1979 in Case 120/78 ('Cassis de Dijon') [1980] OJ C256/2. See subsequently Mutual Recognition Regulaton 764/2008 [2008] OJ L218/21.

new approach directives and its regime on qualifications and driving licences, as well as subsequently being rolled out to the area of freedom, security and justice.[7]

But the Commission's activity embracing *Cassis* was not just about legislation. As Marcus Gehring has shown, the Commission built on the decision in *Cassis* through enforcement actions. Overall, from the *Cassis de Dijon* decision in 1979 to the signature of the Single European Act seven years later, 37 cases were brought to the Court of Justice challeging infringement of the Treaty provision on free movement of goods, of which 90 per cent were lost by the defendant Member State.[8] In addition, 24 infringement cases were brought but withdrawn by the Commission when the Member State involved agreed to take action before the case was heard (see Figure 1.1[9]).

**Figure 1.1** Infringement actions on free movement of goods

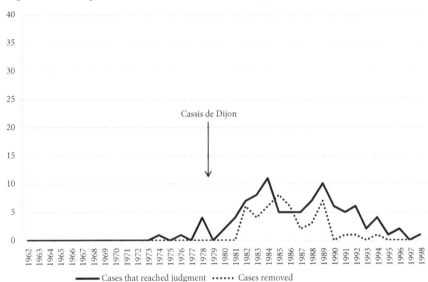

Cassis de Dijon

—— Cases that reached judgment   •••••• Cases removed

[7] See further K Lenaerts, 'The Principle of Mutual Recognition in the area of Freedom, Security and Justice', available at http://www.monckton.com/publication/sir-jeremy-lever-lecture-2015-principle-mutual-recognition-area-freedom-security-justice/. See also L Larsen, 'Mutual Recognition in the field of Criminal Law – A short-cut with Obstacles', *Europa Working Paper No 2014/10*; M Möstl, 'Preconditions and limits of Mutual Recognition' (2010) 47 *CML Rev* 405; J Thomas, 'The principle of mutual recognition – success or failure' (2013) 13 *ERA Forum* 585; A Hoogenboom, 'Origin and Meaning of Mutual Recognition as Foundational Principle in the European Integration process', available at http://papers.ssrn.com/sol3/papers.cfm?abstract_id=2477453; C Janssens, *The Principle of Mutual Recognition in EU Law* (Oxford, Oxford University Press, 2013).
[8] Data compiled by Markus Gehring and Alec Stone Sweet from the European Court Reports, the *Official Journal of the EC*, and the *Official Journal of the EU*.
[9] This figure has been produced by Estelle Wolfers, PhD student at the University of Cambridge, drawing on her own data. Some of the material that follows draws on her work.

So, in the immediate aftermath of *Cassis de Dijon*, approximately one in three infringement cases brought to the ECJ concerned the free movement of goods and were assessed according to the *Cassis* parameters.[10]

The rise in infringement actions on the free movement of goods and, in particular, the *Cassis* criteria can be compared to the spikes in preliminary references on the topics of the free movement of goods and measures equivalent to quantitative restrictions that followed *Cassis de Dijon* (Figure 1.2; same scale for comparison). If anything, the spike in infringement cases is more marked, although it can be suggested that the difference reflects the more contingent way in which preliminary references reach the Court of Justice.[11] Thus it can be argued that the Commission's use of infringement proceedings is a more straightforward route to the achievement of (negative) integration despite the more prolific nature of the preliminary reference case law.

**Figure 1.2** Preliminary references on free movement of goods

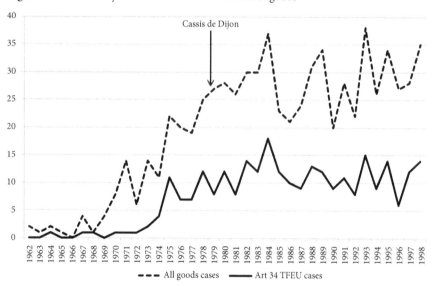

The Commission's adoption of the *Cassis* criteria also enabled it to address a further problem that systematically arises from relying on preliminary references to counter national non-compliance with EU legislation, which is the very uneven rate of referral between the Member States. As Table 1.1 indicates, some Member States see a high rate of preliminary references (PR) by their national

---

[10] Data compiled by Markus Gehring and Alec Stone Sweet from the European Court Reports, the *Official Journal of the EC*, and the *Official Journal of the EU*.

[11] A case has to be brought before a national court; the litigant has to raise an argument that falls within the scope of EU law; and the national court has to decide that the case is outside its existing understanding of EU law.

courts as well as being the recipients of a relatively large number of direct actions by the Commission: for instance, France and Germany. Others, most notably the Netherlands and the UK, have been the subject of few actions by the Commission and have seen a high rate of preliminary references emerging from their courts. Member States such as Denmark, as well as Austria and Finland, that joined the EU only in 1995, have the reputation of being prompt and effective in their transposition and application of EU measures. These Member States are probably in the same position, in that the Commission has rarely, if ever, found it necessary to bring infringement actions against them.

**Table 1.1** Litigation on free movement of goods

| 1961–1998 | Art 226 cases completed | Art 226 cases removed | PRs |
|---|---|---|---|
| Belgium | 10 | 6 | 26 |
| France | 16 | 15 | 59 |
| Germany | 15 | 4 | 47 |
| Italy | 23 | 11 | 38 |
| Luxembourg | 0 | 1 | 5 |
| Netherlands | 4 | 0 | 51 |
| Denmark | 1 | 0 | 8 |
| Ireland | 8 | 4 | 0 |
| UK | 5 | 0 | 21 |
| Greece | 14 | 6 | 2 |
| Portugal | 0 | 0 | 1 |
| Spain | 2 | 0 | 3 |
| Austria | 0 | 0 | 6 |
| Finland | 0 | 0 | 2 |
| Sweden | 0 | 0 | 6 |
| Total | 98 | 47 | 275 |

As Wolfers has argued,[12] of the Member States that typically receive high numbers of actions from the Commission, however, Greece and Italy stand in contrast to each other. The litigation pattern with respect to Italy's infringements resembles that of the other large founding Member States, in that there are large numbers of both direct actions by the Commission and preliminary references from the national level. Greek courts, however, have referred very few questions on the free movement of goods to the ECJ. In the case of Greece, therefore, almost all litigation on the topic has been initiated by the Commission, and it can be argued that

---

[12] See n 9.

the application of the *Cassis* ruling has been the main means by which compliance with EU law relating to the free movement of goods has been enforced.

## III. The Best Days of *Cassis de Dijon*?

The orthodoxy of EU law identifies *Cassis de Dijon* as one of the leading cases of EU law.[13] These leading cases, to use the (hyperbolic) words of Clark Hare and Wallace, are the 'great "lighthouses of the law", which never fail, are never dimmed, and are most visible in those times when the need for a guide is mostly felt'.[14] But given that this case is so well known, why revisit it? Is there anything left to say? As this volume shows, there is. The 40th anniversary of the Court's decision provides us with an opportunity to show how *one* case of crucial significance in the EU law orthodoxy can be re-examined by drawing on a range of diverse and multi-disciplinary angles.

## A. The Context

The application of relative mutual recognition to the single market had two important consequences. On the one hand, this principle enabled the management of diverse rules reflecting local, regional and national preferences. The *Cassis* decision did *not* impose uniformity: it allowed for the continued existence of regional products, retaining the local character of beverages, as encapsulated by the image on our book cover. *Cassis de Dijon* enabled the wider dissemination and marketing of products associated with local, regional and national identities, in the emerging single market. In the same way, the decision fulfilled a key objective of the Commission to avoid the creation of homogeneous 'Euro-products'.[15] In other words, it facilitated regional diversity, localism and even subsidiarity. In many ways it was a decision ahead of its time. It also unlocked the new approach to legislation precipitated by the desire to achieve the single market, a desire that, it is worth remembering in these Brexit days, was championed by the UK. Sir Stephen Wall, Head of the Foreign Office's European Community Department at the time, noted that 'Charles Moore[16] thinks MT [Margaret Thatcher] would almost certainly have heard of the *Cassis de Dijon* case. As do I, since it was much mentioned in the context of the SEA [Single European Act].' Sir Stephen adds, 'Charles doubts whether MT would have drunk the drink, not liking "foreign concoctions". She did drink white wine, but preferred whisky.'[17]

---

[13] See n 2.

[14] JI Clark Hare and HB Wallace, *American Leading Cases* (1847), cited in AWB Simpson, *Leading Cases in the Common Law* (Oxford, Clarendon, 1995) 6.

[15] See Brigitte Leucht's chapter in this book (ch 4) and especially A Mattera Ricigliano, 'L'arrêt «Cassis de Dijon»: une nouvelle approche pour la réalisation et le bon fonctionnement du marché intérieur' (1980) *Revue du marché commun* 505.

[16] Margaret Thatcher's biographer.

[17] Private correspondence on file with the authors.

On the other hand, the internal market remains incomplete, precisely as a result of non-absolute mutual recognition. As Jukka Snell has argued:

> At 40, it is not yet time for *Cassis* to retire, even if its best days may be over. Mutual recognition undoubtedly still has a place in the market integration project. It just cannot take the leading role anymore if we hope to move towards a genuine economic union capable of supporting the single currency.[18]

This assessment might hold true in the context of the internal market and with the longer-term objective of developing an economic union – however compromised this objective has become following the EU's hesitant response to the global financial crisis from 2008, Brexit and ongoing challenges to the rule of law in some of the Member States. The May 2020 judgment of the 2nd Senate of the German Federal Constitutional Court challenged the independent European Central Bank *and* the primacy of EU law,[19] adding further doubt to the likelihood of further integration between the Member States, albeit that the EU's Recovery Plan for Europe, agreed in July 2020 in the wake of the Coronavirus pandemic, showed just what the EU can achieve (in the absence of the UK). However, this book challenges the notion that 'the best days' of *Cassis* 'may be over'.

## B. The Structure of the Book

The contributions to this volume have been grouped into two main parts dealing with the *making* and the *impact* of the landmark decision. The three chapters in Part I – by Robert Schütze, Catherine Barnard and Brigitte Leucht – develop new perspectives on the historical context of the decision in *Cassis de Dijon*. The chapters are shaped by the different disciplinary approaches and methods of the authors but share a commitment to contextualising *Cassis de Dijon* in a wider legal and historical framework. Schütze (chapter 2) argues that *Cassis de Dijon* was the ground-breaking decision in the field of free movement of goods. Through a careful analysis of contemporary decisions, he posits that *Dassonville*, so often seen as paving the way, was in fact a decision with a much more limited ambition.

Catherine Barnard (chapter 3) tries to understand what inspired the judges at the Court of Justice to come up with the concepts of mutual recognition and mandatory requirements in *Cassis*. Through an exercise in legal archaeology, she examines the submissions of the parties, the key players and the wider legal context to appreciate the source of these highly influential doctrines.

---

[18] J Snell, 'Cassis at 40' (2019) 44(4) *EL Rev* 445.
[19] BVerfG, Urteil des Zweiten Senats vom 05. Mai 2020–2 BvR 859/15 -, Rn (1-237), available at www.bverfg.de/e/rs20200505_2bvr085915.html. See FC Mayer, 'Auf dem Weg zum Richterfaustrecht?: Zum PSPP-Urteil des BVerfG' *VerfBlog* (7 May 2020), available at https://verfassungsblog.de/auf-dem-weg-zum-richterfaustrecht/.

Brigitte Leucht (chapter 4), coming at the decision from a historian's perspective, grapples with similar issues through a close examination of the archives. She looks at the personalities involved in the decision, particularly Gert Meier, Rewe's influential in-house lawyer, the lawyers for the German Government, Sedemund and Deringer, and the role of Pescatore as *juge rapporteur*, before examining how the Commission, led by Ehlermann, Matthies and Mattera, picked up and ran with the judgment in the Commission's famous communication of 1980.

Part II of the book assembles six chapters that address the influence of the *Cassis de Dijon* decision in EU law.

Inge Govaere (chapter 5) spells out the regulatory and constitutional impact of the decision in *Cassis de Dijon*. First, she notes that the principle of mutual recognition prioritised the interests of the (single) exporting state and the exporter over those of the 27 (26) importing states, but thereby created a risk of race to the bottom. Second, she argues that the Court, in its decision in *Cassis de Dijon* constitutionalises the principle of mutual recognition. This is because, as a binding interpretation of the primary law, the Court of Justice's ruling in *Cassis de Dijon* can no longer be altered by EU secondary law even if it is precisely the absence of the latter for which it sought to compensate. Finally she notes the impact of this judge-made principle on the democratic process and democratic legitimacy of the European integration process. She notes *Cassis de Dijon* has also been instrumental in developing a new approach to EU harmonisation, combining negative and positive harmonisation.

Stephen Weatherill (chapter 6) examines the crucial issue of whether, for all its iconic status, *Cassis de Dijon* really made a difference. In particular, he highlights a line of impact of the *Cassis* decision that has been comparatively less explored than others. Thus he argues that despite the fact that the judgment has been perceived as a beacon for de-regulation, the reality is that it triggered a legislative response and, in doing so, ultimately emphasised the need for harmonised rules in the internal market because of the uncertainties associated with a non-absolute model of mutual recognition.

Chapter 7 by Albertina Albors-Llorens deals with the impact of *Cassis de Dijon* on EU competition law and seeks to appraise the effects that this decision might have had in the interpretation of the Treaty anti-trust prohibitions. It does so taking into account the shared single market goal of the free movement and the competition rules, as well as the important differences between these two areas of law. It argues that the impact of this decision in EU competition law might be traced in three domains. These are the policy shift from a form- to an effects-based approach, the appearance of public interest considerations in the interpretation of Article 101(1) TFEU and the development of the notion of objective justification in the application of both Articles 101 and 102 TFEU.

Peter Oliver started working in the Commission's legal service shortly before the hearing in *Cassis*. Matthies ('a brilliant and forbidding German official of the old school') was his director and a key player in *Cassis* and its aftermath. In chapter 8 he discusses some 'open conundrums' from the judgment, in particular the thorny question of whether the key phrase actually used for mutual recognition in paragraph 14 of *Cassis*, 'lawfully produced *and* marketed in one of the Member States', is still good law. He notes that the phrase has 'scarcely been addressed in the case law – let alone elucidated – after forty years. With hindsight, it is plain that this phrase never meant what it said.'

The final chapters in Part II focus on the impact of mutual recognition. They include two contributions – by Georges Baur (chapter 9), and by Emilija Leinarte and Catherine Barnard (chapter 10) – examining the principle of mutual recognition within a wider international trade framework.

Georges Baur provides a fascinating insight into the application of the principle of mutual recognition and the case law that has followed in three of the European Free Trade Association (EFTA) states – Iceland, Liechtenstein and Norway – by virtue of the European Economic Area (EEA) Agreement. Further, he explores the special position of the fourth EFTA state, Switzerland, which does not benefit directly from the *Cassis de Dijon* principle of mutual recognition because of its much weaker link with the EU, but which nonetheless decided to introduce this principle thorough an autonomous adaptation of Swiss Law. This chapter examines in detail the consequences of such a unilateral adoption of the principle of mutual recognition and shows only too well the price that there is to pay in maintaining independence from the EU while wanting to partake of some of its benefits.

Emilija Leinarte and Catherine Barnard look closely at the development of mutual recognition agreements (MRAs), which help facilitate international trade by eliminating duplicate product safety testing. As they note, MRAs have received very little attention from legal scholars, as compared to, for example, free trade agreements (FTAs) or bilateral investment protection treaties, yet it is likely they will become an important issue in any future UK/EU trading arrangement. The chapter examines the nature and different types of MRAs, and some of the incentives for concluding them. They note that past experience shows that negotiating MRAs is a complex and sensitive process that requires a high degree of trust between the parties, the very trust that the Court of Justice had identified in *Opinion 2/13*[20] as key to the successful operation of mutual recognition in the EU context.

In Part III of the book (chapter 11), Karen Alter offers her view on 40 years of *Cassis de Dijon* in the landscape of European legal and market integration by providing a critical reflection and a first assessment of the contributions to the volume. And in so doing she reflects on her own seminal contribution to the field, her article on *Cassis de Dijon* (co-authored with Sophie Meunier),[21] which continues to serve as a key point of reference, as is evidenced by the multiple citations of the article throughout the book.

Against this backdrop, we are proposing two arguments in favour of re-examining the *Cassis de Dijon* decision, which will be developed in the

---

[20] *Opinion 2/13*, ECLI:EU:C:2014:2454.
[21] K Alter and S Meunier-Aitsahalia, 'Judicial Politics in the European Community. European Integration and the Path-Breaking *Cassis de Dijon* Decision' (1994) 26 *Comparative Political Studies* 535.

remainder of this Introduction. The first argument highlights the potential for an integrated interdisciplinary research agenda to examine the development, transfer and circulation of legal ideas in EU law over time going beyond this landmark case. The second argument stresses the potential of mutual recognition in a post-Brexit and wider international trade context. These arguments are not mere summaries of the chapters that follow; instead they aim to encourage the reader to join us in thinking about future avenues for interdisciplinary research on landmark cases (section IV) and about fruitful applications of *Cassis de Dijon*, and mutual recognition in particular (section V). In short, we propose that the best days of *Cassis de Dijon* are yet to come.

# IV.  Interdisciplinary Research and the Origins, Transfer and Circulation of Legal Ideas

The call for developing an integrated interdisciplinary research agenda to re-examine landmark cases builds on a growing body of research on EU law written from diverse disciplinary angles. For a long time, the study of EU law has been almost exclusively the domain of legal scholars and political scientists. While lawyers tend to examine the system of juridical norms independently of power relations, political scientists have introduced power and agency into the study of the jurisprudence of the Court.[22] Only a little over a decade ago, political sociologists and historians joined the conversation and began developing new perspectives on the study of EU law.

## A.  New Perspectives on EU Law by Political Sociology and History

A group of predominantly French political sociologists, inspired by Pierre Bourdieu's theory of the legal field,[23] began reconstructing the 'EU legal field' over time. Antoine Vauchez and others have demonstrated that EU law was indeed shaped by judges, lawyers, legal advisers to the European institutions and others with an interest in building Europe,[24] which sometimes went back to the interwar period.[25]

---

[22] ibid.

[23] P Bourdieu, 'The Force of Law: Toward a Sociology of the Juridical Field' (1986–87) 38 *Hastings Law Journal* 814. See B Leucht, 'Beyond Morgenthau: the Transnational Turn and the Potential of Interdisciplinary Approaches for International History' in B Haider-Wilson, WD Godsey and W Mueller (eds), *International History in Theory and Practice* (Vienna, Austrian Academy of Sciences, 2017) 289.

[24] A Vauchez, *Brokering Europe: Euro-Lawyers and the Making of a Transnational Polity* (New York, Cambridge University Press, 2015).

[25] A Cohen, 'Constitutionalism without Constitution: Transnational Elites Between Political Mobilization and Legal Expertise in the Making of a Constitution for Europe (1940s–1960s)' (2007) 32(1) *Law and Social Inquiry* 109, 109–13.

Around the same time as political sociologists started to take an interest in EU law, historians 'discovered' EU law too. Bill Davies published a pioneering study on the reception of EU law in West Germany.[26] Building on Karen Alter's book on the national judicial reception of the supremacy of EU law in Germany and France,[27] he provided an archive-based, in-depth study accentuating the importance of the wider legal *and* non-legal discourse in accounting for the reception of EU law in Germany.

The Danish academic Morten Rasmussen also initiated a research programme focusing on how the international treaties establishing the European Coal and Steel Community (1951) and the European Economic Community (EEC, 1957) could lead to the establishment of a 'constitutional practice'.[28] This approach shares with the legal and social science literature the focus on the Court decisions relating to direct effect and supremacy, but draws attention to the power struggles in the development and the reception of this case law. An innovative archival strategy, combining the examination of the records of the Legal Service of the High Authority and the European Commission with that of the personal papers of key actors, such as the director of the Legal Service of the European Communities executives, Michel Gaudet, enabled Rasmussen and others to recast the role of the Court of Justice in the genesis of the doctrines of direct effect and supremacy.[29] These works have revealed the crucial role of the Legal Service of the High Authority and the Commission in advancing the Court's constitutional practice, and have generated 'thick descriptions' of the *Van Gend en Loos* and *Costa* decisions by placing these landmark cases in their wider legal, societal and political context.[30]

Davies and Rasmussen joined forces and co-authored the programmatic introduction to a special journal issue of *Contemporary European History*, in which they called for the establishment of a 'New History of European Law'. This call aimed at repositioning the development of EU law at the centre of (archive-based) historical

---

[26] B Davies, *Resisting the European Court of Justice. West Germany's Confrontation with European Law, 1949–1979* (Cambridge, Cambridge University Press, 2012).

[27] KJ Alter, *Establishing the Supremacy of European Law: The Making of an International Rule of Law in Europe* (Oxford, Oxford University Press, 2001).

[28] *Towards a New History of European Public Law – Battles over the constitutional practice, 1950 to 1993*, available at https://europeanlaw.saxo.ku.dk/about_the_project/ (2012–15); A Boerger and M Rasmussen, 'Transforming European law: The establishment of the constitutional discourse from 1950 to 1993' (2014) 10(2) *European Constitutional Law Review* 199.

[29] M Rasmussen and A Boerger, 'The Making of European Law: Exploring the Life and Work of Michel Gaudet' (2017) 57/1 *American Journal of Legal History* 51; M Rasmussen, 'Establishing a Constitutional Practise of European Law: The History of the Legal Service of the European Executive, 1952–1965' (2012) 21 *Contemporary European History* 237.

[30] The state of the art on the two cases is summarised in A Vauchez, 'EU Classics in the Making. Methodological Notes on *Grand arrêts* at the European Court of Justice' in Nicola and Davies (n 2) 21, 22–23.

research on European integration.[31] It might come as a surprise to many legal scholars that this call had to be articulated at all – and that it came as late as 2012.

There are a number of reasons, however, why historians had not yet contributed to the scholarship examining the jurisprudence of the Court. *First*, until very recently the archives of the Court of Justice were inaccessible. This only changed in December 2015, when the archives of the Court were opened and made available in the Historical Archives of the EU at the European University Institute.[32] *Second*, the historiography of European integration focused for a long time on diplomatic and economic history, which reflected the training and background of the historians who established the field of EU history from the 1970s and 1980s.[33] This is not to say that there were no archive-based studies on the negotiations of the EU founding Treaties.[34] There is also a substantive body of literature on important EU policies.[35] But what was missing from the historiographical picture was the jurisprudence of the Court.

A *third* reason why historians of the EU perhaps shied away from engaging with the case law can be extrapolated from Bourdieu's description of the legal field. He argued that the legal field operated on the basis of the social division between legal professionals and non-specialists. There is an assumed 'unity of discourse' between judges and legal scholars that crucially is not open to those outside of the legal community.[36] Legal scholars argue with the Court about the rationale adopted and the conclusions reached when they comment on specific cases, but this discourse is exclusive and it is not open to other disciplines. The division of labour between lawyers and non-lawyers is also reflected in the institutionalisation of legal history, which, to this day, is taught in law departments. Legal history is the domain of legal scholars, while approaches to the law by non-lawyers have never been institutionalised within their home disciplines.

*Fourth*, compounding this division, history as a discipline has not provided much incentive for institutionalising legal history. Legal history is regarded as

---

[31] M Rasmussen and B Davies, 'Towards a New History of European Law' (2012) 21 *Contemporary European History* 305. Cf also M Rasmussen and B Davies, 'From International Law to a European Rechtsgemeinschaft: Towards a New History of European Law, 1950–1979' in J Laursen (ed), *The Institutions and Dynamics of the European Community, 1973–1986* (London, Nomos/Bloomsbury, 2015) 97.

[32] Cf Council Regulation (EU) 2015/496; for an overview of the files, see at https://archives.eui.eu/en/fonds/230050?item=CJUE.

[33] See, for an assessment of recent trends in the historiography, KK Patel, 'Widening and deepening? Recent advances in European Integration History' (2019) 64(2) *Neue Politische Literatur* 327, 333–35.

[34] See the publications by the Groupe de liaison des historiens auprès la Communauté européenne, esp K Schwabe (ed), *Die Anfänge des Schuman Plans 1950/51 (The Beginnings of the Schuman Plan)*, (Baden-Baden, Nomos, 1988); and E Serra, *Il rilancio dell'Europa e i trattati di Roma (The relaunching of Europe and the Treaties of Rome)* (Baden-Baden, Nomos, 1989). More recently, A Boerger, 'Negotiating the Foundations of European Law, 1950–1957: The Legal History of the Treaties of Paris and Rome' (2012) 21(3) *Contemporary European History* 339, 351–55.

[35] Cf W Kaiser and A Varsori (eds), *European Union History: Themes and Debates* (Basingstoke, Palgrave Macmillan, 2010).

[36] Leucht, 'Beyond Morgenthau' (n 23). Cf also RA Posner, *How Judges Think* (Cambridge, MA and London, Harvard University Press, 2008).

niche, dry and too technical[37] – perhaps even more so if this is the legal history of the EU. It is quite telling that the historians engaging with the 'New History of European Law' tend to publish in law journals rather than mainstream history journals.[38] In short, for historians, it is not necessarily a smart move to engage with the jurisprudence of the Court of Justice. Following Bourdieu's field logic, writing legal history does not hold the promise of accumulating social capital in the discipline of history.

Against the background of so much critical introspection we might rightly ask: why bother? Why this plea for *more* interdisciplinary research? Why the call for developing not only multi-disciplinary perspectives on a landmark case but, in the future, fully integrated research designs?[39] We argue that there are at least two good reasons to take the interdisciplinary cooperation between legal scholars, historians and social scientists with an interest in the temporal dimension of EU law to the next level. These will be considered in the next section.

## B.  Towards Integrated Interdisciplinary Research Designs

The *first* reason for developing integrated interdisciplinary research designs is that the ground has been prepared for this. We can build on a growing interest in revisiting landmark cases that has been developed over recent years. This trend is evident in two publications written from different disciplinary backgrounds. The first of these works is *The Past and Future of EU Law*, by Miguel Poiares Maduro and Loïc Azoulai[40] – a collection assembling predominantly legal scholars and practitioners, as well as a handful of social scientists and one historian, to revisit the Court's landmark cases on the 50th anniversary of the Treaty of Rome. Another, more interdisciplinary collection re-examining landmark cases in EU law was published by Fernanda Nicola and Bill Davies.[41]

These two collections offer food for thought about the notion of a 'landmark case', and they encourage us to consider the contextual issues the 'great lighthouses of the law' seek to address more consistently. Antoine Vauchez has stressed that there is no common understanding of what constitutes a landmark case: 'Just as there is no *ex ante* definition of what a "classic" is in art or literature, there is no

---

[37] Laura Edwards has argued that legal history is marginalised by historians 'because they consider scholarship on law, even legal history, to be separate from history'. LF Edwards, 'The History in "Critical Legal Histories": Robert W Gordon. 1984. Critical Legal Histories. "Stanford Law Review" 36:57–125' (2012) 37(1) *Law & Social Inquiry* 187, 197. On the broader question of interdisciplinarity between law and the humanities, see D Feenan, 'Foreword: Socio-Legal Studies and the Humanities' (2009) 5(3) *International Journal of Law in Context* 235–42.

[38] Cf the references to historical works in this Introduction. Davies' and Rasmussen's special issue in *Contemporary European History* (n 31) remains an exception.

[39] See, for an argument to go beyond multidisciplinarity, A Warleigh-Lack, 'Interdisciplinarity in Research on the EU. Politics, History and Prospects for Collaboration' in W Kaiser, B Leucht and M Rasmussen (eds), *The History of the European Union. Origins of a trans- and supranational polity, 1950–72* (New York and London, Routledge, 2009) 206, 216–17.

[40] See n 2.

[41] See n 2.

general and transhistorical notion of the intrinsic properties of a *grand arrêt* that does not eventually end up with tautological definitions of "greatness."[42] Notably, moreover, *Cassis de Dijon* is examined together with the earlier *Dassonville* decision (1974)[43] in Maduro and Azoulai's collection. *Dassonville* provided a wide definition of the 'measures having equivalent effect to quantitative restrictions' of Article 34 TFEU.[44] Following the well-established doctrinal relationship between the two landmark cases, *Dassonville* served as the foundation,[45] but it was *Cassis de Dijon* that made the broad '*Dassonville* formula' manageable.[46]

Our book is a rarity in that it is devoted to *one* specific landmark case. Revisiting *Cassis de Dijon* from a temporal perspective encourages us to consider change over time. The three chapters in our book dealing with the *making* of the *Cassis de Dijon* decision (Part I) provide different perspectives on how and why *Cassis de Dijon* became a landmark case; and they also recast the doctrinal link between *Cassis de Dijon* and the earlier *Dassonville* decision (especially chapter 2 by Robert Schütze). The chapters evaluating the *impact* of *Cassis de Dijon* in Part II of the book address the spatial dimension of our landmark case. They trace the development of legal ideas outside of the primary legal context in which they were conceived, both within the broad area of EU law and within other legal systems.

The chapters in this book are all written from distinct disciplinary perspectives, but they cross disciplinary divides. A case in point is Catherine Barnard's chapter on 'legal archaeology' (chapter 3), which approaches the connections between different legal sources combining legal expertise with historical thinking. Another example is Robert Schütze's chapter, with his emphasis on the context of the jurisprudence of the Court. A productive future development of these emergent synergies could be the targeting of archival research to integrate further interdisciplinary scholarship. Brigitte Leucht brings this historical perspective in to chapter 4.

There is, in fact, one recent collection in which legal scholars and historians co-authored chapters on key questions in the development of EU competition law and policy.[47] The book, edited by Kiran Patel and Heike Schweitzer, did not focus on landmark cases but identified a catalogue of research questions to revisit

---

[42] Vauchez, 'EU Classics in the Making' (n 30).

[43] Case 8/74 *Procureur de Roi v Benoît et Gustave Dassonville; et SA Ets Fourcroy et SA Breuval et Cie v Benoît et Gustave Dassonville*, ECLI:EU:C:1974:82. Kalypso Nicolaïdis' chapter on *Cassis de Dijon* in Nicola and Davies' book provides a fascinating account of the author's professional trajectory through the landscape of mutual recognition. K Nicolaïdis, 'The *Cassis* Legacy: Kir, Banks, Plumbers, Drugs, Criminals and Refugees' in Nicola and Davies (n 2) 278–300.

[44] Originally Art 30 of the Treaty establishing the EEC, the provision read (emphasis added) 'Quantitative restrictions on imports and *all measures having equivalent effect* shall, without prejudice to the following provisions, be prohibited between Member States.'

[45] The Court stipulated that 'All trading rules enacted by Member States which are capable of hindering, directly or indirectly, actually or potentially, intra-Community trade are to be considered as measures having an effect equivalent to quantitative restrictions.' *Dassonville* (n 43) 852.

[46] See, JHH Weiler, 'The Constitution of the Common Market Place: Text and Context in the Free Movement of Goods' in P Craig and G de Búrca (eds), *The Evolution of EU Law* (Oxford, Oxford University Press, 1999) 349.

[47] K Patel and H Schweitzer (eds), *The Historical Foundations of EU Competition Law* (Oxford, Oxford University Press, 2013).

competition law and policy. Crucially, this cooperation extended over a series of workshops in which the research agenda was jointly developed by the contributors to the book and draft chapters were shared in various versions. This type of integrated interdisciplinary cooperation is intellectually rewarding and productive in terms of enhancing understanding, but time – and resource – intensive.

The *second* reason for developing integrated interdisciplinary research designs is that we still need to understand key issues relating to the development of the single market. As indicated above, we have a full picture now of how multiple actors constructed the *Van Gend en Loos* and *Costa* decisions that established the supremacy and direct effect of EU law. We also have a much better understanding of why, how and to what extent some Member States – for example Germany – pushed back against the jurisprudence of the Court of Justice.[48] In contrast, we know very little about the 'substantive constitution' of the EU and the role of law in the development of the single market from a historical perspective.[49] Archive-based historical research is now moving into the era of the Single European Act and will soon be moving to the Maastricht Treaty. This is the time to develop research questions concerning the wider jurisprudence of the Court, which place the case law within a broader political and societal context.

One point that should be included in this research agenda concerns the precise links between *Cassis de Dijon* and mutual recognition and the negotiations on Article 114 TFEU, which is addressed in the conclusions to Brigitte Leucht's chapter in this book. Arguably, Member States chose to expand the scope of qualified majority voting to increase the competitiveness of companies established in the EU by enlarging the home markets.[50] We also know that the European Commissioner Arthur Cockfield played an important role here.[51] But the process of how mutual recognition – as a doctrine or legal idea – moved through the landscape of position papers, negotiations and draft treaty provisions has never been traced on the basis of archival sources.

Having highlighted the benefits of an integrated interdisciplinary research agenda for EU law, we shall now turn to our second argument as to why the best days of *Cassis de Dijon* are yet to come, by sketching future applications of mutual recognition.

## V. Mutual Recognition after Brexit and beyond the EU

Mutual recognition was not born in 1979. Quite the contrary. The Asian Development Bank (ADB) finds the earliest MRA to date back to 1892. It, like

---

[48] Davies, *Resisting the European Court of Justice* (n 26).

[49] Among the works beginning to address this agenda are B Leucht, 'The policy origins of the European economic constitution' (2018) 24(2–3) *European Law Journal* 191; and, for *Competition Law (and Policy)*, Patel and Schweitzer, *The Historical Foundations* (n 47) 41; L Warlouzet and T Witschke, 'The Difficult Path to an Economic Rule of Law: European Competition Policy, 1950–91' (2012) 21(3) *Contemporary European History* 437.

[50] L Warlouzet, 'The Interdisciplinary Challenge in European Integration History' (2014) 49(4) *Journal of Contemporary History* 837, 841.

[51] Lord Cockfield, *The European Union: Creating the Single Market* (Chichester, Wiley, 1994).

many others, focused on mutual recognition of qualifications. Proliferation of academic qualification MRAs peaked in the 1970s and 1980s, and the original EEC Treaty contained an express provision for this in Article 57. *Cassis de Dijon* seems like a significant departure in that it extended mutual recognition to goods, but as Catherine Barnard's chapter shows (chapter 3), even this is an oversimplification, because a number of EU measures had been applying the principle to technical standards. Perhaps all we can say is that *Cassis de Dijon* contained the most visible and public commitment to mutual recognition, a commitment seized on with alacrity by the Commission in the 1980 Communication.

We know that, as Snell has indicated, mutual recognition, on its own, has not delivered quite what some of its advocates had hoped. Increasingly, as Weatherill's chapter shows (chapter 6). it has had to be supplemented by legislation. However, mutual recognition has been rolled out in MRAs, a key pillar in international regulatory cooperation.[52] Brito et al produce the following classification on the implications of mutual recognition in the EU:

1. In case of judicial mutual recognition there is no EU regulation, only national regulation, but there are no longer technical barriers to trade (TBTs) either ['the pure *Cassis* situation'].

2. In case of regulatory mutual recognition, there is 'light' harmonisation of objectives only, sometimes complemented with a few basic technical requirements when the complexity of the sector demands such; but the relevant European standards facilitate market access as adherence allows the affixing of a CE mark (indicating conformity with EU requirements). In many instances, the CE mark can be based on a Supplier Declaration of Conformity (SDoC), backed up by a technical file (authorities can demand this file for verification); in some cases of higher risk, CE marks can only be affixed after 3rd party certification by a so-called Notified Body, accredited via the European Co-operation for Accreditation system (EA).

3. Given 1. and 2., MRAs inside the EU are not necessary. Notified Bodies are Conformity Assessment Bodies (CABs) which are accredited by the EU's EA system, and the underlying rules, standards and procedures are identical. For the Old Approach regulating higher risks sectors, all detailed specifications tend to be included in directives, and procedures for conformity assessment (including inspection or type approval) are identical. Thus, also here no MRAs are needed inside the EU.

4. With third countries, like the US, Canada, Australia and New Zealand as well as Japan, MRAs have been concluded in the late 1990s. For 'associated' or candidate countries expressing a desire to be 'part of the EU internal market', so-called 'enhanced MRAs' have been concluded on a sector by sector basis. This is logical as the regulatory 'acquis' (the rules and market institutions of the EU) is adopted by these countries, and at some point 'free movement' can be applied. For candidate countries, some sectors might be advanced in the 'pre-accession process' and Agreements on Conformity Assessment and Acceptance of Industrial Product

---

[52] *International Regulatory Co-operation – Addressing Global Challenges* (OECD Publishing, Paris, 2013).

(ACAA) in sector x or y might ensure market access without further conformity assessment. For neighbourhood countries, there is usually no hard promise of EU membership, or it is impossible as they are not European countries, so that MRAs are unavoidable. However, the EU only accepts such MRAs (also called ACAAs) in sectors where regulations and conformity procedures have been aligned with the EU, and the CABs recognised as Notified Bodies (or otherwise designated).[53]

All of this shows that mutual recognition has a life beyond *Cassis de Dijon*. The interesting question is whether the mutual recognition principle has a life outside the EU. Baur's chapter (chapter 9) shows how mutual recognition has developed a life of its own in Switzerland. The UK wants to learn from the Swiss, Spanish and Australian experience (but no mention is made of the EU or the strong EU origins of the principle advocated in the White Paper[54]) in developing its own internal market post Brexit. The White Paper says:

129. The government believes that a system of mutual recognition supported by a non-discrimination principle will provide an effective legislative means to deliver a smooth and fair trading space within the UK.

130. The fundamental aim of all mutual recognition systems is to ensure that compliance with regulation in one territory is recognised as compliance in another. This is useful to prevent discrimination against businesses from other parts of the UK, and to ease the burdens associated with complying with 2 sets of requirements. Mutual recognition is a known and well-tested system, used in countries such as Australia and Switzerland.

131. The experience of mutual recognition in other countries shows that it can provide a low-cost and decentralised way of dealing with differences in regulation. A mutual recognition system does nevertheless protect the ability of administrations to regulate domestically produced goods, professionals and services originating from their territory, while ensuring that any differences in regulation that emerge between jurisdictions do not result in unnecessary barriers to trade.[55]

The areas identified for the application of the mutual recognition principle are goods, professional qualifications and services, the three areas in which it was first deployed in the EU, as Barnard's chapter shows. Ironically, for all the UK's attempts to distance itself from the EU principle, EU language is used and abused. Take, for example, paragraph 133 of the White Paper on goods:

[M]utual recognition of goods means that a good which can be lawfully sold in one territory, can be lawfully sold in other territories without having to comply with that other territory's requirements (that would otherwise apply). *Mutual recognition will cover mandatory requirements* relating to lawful sale, ie product requirements and their related processes and production methods (for example, requirements on production, composition, quality, packaging or labelling).[56]

---

[53] See at www.oecd.org/regreform/WP2_Contribution-of-mutual-recognition-to-IRC.pdf.
[54] *Cassis* is mentioned only once, on p 99, in the context of the Swiss experience.
[55] See at www.gov.uk/government/publications/uk-internal-market.
[56] ibid para 133 (emphasis added).

'Product requirements' is terminology derived from paragraph 15 of the Court of Justice's decision in *Keck*[57] when describing the ratio in *Cassis de Dijon*, and the examples given in paragraph 133 of the White Paper broadly map on to the list in paragraph 15 of *Keck* ('designation, form, size, weight, composition, presentation, labelling, packaging'). 'Mandatory requirements', as used in paragraph 133, is a synonym for 'product requirements' and not, as is usually understood from *Cassis de Dijon* and beyond, as the exceptions to the rule.[58] There is no evidence of a fully-fledged mandatory requirements regime being proposed, and the Internal Market Bill confirmed that this is the case. The UK's version of mutual recognition[59] is closer to absolute mutual recognition (albeit with a caveat for protection against serious threats to human, animal or plant health).[60]

The Scottish Government is not impressed and sees mutual recognition as a vehicle to undermine the devolution settlement and regulatory diversity.:

> The introduction of a mutual recognition regime of the type we understand you wish to bring forward would mean that a reduction in standards in one part of the UK would have the effect of pushing down standards elsewhere in the UK, in direct contradiction of the preferred approaches of stakeholders and decisions taken by the devolved parliaments. Mutual recognition could be applied to a range of devolved policy choices such as food standards.

> This proposal is not only unacceptable: it also ignores the reality and history of devolution. These have shown that the market can successfully operate across the UK with variations in standards, in ways that allow for positive differences in ambition to be pursued by the four nations. It would be extremely damaging if these freedoms were lost, or we could no longer make choices. Your approach would work against the interests of producers and consumers, and ignore the need to reflect natural variations in our geographies, sectors and communities which is a cornerstone of devolution.[61]

These claims – of mutual recognition leading to negative competition and ultimately deregulation – resonate with the arguments made by the German Government at the time of *Cassis de Dijon*, as Barnard notes in her chapter. In their paper on the current European interest in the ordo-liberal tradition, Hien and Joerges recognise that phenomenon:[62]

> The principle of 'mutual recognition' of product standards and regulations, which was introduced by the ECJ's legendary *Cassis* ruling and systematically developed in the

---

[57] Case C-268/91 *Keck and Mithouard* [1993] ECR I-6097.

[58] See further ch 3 by Barnard in this volume for an explanation.

[59] Clause 2(1) provides 'The mutual recognition principle for goods is the principle that goods which – (a) have been produced in, or imported into, one part of the United Kingdom ("the originating part"), and (b) can lawfully be sold there, because the goods comply with the relevant requirements that would apply to their sale (or there are no such requirements), should be able to be sold in any other part of the United Kingdom, free from any relevant requirements that would otherwise apply to the sale.'

[60] Sch 1, 'Exclusions from Market Access Principles'.

[61] Letter from Michael Russell MSP to Michael Gove MP, 3 July 2020, available at https://cdn.prgloo.com/media/download/42431953a37d47b3b4a43fb665f834ab. See M Dougan et al, UK Internal Market Bill: Devolution and the Union, 2020 https://www.centreonconstitutionalchange.ac.uk/publications/uk-internal-market-devolution-and-union.

[62] J Hien and C Joereges, 'Dead man walking: Current European interest in the ordoliberal tradition' *EUI Working Paper 2018/03*, available at https://cadmus.eui.eu/bitstream/handle/1814/51226/LAW_2018_03.pdf?sequence=1.

Commission's White Paper, was understood as institutionalising a regulatory competition which was to expose national laws to an international competition for the 'best' regulation.

In other words, they saw the *Cassis de Dijon* decision as fitting into the second generation of German post-war ordoliberalism, with von Hayek's 'competition as a discovery procedure' as the 'new guiding star'. In fact, as Weatherill notes in chapter 6, the non-absolute nature of mutual recognition, due to the introduction of mandatory requirements, diluted the deregulatory trajectory of *Cassis de Dijon*, and increasing use of EU legislation clipped its deregulatory wings still further. This is a reminder that the EU has never been simply a market order but a '*social market economy*',[63] a more Polanyian 'market society'.[64] And so is the UK.

For mutual recognition to work, even in its most narrow form in respect of recognition of testing, it is dependent on trust between nations, regulatory bodies within those nations and between conformity assessment bodies. Inside the EU that trust comes bottom up from membership of a highly integrated club. But it also comes top down due to rigorous enforcement of EU rules, both through proceedings brought by claimants relying on the principles of direct effect and primacy of EU law in the national courts, which can make references to the Court of Justice, and through enforcement proceedings brought by the Commission as Gehring and Wolfers reminded us above. This point was expressly recognised by the Court of Justice in *Opinion 2/13 (ECHR)*:

> 167. These essential characteristics of EU law [direct effect, supremacy] have given rise to a structured network of principles, rules and mutually interdependent legal relations linking the EU and its Member States, and its Member States with each other, which are now engaged, as is recalled in the second paragraph of Article 1 TEU, in a 'process of creating an ever closer union among the peoples of Europe'.

> 168. This legal structure is based on the fundamental premiss that each Member State shares with all the other Member States, and recognises that they share with it, a set of common values on which the EU is founded, as stated in Article 2 TEU. That premiss implies and justifies the existence of mutual trust between the Member States that those values will be recognised and, therefore, that the law of the EU that implements them will be respected.[65]

The Court added:

> [I]t should be noted that the principle of mutual trust between the Member States is of fundamental importance in EU law, given that it allows an area without internal borders to be created and maintained. That principle requires … each of those States, save in exceptional circumstances, to consider all the other Member States to be complying with EU law and particularly with the fundamental rights recognised by EU law.[66]

---

[63] Art 3(3), Treaty on European Union (TEU) (emphasis added).
[64] K Polanyi, *The Great Transformation: The Political and Economic Origins of Our Time* (Boston, MA, Beacon Press, 2001) (orig 1944).
[65] *Opinion 2/13 (ECHR)*, EU:C:2014:2454.
[66] ibid para 191.

But what about outside the EU where these ties are much weaker? As Leinarte and Barnard show in chapter 10, there are various mechanisms that need to be introduced artificially to help develop trust in the absence of the mechanisms used to buttress trust in the single market. Internally, within an evermore devolved UK, similar mechanisms will be required.

## VI. Conclusions

What will be the relevance of *Cassis de Dijon* by the time of the 50th anniversary of the decision in 2029? This Introduction has posited that 'the best days of *Cassis* are yet to come'. We would therefore expect legal scholars and historians returning to our landmark case in the future to identify new avenues for research, much in the same way as the contributions to this volume demonstrate the benefits of re-examining *Cassis* from a range of diverse and multi-disciplinary angles. If the interdisciplinary research agenda and the potential of the *Cassis de Dijon* decision and mutual recognition in particular are to be realised, there is little to suggest professional academic interest in the Court's 1979 decision would wane any time soon. As Alter shows (chapter 11), more dots will become available to join up and the globalisation of the principle may become more – or less – apparent.

What is more, the emergence of new global challenges and new uncertainties, which include the various internal and external challenges to EU integration, will render the legacy of the *Cassis de Dijon* decision discussed in this book enduringly relevant. The pursuit of merging markets and market harmonisation will continue to respond to, accommodate and shape the shifting and overlapping allegiances people have to a specific place, a region, a state and the EU. From this perspective, the image of our book that addresses boundaries between different forms of identity, while leaving room for the idea of diversity, will be as relevant as it was at the time of writing.

## PART I

# The Making of a Landmark Decision

# 2

# From *Dassonville* to *Cassis*: The Revolution That Did *Not* Take Place

ROBERT SCHÜTZE*

## I. Introduction

Where did *Cassis de Dijon* come from; and what is its historic relationship to *Dassonville*? The traditional *Dassonville–Cassis* story insists that the European Court of Justice (ECJ) abruptly abandoned the international trade law model in *Dassonville* by giving Article 34 TFEU a radically wide scope, while *Cassis* subsequently limited the consequences of this market-liberalising revolution through the introduction of implied exemptions originally called mandatory requirements.[1] The best-known popularisation of this orthodox view has come from the pen of Joseph Weiler. For him, the *Dassonville* Court 'explicitly or implicitly reject[ed] the GATT philosophy' in an attempt to create a common market that 'has as its implicit ideal type a transnational market-place which is identical to a national market-place'.[2]

The view that *Dassonville* was intended to introduce a 'national' market model, according to which *all* restrictions of trade fall within the scope of Article 34, can equally be found in the standard textbooks. In Catherine Barnard's well-known manual on the EU internal market, we thus read that *Dassonville* 'provide[d]

---

*This chapter constitutes a second 'instalment' from 'Framing *Dassonville*: Text and Context in European Law' (in preparation). Parts of the 'Introduction' and 'Conclusion' overlap with my '"Re-reading" *Dassonville*: Meaning and Understanding in the History of European Law' (2018) 24 *European Law Journal* 376.

[1] For representative examples of the 'traditional' view in English, see JHH Weiler, 'The Constitution of the Common Market Place: Text and Context in the Evolution of the Free Movement of Goods' in P Craig and G de Búrca (eds), *The Evolution of EU Law* (Oxford, Oxford University Press, 1999) 349; C Barnard, *The Substantive Law of the EU: The Four Freedoms* (Oxford, Oxford University Press, 2016); as well as M Maduro, 'Revisiting the Free Movement of Goods in a Comparative Perspective' in Court of Justice of the European Union, *The Court of Justice and the Construction of Europe: Analysis and Perspectives on Sixty Years of Case Law* (The Hague, Asser, 2013) 485. For the German literature, see U Haltern, *Europarecht* (Tübingen, Mohr Siebeck, 2005) ch 14.

[2] JHH Weiler, 'Epilogue: Towards a Common Law of International Trade' in JHH Weiler (ed), *The EU, The WTO and the NAFTA: Toward a Common Law of International Trade* (Oxford, Oxford University Press, 2000) 201, 215.

individual traders with a vehicle to challenge *any national rule* which – even potentially and indirectly – stands in their way'; and that such a revolutionary solution was justified because '[l]ooked at in its historical context, *Dassonville* was an effective tool to cull the dead wood of centuries of accumulated legislation'.[3] Seen against this background, *Cassis* tends to become, as for Weiler, a 'corrective' judgment that returns important regulatory powers to the Member States.[4]

Hardly ever was there so much agreement among European law scholars; and it is therefore hardly surprising that political scientists, working on the internal market, have equally come to embrace the traditional legal interpretation. In the most outstanding treatment of *Cassis de Dijon* here, the conventional legal interpretation is thus devotedly accepted – despite running counter to its own internal logic.[5] And in one of the more recent presentations of the standard political science narrative we read:

> [L]awyers know that the real radical breakthrough came in 1972 [*sic*] with *Dassonville* … At the time, it boldly struck down a Belgian provision (requiring that imported goods bearing a designation of origin be accompanied by a certificate of origin) with a sweeping approach: 'all measures with an equivalent effect to quotas' [*sic*] were to be struck down! *This was already and much more radical than* Cassis *in terms of result, an obligation of recognition. But it did not enunciate mutual recognition, and was in fact set aside as too bold. In this sense,* Cassis *was not a continuation but a break from* Dassonville, *which sought to impose an obstacles-based approach to national regulation, whereby all national rules are potentially subject to an assessment of illegality.*[6]

This chapter argues that this common reading of the *Dassonville–Cassis* story is flawed. For not only do the traditional accounts ignore the original meaning of the *Dassonville* judgment.[7] The philosophy behind the European Union's (EU)

---

[3] Barnard, *The Substantive Law of the EU* (n 1) 74 (emphasis added).

[4] Weiler, 'Epilogue' (n 2) 231.

[5] KJ Alter and S Meunier-Aitsahalia, 'Judicial Politics in the European Community: European Integration and the Pathbreaking *Cassis de Dijon* Decision' (1994) 26 *Comparative Political Studies* 535, 540: 'Instead [!], legal scholars point to the landmark *Dassonville* (1974) ruling, which established a legal basis for challenging the validity of national laws that create nontariff barriers. To the extent that the *Cassis* decision ruled invalid a national law on the basis that it created a nontariff barrier, it was a straight application of the jurisprudence established in the *Dassonville* decision. In fact, rather than moving beyond the *Dassonville* decision, the legal innovation of the *Cassis* verdict, the rule of reason, actually softened the Court's position regarding nontariff barriers. In extending the rights of the member states to maintain all reasonable national policies, which had the effect of creating nontariff barriers, the Court seemingly opened a huge loophole, albeit a loophole which could be controlled exclusively by the Court itself.' For Alter's sincere devotion to Weiler's teaching, see Chapter 11 below.

[6] K Nicolaïdis, 'The *Cassis* Legacy: Kir, Banks, Plumbers, Drugs, Criminals and Refugees' in F Nicola and B Davies (eds), *EU Law Stories: Contextual and Critical Histories of European Jurisprudence* (Cambridge, Cambridge University Press, 2017) 278, 281 (emphasis added). Not only is the year of *Dassonville* wrong; the author quotes a passage that cannot be found in the *Dassonville* judgment. Alas, if political scientists – rightly – chastise lawyers for not reading enough non-legal materials, can we lawyers not equally complain if political scientists are unable to closely read (if they do read them at all) the fundamental judgments they go on to write a great deal about?

[7] R Schütze, '"Re-reading" *Dassonville*: Meaning and Understanding in the History of European Law' (2018) 24 *European Law Journal* 376.

internal market remained, in general, loyal to the traditional categories of the General Agreement on Tariffs and Trade (GATT) until *Cassis de Dijon*. It is only through this *truly* revolutionary judgment that the scope of Article 34 becomes finally dissociated from the 'ordinary' international law logic.

In order to prove this thesis, the chapter will, microscopically yet systematically, analyse the case law on Articles 34/35 during the historical period starting with *Dassonville* and finishing with *Cassis*. (For a list of all free movement of goods cases during this period, see Table 2.1.[8]) It will show that the traditional *Dassonville–Cassis* story is (very) hard – if not impossible – to defend when measured against the 'empirical' and historical record. The chapter thereby classifies the relevant case law into four broad categories. Following the GATT conceptualisation, we shall first distinguish between 'border measures' and 'internal measures'. The former concept refers to measures that distinctly affect 'imports' *as imports* or 'exports' *as exports*, whereas internal measures apply indistinctly to both imports and domestic goods.[9] Within the internal measures group, second, we need to further distinguish between industrial goods and agricultural goods; and the reason for that distinction lies in the exceptional principles that the EU Treaties established for agricultural goods from the start.[10] Of particular importance in the category of internal measures dealing with industrial goods, finally, are national laws on the protection of industrial property rights.

For each of the resulting four categories, the Court develops a distinct form of judicial reasoning; and, depending on the category, a distinct substantive test as to what measures will fall within Article(s) 34 or 35 is established. How do these distinct tests relate to the *Dassonville* formula; and can we find traces of *Cassis de Dijon*-reasoning already in the pre-1979 case law? Does the Court bring an absolute restriction test or a relative discrimination test, or both, to national measures hindering trade in goods? Let us explore these questions by examining each of our four categories individually. A 'Conclusion' will, in a last step, bring the various jurisprudential lines together in order to evaluate the empirical case for or against the traditional *Dassonville–Cassis* account.

## II.  Case Category 1: 'Border Measures' and the *Dassonville* Formula

In the period between *Dassonville* and *Cassis de Dijon*, the Court dealt with seven Articles 34/35 cases that concern – in GATT terminology – 'border measures'.

---

[8] Table 2.1 omits a number of cases that mention Art 34 or Art 35 TFEU but do not directly concern these provisions, eg Case 29/75, *Kaufhof v Commission*, ECLI:EU:C:1976:55; or Case 5/77, *Tedeschi v Denkavit*, ECLI:EU:C:1977:144.

[9] See especially Annex I, Ad Art III GATT. The GATT jurisprudence thus distinguishes between 'import bans', ie bans that apply to imports *as imports* at the border, and 'sales bans' or 'marketing bans' that indistinctly apply to imported and domestic products and are thus internal measures.

[10] R Schütze, *European Union Law* (Cambridge, Cambridge University Press, 2018) ch 14, section 4.

**Table 2.1** Jurisprudence on Articles 34 and 35 between *Dassonville* and *Cassis de Dijon*

| Border Measures | Internal Measures | | | |
| --- | --- | --- | --- | --- |
| | Industrial Products | | Agricultural Cases | |
| | General Aspects | Industrial Property | | |
| Rewe, Case 4/75 | *Germany*, Case 12/74 | *Centrafarm*, Case 15/74 | *Van Haaster*, Case 190/73 | *Kramer*, Cases 3, 4, 6/76 |
| Simmenthal, 35/76 | *De Peijper*, Case 104/75 | *Centrafarm*, Case 16/74 | *Galli*, Case 31/74 | *Van den Hazel*, Case 111/76 |
| Donckerwolcke, Case 41/76 | *Bouhelier*, Case 53/76 | *EMI Cases*[11] | *Charmasson*, Case 48/74 | *Ramel*, Case 80-81/77 |
| Bouhelier, Case 53/76[12] | *Ianelli*, Case 74/76 | *Terrapin*, Case 119/75 | *Van der Hulst*, Case 51/74 | *Dechmann*, Case 154/77 |
| France, Case 68/76 | *GB-Inno*, Case 13/77 | *Hoffmann La Roche*, Case 102/77 | *French Wine Cases*[13] | *Bussone*, Case 31/78 |
| Cayrol, Case 52/77 | *Van Tiggerle*, Case 82/77 | *Centrafarm*, Case 3/78 | *Tasca*, Case 65/75 | *Redmond*, Case 83/78 |
| Thompson, Case 7/78 | *Eggers*, Case 13/78 | | *Sadam*, Joined Cases 88-90/75 | *Sukkerfabriken*, Case 151/78 |
| Category 1 | Category 2 | Category 3 | | Category 4 |

[11] This is a collection of three cases, namely: Case 51/75, *EMI Records v CBS United Kingdom*, ECLI:EU:C:1976:85; Case 86/75, *EMI Records v CBS Grammofon*, ECLI:EU:C:1976:86; and Case 96/75, *EMI Records v CBS Schallplatten*, ECLI:EU:C:1976:87.

[12] In order to help distinguish between Art 34 and Art 35 cases, the names of all export cases are not italicised in Table 2.1.

[13] This is a collection of three (joined) cases: Cases 10–14/75, *Procureur de la République at the Cour d'Appel Aix-en-Provence and Fédération Nationale des Producteurs de Vins de Table and Vins de Pays v Paul Louis Lahaille and others*, ECLI:EU:C:1975:119; Joined Cases 89–74, 18 and 19–75, *Procureur Général at the Cour d'Appel Bordeaux v Robert Jean Arnaud and others*, ECLI:EU:C:1975:118; Case 64/75, *Procureur Général at the Cour d'Appel Lyon v Henri Mommessin and others*, ECLI:EU:C:1975:171.

The latter are measures that *distinctly* apply to imports or exports in that they are specifically designed to deal with *international* trade (and, as such, they will typically be applied at the national border). A typical case for the EU here is *Rewe*,[14] where the Court was asked to assess phytosanitary inspections at the national border with regard to imports of apples. These border inspections were easy prey. Dutifully reciting the *Dassonville* formula,[15] the Court nevertheless did not reach its conclusion on the basis of *Dassonville*. Instead, it grounded its reasoning in Article 2(2) of Directive 70/50 and held:

> It is clear from the questions put that the phytosanitary inspections in question *only concern importations* of plant products and that similar domestic products, such as apples, are not subject to comparable compulsory examinations for the purpose of distribution. *These inspections thus amount to a condition which is required in respect of imported products only, within the meaning of Article 2(2) of the abovementioned directive* … It follows that phytosanitary inspections *at the frontier* which plant products, such as apples, coming from another Member State are required to undergo, constitute measures having an effect equivalent to quantitative restrictions within the meaning of Article [34] of the Treaty, and are prohibited under that provision subject to the exceptions laid down by [Union] law.[16]

This substantive test for *frontier* inspections was elaborated in *Simmenthal*.[17] Quoting once more its *Dassonville* formula,[18] the Court held that 'veterinary and public health inspections *at the frontier* – whether carried out systematically or not – *on the occasion of the importation*' constitute a violation of Article 34 of the Treaty.[19] Importantly, this absolute rule would equally apply to exports. The Court thus subsequently confirmed that 'the imposition of any special *export* formality constitutes an obstacle to trade by the delay which it involves and the dissuasive effect that it has upon exporters'.[20] Within the context of border measures, then, the Court generally applied an absolute restriction test that was often rhetorically expressed through the *Dassonville* formula.

Would this absolute restriction test apply to all goods – including third-country goods? Ever since *International Fruit* it had been clear that special considerations would apply to goods coming from third countries;[21] and *Dassonville* itself had clarified that this exceptional status would even extend to third-country goods in

---

[14] Case 4/75, *Rewe-Zentralfinanz eGmbH v Landwirtschaftskammer*, ECLI:EU:C:1975:98.

[15] The Court cites the formula in para 3 of the judgment: 'For the purposes of this prohibition it is enough for the measures in question to be capable of acting as a direct or indirect, real or potential hindrance to imports between Member States.'

[16] ibid paras 3–5.

[17] Case 35/76, *Simmenthal SpA v Ministero delle Finanze italiano*, ECLI:EU:C:1976:180.

[18] ibid para 7: 'To come within the prohibition contained in these provisions it is enough for the measures in question to be capable of acting as a direct or indirect, real or potential hindrance to imports between Member States.'

[19] ibid para 8 (emphasis added).

[20] Case 68/76, *Commission v France*, ECLI:EU:C:1977:48, para 16 (emphasis added).

[21] Case 51-54/71, *International Fruit Company NV and others v Produktschap voor groenten en fruit*, ECLI:EU:C:1971:128.

free circulation.[22] Border measures that Member States imposed on third-country goods, therefore, seemed *not* to be subject to an absolute restriction test but rather to a different – softer – test.

This softer test was expressly confirmed in *Donckerwolke*.[23] Belgian traders had imported Lebanese and Syrian textile products from Belgium into France. The importation of these goods had violated French customs legislation, which required third-country goods to be accompanied by a certificate of origin.[24] Were these certificates allowed in the EU's customs union? According to Article 28 (2) TFEU, they were not;[25] yet the Court made this *theoretical* solution 'conditional upon the establishment of a common commercial policy',[26] and held:

> *The assimilation to products originating within the Member States of goods in 'free circulation' may only take full effect if these goods are subject to the same conditions of importation both with regard to customs and commercial considerations, irrespective of the State in which they were put in free circulation.* Under Article [207] of the Treaty this unification should have been achieved by the expiry of the transitional period and supplanted by the establishment of a common commercial policy based on uniform principles. The fact that at the expiry of the transitional period the [Union] commercial policy was not fully achieved is one of a number of circumstances calculated to maintain in being between the Member States differences in commercial policy capable of bringing about deflections of trade or of causing economic difficulties in certain Member States.[27]

In essence: since the third-country goods in question did not yet come within the positively harmonised Common Commercial Policy (CCP),[28] the Member States were '*not* prevented from requiring from an importer a declaration concerning the actual origin of the goods in question even in the case of goods put into free circulation in another Member State'.[29] In the absence of Union harmonisation, there was consequently no absolute restriction test for import or export formalities for third-country goods. On the contrary, a softer test triggering Article 34 was to apply; yet the extra freedom for the Member States was – just like in *Dassonville* – subject to a rule-of-reason test.[30] While the certificate of origin in *Donckerwolke* would thus

---

[22] On this point, see R Schütze, 'Re-reading Dassonville' (n 7) esp 399. It will be recalled that the EU internal market is based on a customs union; and it accordingly aims to guarantee free movement not just for Union goods but, in principle, also third-country goods 'in free circulation'. This customs-union principle is set out in Art 28(2) TFEU; and according to Art 29 TFEU, third-country goods are in free circulation, where the import formalities have been complied with' and any customs duties or charges having equivalent effect have been paid in the Member State of first importation.

[23] Case 41/76, *Suzanne Criel, née Donckerwolcke and Henri Schou v Procureur de la République au tribunal de grande instance de Lille and Director General of Customs*, ECLI:EU:C:1976:182.

[24] ibid para 12.

[25] ibid paras 14–23. The main elements of the Court's reasoning here were, in addition to Art 28(2), the *Dassonville* formula (ibid para 19), and the more specific judgment in *International Fruit* (ibid para 20).

[26] ibid para 24.

[27] ibid paras 25–27 (emphasis added).

[28] ibid para 6.

[29] ibid para 33.

[30] ibid para 35: 'Nevertheless the Member States may not require from the importer more in this respect than an indication of the origin of the products in so far as he knows it or may reasonably be expected to know it.'

'*not in itself* constitute a measure equivalent to a quantitative restriction',[31] it would violate Article 34 if it were excessive in the means to achieve its given end.[32] The Court thus confirmed that the scope of Articles 34/35 was – in the absence of a unified CCP – to be narrower for third-country goods.[33] Indeed, in the absence of Union harmonisation, a rule-of-reason test would here apply.

## III.  Case Category 2: 'Internal Measures' and the Discrimination Test

With regard to indistinctly applicable measures formally regulating both foreign and domestic goods, two categories must be distinguished within the early European case law: intellectual property cases and all other cases dealing with internal measures. The latter – residual – category will be analysed in this section. It itself includes two major subgroups of cases that, respectively, relate to national price-fixing measures and national market regulations.

The regulation of prices was seen as a core problem for Article 34 from the very beginning: Directive 70/50 indeed listed a whole range of possible price regulations that could constitute measures having equivalent effect to quantitative restrictions (MEEQRs). When dealing with national measures *not* equally applicable to domestic and imported goods, Article 2 of Directive 70/50 thus stated:

> The measures referred to must be taken to include those measures which:
>
> (a)  lay down, *for imported products only*, minimum or maximum prices below or above which imports are prohibited, reduced or made subject to conditions liable to hinder importation;
>
> (b)  lay down *less favourable prices for imported products* than for domestic products;
>
> (c)  fix profit margins or any other price components *for imported products only* or fix these differently for domestic products and for imported products, to the detriment of the latter;
>
> (d)  preclude any increase in the price *of the imported product* corresponding to the supplementary costs and charges inherent in importation;
>
> (e)  fix the prices of products *solely on the basis of the cost price or the quality of domestic products* at such a level as to create a hindrance to importation[.][34]

---

[31] ibid para 41.

[32] ibid para 42. See also Case 52/77, *Leonce Cayrol v Giovanni Rivoira & Figli*, ECLI:EU:C:1977:196, where the Court confirmed this result at esp paras 33–36.

[33] The Court had already indicated this solution in Case 86/75, *EMI Records Limited v CBS Grammofon*, ECLI:EU:C:1976:48 in the context of intellectual property rights. For a more extensive discussion on the status of third-country goods in the common market, see R Schütze, 'Third Country Goods in the EU Internal Market' in F Amtenbrink et al (eds), *The Internal Market and the Future of European Integration* (Cambridge, Cambridge University Press, 2019) 200.

[34] (Commission) Directive 70/50/EEC on the abolition of measures which have an effect equivalent to quantitative restrictions on imports and are not covered by other provisions adopted in pursuance of the EEC Treaty, (1970) OJ English Special Edition: Series I 17, Article 2 (a)–(e) (emphasis added).

These categories of price measures were perceived as *distinctly* applicable to imports; but the question remained how the Court would deal with *indistinctly* applicable price measures.[35] The most famous case between *Dassonville* and *Cassis* here is *GB INNO*.[36] It concerned a Belgian measure that imposed a fixed consumer price for tobacco products. The Court began its Article 34 analysis with a reference to the *Dassonville* formula,[37] then pointed to Directive 70/50,[38] but finally settled on the following solution:

> *Although a maximum price applicable without distinction to domestic and imported products does not in itself constitute a measure having an effect equivalent to a quantitative restriction*, it may have such an effect, however, when it is fixed at a level such that the sale of imported products becomes, *if not impossible, more difficult than that of domestic products.*

> On the other hand a system whereby the prices are freely chosen by the manufacturer or the importer as the case may be and imposed on the consumer by a national legislative measure, and whereby no distinction is made between domestic products and imported products, *generally has exclusively internal effects.*

> However, the possibility cannot be excluded that in certain cases such a system may be capable of affecting intra-[Union] trade.[39]

In essence, the Court thus held that indistinctly applicable price measures would *not* in themselves constitute MEEQRs, because they were generally regarded as having exclusively *internal* effects, that is effects that were not distinctive on external or international trade. Yet these measures could still fall within the scope of Article 34 where they (materially) *discriminated* against imports; and this was the case where the sale of imported goods would become 'if not impossible, more difficult than that of domestic products'.

This solution was subsequently confirmed in *Van Tiggere*.[40] A Dutch victualler had been accused of selling gin at a price below the minimum price set by the Netherlands. In the course of the national court proceedings he argued that Article 34 was violated; and when asked about this, the Court of Justice emphatically

---

[35] For two brilliant early academic discussions of this question, see M Waelbroeck, *Les réglementations nationales de prix et le droit communautaire* (Brussels, Université de Bruxelles, 1975) esp 40 et seq; as well as K Winkel, 'Die Vereinbarkeit staatlicher Preislenkungsmaßnahmen mit dem EWG-Vertrag' (1976) 45 *Neue Juristische Wochenschrift* 2048.

[36] Case 13/77, *GB-INNO-BM v Association des détaillants en tabac (ATAB)*, ECLI:EU:C:1977:185.

[37] ibid para 28, but esp paras 46–47: 'Article [34] of the Treaty prohibits in trade between Member States all measures having an effect equivalent to quantitative restrictions. For the purpose of this prohibition it is sufficient that the measures in question are likely to hinder, directly or indirectly, actually or potentially, imports between Member States.'

[38] ibid para 48: 'It should be pointed out that, as stated in Commission Directive No 70/50 … "measures, other than those applicable equally to domestic or imported products, which hinder imports which could otherwise take place, including measures which make importation more difficult or costly than the disposal of domestic production" are measures which have an effect equivalent to a quantitative restriction on imports.'

[39] ibid paras 52–54 (emphasis added).

[40] Case 82/77, *Openbaar Ministerie (Public Prosecutor) of the Kingdom of the v Jacobus Philippus van Tiggele*, ECLI:EU:C:1978:10.

underlined that 'national price-control rules applicable without distinction to domestic products and imported products *cannot in general produce such an effect*'; and that they could do so only '*in certain specific cases*'.[41] Yet since the marketing rule in question applied to domestic and imported products alike, it 'cannot produce effects detrimental to the marketing of *imported products alone* and *consequently* cannot constitute a measure having an effect equivalent to a quantitative restriction on imports'.[42] Only where a specific form of *discrimination* could be shown would the national measure violate Article 34.[43]

This discrimination criterion was further developed in a second subgroup of cases that concern quality-ensuring measures. In *Commission v Germany (Sekt & Weinbrand)*,[44] the Court had thus been asked to review a German law that reserved the appellations 'Sekt' (sparkling wine) and 'Weinbrand' (brandy) to wines produced in Germany or from a fixed amount of German grapes. The solution suggested by Directive 70/50 was clear: national laws that 'confine names which are not indicative of origin or source to domestic products only' were *distinctly* applicable measures that would constitute measures having an equivalent effect to quantitative restrictions.[45] And rejecting the German argument that the appellations were true geographic indications of origins,[46] the Court had no scruples in finding that the German law was 'calculated to favour the disposal of the domestic products on the German market to the detriment of the products of other Member States'.[47] Without even citing *Dassonville*, the Court exclusively based its analysis on the presence of formal discrimination.

This solution was confirmed in *Eggers*,[48] where the Court essentially dealt with the same questions.[49] This time, however, the bone of contention was the German condition that *home*-produced brandies could use the designation 'Weinbrand' only if 85 per cent of the alcoholic content was derived from wine distillate whose distillation had taken place inside the national territory. This element was new, since the German rule was confined to the designation of *German* products. Yet the Court followed its previous reasoning and insisted that while the Member States were 'empowered to lay down quality standards for products marketed on their territory and may make use of designations of quality subject to compliance with such standards', this was 'dependent solely on the existence of the intrinsic

---

[41] ibid para 13.

[42] ibid para 16 (emphasis added).

[43] ibid para 18.

[44] Case 12/74, *Commission v Germany (Sekt & Weinbrand)*, ECLI:EU:C:1975:23.

[45] Art 2(3)(s) Directive 70/50 (n 34).

[46] Case 12/74, *Commission v Germany* (n 44) para 7. See also ibid para 12: 'It results from the foregoing considerations that the appellations "Sekt" and "Weinbrand" do not constitute indications of origin.'

[47] ibid para 14.

[48] Case 13/78, *Eggers Sohn & Co v Freie Hansestadt Bremen*, ECLI:EU:C:1978:182.

[49] Interestingly, the Court now refers to the *Dassonville* formula in ibid para 23, yet immediately reverts to Directive 70/50 and in particular its Art 2(3)(s). The subsequent analysis then reproduces extensively the ruling in Case 12/74, *Commission v Germany* (n 44).

objective characteristics which give the product the quality required by law'.[50] To thus insist that part of a production process had to take place within Germany was to *formally* discriminate against production processes in other Member States and thus clearly constituted an MEEQR.[51]

This discrimination criterion equally applied to export restrictions – a choice confirmed in *Bouhelier*.[52] A French law required exporters of quality watches to obtain an export licence or, in the alternative, a 'standards certificate' issued by a French Centre for Industry. With regard to the export licence, the Court could of course simply refer to its earlier (absolute) rule for border measures; yet since the standards certificate was an internal measure, this jurisprudential line involving an absolute restriction test was not available. The Court thus reverted to a discrimination analysis;[53] and it was only thanks to the latter that the second aspect of the national measure was 'capable of constituting a direct or indirect, actual or potential obstacle to intra-[Union] trade'.[54]

# IV.  Case Category 3: 'Industrial Property Laws' and Article 36

A sizable number of Article 34 cases between *Dassonville* and *Cassis* concerned national industrial or intellectual property rights.[55] These post-*Dassonville* cases continued the jurisprudential line that had previously started with *Deutsche Gramophone* and *Hag*.[56] And indeed, in a powerful illustration of judicial path dependency, the post-*Dassonville* development of this special jurisprudential line exclusively draws on the doctrinal tools invented in the pre-*Dassonville* era. The judicial logic and rhetoric of these cases is thereby so different from the rest of the indistinctly applicable 'internal' measures cases that they deserve their own category. The reason for this difference lies, in my view, in the fact that the Court had originally developed its intellectual property cases in the context of EU

---

[50] Case 13/78, *Eggers* (n 48) para 25.

[51] ibid para 26.

[52] Case 53/76, *Procureur de la République de Besançon v Les Sieurs Bouhelier and others*, ECLI:EU:C:1977:17.

[53] ibid paras 13–15.

[54] ibid para 16.

[55] See Table 2.1. For an early academic analysis of this special jurisprudential line, see especially J Andermann, *Territorialitätsprinzip im Patentrecht und Gemeinsamer Markt* (Berlin, Duncker & Humblot, 1975); FA Mann, 'Industrial Property and the EEC Treaty' (1975) 24 *International and Comparative Law Quarterly* 31; EA van Nieuwenhoven Heldbach, 'Industrial Property, The *Centrafarm* Judgments' (1976) 13 *CML Rev* 37; B Harris, 'The Application of Article 36 to Intellectual Property' (1976) 1 *EL Rev* 515; C von Bar, *Territorialität des Warenzeichens und Erschöpfung des Verbreitungsrechts im gemeinsamen Markt* (Frankfurt am Main, Alfred Metzner Verlag, 1977); A Deringer, 'Gewerbliche Schutzrechte und freier Warenverkehr im Gemeinsamen Markt' (1977) 46 *Neue Juristische Wochenschrift* 469.

[56] Case 78/70, *Deutsche Grammophon v Metro-SB-Großmärkte*, ECLI:EU:C:1971:59; and Case 192/73, *Van Zuylen frères v Hag AG*, ECLI:EU:C:1974:72.

competition law, where it could not concentrate on the legality of the *state* measure as such, but where it had to instead focus on the legality of *private* actions of individual parties. This intricate and dynamic relationship between the internal market and competition law will be further picked up and wonderfully explained in chapter 7.

## A. The Specific-Subject-Matter and Exhaustion Doctrines: *Centrafarm I* and *II*

Prior to 1970, the Court had tried to fight restrictions on (parallel) imports caused by intellectual property rights under the EU competition law rules. But once the free movement of goods provisions became directly effective, after the end of the transitional period, the Court swiftly started to shift its analytical efforts to Article 34. The tools originally developed for intellectual property cases within the competition law context were then simply 'imported' into Article 34 by *Hag*; and the *Hag* legal transplant was – after *Dassonville* – further elaborated on in the two *Centrafarm* judgments.[57]

In both *Centrafarm* judgments the Court was asked to determine the exclusionary scope of national intellectual property rights. *Centrafarm I* involved an American company – Sterling Drug – that held parallel patents for the sale of pharmaceuticals in the United Kingdom and the Netherlands. One British and one Dutch subsidiary had been licensed to manufacture the drugs in the two Member States, respectively. Due to governmental price restrictions, the British drugs were thereby much cheaper than the Dutch drugs, and a third party – Centrafarm – decided to exploit these price differences by importing British goods into the Netherlands. The sale of these parallel imports was opposed on the basis of Sterling's *Dutch* patent, because the patent holder had not *itself* placed the goods on the *Dutch* market. The question before the European Court was thus this: could a patent holder with two parallel patents within two Member States block the sale of goods within each of these national markets by third parties, even though these goods had been lawfully marketed by the same patent holder in each of these national markets? In *Centrafarm II* – a case decided on the same day as *Centrafarm I* – this question was extended from national patents to national trademark legislation.

Without any reference to *Dassonville*, the Court quickly drew on its earlier distinction – famously developed for EU competition law in *Consten and Grundig* – between the existence and the exercise of an intellectual property right. Finding that exercises of intellectual property rights can only be justified (!) under Article 36 when they fall into the 'specific subject matter' of that intellectual

---

[57] Case 15/74, *Centrafarm and de Peijper v Sterling Drug* (*Centrafarm I*), ECLI:EU:C:1974:114; and Case 16/74, *Centrafarm and de Peijper v Winthrop* (*Centrafarm II*), ECLI:EU:C:1974:115.

property right, the Court dutifully defined the specific subject matter for patents (and trademarks). Defining this to be the exclusive right to *market the product for the first time*,[58] the Court subsequently claimed that once these rights were exhausted in specific national markets,[59] national intellectual property laws could no longer be used to ban parallel imports. In the famous words of *Centrafarm* I:

> [A] derogation from the principle of the free movement of goods *is not, however, justified where the product has been put onto the market in a legal manner, by the patentee himself or with his consent, in the Member State from which it has been imported*, in particular in the case of a proprietor of parallel patents.
>
> In fact, if a patentee could prevent the import of protected products marketed by him or with his consent in another Member State, he would be able to partition off national markets and thereby restrict trade between Member States, in a situation where no such restriction was necessary to guarantee the essence of the exclusive rights flowing from the parallel patents.[60]

When viewed against an international law frame,[61] the emerging doctrine of Union exhaustion was a major development for the European 'common market'. For the insistence on the internal sovereignty of states is replaced by a quasi-federal perspective that explores the relationship between two national markets within the Union. However, and fundamentally, this quasi-federal perspective is only triggered by (and confined to) the *personal conduct of the individual right holder*. Where a patent holder has placed her goods onto *two* separate Member State markets, parallel imports *between these two national markets* cannot be blocked by the right holder.

The doctrine of Union exhaustion is consequently rooted in an estoppel rationale: a person who has consented to exploit her patents in more than one national market within the Union, cannot block the free circulation of goods between these national markets! And since the key characteristic for the doctrine of exhaustion is the *consensual* marketing *in another Member State*, Union exhaustion is triggered

---

[58] In *Centrafarm I*, we thus read (ibid para 9 (emphasis added)): 'In relation to patents, the specific subject matter of the industrial property is the guarantee that the patentee, to reward the creative effort of the inventor, has the exclusive right to use an invention with a view to manufacturing industrial products and *putting them into circulation for the first time, either directly or by the grant of licences to third parties, as well as the right to oppose infringements*.' With regard to trademarks, *Centrafarm II* states (ibid para 8 (emphasis added)): 'In relation to trade marks, the specific subject-matter of the industrial property is the guarantee that the owner of the trade mark has the exclusive right to use that trade mark, *for the purpose of putting products protected by the trade mark into circulation for the first time, and is therefore intended to protect him against competitors wishing to take advantage of the status and reputation of the trade mark by selling products illegally bearing that trade mark*.'

[59] For Union limits to the specific-subject-matter and exhaustion doctrines, see however, Case 102/77, *Hoffmann-La-Roche*, ECLI:EU:C:1978:108; as well as Case 3/78, *Centrafarm BV v American Home Products Corporation (Centrafarm III)*, ECLI:EU:C:1978:174. In these cases, the Court defended a trademark holder's right to object to some forms of repackaging and reaffixing of a trademark.

[60] *Centrafarm I* (n 57) paras 11–12. For the equivalent statement in *Centrafarm II* (n 57), see paras 9–11.

[61] According to the 1883 Paris Convention for the Protection of Industrial Property, 'parallel' rights are absolute rights and independent of each other. They flow from the internal sovereignty of each signatory state, with the result that there is no principle of exhaustion (see esp ibid Art 4 *bis*).

only by specific *private party actions*; and as such it did not, strictly speaking, follow a federal – let alone national – market philosophy. For it would not affect the rights of parallel patent holders in Member States *where they had not consented to the marketing of their product*; nor would their rights – as under a national market model – be exhausted whenever they had marketed their products in a single Member State.

## B.  Locating Violations: Article 36 and Arbitrary Discriminations

The jurisprudential line on intellectual property would, for a long time, remain different and distinct from all other Article 34 cases. What were the doctrinal steps the Court employed here? The terse rhetoric within the early intellectual property cases makes it hard to decipher the Court's 'reasoning'. Markedly, the early Court never really concentrated on whether the national intellectual property law constituted a MEEQR within Article 34; instead, it exclusively explored whether the private 'exercise' of such a right constituted an 'arbitrary discrimination' (or a disguised restriction on trade) under Article 36.

A good example for this doctrinal reductionism is *Terrapin v Terronova*.[62] The case involved the owner of the British trademark 'Terrapin', who had appealed against a decision of a German court finding that the British trademark was confusingly similar to the German trademark 'Terranova'. There was no dishonest intent to free-ride on the commercial reputation of the other party; the obstacle to trade simply arose from the parallel co-existence of two – unharmonised – national intellectual property regimes. Would such an obstacle arising from the disparities in national laws violate Article 34 and therefore be in need of justification under Article 36? The Court's answer was this:

> [I]n the present state of [Union] law an industrial or commercial property right legally acquired in a Member State may legally be used to prevent under the first sentence of Article 36 of the Treaty the import of products marketed under a name giving rise to confusion where the rights in question have been acquired by different and independent proprietors under different national laws. If in such a case the principle of the free movement of goods were to prevail over the protection given by the respective national laws, the specific objective of industrial and commercial property rights would be undermined.[63]

On its surface, the judicial argument here seemed to imply that obstacles arising from the (un-harmonised) co-existence of national laws would fall within the scope of Article 34 but could equally, under the (then) state of Union law, automatically

---

[62] Case 119/75, *Terrapin (Overseas) Ltd v Terranova Industrie CA Kapferer & Co*, ECLI:EU:C:1976:94.
[63] ibid para 7.

be justified under Article 36. In one sense, therefore, the post-*Dassonville* intellectual property right cases may be seen as an interesting precursor to the inclusion of non-discriminatory national measures in *Cassis* – unless one sees the exclusionary right granted under a *national* intellectual property law as a distinct form of indirect discrimination or as a quasi-border measure.

# V. Case Category 4: 'Agricultural Legislation' and *Dassonville* Pre-emption

The EU Treaty title on agriculture constituted – from the very beginning – a collective *lex specialis* within the law governing the free movement of goods. The reason for this special treatment was the close connection between negative and positive integration established for this part of the Rome Treaty;[64] and the strong nexus between the creation of a common *market* and the creation of a common *policy* had been clarified by the very first provision for the Common Agricultural Policy (CAP).[65] Much of the early case law on agricultural goods is therefore concerned with EU legislation designed to offer a comprehensive legislative 'framework' for goods falling within its scope. The application of the *Dassonville* formula for this case category must be seen in this special – legislative – context.

## A. Export Restrictions and *Dassonville* Pre-emption

The first case to be decided after *Dassonville* was indeed an agricultural case: *van Haaster*.[66] A Dutch law had made the production of flower bulbs subject to a cultivation licence; and a Dutch producer that had nonetheless (and illegally) grown hyacinth bulbs was consequently prosecuted under national law. In the course of the national proceedings, the grower argued that the Dutch production system violated Regulation 234/68 establishing a 'common organisation of the market in live trees and other plants, bulbs, roots and the like, cut flowers and ornamental foliage',[67] and in particular Article 10 of the Regulation prohibiting quantitative restrictions and all measure having an equivalent effect on exports.[68]

---

[64] See n 10.

[65] Art 38(4) TFEU: 'The operation and development of the internal market for agricultural products must be accompanied by the establishment of a common agricultural policy.'

[66] Case 190-73, *Officier van Justitie v JWJ van Haaster*, ECLI:EU:C:1974:113. While the case was registered before *Dassonville*, it was only decided after it.

[67] Regulation 234/68 on the establishment of a common organisation of the market in live trees and other plants, bulbs, roots and the like, cut flowers and ornamental foliage (1968) OJ English Special Edition: Series I, 26.

[68] ibid Art 10(1) stated: 'The following shall be prohibited in the internal trade of the [Union]:– the levying of any customs duty or charge having equivalent effect; – any quantitative restriction or measure having equivalent effect[.]'

This was a novel argument, for the idea that Article 35 TFEU – which obviously stood behind Article 10 of the Regulation – could cover *production* measures was new.[69] The Dutch Government opposed such an extensive interpretation and argued that since the notion of MEEQR 'only refers to regulations relating to *trade*', it could 'not extend to measures relating to production itself';[70] and it thereby made no difference whether the concept was used in the context of primary or secondary Union law. The Commission concurred and proposed a solution (implicitly) based on Article 3 of Directive 70/50:

> *The fact that measures regulating or limiting production have an effect upon the quantity and, if applicable, the quality of products capable of being the subject of trade within the [Union], is not in itself sufficient to place them on a par with quantitative restrictions or measures having an equivalent effect, directed at trade.* Many measures, despite their restrictive effect upon trade, are not incompatible with Articles [34 and 35]: they fall within the framework of the powers or possibilities which the Treaty has implicitly or explicitly left to Member States and a restrictive effect upon trade is inherent in them ...

> The terms 'quantitative restriction or measure having an equivalent effect' referred to in Article 10 of Regulation No 234/68 do not apply to measures by which a Member State limits production, unless these measures act as a greater brake upon exports than upon the flow of the goods in question to the market of the Member State concerned *and unless this restrictive effect exceeds the effects proper to such measures, as would be the case if the latter pursued an object incompatible with the Treaty.*[71]

How did the Court decide? The Court acknowledged that Article 10 of the Union Regulation principally related to *marketing* measures, whereas the national law squarely concerned the *production* process.[72] Yet the Court nevertheless chose to place Article 10 of the Regulation 'back into the global system of the organization of the market';[73] and '[i]n the absence of express provisions as to the compatibility of a national regulation restricting production with the organization of the market', it explored the aims and objectives of the Union market organisation.[74] Having found that 'the organization of the market also involves diverse provisions applicable to the production stage',[75] the Court then identified the wish of the Union

---

[69] For a subsequent confirmation of this ruling, see Joined Cases 3, 4 and 6/76, *Kramer and others*, ECLI:EU:C:1976:114, which dealt with national measures fixing the catch quota for fish against the backdrop of the relevant common market organisation. However, the Court here ingeniously avoided ruling that the national measure was a MEEQR by insisting that a quota was not a measure limiting production in the long term because it was designed to preserve and thus enhance the future 'production' of fish.

[70] Case 190/73, *van Haaster* (n 66), Written Submissions at 1126.

[71] ibid 1127. This was further elaborated during the oral proceedings (ibid 1129): 'As regards the cultivation licences it is right to point out – and on this point the Commission would like to define more clearly its written observations – that national measures for restricting production cannot as such and by themselves amount to measures having an effect equivalent to quantitative restrictions.'

[72] Case 190/73, *van Haaster*, Judgment, para 5: 'The national system in question and the provision under [Union] law of which the interpretation is requested relate to different stages of the economic process, that is to say to production and to marketing respectively.'

[73] ibid para 6.

[74] ibid para 7.

[75] ibid para 11.

legislator to provide for 'a totality of [Union] measures on the introduction of common quality standards'.[76] And from there, the Court found as follows:

> [A]s regards the internal trade of the [Union], the organization of the market for the products in question is based upon freedom of commercial transactions under conditions of genuine competition, thanks to stabilization of the quality of the products.
>
> *Such a system excludes any national system of regulations which could impede directly or indirectly, actually or potentially, trade within the [Union].*
>
> A national organization having the purpose of rationing production affects – or is at any rate capable of affecting – the system of trade thus defined, and must accordingly be considered a measure having an effect equivalent to quantitative restrictions *within the meaning of the Regulation.*[77]

The very last words within the quotation are essential and decisive: the Court held the national law to be a MEEQR on exports *within the meaning of the Regulation*. This, however, crucially did not mean that this wide definition of a MEEQR would also be projected onto Article 35 TFEU. For Article 10 of the Regulation was, as the Advocate General in this case expressly counselled,[78] much wider than Article 35 of the Treaty. It was wider *because* it was placed within a comprehensive legislative scheme established by the Union. And it was this legislative scheme that pre-empted any national law that directly or indirectly, actually or potentially, interfered with the quality system established by the common market organisation.[79]

## B.  Import Restrictions and *Dassonville* Pre-emption

This legislative pre-emption logic was extended to imports in *Galli*.[80] The case involved Regulation 120/67 on the common market organisation in cereals.

---

[76] ibid para 13.

[77] ibid paras 15–17.

[78] In the words of Advocate General Mayras (Case 190/73, *van Haaster*, ECLI:EU:C:1974:93 at 1139), 'I consider therefore that the prohibition in Article 10 of the Regulation has a scope wider than that of Article [35 TFEU], all the more so, since it appears in a common organization of the market.'

[79] For the same solution, in the context of Regulation 123/67 on the common market organisation in poultrymeat, see Case 111/76, *Officier van Justitie v Beert van den Hazel*, ECLI:EU:C:1977:83, where the Court held (paras 13 and 18–19): 'Once the [Union] has, pursuant to Article 40 of the Treaty, legislated for the establishment of the common organization of the market in a given sector, Member States are under an obligation to refrain from taking any measure which might undermine or create exceptions to it … It thus follows from the general tenor of the regulation that, as regards the internal trade of the [Union], the organization of the market in the product in question is based upon freedom of commercial transactions under conditions of genuine competition. Even if the national restrictions on slaughter must be regarded as referring to the production and not to the marketing of the products they are also prohibited by Article 2 of Regulation No 123/67 as amounting to withdrawal of the products from the market and as constituting quantitative restrictions capable of affecting, potentially at any rate, the system of trade as it has been set up by the organization of the market established by Regulation No 123/67.'

[80] Case 31/74, *Galli*, ECLI:EU:C:1975:8.

The latter had, again, been adopted to establish 'a framework of organization calculated to meet all foreseeable situations';[81] and it had in particular created a 'price system' so as 'to make possible complete freedom of trade within the [Union] and to regulate external trade'.[82] Galli had been accused of breaching an Italian law fixing maximum prices for cereal goods; and in his defence, he pleaded that the Italian legislation was pre-empted by the Union legislative system. The Court found that this was indeed the case:

> So as to ensure the freedom of internal trade the regulation comprises a set of rules intended to eliminate both the obstacles to free movement of goods *and all distortions in intra-[Union] trade due to market intervention by Member States other than that authorized by the regulation itself ...*
>
> *Such a system excludes any national system of regulation impeding directly or indirectly, actually or potentially, trade within the [Union].* Consequently, as concerns more particularly the price system, any national provisions, the effect of which is to distort the formation of prices as brought about within the framework of the [Union] provisions applicable, *are incompatible with the regulation.*
>
> Apart from the substantive provisions relating to the functioning of the common organization of the market in the sector under consideration, Regulation No 120/67 comprises a framework of organization designed in such a way as to enable the [Union] and Member States to meet all manner of disturbances.[83]

The Court here, again, used the *Dassonville* formula to delineate the pre-emptive scope of Union *legislation*. This total pre-emption was justified on the basis that 'the very existence of a common organization of the market' had 'the effect of precluding Member States from adopting in the sector in question unilateral measures capable of impeding intra-[Union] trade'.[84] Yet this 'conceptualist-federalist' approach to Union pre-emption was, as the insightful analysis by Waelbroeck has

---

[81] ibid para 9.

[82] ibid paras 9 and 11.

[83] ibid paras 12–16. In a second part of the judgment the Court even extended this to Common Market Organisations (CMOs) that would not include a 'price system' (ibid paras 26–27).

[84] ibid para 27. See also Case 51/74, *PJ van der Hulst's Zonen v Produktschap voor Siergewassen*, ECLI:EU:C:1975:9, esp para 25: 'Once the [Union] has, pursuant to Article 40 of the Treaty, legislated for establishment of a common organization of the market in a given sector, Member States are under an obligation to refrain from taking any measure which might undermine or create exceptions to it.' See further Case 83/78, *Pigs Marketing Board v Raymond Redmond*, ECLI:EU:C:1978:214, paras 55 and 58: 'It follows that, having regard to the structure of Regulation No 2759/75, which is now in force, the provisions of the Treaty relating to the abolition of tariff and commercial barriers to intra-[Union] trade and in particular Articles [34 and 35] on the abolition of quantitative restrictions and of all measures having equivalent effect on imports and exports are to be regarded as an integral part of the common organization of the market ... Hence any provisions or national practices which might alter the pattern of imports or exports or influence the formation of market prices by preventing producers from buying and selling freely within the State in which they are established, or in any other Member State, in conditions laid down by [Union] rules and from taking advantage directly of intervention measures or any other measures for regulating the market laid down by the common organization are incompatible with the principles of such organization of the market.'

shown, subsequently complemented by a 'pragmatic' approach.[85] In *Sadam*, the Court thus held:

> Article [34] of the Treaty prohibits in trade between Member States all measures having an effect equivalent to quantitative restrictions and this prohibition is repeated in Article 35 of Regulation No 1009/67 as regards the market in sugar. *For the purposes of this prohibition it is sufficient that the measures in question are likely to constitute an obstacle, directly or indirectly, actually or potentially, to imports between Member States.* Although a maximum price applicable without distinction to domestic and imported products *does not in itself constitute a measure having an effect equivalent to a quantitative restriction*, it may have such an effect when it is fixed at a level such that the sale of imported products becomes, if not impossible, more difficult than that of domestic products.[86]

What is interesting about the 'pragmatic' approach here is that the Court, after having defined the scope of the *legislative* prohibition on import restrictions via the *Dassonville* formula, held that measures 'applicable without distinction to domestic and imported products' would generally *not in themselves* constitute import restrictions. On the contrary, the Court would in future cases have recourse to a classic discrimination analysis so as to see whether such indistinctly applicable measures would fall within the scope of the specific Regulation.[87]

# VI.  Conclusion: Towards a Re-reading of *Cassis*

What meaning can be given to the judicial 'raw material' presented in the previous four sections? And to what extent can they shed new light on the meaning of *Dassonville* and its famous formula? The following conclusions from the case law up to *Cassis* can immediately be drawn.

*First*, the Court clearly analysed Article 34 and Article 35 TFEU in the same manner. The notions of MEEQR in Article 34 and Article 35 were regarded as identical. This parallelism is particularly apparent when the Court uses the *Dassonville* formula for Article 35 cases.[88]

*Second*, despite its common approach towards Articles 34 and 35, the Court develops a plurality of jurisprudential lines that follow their own distinctive logic

---

[85] The two approaches were famously identified by M Waelbroeck, 'The Emergent Doctrine of Community Pre-emption – Consent and Re-delegation' in T Sandalow and E Stein, *Courts and Free Markets: Perspectives from the United States and Europe*, vol 2 (Oxford, Clarendon Press, 1982) 548.

[86] Joined Cases 88 to 90/75, *Società SADAM and others v Comitato Interministeriale dei Prezzi and others*, para 15. For an extensive early discussion of *SADAM*, see M Waelbroeck, 'Annotation on SADAM' (1977) 14 *CML Rev* 89. See also Case 65/75, *Tasca*, ECLI:EU:C:1976:30.

[87] For such a discrimination rationale, see Joined Cases 10–14/75, *Procureur de la République at the Cour d'Appel Aix-en-Provence and Fédération Nationale des Producteurs de Vins de Table and Vins de Pays v Paul Louis Lahaille and others*, ECLI:EU:C:1975:119; Joined Cases 89/74, 18 and 19/75, *Procureur Général at the Cour d'Appel Bordeaux v Robert Jean Arnaud and others*, ECLI:EU:C:1975:118; as well as Case 64/75, *Procureur Général at the Cour d'Appel Lyon v Henri Mommessin and others*, ECLI:EU:C:1975:171.

[88] eg Case 53/76, *Procureur de la République de Besançon v Les Sieurs Bouhelier and others* (n 52) para 16.

and rhetoric.[89] The judicial analysis of 'border measures' thus follows a different line of reasoning than that for 'internal measures'; and within the category of internal measures, the judicial reasoning with regard to intellectual property rights is fundamentally different from all other internal measures.

*Third*, in the context of border measures, the Court does not apply a discrimination test but an absolute restriction test. That absolute restriction test is often expressed via the *Dassonville* formula. However, the Court here also elaborates a distinction that it had previously made in *International Fruit*: border measures hindering goods produced in Member States are per se prohibited, while border measures for third-country goods are subject to a 'rule of reason'. Yet importantly, this rule of reason was originally specific and exclusive to this third-country context.[90]

*Fourth*, internal measures are, in the absence of Union harmonisation, subject to a discrimination test.[91] With regard to indistinctly applicable measures, the Court thus expressly examines whether the national measure formally or materially discriminates against imports or exports. An important – but limited – interpretative pointer here is Directive 70/50, but only with regard to one category of national measures.[92]

*Fifth*, there appears to exist one important exception to the discrimination test for internal measures: national intellectual property laws. The reasons behind the special treatment given to national intellectual property rights probably lie in their nature as *exclusive national* rights, and the Court consequently comes to treat them as analogous to 'import' bans. National intellectual property laws are

---

[89] This point was perhaps first made by Luigi Daniele, who argued in 1984 that there was not one but many notions of MEEQR (L Daniele, 'Réflexions d'ensemble sur la notion de mesure ayant un effet équivalant à une restriction quantitative' (1984) 281 *Revue du Marché commun* 477, 481, 'Notre examen nous permit, en effet, de constater que la Cour a dû, au cours des années, adopter des approches sensiblement différentes, selon le type de mesure examinée et selon le domaine visé. L'impression que l'on retire de la jurisprudence des dernières années est que l'unité de la notion de mesure d'effet équivalent, telle que consacrée dans la « formule *Dassonville* », n'a pas résiste à l'épreuve des fait que dans une mesure limitée, et qu'à l'heure actuelle il ne serait pas hasardeux de parler, tout au moins sue le plan de l'application pratique, d'une pluralité de notions, toutes rapportables, plus ou moins directement, à la « formule *Dassonville* », mais en même temps toutes suffisamment diversifiées les unes des autres pour qu'elles soient examinées séparément.'

[90] This is a point that hardly any of the post-*Cassis* commentators on *Dassonville* picked up; and because this was not realised, it was (wrongly) assumed that the *Dassonville* rule-of-reason applied to all measures falling within Art 34; and this, in turn, led to the mistaken view that *Cassis* simply placed the *Dassonville* rule-of-reason approach on firmer ground. One of the early 'culprits' in this context is probably L Gormley, *Prohibiting Restrictions on Trade within the EEC: The Theory and Application of Articles 30–36 of the EEC Treaty* (Amsterdam and New York, North Holland, 1985) 51.

[91] In this sense, see also W Veelken, 'Maßnahmen gleicher Wirkung wie mengenmäßige Beschränkungen' (1977) 12 *Europarecht* 311. For the opposite view, see L Gormley, *Prohibiting Restrictions in Trade within the EEC* (n 90) 22, where it is claimed that through *Dassonville*, '[t]he discrimination criterion was firmly rejected'. For the modern version of this reading, see inter alia Barnard, *The Substantive Law of the EU* (n 1) 74, as well as Maduro, 'Revisiting the Free Movement of Goods' (n 1) 490.

[92] The Directive is only relevant for category 2 cases (four out of seven cases); it hardly plays any role within the other case categories. There indeed appears to be only one case in which the Directive was invoked for border measures (*Rewe*), while there seem to be no intellectual property or agricultural cases invoking the Directive.

therefore treated as automatic violations of Article 34, which require justification under Article 36.

*Sixth*, and finally, with regard to national agricultural laws, a completely different jurisprudential logic altogether is developed. The prohibition of quantitative restrictions on imports or exports is here embedded in positive Union legislation; and due to the CAP's aim to establish a complete Union scheme, the legislative (!) prohibition on quantitative restrictions generally receives a broader scope – a scope that may include all measures that 'directly or indirectly, actually or potentially' interfere with the Union legislative system.

What do these six conclusions mean for the traditional *Dassonville–Cassis* story – told and retold in the 'authoritative' accounts of European law? That story is based on a serious misreading when it argues, as the 'Introduction' to this chapter set out, that the *Dassonville* Court radically abandoned the international GATT categories by giving Article 34 a 'national' scope.[93] In light of the empirical evidence and the systematic analysis of the case law submitted above, it is impossible to agree with such a reading. Indeed, the normative solution that emerged from the early jurisprudence was this: in the absence of a textual equivalent to Article III:4 GATT, Article 34 TFEU assumed two functions. In addition to outlawing 'border measures' à la Article XI GATT that would directly or indirectly affect international trade, Article 34 TFEU would also outlaw 'internal measures' – but only when they discriminated against imports. This solution ingeniously filled the textual gap that the EU Treaty-makers had left open. But by importing the Article III:4 GATT solution into Article 34 TFEU, the Court in no way challenged the conceptual pillar of international trade law – the internal sovereignty of a state to regulate its national market.

This doctrinal frame would only be fundamentally challenged in *Cassis de Dijon* – the subject of this book. Through *Cassis*, a true – *federal* – revolution would take place. The opposite reading, according to which *Cassis* is but a 'conservative' judgment that returns regulatory powers to the Member States, must, by contrast, be rejected as untenable.[94] It shows, once more, that each generation of European law scholars must 're-read' the classics in order to critically engage with the 'traditional' interpretations that are 'given to us' by the past 'authorities' of European law. And more importantly still, it also means that any EU law 'theory' worthy of that name must first establish its 'facts' and the concrete 'order(s)' through which they are transmitted to us before moving into the abstract heights of speculative 'philosophical' thought. We need, to quote Quentin Skinner, 'more history' and 'less philosophy' – and, if I may politely add, 'no theology' – in the study of the EU. The internal market constitutes an excellent starting point for such a 'critical' programme. For no other area of European law was historically more essential – both in substantive *and* constitutional terms – for the changing *normative* and *decisional* structures of European law.

---

[93] For representatives of this view, see n 1.

[94] Weiler, 'Epilogue' (n 2) 231. For a detailed discussion of where 'Cassis' potentially comes from, see Schütze, 'Framing *Dassonville*' (n *), as well as ch 3 of this volume by Catherine Barnard.

# 3

# The Missing Ingredient in *Cassis de Dijon*: An Exercise in Legal Archaeology

CATHERINE BARNARD

## I. Introduction

It is bread and butter for most EU lawyers that the principle of mutual recognition was first recognised by the Court of Justice in the seminal decision of *Cassis de Dijon*,[1] and since then it has formed the cornerstone of EU judicial and legislative activity, not just in supporting the free movement of goods but in fields as diverse as the recognition of qualifications and criminal matters.[2] It is also well known that the Court developed the doctrine of mandatory requirements in *Cassis de Dijon* as a limit to the consequences of mutual recognition.

Like many EU lawyers, I have taught this case for years. But I have often had a queasy feeling: is my interpretation and presentation of this case in fact correct? This queasiness ultimately provided a spur to research what eventually became this chapter. There were four questions I wanted to find answers to. First, to what extent did *Cassis de Dijon* actually establish the principles of mutual recognition and mandatory requirements? Second, if *Cassis de Dijon* did establish those two principles, why did the Court choose this case to develop them? Third, what was the inspiration for those principles? Fourth, why and how did the principle of mutual recognition start somewhat in the shadows of the judgment in *Cassis* only to emerge into the sunshine in subsequent case law and policy? I assumed there were simple answers to these simple questions. I was wrong.

---

[1] Case 120/78 *Rewe Zentral AG v Bundesmonopolverwaltung für Branntwein (Cassis de Dijon)*, ECLI:EU:C:1979:42.
[2] See, eg, L Larsen, 'Mutual recognition in the field of criminal law – A short-cut with obstacles' *Europa Working Paper 2014/10*: M Moestl, 'Preconditions and Limits of Mutual Recognition' (2010) 47 *CML Rev* 405; Sir John Thomas, 'The Principle of Mutual Recognition – success or failure?' (2013) 13 *ERA Forum* 585; K Lenaerts, *The Principle of Mutual Recognition in the area of Freedom, Security and Justice*, Fourth Annual Sir Jeremy Level Lecture, University of Oxford, 2015.

Why is it interesting to answer these questions? In part, it is because I was curious about the people involved in the case, as parties, judges and subsequent players.[3] What motivated the parties to litigate, and why did they not simply comply with German rules? How did the parties conceive of the legal issues involved? Who and what drove the Court to decide as it did? Why did the principle of mutual recognition, now so important in the jurisprudence, make such a brief appearance in *Cassis*.

Brian Simpson might be pleased about the light being shone on *Cassis de Dijon* in this way.[4] He notes that there is something very peculiar about the tradition in legal academia of suppressing curiosity about cases.[5] He explains it on the basis of the theory of adjudication – where 'most contextual information about cases is simply irrelevant'. Yet, as he notes, much of the information that is excluded has explanatory value: 'for example, what looks like an isolated piece of litigation may be in reality a mere skirmish in a long-standing feud, or an agreed test case'.[6] He toyed with the idea of using the term 'legal archaeology' to describe his contextual study of cases.[7] He argued that a reported case does in some ways resemble those traces of past activity such as crop marks, the footings of walls, pottery shards – from which the archaeologist attempts, 'by excavation, scientific testing, comparison and analysis to reconstruct and make sense of the past'.[8] He continued:

> Cases need to be treated as what they are, fragments of antiquity, and we need, like archaeologists, gently to free these fragments from the overburden of legal dogmatics, and try, by relating them to other evidence, which has to be sought outside the law library, to make sense of them as events in history and incidents in the evolution of the law.[9]

I like this description of the activity I have tried to undertake in my approach to *Cassis de Dijon*. However, for me, a lot of the evidence I rely on comes from within the case itself rather than outside it, and from looking at other cases of this period. By piecing together these fragments it is possible to construct a particular understanding of the decision in *Cassis de Dijon* and its place in the history of European integration. In this way this chapter provides a legal complement to the archival work conducted by the historian Brigitte Leucht in chapter 4. By reconstructing the context in which *Cassis de Dijon* was decided, it is possible to see that the principles articulated in the case can be traced back to earlier decisions, to earlier legislation, and to earlier principles. *Cassis de Dijon* was no bolt from the blue.

---

[3] See further ch 11 by Karen Alter in this volume on how lawyers view cases.
[4] AW Brian Simpson, *Leading Cases in the Common Law* (Oxford, Clarendon, 1995) 10.
[5] ibid 10.
[6] ibid 11.
[7] ibid 12. Cf W Twining, 'What is the point of legal archaeology?' (2012) 3 *Transnational Legal Theory* 166.
[8] ibid.
[9] ibid.

The chapter is structured as follows. It begins by looking at the judgment in *Cassis de Dijon* and how the Court reasoned the case, to see if it did in fact establish the two principles for which it is famed. It will argue that while *Cassis* did establish the principle of mandatory requirements in respect of goods, the introduction of mutual recognition is significantly more tentative (section II). The chapter then considers the extent to which the key players in the litigation persuaded the Court in *Cassis de Dijon* to make an apparently significant departure from its earlier case law, and why the Court decided to make that jump (section III). It will suggest that a combination of circumstances, not least the constant failure of the Member States to comply with their Treaty obligations, despite repeated programmes on the removal of technical obstacles to trade, eventually forced the Court to act. This raises the question as to the origins of the ideas of mutual recognition and mandatory requirements. It will be argued that while the source of the idea of mandatory requirements is easily identifiable, not least by looking at the submissions of the parties and of the Commission, this is not the case with the principle of mutual recognition. It will be suggested that there are a number of potential sources, both internal and external to the EU, for the principle of mutual recognition, but the internal sources are more likely to have served as inspiration for the Court in *Cassis de Dijon* (section IV). Section V then looks at how the principle of mutual recognition moved from almost a throw-away line in *Cassis* to a free-standing principle in its own right. Section VI concludes.

# II. The Judgment and What it Established

## A. Introduction

The facts of *Cassis de Dijon* are very well known: a German importer, Rewe, challenged a German regulation that stopped it from importing into Germany French Cassis, manufactured in accordance with French law but with a lower alcohol content than that specified by German law. As Alter and Meunier-Aitsahalia noted,[10] the German law had already been challenged in 1974 infringement proceedings brought by the Commission in a case involving French Anisette, whose alcohol content was also too 'low'. The infringement proceedings were dropped the following year after a political settlement was reached under which the Anisette was allowed on to the German market. However, the German law remained intact. Alter and Meunier-Aitsahalia argued that *Cassis* was selected as a test case by the claimant's lawyer, Dr Gert Meier, a key figure in this drama, to

---

[10] K Alter and S Meunier-Aitsahalia, 'Judicial Politics in the European Community. European Integration and the Path-Breaking *Cassis de Dijon* Decision' (1994) 26 *Comparative Political Studies* 535, 538.

challenge the Commission/Germany agreement and to provoke harmonisation of the alcohol industry. As Leucht's chapter demonstrates, Meier took an active interest in questions of European integration. She notes that he

> published an article on the problems involved in devising a legal framework for [an EU]-wide alcohol market; co-authored a work on the Rewe group, the wholesale chain he represented when he invoked EU law ... [in] the *Cassis de Dijon* decision; and later on, he contributed to the discussion on food law in law journals.[11]

I am told by the lawyers working at the time that Meier imported four boxes of Cassis de Dijon from France in order to have them seized by the German Custom officers at Frankfurt Airport.[12] So, on behalf of Rewe, he asked the German Bundesmonopolverwaltung für Branntwein (Federal Monopoly Administration for Spirits) to make the same exception for Cassis as it had for Anisette. When it refused, Rewe challenged this decision before the Verwaltungsgericht Darmstadt, which referred the case to the Hessisches Finanzgericht, which in turn decided to refer the case to the Court of Justice.

## B. The Judgment

So what did the Court actually say in *Cassis*? It began by recasting the referring court's question at paragraph 6:

> The national court is thereby asking for assistance in the matter of interpretation in order to enable it to assess whether the requirement of a minimum alcohol content may be covered ... by the prohibition on all measures having an effect equivalent to quantitative restrictions in trade between Member States contained in [Article 34] of the Treaty ...[13]

In paragraph 8 the Court introduced the notion of mandatory requirements, which Member States could invoke to justify their restrictive rules (emphasis added):

> In the absence of common rules relating to the production and marketing of alcohol – a proposal for a regulation submitted to the Council by the Commission on 7 December 1976 (Official Journal C 309, p 2) not yet having received the Council's approval – it is for the Member States to regulate all matters relating to the production and marketing of alcohol and alcoholic beverages on their own territory.

> Obstacles to movement within the Community resulting from disparities between the national laws relating to the marketing of the products in question must be accepted

---

[11] Ch 4 of this volume, section II.A (footnotes omitted).

[12] Interview on file with the author.

[13] The referring court also asked at para 6 about the compatibility of the rule with Art 37 EEC, but the Court said at para 7 that that provision was 'irrelevant with regard to national provisions which do not concern the exercise by a public monopoly of its specific function – namely, its exclusive right – but apply in a general manner to the production and marketing of alcoholic beverages, whether the latter are covered by the monopoly in question'.

in so far as those provisions may be recognized as being necessary in order to satisfy *mandatory requirements* relating in particular to the effectiveness of fiscal supervision, the protection of public health, the fairness of commercial transactions and the defence of the consumer.

In paragraphs 9–13 the Court demolished the German Government's defence of its rules on grounds of public health and fairness of commercial transactions. The Court thought suitable labelling would be enough. This led it to conclude in paragraph 14:

> It is clear from the foregoing that the requirements relating to the minimum alcohol content of alcoholic beverages do not serve a purpose which is in the general interest and such as to take precedence over the requirements of the free movement of goods, which constitutes one of the fundamental rules of the [Union].
>
> In practice, the principle [*sic*] effect of requirements of this nature is to promote alcoholic beverages having a high alcohol content by excluding from the national market products of other Member States which do not answer that description.

The Court therefore concluded that 'the unilateral requirement imposed by the rules of a Member State of a minimum alcohol content for the purposes of the sale of alcoholic beverages constitutes an obstacle to trade which is incompatible with the provisions of Article [34] of the Treaty'. Then, at the end of paragraph 14, apparently as an afterthought,[14] the Court added what became known subsequently as the principle of mutual recognition:[15]

> There is therefore no valid reason why, provided that they have been lawfully produced and marketed in one of the Member States, alcoholic beverages should not be introduced into any other Member State; the sale of such products may not be subject to a legal prohibition on the marketing of beverages with an alcohol content lower than the limit set by the national rules.

The Court did not need the principle of mutual recognition to answer the question; it seems to have thrown it in to buttress its arguments on justification. Nevertheless, the principle does appear again in the conclusions:

> [T]he concept of 'measures having an effect equivalent to quantitative restrictions on imports' contained in Article [34] of the Treaty is to be understood to mean that the fixing of a minimum alcohol content for alcoholic beverages intended for human consumption by the legislation of a Member State also falls within the prohibition laid

---

[14] Cf T Hartley, *The Foundations of European Community Law* (Oxford, Oxford University Press, 1988) 78–79: 'A common tactic is to introduce a new doctrine gradually … if there are not too many protests it will be reaffirmed in later cases.'

[15] There is much dispute over the accuracy of this term: see, eg, JHH Weiler, 'Mutual Recognition, Functional Equivalence and Harmonization in the Evolution of the European Common Market and the WTO' in F Padoa Schioppa (ed), *The Principle of Mutual Recognition in the European Integration Process* (Basingstoke, Palgrave Macmillan, 2005) 45, who prefers 'functional parallelism' or 'functional equivalence', but since 'mutual recognition' is the term most commonly in use, it will be used in this chapter. See also P Oliver, 'Measures of Equivalent Effect: a reappraisal' (1982) 19 *CML Rev* 217 on the use of the term 'mutual recognition'.

down in that provision where the importation of alcoholic beverages lawfully produced and marketed in another Member State is concerned.[16]

The case itself could easily have been dealt with under the existing principles in Articles 34 and 36 TFEU.[17] By preventing the lower-alcohol French Cassis from being sold on the German market, Germany's rules clearly interfered with the free movement of goods. *Dassonville*[18] had already made clear that all trading rules that hindered, directly or indirectly, actually or potentially, inter-state trade breached Article 34 TFEU.[19] This forced the German Government to come up with a defence based on one of the express derogations under Article 36 TFEU. It relied on a public-health argument – rightly rejected – but that would surely have been enough. The Court could have stopped there but it did not. So why did it do what it did, and where did the ideas come from?

## III.   The Parties, the Interveners and the Advocate General

So to what extent were the parties, the interveners and the Advocate General responsible for prompting the Court to make this remarkable shift? As we shall see, there is a case to be made for the Commission's and the Advocate General's influencing the introduction of mandatory requirements in the field of goods, but it is harder to trace their influence on the creation of mutual recognition. The Advocate General's Opinion can also be read as a call to arms for the Court to intervene to deal with the legislative blockage in remedying technical barriers to trade, but it is hard to construe his Opinion as developing the contours of the principle of mutual recognition.

### A.   The Parties and the Interveners

#### i.   *The Claimant/Dr Gert Meier*

Dr Gert Meier, on behalf of Rewe, the German claimant, made a beguilingly simple argument:

> To prohibit the marketing of a product from one Member State in another Member State hinders the importation of that product in a direct and immediate manner; it is therefore a measure having an effect equivalent to a quantitative restriction on imports prohibited by Article [34 TFEU], subject to the exceptions laid down by [Union] law.[20]

---

[16] *Cassis de Dijon* (n 1) para 15.
[17] The Advocate General seems to have thought this too: ibid para 3.
[18] Case 8/74 *Procureur du Roi v Dassonville* [1974] ECR 837, para 5.
[19] Cf Schuetze's chapter in this volume (ch 2), where he argues that *Dassonville* applies to distinctly applicable border measures and focuses only on discrimination between imports (direct and indirect).
[20] *Cassis de Dijon* (n 1) 652.

This idea is also mentioned by the referring court in its first question to the Court of Justice:

> Must the concept of measures having an effect equivalent to quantitative restrictions on imports contained in Article [34 TFEU] be understood as meaning that the fixing of a minimum wine-spirit content for potable spirits laid down in the German *Branntweinmonopolgesetz*, the result of which is that traditional products of other Member States whose wine-spirit content is below the fixed limit cannot be put into circulation in the Federal Republic of Germany, also comes within this concept?[21]

The Court reproduced Rewe's submission in its judgment:

> The [claimant] takes the view that the fixing by the German rules of a minimum alcohol content leads to the result that well-known spirits products from other Member States of the Union cannot be sold in the Federal Republic of Germany and that the said provision therefore constitutes a restriction on the free movement of goods between Member States which exceeds the bounds of the trade rules reserved to the latter.[22]

Rewe also referred to Article 3 of Directive 70/50[23] (the Court did not). Although the ninth recital suggests that equally applicable rules are lawful,[24] Article 3 says that there are circumstances where 'measures governing the marketing of products which deal, in particular, with shape, size, weight, composition, presentation, identification or putting up and which are equally applicable to domestic and imported products' may be unlawful. Rewe continued that the German regulation on the minimum wine-spirit content of potable spirits (ie a measure concerning the composition of the good) 'renders it impossible, in that country [Germany], to market and therefore to import from other Member States certain liqueurs which are known and marketed there in that form, including "Cassis de Dijon".[25] The manufacture of those liqueurs in a form specifically designed for the German market would make their importation more difficult and more costly in relation to the disposal of national products.

With hindsight, it could be argued that Rewe made an appealing argument that paved the way for the principle of mutual recognition: German law precluded the marketing of a very fine, traditional well-known product from another Member State. Why did that product have to be changed, without good reason, before it could be marketed in Germany? In the absence of harmonisation, why did German law, not French law, apply?

---

[21] ibid.

[22] ibid para 4.

[23] *Official Journal*, English Special Edition 1970 (I), p 17.

[24] 'Whereas effects on the free movement of goods of measures which relate to the marketing of products and which apply equally to domestic and imported products are not as a general rule equivalent to those of quantitative restrictions, since such effects are normally inherent in the disparities between rules applied by Member States in this respect …'

[25] *Cassis de Dijon* (n 1) 653.

## ii. The German Government

It was, of course, not in the German Government's interests to advocate any principle of mutual recognition; it had to defend its rules. Its arguments ran as follows. First, it said that the Treaty prohibited only discriminatory rules; the rule at issue in *Cassis de Dijon* was equally applicable and therefore Article 34 TFEU did not apply. It said any obstacles to trade were due to the co-existence of two legal orders of two Member States that have

> traditionally laid down different minimum requirements in relation to the alcohol content of various spirits. The mere fact that German law contains stricter minimum requirements,which, when viewed objectively, give no advantage to national producers, cannot constitute a material discrimination within the meaning of Article [34] of the Treaty.[26]

Second, it invoked the (nightmare, to Germany) scenario of what might occur if Rewe was right:

> [I]t should be noted that its consequence would be that the minimum alcohol content of a given product in the Federal Republic of Germany would no longer be governed by German law but by French law; in consequence, the lower minimum alcohol content fixed by French law should also be extended to the whole of German national production. … The result would be to lower minimal requirements to the lowest level set in any given national rules, in the absence of the authorization required by Article [115 TFEU], which presupposes the consent of the Member States.[27]

In other words, there would be *de facto* extraterritorial application of French law and a race to the bottom in terms of setting standards.

## iii. The Danish Government

While Germany was obviously against any nascent idea of mutual recognition, the Danish Government intervened to draw the Court's attention to the fact that fruit-based wines, such as the Danish cherry wine, were also affected by the marketing prohibition under the German rules in relation to the minimum wine-spirit content of potable spirits. It therefore supported Rewe's position and called for an affirmative answer to the question referred.[28]

## iv. The Commission

It might have been thought that the Commission would have been the principal advocate for the principle of mutual recognition, given its subsequent enthusiastic

---

[26] ibid 656.
[27] ibid.
[28] ibid 658.

support for the idea. However, there is not much evidence for this in its submissions. According to the report for the hearing, the Commission's starting point – like the Court's subsequently – was the question of justification:

> In so far as provisions relating to the composition or nature of the components of certain beverages or foodstuffs are not designed to ensure protection of health, restrictions on trade may be justified, in accordance with Article 36 [TFEU], only on the basis of the principle of the protection of the consumer (consumer information and protection against fraud) and that of fair competition between producers.[29]

Thus, the Commission suggested that Article 36 TFEU was wide enough to include justifications based on consumer protection and fair competition between producers. As we now know, the Court dealt with the issue in a different way, by agreeing to widen the justifications through creating a separate list of mandatory requirements.

The Commission was also worried about proportionality: would a labelling requirement be more proportionate than a total prohibition on sale? Given the sensitivity of the issue, the Commission thought that rules concerning the minimum wine spirit content might 'contribute to ensuring fair competition and consumer protection'.[30] It added, 'Where suitable designation or labelling of the product is not sufficient to avoid any error on the part of the consumer or where it is wholly or largely impossible to supply the requisite information, a prohibition on sale may be justified.'[31] Yet, in *Cassis de Dijon* itself the Commission concluded that the answer to the national court's question should be that the fixing of an equally applicable minimum wine-spirit level in alcoholic drinks could be 'justified in the interests of consumer protection and fair competition between producers of potable spirits'.[32] However, it continued,

> such rules are excessive and therefore constitute a prohibited measure having an effect equivalent to quantitative restrictions on imports where their consequence is that, notwithstanding a suitable indication, typical products from other Member States, manufactured according to a particular process and characterized traditionally by an alcohol content which is lower than the limit fixed may not be put into circulation in the Member State concerned or may be put into circulation there only if they conform to unreasonable requirements.[33]

Thus, the Commission suggested that the German rules in this case, while justified, were not proportionate.

Three points may be made about the Commission's observations. First, they show that the Commission saw *Cassis de Dijon* primarily as a case about justification and proportionality (an approach that, as we have seen, the Court largely

---

[29] ibid 658–59.
[30] ibid 659.
[31] ibid.
[32] ibid.
[33] ibid.

followed), not mutual recognition. The fact that so much emphasis was placed on justification was not altogether surprising – the Court had already shown the way in its earlier decision in *Van Binsbergen*,[34] where it had recognised, for the first time, public interest requirements in the field of free movement of services. This is considered further in section III.C.

Second, despite its preoccupation with justification and proportionality, the Commission does seem to countenance some (weak) idea of mutual recognition ('typical products from other Member States, manufactured according to a particular process and characterized traditionally by an alcohol content which is lower than the limit fixed may not be put into circulation in the Member State concerned'), but there is no evidence that the Commission legal service laid any store by it in *Cassis de Dijon* itself. That said, ideas about mutual recognition were in circulation at the time. As Karen Alter notes:[35]

> Although the idea of mutual recognition was not totally new[36] and the notion that mutual recognition might be applied to goods had been evoked previously in some Commission circles [no citation], it was never acted on or even officially suggested because of the member states' opposition.

This fact might help to explain why the Commission (led by Matthies in the legal service) was so reticent in its submissions in *Cassis de Dijon* on the mutual recognition point but so enthusiastic about it in subsequent communications (led by Alfonso Mattera ('Mr Cassis'[37])/DG Internal Market).[38]

Third, the Commission's caution towards how to address what became known much later as 'product requirements'[39] (measures 'applicable without distinction to domestic and imported products'[40]) might be explained, as Advocate General Capotorti suggested, by the fact that the Commission felt it had its hands tied by its own Directive 70/50. As we have seen, the ninth recital of Directive 70/50 said that such rules were *not*, as a general rule, equivalent to those of quantitative restrictions.

---

[34] Case 33/74 *Johannes Henricus Maria van Binsbergen v Bestuur van de Bedrijfsvereniging voor de Metaalnijverheid*, ECLI:EU:C:1974:131, [1974] ECR 1299. See further ch 7 by Albertina Albors-Llorens in this volume.

[35] K Alter, *The European Court's Political Power: Selected Essays* (Oxford, Oxford University Press, 2009) 152.

[36] Her footnote says 'The expression *mutual recognition* was used in the Treaty of Rome in Article 57 with reference to diplomas and professional qualifications. It was also used during the 1970s with respect to financial services. At the time of *Cassis*, however, the expression was not used with reference to goods; only the terms *harmonization, approximation,* or *coordination* were applied to goods.'

[37] B Leucht, 'The Policy Origins of the European Economic Constitution' (2018) 24 *ELJ* 191.

[38] Notably Commission, 'Communication from the Commission regarding the *Cassis de Dijon* judgment' [1980] OJ C256/2, considered by L Gormley, '*Cassis de Dijon* and the Communication from the Commission' (1981) 6 *EL Rev* 454. For a full list of Commission follow-up measures, see P Oliver, *Oliver on the Free Movement of Goods in the European Union*, 5th edn (London, Sweet & Maxwell, 2010) 231.

[39] Joined Cases C-267/91 and C-268/91 *Keck and Mithouard* [1993] ECR I-6097, para 15.

[40] Ninth recital of Directive 70/50.

The Advocate General also noted that the Commission

> opts for prudence (or perhaps for a limited interpretation of Article [34]) on the subject of the formalities upon the completion of which importation is made conditional, stating (in the third recital of the preamble to the directive under consideration) that those formalities do not as a general rule have an effect equivalent to that of 'quantitative restrictions'.[41]

He said that that argument had subsequently been rejected by the Court of Justice in *Donckerwolke*.[42] He continued:

> However, once the transitional period was over and the prohibition on quotas and measures having equivalent effect had thereby become absolute that attitude of prudence was no longer justified.[43]

In a similarly robust vein, the Advocate General said that the statement in the ninth recital of the directive (that the Treaty does not adversely affect the powers of the Member States to regulate trade) had to be 'taken with a pinch of salt'. He said '[s]uch powers have indeed not been transferred to the [Union] but [Union] law is capable of limiting the exercise of them and in fact limits that exercise by means of numerous rules, including Article [34 TFEU]'.[44] The Advocate General thus provided the context for the Court to depart from the constraints of Directive 70/50 and do something new.

## B.  The Advocate General

The Advocate General's Opinion is interesting for what it does – and does not – tell us. He set the context clearly in his opening sentence and provides a significant hint that now is the time for the Court to act to deal with the problem of national regulation of product requirements:

> This new Rewe case presents the Court with the opportunity to tackle the problem of the limits within which the Member States are still free to make the marketing of certain categories of products, whether national or imported, conditional upon the presence of certain characteristics, thereby creating an obstacle to the importation of foreign products within those categories which do not possess the requisite characteristics.[45]

As we have seen, he also thought that Directive 70/50 was, if not a retrograde step, at least a document of the past. He identified the lamentable failure of the Member States to address the problems with non-tariff barriers. He described

---

[41] Opinion of AG Capotorti, *Cassis de Dijon* (n 1) 670.
[42] Case 41/76 *Suzanne Criel, née Donckerwolcke and Henri Schou v Procureur de la République au tribunal de grande instance de Lille and Director General of Customs* [1976] ECR 1921.
[43] Opinion of AG Capotorti, 670, para 4.
[44] ibid.
[45] ibid 666, para 1.

how, on 28 May 1969, the Council drew up a general programme for the removal of technical obstacles[46] and, in particular, a resolution concerning foodstuffs. He pointed out in *Cassis de Dijon* that the 1969 programme made provision, inter alia, for the adoption by the Council before 1 January 1971 of directives in the spirits sector, and it was accompanied by an agreement between the representatives of the governments of the Member States meeting within the Council to establish a provisional system preserving the status quo. The timetable adopted in May 1969 was later replaced by another, annexed to the Council Resolution of 17 December 1973,[47] which postponed until 1 January 1978 the final date for the adoption by the Council of the Commission's proposals relating to spirits. The foot-dragging continued: '[I]t appears that proposals in that field have not yet been submitted to the Council.'[48]

This careful setting out of context by its Advocate General may have persuaded the Court to take a more interventionist approach to free movement of goods, in much the same way as it had been doing in the field of services. Some of the cases coming before the Court in that period had demonstrated to the Court the obstacles experienced by importers.[49] The Commission had also published a Communication, 'Safeguarding free trade in the Community' on 6 November 1978, which emphasised that free movement of foods was being interfered with by an increasing number of restrictive measures.

Alter also notes the Commission's concerns about the failure by the Member States to take action to address non-tariff barriers:[50]

> Under Commissioner Davignon's leadership in the late 1970s, the Commission increased its vigilance over barriers to trade, actively attempting to redirect its harmonization policy.[51] Whereas in 1974, the time of the *Dassonville* ruling, the Commission was still hopeful that a recently adopted directive [Directive 70/50] designed to confront the problem of non-tariff barriers would rectify the situation,[52] by 1979 it was ready for a radical change.

The rest of Advocate General Capotorti's Opinion in *Cassis de Dijon* was devoted to the question of justification. He focused mainly on what could be achieved under Article 36 TFEU. He did, however, observe that in Directive No 75/726 on the approximation of laws concerning fruit juices,[53] the prohibition on the

---

[46] [1969] OJ C76/1.
[47] Council Res on Industrial Policy [1973] OJ C117/1.
[48] Opinion of AG Capotorti, *Cassis de Dijon* (n 1) 671, para. 4.
[49] See eg Case 12/74 *Commission v Germany (Sekt)* [1975] ECR 181; Case 104/75 *De Peijper* [1976] ECR 613.
[50] Alter, *Selected Essays* (n 37) 153.
[51] Her footnote reads, 'In 1978, the Commission complained to the member states about the increasing number of restrictive and protectionist measures and informed them that it was investigating over 400 cases of barriers to free movement of goods (Communication from the Commission to the Parliament and the Council, 10 November 1978).'
[52] This view is supported by, for example, Case 12/74 *Commission v Germany (Sekt)* [1975] ECR 181, where the Court relied on Directive 70/50 to reject the German designation of origin.
[53] [1975] OJ L311/40.

creation of obstacles to intra-Union trade in those products by non-harmonised provisions concerning the composition, manufacturing specifications, packaging or labelling of those products ('product requirements' in modern parlance) (Article 12(1)) did not apply to provisions justified on grounds of 'the repression of unfair competition, in addition to those of the protection of public health, the repression of frauds, the protection of industrial and commercial property, of indications of source and appellations of origin' ('mandatory requirements' in modern parlance) (Article 12(2)).[54] He thus seemed to offer a textual basis to justify the Court's extending the list of derogations to indistinctly applicable product requirements. As we know, the Court followed his lead and created a new non-exhaustive list of 'mandatory requirements', which are rather reminiscent of those in Article 12(2) of Directive 75/726.

At the end of his Opinion the Advocate General added:

> From the point of view of [Union] law, there is nothing to prevent a Member State from fixing a minimum alcohol content for nationally produced spirits or liqueurs, at the same time requiring that the corresponding foreign products should bear a clear indication as to their origin and alcohol content (obviously without misappropriating duly protected national designations).[55]

This almost throwaway comment suggests that the Advocate General thought – like the Commission – that French goods should be able to be sold in Germany without adaptation, provided an adequate label was attached.

## C. Preliminary Conclusions

So where does this leave us? It is possible to see the clear footprint of mandatory requirements in the Advocate General's Opinion. For the Court it was a fairly easy jump to develop mandatory requirements in the field of goods, having recently done so in the field of services. In *Van Binsbergen*,[56] the Court had already paved the way for some additional exceptions to the free movement provisions.[57] There, the Court said:

> However, taking into account the particular nature of the services to be provided, specific requirements imposed on the person providing the service cannot be considered incompatible with the Treaty where they have as their purpose the application of professional rules justified by the general good – in particular rules relating to organization, qualifications, professional ethics, supervision and liability – which are binding upon any person established in the State in which the service is provided.[58]

---

[54] Opinion of AG Capotorti, *Cassis de Dijon* (n 1) 672, para 5.

[55] ibid 674, para 5.

[56] Case 33/74 *Van Binsbergen v Bestuur van de Bedrijfsvereniging voor de Metaalnijverheid*, ECLI:EU:C:1974:131, [1974] ECR 1299.

[57] See also Case 71/76 *Thieffry v Conseil de l'Ordre des avocats à la cour de Paris* [1977] ECR 765, paras 12 and 15.

[58] *Van Binsbergen* (n 56) para 12.

In *Van Wesemael*,[59] again in the field of services, the Court elaborated on this. Not only did the Court reiterate the principle that national restrictions can be 'justified by the general good or by the need to ensure the protection of the entertainer, which are binding upon any person established in the [host] State', but it added 'in so far as the person providing the service is not subject to similar requirements in the Member State in which he is established'.[60] This case was decided on 28 January 1979, a month before *Cassis de Dijon* and by the same judges sitting in *Cassis de Dijon*. Free movement of services and free movement of goods share a common feature: both essentially concern home state control, and thus only a temporary engagement with the host state's legal order.

While it is possible to see some elements of mutual recognition at the tail end of *Van Wesemael*, it is hard to explain the introduction of the mutual recognition principle in *Cassis* on this basis alone. It is certainly possible to find traces of the principle of mutual recognition in *Cassis de Dijon* in the submissions of Rewe, the Commission and the Advocate General, but it is not possible to find the pithy statement on mutual recognition provided by the Court in paragraph 15 of *Cassis*. So this suggests that the Court itself came up with the idea, if not the name (at the time), of mutual recognition.[61] This is the view of Peter Oliver, a former member of the Commission's legal service and expert on the free movement of goods. In correspondence, he wrote:

> Heinrich Ma[t]thies, who appeared for the Commission [in *Cassis de Dijon*], was my boss at the time. Although he spoke about the judgment very frequently and wrote various articles on free movement, I do not recall him mentioning mutual recognition. … I also met Gert Meier, the lawyer for Rewe and read some of his writings at the time; again, I do not recall him saying anything about this. So my feeling is that MR [mutual recognition] was an innovation of the judges themselves …

So, it may be that it was the judges, possibly prompted by Dr Meier but probably influenced by Pescatore[62] (the Juge Rapporteur[63]), who came up with the principle of mutual recognition. I shall return to Pescatore's role in section IV.A.

---

[59] Joined Cases 110 and 111/78 *Ministère public and 'Chambre syndicale des agents artistiques et impresarii de Belgique' ASBL v Willy van Wesemael and others* [1979] ECR 35.

[60] ibid, para 28.

[61] For an early example of the express use of the term 'mutual recognition', see Case C–184/96 *Commission v France (foie gras)* [1998] ECR I–6197, para 28 (on the non-use by France of a mutual recognition clause in its legislation). By the time of Case C–110/05 *Commission v Italy (Trailers)* [2009] ECR I–519, para 34, the Court said 'Article [34 TFEU] reflects the obligation to respect the principles of non-discrimination and of mutual recognition of products lawfully manufactured and marketed in other Member States, as well as the principle of ensuring free access of Community products to national markets (see, to that effect, Case 174/82 *Sandoz* [1983] ECR 2445, paragraph 26; Case 120/78 *Rewe-Zentral* ("*Cassis de Dijon*") [1979] ECR 649, paragraphs 6, 14 and 15; and *Keck and Mithouard*, paragraphs 16 and 17).'

[62] See further Leucht and Alter in chs 4 and 11 respectively in this volume. They also document Pescatore's role in the EUI-led *Integration through law* project.

[63] This is not mentioned in the report but can be seen at https://eur-lex.europa.eu/legal-content/EN/ALL/?uri=CELEX:61978CJ0120 and at http://curia.europa.eu/juris/fiche.jsf?id=C%3B120%3B78%3BRP%3B1%3BP%3B1%3BC1978%2F0120%2FJ&language=en (thanks to Brigitte Leucht for pointing this out).

But where did the idea of mutual recognition come from? In the next section I shall argue that by examining the Treaty, legislative and case-law context of the period, it is possible to make a case that the judges were familiar with the idea of mutual recognition and saw how it was working in analogous areas. Furthermore, it was an idea that was gaining traction at international level, although there is less evidence that the judges were aware of this context. I argue that against this background, it was therefore only a relatively small step to extend the principle to free movement of goods more generally, albeit only tentatively, at least at first.

# IV. Sources of Inspiration for the Idea of Mutual Recognition in Free Movement of Goods

## A. EU Law

The most obvious source of inspiration for the mutual recognition principle in goods comes from the Treaty. There were two references to mutual recognition in the Treaty of Rome. The first was in the now repealed Article 220 EEC. This provided (emphasis added):

> Member States shall, so far as is necessary, enter into negotiations with each other with a view to securing for the benefit of their nationals:
>
> ...
>
> –  the *mutual recognition* of companies or firms within the meaning of the second paragraph of Article 58, the retention of legal personality in the event of transfer of their seat from one country to another, and the possibility of mergers between companies or firms governed by the laws of different countries;
> –  the simplification of formalities governing the reciprocal recognition and enforcement of judgements of courts or tribunals and of arbitration awards.

While this would be an obvious source of inspiration for the broader principle of mutual recognition, there is no evidence that any of the judges sitting in *Cassis de Dijon* had any particular interest in, or knowledge of, company law.[64] That said, as Leucht shows in chapter 4, Pescatore had been intimately involved in the negotiations in the Treaty of Rome, albeit specifically on the role of the Court of Justice.

It is more likely that judges drew inspiration from Article 57 EEC (emphasis added):

> In order to make it easier for persons to take up and pursue activities as self- employed persons, the Council shall, on a proposal from the Commission and after consulting the Assembly [European Parliament], acting unanimously during the first stage and by

---

[64] A search was conducted of the judges' biographies, accompanied by a search for their academic works, on Google, Cambridge's Newton Catalogue, Harvard's Hollis Catalogue, LexisNexis, Westlaw and HeinOnline.

a qualified majority thereafter, issue directives for the *mutual recognition* of diplomas, certificates and other evidence of formal qualifications.

Article 57 EEC reflected long-established practice in international agreements, especially in respect of qualifications. A report by the Asian Development Bank, *Reinventing Mutual Recognition Agreements*, notes that 'One of the earliest MRAs dates back to 1892, when representatives from the colonies of New South Wales, Victoria, Queensland, South Australia, Western Australia, and New Zealand unanimously agreed to mutually recognize certificates of competency for surveyors.'[65] According to Nicolaidis, 'Mutual recognition was formally invented in 1958', citing Article 57 EEC.[66] Crucially, the type of recognition envisaged by Article 57 EEC was 'enhanced recognition', that is mutual recognition of standards, not just of testing regimes.[67] We return to the significance of this point later in this section.

The Court of Justice was clearly familiar with Article 57 EEC. It expressly referred to Article 57 EEC in *Reyners*,[68] when considering whether (what is now) Article 49 TFEU was 'directly applicable'. The Court referred to it again in *Van Binsbergen* (1974)[69] and *Patrick* (1977).[70]

Article 57 EEC was the legal basis for Council Directive 78/1026 concerning the mutual recognition of diplomas, certificates and other evidence of formal qualifications in veterinary medicine.[71] This was at issue in *Auer*,[72] where the Court, after a careful consideration of the Directive, said that for the period prior to the date on which the Member States were required to implement the Directive, the nationals of another Member State could not rely on Article 49 TFEU to practise as a vet in the host state on any conditions other than those laid down by national legislation.

---

[65] Available at www.adb.org/sites/default/files/publication/224071/reinventing-mras-asean.pdf, citing Australian Government Productivity Commission, Mutual Recognition Schemes: Productivity Commission Research Report (Canberra: Australian Government Productivity Commission, 2015), at http://www.pc.gov.au/inquiries/completed/mutual-recognition-schemes/report/mutual-recognition-schemes.pdf. In Latin America too, 'recognition agreements are common and date back to the start of the 20th century': J Nielson, 'Trade Agreements and Recognition', available at https://www.oecd.org/education/skills-beyond-school/33729996.pdf, 168. See also K Nicolaidis, 'Globalization with Human Faces: Managed Mutual Recognition and the Free Movement of Professionals' in F Schioppa (ed), *The Principles of Mutual Recognition in the European Integration Process* (Basingstoke, Palgrave MacMillan, 2005) 129. On the philosophical origins of the principle, see F Guiot, 'Le principe de reconnaissance mutuelle: un mécanisme d'exception(s) multiscalaire au service d'une intégration différentielle' in G Marti and E Carpano (eds), *L'exception en droit de l'Union européenne* (Brussels, Bruylant, 2019).

[66] K Nicolaidis, 'Managed Mutual Recognition: The New Approach to the Liberalization of Professional Services', available at http://users.ox.ac.uk/~ssfc0041/managemr.htm, para 12.

[67] See further Leinarte and Barnard in ch 10 of this volume; and K Nicolaidis and G Schaffer, 'Transnational Mutual Recognition Regimes: Governance without global government' (2005) 68 *Law and Contemporary Problems* 267, 278.

[68] Case 2/74 *Reyners v Belgian State* [1974] ECR 631, para 20.

[69] *Van Binsbergen* (n 57) para 21.

[70] Case 11/77 *Richard Hugh Patrick v Minister for Cultural Affairs*, EU:C:1977:113, para. 17.

[71] [1978] OJ L 362/1. See also the note by K Nicolaidis, 'The *Cassis* Legacy. *Kir, Banks, Plumbers, Drugs, Criminals and Refugees*' in F Nicola and B Davies (eds), *EU Law Stories: Contextual and Critical Histories of European Jurisprudence* (Cambridge, Cambridge University Press, 2017), 278, 281, 'the whole philosophy was defended with great passion by Ralph Dahrendorf, who was able to make limited progress in applying mutual recognition in the professions when he became Commissioner in 1974'.

[72] Case 136/78 *Auer* [1979] ECR 437.

By implication, following the implementation of the Directive, mutual recognition of qualifications would apply. *Auer* was delivered on 7 February 1979 by the Court (Kutscher, Mertens de Wilmars, Mackenzie Stuart, Donner, Pescatore, Sørensen, O'Keeffe, Bosco and Touffait, the same judges as were in *Cassis de Dijon*), two weeks before the decision in *Cassis de Dijon* (20 February 1979). Two years earlier, in *Thieffry*,[73] the Court had contemplated a limited form of mutual recognition of qualifications even in the absence of any EU legislation, based on the states' obligations under Article 5 EEC (now Article 4(3) TEU).[74]

It was not just qualifications that were the subject of the mutual recognition principle: so were driving licences. Although the secondary legislation had not been adopted at the time of the decision in *Choquet*,[75] delivered on 28 November 1978 (three months before the decision in *Cassis*), the Court (Kutscher, Mertens de Wilmars, Mackenzie Stuart, Donner, Pescatore, Sørensen, O'Keeffe, Bosco, all judges who were in *Cassis de Dijon*) was aware of a draft measure[76] whose aim was to introduce a '[Union] driving licence which could be issued on an optional basis ... which, as it would be valid throughout [Union] territory, would in practice be tantamount to mutual recognition of national driving licences by the Member States'. The Court itself referred to this draft and noted that 'national rules relating to the issue and mutual recognition of driving licences by the Member States exert an influence, both direct and indirect, on the exercise of the rights guaranteed by the provisions of the Treaty relating to freedom of movement'.[77]

However, the Court went on to say that a comparative study of the laws of the Member States revealed such difference on the issue of driving licences (eg the nature of driving tests, medical examinations) that the mere recognition of driving licences could not be contemplated unless the requirements for the issue of those driving licences were harmonised to a sufficient extent. Thus, the Court found that the host state could require a migrant to obtain a host state driving licence, provided the conditions for obtaining it were not disproportionate.

These cases show that the judges in *Cassis de Dijon* were well aware of the principle of mutual recognition in the field of free movement of *persons*. But it was not just the persons case law where the principle of mutual recognition had already been raised. I would like to argue that the judges were also aware of the application of the mutual recognition principle in specific sectors in the field of free movement of goods, through a number of less well-known cases decided in the period leading up to *Cassis*.

In *Cassis de Dijon*, Advocate General Capotorti mentioned a 1969 programme. The full title of this programme, which he did not name but was mentioned by the

---

[73] Case 71/76 *Thieffry v Conseil de l'ordre des avocats à la cour de Paris* [1977] ECR 765.
[74] ibid para 16.
[75] Case 16/78 *Choquet* [1978] ECR 2293.
[76] See the summary of the facts and issues (ibid 2299, citing [1976] OJ C8/2).
[77] *Choquet* (n 75) para 5.

Commission in its submissions in the 1978 decision of *Commission v Netherlands (Metrology)*,[78] was the General programme for the elimination of technical barriers to trade in industrial products, foodstuffs and with a view to the *mutual recognition* of inspections.[79] Thus mutual recognition was already being applied in the field of goods, albeit a thinner type of mutual recognition based on the recognition of *inspections*. This was more the norm in international trade[80] than the enhanced mutual recognition (of standards) envisaged by Article 57 EEC. Nevertheless, it does show the relevance of mutual recognition in the field of goods and its importance. As the Full Court (Kutscher, Sørensen, Bosco, Donner, Mertens de Wilmars, Pescatore, Mackenzie Stuart, O'Keeffe and Touffait (again the same judges who heard *Cassis*)) said in *Commission v Netherlands*:

> This general programme was implemented by an outline directive of the Council, Directive No 71/316/EEC … on the approximation of the laws of the Member States relating to common provisions for both measuring instruments and methods of metrological control … whose aim was essentially to harmonize the national provisions relating to the control of those instruments and which was based on the *fundamental principle of mutual recognition* of controls.[81]

Similarly, *Commission v Italy (Agricultural Tractors)*[82] concerned the non-implementation by Italy of Directive 74/150 on the approximation of laws on the type approval of wheeled agricultural or forestry tractors, which introduced a system of EEC type approval based on the principle of *mutual recognition* of checks carried out and of certificates of conformity issued by competent national authorities.[83] The case was heard by the same judges as in *Metrology*, except Mertens de Wilmars and Touffait. The nature of the Directive (mutual recognition of checks and conformity) was noted in the Court's statement of facts.[84] Again, this Directive refers to the thinner form of mutual recognition, namely checks by the exporting state confirming that the exports comply with the importing state's standards.

The principle of mutual recognition was also well established in respect of documents used for import and exports. This was mentioned in Advocate General Mayras' Opinion in *De Peijper*.[85] He described how Article 22 of Directive 75/319 on the approximation of provisions laid down by Law, Regulation or Administrative Action relating to proprietary medicinal products[86] provided that, in the case of the export of any batch of a registered medicinal preparation, the manufacturer

---

[78] Case 95/77 *Commission v Netherlands (metrology)* [1978] ECR 863. This was also repeated in Case 100/77 *Commission v Italy (metrology)* [1978] ECR 879, para. 3.
[79] 1969 Programme (n 46) (emphasis added).
[80] See ch 10 by Leinarte and Barnard in this volume.
[81] *Commission v Netherlands* (n 79) para 3 (emphasis added).
[82] Case 69/77 *Commission v Italy (Agricultural Tractors)* [1978] ECR 1749.
[83] [1974] OJ L84/10.
[84] *Agricultural Tractors* (n 83) 1750.
[85] Case 104/75 *De Peijper* [1976] ECR 613.
[86] [1975] OJ L147/13.

had to enclose a document relating to the product's preparation and supervision.[87] He added:

> By way of compensation facilities are granted to manufacturers with a view to effecting *mutual recognition* of authorizations. This arrangement is designed to allow free movement of medicinal preparations for the maximum benefit of public health so long as the pharmacopoeia of the Member States have not been harmonized.[88]

Likewise, as the Commission noted in its intervention in the Full Court decision in *Simmenthal*,[89] the procedure of the mutual recognition of inspections had been adopted in several harmonisation directives on the trade in animals and meat. The Court itself ruled that:

> The harmonized system of veterinary and public health inspections introduced by the directives is based on the principle that the veterinary and public health guarantees required by each of the Member States are equivalent in nature and it is this principle which guarantees both the protection of health and the equal treatment of products.[90]

These cases show that not only was the principle of mutual recognition reasonably well established in the field of goods, albeit only in specific sectors and concerning controls, inspections and certifications – the thinnest form of mutual recognition – but also that the Court was well aware of its operation. It was a leap, but not such a great leap, to extend it to goods more generally, and to the recognition of standards, as had been done in the field of services.

It is also striking that Judge Pescatore sat on each of these cases. While it is not possible to prove his direct influence, one of my interviewees observed:

> Within the Court the Luxemburger judge, Pierre Pescatore, who enjoyed a huge authority vis-à-vis his colleagues, was convinced by the pleadings of Dr Meyer [sic] [in *Cassis de Dijon*] and persuaded them one after one all the other judges of the Court as to the interpretation of (at the time) Article 30 of the EEC Treaty as enshrining the principle of 'mutual recognition' of products legally traded in other Member States.[91]

And as Leucht shows in chapter 4 in this volume, Pescatore played a crucial role in the creation of the 'constitutional discourse'; and she observes that 'it was no coincidence then that Pescatore was the juge rapporteur in *Cassis de Dijon*'.

## B.  Influences Outside the EU?

As we have already seen, the principle of mutual recognition has a long history in international trade agreements. The requirement of mutual recognition (but again,

---

[87] AG Mayras' Opinion in *De Peijper* (n 85) 653.
[88] ibid (emphasis added).
[89] Case 35/76 *Simmenthal v Italian Minister for Finance* [1976] ECR 1871, 1876.
[90] ibid para 19.
[91] Interviewee asked to remain anonymous but record on file with the author.

without the label) became part of the 9 GATT (General Agreement on Tariffs and Trade) Standards Code, later strengthened and clarified by the 1994 Technical Barriers to Trade (TBT) Agreement. The Standards Code, adopted[92] the same year as *Cassis de Dijon*, aimed to address 'the serious and complex problem of non-tariff distortions of trade'.[93] Among the most complex are 'distortions due to disparities between national standards and technical regulations and the certification, testing and approval procedures which frequently accompany them'.[94] The key provision was Article 5. Article 5(1) considered the question of obstacles to international trade created by technical standards, and specifically the non-discrimination principle:

> Parties shall ensure that technical regulations and standards are not prepared, adopted or applied with a view to creating obstacles to international trade. Furthermore, products imported from the territory of any Party shall be accorded treatment no less favourable than that accorded to like products of national origin and to like products originating in any other country in relation to such technical regulations or standards. They shall likewise ensure that neither technical regulations nor standards themselves nor their application have the effect of creating unnecessary obstacles to international trade.[95]

Article 5(2) then lays down the principle of mutual recognition, albeit in the limited context of conformity assessment.[96] It provides that the Parties are required

> to ensure, whenever possible, that their central government bodies:
> - accept test results, certificates or marks of conformity issued by relevant bodies in the territories of other Parties; or
> - rely upon self-certification by producers in the territories of other Parties;
>
> even when the test methods differ from their own, provided they are satisfied that the methods employed in the territory of the exporting Party provide a sufficient means of determining conformity with the relevant technical regulations or standards.

According to Middleton,[97] mutual recognition had successfully been applied in the European Free Trade Area (EFTA) to the removal of technical barriers to trade, through intergovernmental agreements on recognition of tests. Its potential success in the multilateral context was demonstrated by the fact that since the conclusion of these EFTA agreements, a number of non-EFTA countries have acceded to them.

So at least a limited form of mutual recognition of testing, if not of standards themselves, was on the political agenda around the time of the decision in *Cassis*, but it is not clear whether the judges – or their référendaires – were in any way

---

[92] This agreement was negotiated as part of the Tokyo Round, which took place in 1973–79. Around 100 countries participated in the Tokyo Round, but only 32 were signatories to the TBT Agreement, including most OECD (Organisation for Economic Cooperation and Development) countries, which included EU Member States.

[93] RW Middleton, 'The GATT Standards Code' (1980) 14 *World Trade Law Journal* 201, 201.

[94] ibid.

[95] See now Art 2.2 TBT.

[96] See further ch 10 by Leinarte and Barnard in this volume.

[97] Middleton, 'The GATT Standards Code' (n 93).

aware of this discourse or, if they were, whether they were influenced by these developments.

Likewise, there is little evidence that the Court was influenced by US Constitutional law, in particular Article IV requiring Full Faith and Credit to be given in each State to the public Acts, Records and judicial Proceedings of every other State.[98] There is evidence that at least two of the judges had an interest in US Constitutional law: Pierre Pescatore wrote the Foreword (in 1988) to a book entitled *Le juge et la Constitution aux Etats-Unis d'Amérique et dans l'ordre juridique euro-péen* by Koen Lenaerts, and Max Sørensen wrote an article in the *American Journal of International Law* entitled 'Federal States and the International Protection of Human Rights'.[99] However, it is not clear how this may have shaped their thinking. The full faith and credit clause may have influenced the drafters of the original Article 220 EEC but not the Court in *Cassis*. This is the view of Laurence Gormley, one of the leading writers in the field of free movement of goods. He said 'I am not aware of American influence in [*Cassis*] (unlike for *Blesgen* where the Legal Secretaries looked at Larry Tribe's American Constitutional Law).'[100]

## C. Preliminary Conclusions

So, by way of conclusion, it looks increasingly likely that the Court itself initiated the introduction of the (enhanced) mutual recognition principle in *Cassis de Dijon*, based on earlier developments of EU law rather than on influences from outside the EU. Most strikingly, it was the fullest form of mutual recognition, namely of the standards of the home state, not just the testing, that the Court recognised. This was a significant departure. And it may be for this reason that the Court recognised that the control lost by the host states by way of the introduction of enhanced mutual recognition, was regained by way of mandatory requirements. This might help to explain why the mandatory requirements achieved such prominence in the decision. This brings me to my final question: how did the principle of mutual recognition move from the shadows in paragraph 14 of *Cassis* to centre-stage in today's analysis of the jurisprudence?

# V. The Subsequent Elevation of the Principle of Mutual Recognition

For Peter Oliver, the doyen of free movement of goods, 'the principle of mutual recognition is undoubtedly a manifestation of two fundamental

---

[98] Its origins lay in Art 4 of the Articles of Confederation, which was 'chiefly intended to oblige each state to receive the records of another as full evidence of such acts and judicial proceedings': *James v Allen*, 1 Dall (1 US) 188, 191–92.

[99] M Sørensen, 'Federal States and the International Protection of Human Rights' (1952) 46 *AJIL* 195.

[100] Private correspondence on file with the author.

principles: proportionality; and the duty of sincere cooperation under Art 4(3) TEU'. There is no contemporaneous evidence that Article 4(3) TEU shaped paragraph 14 of *Cassis* at the time, although, as we saw, its predecessor (Article 5 EEC) was referred to in *Thieffry*. Instead, proportionality was seen as the guiding principle. Put simply, a failure to recognise the regulatory conditions of the home state meant the host state measure requiring the application of an entirely different (host state) legal regime was disproportionate. A number of authors continue to see mutual recognition in this way.[101] The focus on mutual recognition as an aspect of the proportionality principle perhaps explains why there was no elaborate discussion about the underlying ideas of mutual trust that became so important in *Opinion 2/13 (Accession to the ECHR)*.[102] It was simply assumed that states would cooperate with each other under the duty of loyal cooperation to deliver a proportionate outcome (mutual recognition).[103]

Viewing the principle of mutual recognition as an aspect of the proportionality assessment helps to explain why mutual recognition appears in paragraph 14 of the *Cassis* judgment, not paragraph 8. The role of the proportionality principle in respect of any assessment of what we now term 'product requirements' was the approach adopted in Article 3 of Directive 70/50 (to which the Advocate General in *Cassis* had referred).[104] It provides (emphasis added):

> This Directive also covers measures governing the marketing of products which deal, in particular, with shape, size, weight, composition, presentation, identification or putting up and which are equally applicable to domestic and imported products, *where the restrictive effect of such measures on the free movement of goods exceeds the effects intrinsic to trade rules.*

---

[101] See, eg, P Oliver, 'Free movement of goods' in C Barnard and S Peers, *European Union Law* (Oxford, Oxford University Press, 2014) 325; and JHH Weiler, 'The Constitution of the Common Market Place: Text and Context in the Evolution of the Free Movement of Goods' in P Craig and G De Búrca (eds), *The Evolution of EU Law* (Oxford, Oxford University Press, 1999) 367, who says mutual recognition is 'not a radical hermeneutic departure, but in fact a very conservative and fully justified application of the principle of proportionality'.

[102] *Opinion 2/13 (Accession to the ECHR)*, ECLI:EU:C:2014:2454.

[103] Although cf Case 46/76 *WJG Bauhuis v The Netherlands State*, ECLI:EU:C:1977:6, para 22: 'This system is based on the trust which Member States should place in each other as far as concerns the guarantees provided by the inspections carried out initially by the veterinary and public health departments of the Member States from which the animals are exported.'

[104] See also A Mattera, 'The principle of mutual recognition and respect for national, regional and local identities and traditions' in Padoa Schioppa (ed), *The Principle of Mutual Recognition* (n 15) 7, who notes a 'profound similarity' between the provisions of Directive 70/50, especially Arts 8, 9, 10 and 11, with the principles laid down in *Cassis de Dijon*. He also cites former Judge R Joliet, 'La libre circulation des Marchandises, l'arret Keck et Mithouard et les nouvelles orientations de la jurisprudence' (1994) 20 *Journal des Tribunaux du Droit européen* 12 to this effect. Cf A Rosas, 'Life after *Dassonville* and *Cassis*: Evolution but no revolution' in M Poiares Maduro and L Azoulai (eds), *The Past and Future of EU Law: The Classics of EU Law revisited on the 50th anniversary of the Rome Treaty* (Oxford, Hart Publishing, 2010) 440, who sees *Cassis* as a 'clear departure' from Directive 70/50.

Seeing the principle of mutual recognition as an aspect of the proportionality principle means that the focus is on the steps taken by the home state in the name of achieving one of the mandatory requirements, as the Court said expressly in *Van Wesemael*. In the early case law the Court did seem to suggest that in order to distinguish the mandatory requirement case law from the Article 36 derogations, the finding of a proportionate, justified national law meant that no breach of Article 34 TFEU was established[105] (as compared to a distinctly applicable measure that did breach Article 34 TFEU and that needed to be defended under Article 36 TFEU). A steer in this direction might have come from Article 3 of Directive 70/50. However, the Court subsequently abandoned this nicety.

Yet it is striking that in the Commission's 1980 Communication on *Cassis* (the first time the Commission had tried to extract policy from a Court decision[106]), the Commission reversed the order of priority between mutual recognition and mandatory requirements.[107] In paragraph 6 of the Communication, the Commission began by setting out the principle of mutual recognition[108] (again not using the label) and then in paragraph 7 the principle of mandatory requirements. The Commission was even more explicit in its Guide to free movement of goods:

> Thus, the mutual recognition principle in the non-harmonised area consists of *a rule and an exception*:
>
> (1) The general rule that, notwithstanding the existence of a national technical rule in the Member State of destination, products lawfully produced or marketed in another Member State enjoy a basic right to free movement, guaranteed by the [TFEU]; and
> (2) The exception that products lawfully produced or marketed in another Member State do not enjoy this right if the Member State of destination can prove that it is essential to impose its own technical rule on the products concerned based on the reasons outlined in Article 34 TFEU or in the mandatory requirements developed in the Court's jurisprudence and subject to the compliance with the principle of proportionality.[109]

In other words, if the host state does not recognise goods lawfully produced and marketed in the home state, and thus does not respect the principle of mutual recognition, there is a breach of the Treaty and the burden then shifts to the

---

[105] See Weiler, 'The Constitution of the Common Market Place' (n 101).

[106] Alter and Meunier-Aitsahalia, 'Judicial Politics in the European Community' (n 11) 541.

[107] See also A Mattera, 'L'Arret "*Cassis de Dijon*": une nouvelle approche pour la réalisation et le bon fonctionnement du marché intérieur' (1980) 23 *Revue du Marché Commun* 505.

[108] Cf Conseil des Communautés européennes: Service juridique du Conseil des Communautés européennes 1980 no 10690/80, which said that the Commission's generalisation of the principle of mutual recognition went too far.

[109] Commission Staff Working Document, 'Free Movement of Goods – Guide to the application of Treaty provisions governing Free Movement of Goods' (Articles 28–30 EC), SEC (2009) 673, 19 (emphasis added).

host state to justify that breach by reference to mandatory requirements or the Article 36 derogations.[110]

The Court now seems to have adopted this approach itself. As it said in *Trailers*:

> [I]n the absence of harmonisation of national legislation, obstacles to the free movement of goods which are the consequence of applying, to goods coming from other Member States where they are lawfully manufactured and marketed, rules that lay down requirements to be met by such goods constitute measures of equivalent effect to quantitative restrictions even if those rules apply to all products alike (see, to that effect, 'Cassis de Dijon', paragraphs 6, 14 and 15 ...[111]

This shows the influence of the Commission's persistence in determining the shape and meaning of *Cassis de Dijon*, a point developed further by Leucht in this volume (chapter 4). It also helps to explain the shift in perspective on mutual recognition – from an adjunct to the mandatory requirements in *Cassis* to a freestanding independent principle in *Trailers*.

# VI.  Conclusions

Alter and Meunier-Aitsahalia report that 'the Legal Services of the Commission and the German Government were stunned by the *Cassis* verdict. Even the German Government had expected the Court to rule against its regulation but no one anticipated that the Court would draw such wide conclusions from the case.'[112] The legal archaeology conducted for this chapter suggests that the outcome in *Cassis* was, in fact, somewhat less surprising than Alter and Meunier-Aitsahalia suggested. As we have seen, mandatory requirements had already been established in the case law on services; it took little to extend them to goods. Mutual recognition, too, had been around since at least the end of the nineteenth century, and was already relatively well enshrined in the Treaty, especially in Article 57 EEC, and in subsequent technical standards legislation. It was also developing an independent

---

[110] See also Regulation 764/2008 [2008] OJ L218/21, Recital 22: 'In accordance with the principle of mutual recognition, the procedure laid down in this Regulation should provide for the competent authorities to communicate in each case to the economic operator, on the basis of the relevant technical or scientific elements available, that there are overriding reasons of public interest for imposing national technical rules on the product or type of product in question and that less restrictive measures cannot be used. The written notice should allow the economic operator to comment on all relevant aspects of the intended decision restricting access to the market. Nothing prevents the competent authority from taking action after the deadline for the receipt of those comments in the absence of a reply from the economic operator.' See also Commission Working Document, 'The concept of "lawfully marketed" in the Mutual Recognition Regulation (EC) No764/2008' COM(2013) 92, 2–3, 'the Member State of destination of a product must allow the placing on its market of a product lawfully marketed in another Member State or in an [EFTA-EEA] state ... unless the procedural requirements for denying mutual recognition established by the Regulation were met'.

[111] *Trailers* (n 62) para 35.

[112] Alter and Meunier-Aitsahalia, 'Judicial Politics in the European Community' (n 11) 540.

life in GATT and elsewhere in international trade, albeit there is little evidence that this influenced the Court in *Cassis*.

Has my queasiness about reading this case abated? Somewhat. I think it is pretty clear that *Cassis de Dijon* did establish the principles of mutual recognition and mandatory requirements for goods, and that the inspiration for those principles was mainly internal (EU-based), not external (international trade based). I think the Court chose *Cassis* to develop those principles because, as the Advocate General made very clear, the legislature was not delivering and the Member States were blocking inter-state trade. And the evolution of mutual recognition itself owes much to the ambition of the Commission.

But why the hesitation? The legal archaeology does reveal a series of contradictions, inconsistencies and confusions. First, *Cassis* was largely seen at the time as a case about the development of mandatory requirements in the field of goods (and, implicitly, that mandatory requirements applied only to indistinctly applicable measures). Yet these mandatory requirements were not in fact needed to decide the case: Article 34 TFEU was breached, and had the German Government produced a coherent argument based on public health to save its rule, the case could have been decided perfectly well under Article 36 TFEU.

Second, although the principle of mutual recognition can be traced to *Cassis de Dijon*, in the Alice-in-Wonderland world of the EU all is not quite as it seems. The principle of mutual recognition was not called by that name, nor was it used to establish any breach of Article 34 TFEU. It was the Commission, in its 1980 and subsequent Communications, that named mutual recognition as a principle in the field of free movement of goods and explained that when the principle was breached there would be a breach of Article 34 TFEU.

Third, the origins of the mutual recognition principle are not clear, but the most plausible explanation lies with the judges, drawing on their experience in related fields – primarily services and, to a lesser extent, goods – and the promptings of Dr Meier. Yet again, none of this is explained in the decision of the Court.

Fourth, there is no reference to mutual trust as a precursor to mutual recognition. Perhaps the Court assumed that Article 4(3) TEU provided the glue to enable the mutual recognition principle to work in practice. Or perhaps it thought that the obligation of mutual recognition would itself help to foster mutual trust – that due to mutual recognition, mutual trust would grow, organically, from the bottom up. In fact, this has not happened,[113] at least not to the extent its proponents had hoped, despite the significantly expanded use of the mutual recognition principle. And so, 35 years later the Court itself addressed to the question and, in *Opinion 2/13 (Accession to the ECHR)*,[114] recognised mutual trust as a constitutional principle of EU law. From mutual trust flows mutual recognition.

---

[113] Some authors are particularly critical, eg Weiler, who described mutual recognition as 'an intellectual breakthrough but a colossal market failure': Weiler, 'The Constitution of the Common Market Place' (n 101) 49.

[114] See n 99.

Would Simpson approve of this exercise in legal archaeology? Perhaps. I think he would approve of the light it shone on the key players, both in front of the Court (especially Dr Meier), in the Court itself (especially Pescatore) and outside the Court (Mattera and others), and in the developments occurring in the EU and in international trade. I also think a careful excavation into the case law provides a deeper understanding as to what the Court decided in *Cassis* itself, and how it has subsequently been used. I also like to think that by looking at *Cassis* in the broader context of the time we can, as Simpson advocates, make sense of *Cassis* and its progeny, as 'events in history and incidents in the evolution of the law'.

# 4

# The *Cassis de Dijon* Judgment and the European Commission

BRIGITTE LEUCHT*

## I. Introduction

This chapter focuses on the transformation of the *Cassis de Dijon* judgment[1] of 20 February 1979 by the European Commission. It examines how the Commission harnessed the European Court of Justice (ECJ) in its preparations to launch the single market programme, culminating in the 'breakthrough' of the Single European Act in 1986. The chapter will make an innovative contribution to our understanding of the role the Commission played in the ECJ's development of the 'European Economic Constitution'.[2]

This chapter is a further building block in a more comprehensive reassessment of the role of the Court in paving the way for the launch of the single market programme. An article that I published in the *European Law Journal* focused on the debate about the scope of Article 34[3] in the period between 1966 and 1969, which resulted in Directive 70/50. The article approached the development of

* Archival research for this project (2018–19) was made possible by internal funding from the University of Portsmouth. I would like to thank Sylvia Perez from the Archives of the European Commission in Brussels for her patience, expertise and creativity in helping me identify archival sources addressing my very specific questions on decision making and policy making in the Commission. I am also indebted to Robert Schütze for his invaluable feedback on an earlier draft of this chapter.

[1] Case C-120/78 *Rewe Zentral AG v Bundesmonopolverwaltung für Branntwein (Cassis de Dijon)*, ECLI:EU:CL1979:42.

[2] See, for the judicial constitution of the common market, JHH Weiler, 'The Constitution of the Common Market Place: Text and Context in the Free Movement of Goods' in P Craig and G de Búrca (eds), *The Evolution of EU Law* (Oxford, Oxford University Press 1999) 349. See, for a critical view on the notion of the constitutionalisation of the Treaties, the historical literature referenced in ch 1 of this volume. Miguel Maduro discusses the literature on the coordination of the Court's initiatives with those of the Commission's in his seminal work, M Maduro, *We the Court. The European Court of Justice and the European Economic Constitution* (Oxford, Hart Publishing, 1998) 9–10.

[3] Treaty articles, including articles referenced in archival sources, have been brought into line with the Treaty on the Functioning of the European Union (TFEU). Following the established legal writing protocol, the chapter also refers to the European Union (EU), when reference is made to its predecessor organisation, the European Community,

Directive 70/50 from an archive- and actor-based perspective, and added the important policy dimension to the jurisprudential origins of *Cassis de Dijon*. It highlighted that there was a strong continuity in the investment by a small number of key actors in the Commission that focused on Article 34 to create the single market from 1966.[4]

The starting point for this chapter is the written Communication that the Commission addressed to the Member States of the (then) European Community (EC) on 12 September 1980. The Communication translated the *Cassis de Dijon* judgment into a bold action programme for the Commission to advance the creation of the common market. At the core of the Communication, published on 3 October 1980, was a wide interpretation of the 'measures having equivalent effect' to quantitative restrictions of Article 34 TFEU.[5] According to the Commission:

> The principles deduced by the Court imply that a Member State may not in principle prohibit the sale in its territory of a product lawfully produced and marketed in another Member State even if the product is produced according to technical or quality requirements which differ from those imposed on its domestic products.[6]

This provision of the Communication served as the cornerstone of the Commission's 'new approach' to the construction of the Common Market by offering an alternative to relying exclusively on the harmonisation of national laws (Article 115 TFEU). As a result of the fact that unanimity in the Council was required regarding Single Market issues, harmonisation negotiations between the Commission and the Member States had been drawn out and produced only limited results.

The chapter builds on Catherine Barnard's analysis of the origins of the doctrines of mandatory requirements and mutual recognition presented in chapter 3, but shifts the focus from the Court to the European Commission. Furthermore, it shares the approach of Karen Alter and Sophie Meunier, the political scientists who have portrayed the Court as a 'catalyst' that provided the European Commission with a tool to initiate their 'new approach to harmonisation' by introducing the idea of mutual recognition into the European debate.[7] These authors contextualised the *Cassis de Dijon* judgment within the framework of the Commission's attempts to break the harmonisation deadlock and focus on its political consequences. This chapter provides the first archive-based account of the development of the Commission Communication of 1980.

---

[4] B Leucht, 'The Policy Origins of the European Economic Constitution' (2018) 24 *European Law Journal*, 191, available at https://doi.org/10.1111/eulj.12255.

[5] Art 34 TFEU (Art 30 of the Treaty establishing the EEC) reads 'Quantitative restrictions on imports and all measures having equivalent effect shall, without prejudice to the following provisions, be prohibited between Member States.'

[6] Commission Communication of 3 October 1980, [1980] OJ C256/2.

[7] K Alter and S Meunier-Aitsahalia, 'Judicial Politics in the European Community. European Integration and the Path-Breaking *Cassis de Dijon* Decision' (1994) 26 *Comparative Political Studies* 535.

Analysing primary sources from the Archives of the European Commission and the German Government relating to the *Cassis de Dijon* decision,[8] the chapter traces the interaction between the proceedings leading to the judgment and the development of the Commission's position on Article 34, first articulated, following the completion of the customs union (1968), in its Directive 70/50.[9] This archive-based approach allows me to identify a number of individual and collective actors, and to trace how they used the *Cassis de Dijon* decision to develop the 1980 Communication.

The chapter emphasises the significance of the politico-economic context in the development of legal ideas[10] and for reconstructing the essential details of decision and policy making in the departments of the Commission. It will unpick the Commission's development of its new approach in relation to both internal dynamics and external challenges, and will argue that the Commission responded to two developments in particular. The first development concerned the unmanageable workload that the Commission faced as a result not only of harmonisation, but also of protectionism, which Member States resorted to in response to economic challenges. In the aftermath of the oil crisis of 1973, Europe experienced its initial 'shock of the global': European economies and businesses faced a variety of economic challenges, including increasing competition from the US and Japan, low growth rates, high inflation and rising unemployment.[11] In this context, European governments appeared ill-equipped to counter the effects of the economic turmoil and used protectionist measures to strengthen their economies.[12]

The second development facilitating the development of the Commission's new approach were changes in (then) EC governance resulting from the first direct elections to the European Parliament in May 1979. The institution began being accountable to citizens, which informed the approach of parliamentarians to the creation of the Common Market from 1979, as the debates in the European Parliament analysed in this chapter reveal.

---

[8] The chapter is based on archival sources from: The Legal Service of the European Commission and the DG for the Internal Market and Industrial Affairs in the Archives of the European Commission in Brussels; and the German Government in the Federal Archives in Koblenz. Moreover, relevant digitised primary sources, especially speeches, were consulted through the Archive of European Integration at http://aei.pitt.edu/.

[9] Commission Directive 70/50/EEC of 22 December 1969 based on the provisions of Article 33 (7), on the abolition of measures which have an effect equivalent to quantitative restrictions on imports and are not covered by other provisions adopted in pursuance of the EEC Treaty [1970] OJ L13/29.

[10] On the question of methodology, see also N Bernard, 'On the Art of Not Mixing One's Drinks: Dassonville and Cassis de Dijon Revisited' in MP Maduro and L Azoulai (eds), *The Past and Future of EU Law: The Classics of EU Law Revisited on the 50th Anniversary of the Rome Treaty* (Oxford, Hart Publishing, 2010) 456, 456–57; inspired by Quentin Skinner's history of ideas, R Schütze, '"Re-reading" Dassonville: Meaning and understanding in the history of European law' (2018) 24 *European Law Journal* 376, 379–82, doi https://doi.org/10.1111/eulj.12290.

[11] N Ferguson et al (eds), *The Shock of the Global. The 1970s in Perspective* (Cambridge, MA and London, Belknap Press, 2010).

[12] See especially, L Warlouzet, *Governing Europe in a Globalizing World: Neoliberalism and its Alternatives following the 1973 Oil Crisis* (Abingdon, Routledge, 2018).

The chapter adopts a chronological approach and will proceed as follows: Section II analyses the German origins of the *Cassis de Dijon* case from the development of the preliminary reference to the response by the German Government to the questions before the Court. Section III traces the development of the Commission's position on these questions, while section IV picks up from the decision of 20 February 1979, leading up to the Commission Communication of 1980. Finally, section V will present the conclusions of this chapter regarding our understanding of the development of European (market) integration.

## II.  The German Origins of *Cassis de Dijon*: Rewe v the German Government

The German origins of the *Cassis de Dijon* case go back to 1976, when the Cologne-based Rewe-Zentral AG requested authorisation from the German Federal Monopoly Administration for Spirits to import the liqueur Cassis from France into Germany with a view to marketing and selling the spirits there. The Federal Monopoly Administration for Spirits informed Rewe that an authorisation to import was not necessary but that Cassis de Dijon could not be sold in Germany. It argued that according to the German Law on Monopoly in Spirits (*Branntweinmonopolgesetz*), Cassis de Dijon, with its 15–20 per cent wine–spirit by volume, would not fulfil the minimum requirement of 32 per cent for potable spirits to be marketed. Rewe challenged this decision.[13]

## A.  Gert Meier and Rewe's Challenge to the German Government

It has long been alleged that this was a 'test case' developed by the plaintiff's lawyer, Gert Meier, to 'provoke harmonization of the alcohol industry'.[14] A practising lawyer in Cologne, Meier also contributed to the heated debate about the relationship between the European and German legal orders in German academia. Meier contributed to this debate, arguing in favour of the autonomy of the European legal system.[15] Beyond this, he also worked on issues more closely related to *Cassis de Dijon* and its subject matter. For example, Meier published an article on the problems involved in devising a legal framework for a community-wide alcohol market;[16] co-authored a work on the Rewe group, the wholesale chain he

---

[13] *Cassis de Dijon* (n 1) 651.

[14] Alter and Meunier-Aitsahalia, 'Judicial Politics in the European Community' (n 7) 538.

[15] B Davies, *Resisting the European Court of Justice. West Germany's Confrontation with European Law, 1949–1979* (Cambridge, Cambridge University Press, 2012) 78–88, esp 80 and 87.

[16] G Meier, 'Rechtsprobleme einer EG-Alkoholmarktordnung' (1977) 7 *Recht der internationalen Wirtschaft* 410.

represented when he invoked EU law by initiating the preliminary reference to the ECJ leading to the *Cassis de Dijon* decision;[17] and later on, he also contributed to the discussion on food law in law journals.[18]

Archival evidence confirms that Meier prepared the preliminary reference for Case 120/78. The lawyer had earlier already pointed out the incompatibility of the German law fixing an alcohol minimum content with Article 34 TFEU in correspondence to the Darmstadt Administrative Court in the autumn of 1976.[19] Meier invoked the Court of Justice's decision in *International Fruit Company*[20] and stressed that according to this 1971 judgment:

> Quantitative restrictions and measures having equivalent effect under Article [34] and [35] are prohibited for imports and exports. These provisions therefore would prevent national measures that required the licensing of imports and exports or similar procedures, even if only formally.[21]

Meier concluded that it would be necessary to revoke the relevant sections of the German law for intra-Union trade to function properly. The argument developed by Meier echoes the general prohibition of distinctly applicable measures, that is measures differentiating between domestic and imported products, of Directive 70/50, Article 2.

On 27 December 1976, the Darmstadt Administrative Court referred the case to the Hesse Financial Court, and Meier then urged the latter to initiate the preliminary reference procedure to the ECJ.[22] In a letter dated 24 May 1977, he even suggested two questions that might be referred to the Court inquiring into the compatibility of the German law with Articles 34 and 37 TFEU,[23] which shaped the reference for a preliminary ruling the Hesse Financial Court sent to the ECJ. The reference was received at the Court on 22 May 1978[24] and filed as Case 120/78 (or '*Rewe*').

It was Meier who produced the first written submission to the ECJ on 16 June 1978. Building on his earlier efforts, the lawyer wished for the records of the European Commission pertaining to a 1974 complaint brought by the Commission against the German Government under Article 258 TFEU to be admitted as evidence in *Rewe*. In that instance, the Commission had accused Germany of being in breach of Article 34 TFEU by fixing the minimum wine spirit content

---

[17] D Heeger, G Meier and B Menzel, *Die Rewe-Gruppe. Auftrag der Gegenwart* (Cologne, Rewe-Zentral Aktiengesellschaft, 1979).

[18] G Meier, 'Für ein rechtsstaatliches Lebensmittelrecht' (1983) 16(12) *Zeitschrift für Rechtspolitik* 294; cf also G Hohmann, '5. Deutscher Lebensmittelrechtstag am 2/3 April 1992' (1993) 48(5) *JuristenZeitung* 243. Meier chaired the final plenary of the conference.

[19] Letter of 13 October 1976; letter of 9 November 1976; Archives of the European Commission, BAC 371/1991 2454.

[20] Case 51/71 *International Fruit Company NV and others v Produktschap voor groenten en fruit*, ECLI:EU:C:1971:128.

[21] Letter of 9 November 1976; BAC 371/1991 2454; cf also letter 9 May 1977, ibid.

[22] Letter of 9 May 1977; BAC 371/1991 2454.

[23] Letter of 24 May 1977; BAC 371/1991 2454.

[24] *Cassis de Dijon* (n 1) 652.

for liqueurs, including aniseed liquor, at 30 per cent to be marketed and sold. Germany, Meier continued, had followed the Commission's request by specifically reducing the minimum wine spirit for aniseed liquor to 25 per cent (through a regulation of 7 December 1976) without, however, changing the German Law on Monopoly in Spirits.[25] Meier's plea to include the Commission's earlier notification to the German Government may have represented an attempt to bolster a wide interpretation of Article 34 TFEU.

Following on from this request, Meier discussed the first of the two questions submitted to the Court, which asked whether the 'fixing of a minimum wine-spirit content for potable spirits laid down in the German Branntweinmonopolgesetz' would fall under Article 34.[26] It is not surprising that Meier answered the question in the affirmative. His argument and analysis are well known, as they are included in the summary of the written observations submitted to the Court and published with the judgment of the Court. Meier argued:

> The concept of 'quantitative restrictions on imports and all measures having equivalent effect' within the meaning of Article [34] of the … Treaty must be interpreted as meaning that the fixing at national level of a minimum wine-spirit content for potable spirits as a condition for authorization to market within the Member State concerned, where its result is that traditional products of other Member States whose wine-spirit content is below the fixed limit cannot be put into circulation in the Federal Republic of Germany, constitutes such a measure.[27]

Two aspects relating to the development of the preliminary reference and Meier's written submission to the Court are important. The first concerns Meier's answer. While Meier in his proposed answer to the first question submitted to the ECJ did not deal with the *consequences* of the assertion, this is precisely what the German Government would do in their written submission to the Court. Before proceeding to the discussion of the German Government's submission, however, a second aspect relating to Meier's preparation of the argument is relevant.

There is not a single reference to the 1974 *Dassonville* decision[28] in Meier's correspondence and lobbying attempts to send a preliminary reference to Luxembourg; nor can such a reference be found in the subsequent written submission to the Court. This is surprising, given the close link between the *Dassonville*

---

[25] Statement Meier/Rewe to the ECJ [16 June 1978] (recorded entry: 22 June 1978), BAC 371/1991 2453. Meier references the statement by the Commission as COM (75) 373 final. The 1974 infringement proceeding is also acknowledged in Alter and Meunier-Aitsahalia, 'Judicial Politics in the European Community' (n 7) 538.

[26] In full, the question reads (*Cassis de Dijon* (n 1) 652): 'Must the concept of measures having an effect equivalent to quantitative restrictions on imports contained in Article [34] of the … Treaty be understood as meaning that the fixing of a minimum wine-spirit content for potable spirits laid down in the German Branntweinmonopolgesetz, the result of which is that traditional products of other Member States whose wine-spirit content is below the fixed limit cannot be put into circulation in the Federal Republic of Germany, also comes within this concept?'

[27] *Cassis de Dijon* (n 1) 653; Statement Meier/Rewe to the ECJ, 16 June 1978.

[28] Case C-8/74 *Procureur de Roi v Benoît et Gustave Dassonville; et SA Ets Fourcroy et SA Breuval et Cie v Benoît et Gustave Dassonville*, ECLI:EU:C:1974:82.

and the *Cassis de Dijon* judgments established in the leading legal literature,[29] which is critically discussed by Robert Schütze in his contribution to this volume (chapter 2). It is submitted that the apparent 'omission' of *Dassonville* by the pro-integrationist Gert Meier suggests that before *Cassis de Dijon*, the 1974 decision was simply not understood in the context of internal measures but only of border measures, which is in line with the argument developed by Schütze.[30] This chapter's archive-based analysis of the origins of the preliminary reference therefore supports Schütze's reading. Who, if not Meier, would have mobilised *Dassonville* to great effect had it been possible to establish a clear doctrinal link?

## B. The German Government's Response to the First Question before the Court

The authors of the written submission by the German Government were Jochim Sedemund and Arved Deringer,[31] named partners in the firm Deringer, Tessin, Hermann & Sedemund that represented the German Government. While it was Sedemund who represented the German Government before the Court,[32] Deringer provides an important personal link to the debates on Directive 70/50. As a Member of the European Parliament (MEP) and rapporteur of the European Parliament Internal Market Committee, Deringer, back in December 1966, had submitted a written question asking the Commission to clarify its understanding of the measures having equivalent effect. This intervention politicised the legal debate on Article 34 TFEU in the European Commission and gave the decisive input for the Commission to provide a definition through what became Directive 70/50.[33]

In developing the case for the German Government, Sedemund and Deringer warned of the far-reaching consequences of providing an affirmative answer to the first question submitted to the Court:

> [I]n an extreme case, a single Member State could enact legislation for the whole Community, without the collaboration or even the knowledge of the other Member States. The result would be to lower minimal requirements to the lowest level set in any given national rules, in the absence of the authorization required by Article [115] of the Treaty, which presupposes the consent of the Member States.[34]

These consequences, which anticipate a race to the bottom in terms of setting standards in anything but name, would be 'incompatible with the principle of legal

---

[29] Cf Weiler, 'The Constitution of the Common Market Place' (n 2).
[30] Schütze, '"Re-reading" Dassonville' (n 10).
[31] Written submission by the German Government to the Court, JUR (78) D/02752 [4 August and received by the Court on 16 August 1978]; BAC 371/1991 2453; C-120/78, 655–659.
[32] *Cassis de Dijon* (n 1) 660.
[33] Leucht, 'The Policy Origins of the European Economic Constitution' (n 4).
[34] *Cassis de Dijon* (n 1) 656.

certainty' and violate 'the functional separation of powers between the national authorities and the Community authorities'.[35] The authors referenced a book chapter by Claus-Dieter Ehlermann[36] to firm up the argument that in the absence of Union legislation, the competence to legislate would remain with the Member States. They then continued:

> In relation to the interpretation of Article [34], that fundamental principle of the Treaty implies that the application of that provision reaches its limit at the point where the functional exercise of the powers retained by the Member States would be jeopardized. The Member States must continue to be able effectively to exercise those powers, until the achievement of harmonization transfers their freedom of action to the Community.[37]

Advocate General Francesco Capotorti rejected this specific link between Article 34 TFEU and the Treaty provisions on harmonisation (Articles 115–118) in his Opinion.[38] However, the German Government's written submission remains significant in representing the clearest articulation of the likely consequences of arguing that the German law fixing a minimum alcohol content would fall under the provisions of Article 34 TFEU. This was that admitting the German law would constitute a measure having equivalent effect could open the door to a race to the bottom between the Member States.

Summing up this examination of the German origins of *Cassis de Dijon*, if the first question submitted to the Court were decided, as proposed by Meier, and objected to by Sedemund and Deringer, this would: (i) initiate a race to the bottom and create legal uncertainty; and (ii) unsettle the established division of competences between Member States and Community institutions by shifting power away from the Member States and towards the Community. This analysis concludes the discussion of the German origins of the *Cassis de Dijon* case; the chapter will now turn to the position of the European Commission.

## III.  The Commission in the Lead Up to the *Cassis de Dijon* Decision

The starting point for evaluating the Commission's position is the written observations submitted to the Court by this institution.[39]

---

[35] ibid.

[36] Written submission by the German Government to the Court, JUR (78) D/02752. The reference is specifically to C-D Ehlermann, 'Das Verbot der Maßnahmen gleicher Wirkung in der Rechtssprechung des Gerichtshofes' in R Stödter and W Thieme (eds), *Hamburg. Deutschland. Europa. Beiträge zum europäischen Verfassungs-, Verwaltungs- und Wirtschaftsrecht. Festschrift für Hans-Peter Ibsen zum siebzigsten Geburtstag* (Tübingen, Mohr Siebeck, 1977) 579, 579 and 581; *Cassis de Dijon* (n 1) 655–59.

[37] *Cassis de Dijon* (n 1) 656–57.

[38] ibid 670–71.

[39] Written submission by the German Government to the Court, JUR (78) D/02752, BAC 371 1991 2453.

## A.  Heinrich Matthies, Alfonso Mattera and the Written Observations by the Commission

The written observations by the Commission were authored by Heinrich Matthies, a former assistant to Walter Hallstein at the University of Frankfurt and a réfé-rendaire to Judge Karl Roemer between 1954 and 1959. Matthies served as a legal adviser for the High Authority before joining the Legal Service of the Commission. Matthies had already been involved in the drafting of Directive 70/50[40] and was experienced in intervening before the Court.[41] He also represented the Commission in an earlier case brought against the German Government under Article 258 TFEU, regarding the incompatibility of a German wine law with the free move-ment of goods. In this case, the Commission alleged that the German Government acted against EU law by reserving the labels 'Sekt' and 'Weinbrand' for domestic products.[42] In its judgment, the Court of Justice sided with the Commission and argued that these designations had to 'ensure not only that the interests of the producers concerned are safeguarded against unfair competition, but also that consumers are protected against information which may mislead them'.[43] This illustrated not only the importance of regulating the interests of producers and traders, but also the rising significance of consumers in judicial decision making.

It is unclear if, or to what extent, Matthies or, for that matter, officials in the Commission in general were aware of Gert Meier's activities before the prelimi-nary reference for *Cassis de Dijon* reached the Court in May 1978. But it is safe to say that the Commission was extremely well prepared when it became directly involved in the *Cassis* litigation once the Court invited written submissions. Evidence for this assertion is provided by the correspondence Heinrich Matthies initiated, as the Commission's representative in the case, with Alfonso Mattera from Directorate General (DG) III, the Commission's Internal Market Division, on 15 June 1978.[44] At the time, Mattera was an old hand in matters relating to the free movement of goods. The Italian official had joined DG III in 1966 and he was intimately involved in the drafting of Directive 70/50.[45]

To begin with, Matthies' letter of 15 June 1978 enquired into the progress of a planned study on the compatibility of a number of German laws with

---

[40] Cf Leucht, 'The Policy Origins of the European Economic Constitution' (n 4).

[41] Matthies intervened 10 times before the Court between 1959 and 1974. C Marchand and A Vauchez, 'Lawyers as Europe's Middlemen: a Sociology of Litigants Pleading before the European Court of Justice (1954–1978)' in M Mangenot and J Rowell (eds), *A Political Sociology of the European Union. Reassessing Constructivism* (Manchester and New York, Manchester University Press, 2010) 68, 84–85 (fn 9).

[42] Klage der Kommission gegen die Bundesrepublik, eingeleitet 12 June 1974 (JUR/97/74); Case C-12/74 *Commission of the European Communities v the Federal Republic of Germany*, Federal Archives Koblenz, German Economics Ministry B102/244659, ECLI:EU:C:1975:23

[43] *Commission v Germany* (n 42) 194.

[44] Note à l'attention de Monsieur Mattera, 15 June 1978, BAC 304/1993 10.

[45] Leucht, 'The Policy Origins of the European Economic Constitution' (n 4).

Articles 34 et seq, which the Commission had first discussed in October 1977.[46] Mattera confirmed that the study would be compiled and a draft be presented to the Commission in July 1978. He also pointed out that, at that time, only one infringement procedure would be launched against the German Government, concerning Danish cherry wine.[47]

In the same letter, Matthies encouraged Mattera to comment on the traditional characteristics and the quality of the Cassis de Dijon liqueur.[48] Mattera confirmed that Cassis de Dijon would indeed constitute a traditional product. Strictly speaking, however, it could not be considered as a quality product, because its quality was not defined by legislation. There would be no law protecting the name Cassis de Dijon, and French authorities were discussing restricting its use to the Dijon territory.[49] Arguably, recognising the traditional character of the Cassis de Dijon liqueur at this stage in the proceedings represented a point of departure for Mattera's promotion of the principle of equivalence, or mutual recognition, to retain different regional identities in the common market after the *Cassis de Dijon* judgment.[50]

Further, as we shall see, the exchange of information between Matthies and Mattera – between the Legal Service and the Internal Market Division – continued beyond the written submission by the Commission to the Court. In addition to demonstrating that the Commission was very well prepared for *Cassis de Dijon*, the correspondence thus also helps to establish that Matthies and Mattera – the two officials in the Commission who had already been involved in the drafting of Directive 70/50 – were crucial in the development of the legal argument and the transformation of the judgment, respectively.

Turning now to the written observations by the Commission in *Cassis de Dijon*, Matthies first contextualised the question of the incompatibility of the specific German law in question and Article 34 TFEU in the wider framework of national laws on the quality, composition and designation of foodstuffs including alcoholic beverages and Article 34.[51] It might be argued that this approach could be interpreted as providing the basis for a generalisation of the Court's future decision: from the issue of the German law stipulating a minimum alcohol content to provisions relating to the quality, composition and designation of foodstuffs

---

[46] Note à l'attention de Monsieur Mattera, 15 June 1978 (n 44); Commission Meeting, 15 March 1978, COM (78) PV 466, 24–25, BAC 259/1980 1006, available at https://ec.europa.eu/historical_archives/archisplus/getPU.cfm?id=QkFDLTAyNTktMTk4MC0xMDA2.

[47] Note à l'attention de Monsieur Matthies, 6 July 1978 (but likely to have been written earlier given the reference to the 'upcoming Commission meeting on 5 July 1978' in the text of the letter), BAC 304/1993 10.

[48] Note à l'attention de Monsieur Mattera, 15 June 1978 (n 44).

[49] Note à l'attention de Monsieur Matthies, 6 July 1978 (n 47).

[50] A Mattera, 'L'arrêt «Cassis de Dijon»: une nouvelle approche pour la réalisation et le bon fonctionnement du marché intérieur' (1980) 23 *Revue du marché commun* 505; See also P Oliver, 'Measures of equivalent effect: a reappraisal' (1982) 19 *CML Rev* 217, 237.

[51] *Cassis de Dijon* (n 1) 658; JUR (78) D/02752.

in general. This reading would reflect the German Government's interpretation of the possible dangerous consequences. However, in a sketch for the oral plea, drafted in early October 1978, Matthies ruled out such an interpretation, arguing that 'The concerns articulated in the written observations of the German government are unfounded. The Commission does not intend ... to approach the approximation of laws through Art [34] on the basis of the lowest common denominator.'[52]

Second, in the written observations by the Commission, Matthies mobilised the proportionality principle of Article 3 of Directive 70/50, which prohibits certain indistinctly applicable measures, that is measures equally applicable to domestic and imported products. He did so when stating:

> In the final analysis, the essential *question is whether rules which are applicable without distinction concerning the composition of products, in conjunction with the designation of those products, must be considered to be 'out of proportion'*. Where that is not the case restrictions on trade between Member States resulting from disparities between those rules can be abolished only by means of the approximation of laws or the creation of a [Union] law.[53]

For Matthies, the 'great significance' of the anticipated judgment by the Court would be 'to establish criteria for borderline cases in which, exceptionally, the prohibition of Art [34] would apply.'[54]

In his Opinion, Advocate General Capotorti criticised the Commission for its 'prudent' attitude to defining the measures having equivalent effect of Article 34 TFEU. He highlighted the Court's judgment in Case 41/76 *Donckerwolke*,[55] 'according to which such measures include "all trading rules enacted by Member States which are capable of hindering, directly or indirectly, actually or potentially, intra-Community trade".'[56]

The archival evidence scrutinised does not support the idea that the Legal Service of the Commission jumped at the opportunity to argue for a wider reading of the measures having equivalent effect in Article 34 TFEU, at least not in the summer of 1978. Instead, the Commission stayed within the framework of Directive 70/50. At the same time, the Commission was staggering under the workload created by the increasing protectionist tendencies displayed by the Member States. Just how pressing this issue became in the autumn of 1978 is demonstrated by a letter from the Commission to the Member States, which will be discussed in the following section.

---

[52] Heinrich Matthies, Skizze Plädoyer 120/78, 2 October 1978, BAC 304/1993 110. The German original reads 'Die Kommission beabsichtigt ... keine "Angleichung auf kaltem Wege" über Art [34] auf dem niedrigsten gemeinsamen Nenner.'

[53] *Cassis de Dijon* (n 1) 659 (emphasis added).

[54] Matthies, Skizze Plädoyer 120/78 (n 52).

[55] *Donckerwolke and Others v Procureur de la République and Others*, ECLI:EU:C:1976:182.

[56] Opinion of AG Capotorti, *Cassis de Dijon* (n 1) 668.

## B. The Commission's 1978 letter on 'Safeguarding Free Trade within the Community'

On 6 November 1978, Etienne Davignon, the Belgian Commissioner for the Internal Market and Industrial Affairs (1977–81), addressed a letter to the Member States, which was also shared with the European Parliament and the Council of Ministers, drawing attention to 'the problems [then] being raised in the safeguarding of free trade within the Community'.[57] Davignon was one of the trusted commissioners of the British President of the Commission, Roy Jenkins (1976–80),[58] and championed prioritising the completion of the common market to advance European integration from 1979.

While the Commission was preparing its letter to the Member States, the attention of the EU was focused on monetary cooperation. The year when the *Cassis de Dijon* proceedings were launched, 1978, was also the year in which Germany's Social Democratic Chancellor Helmut Schmidt and French President Valéry Giscard d'Estaing, of the newly founded centre-right Union pour la Démocratie Française, resuscitated the drive towards European Monetary Cooperation as a means of advancing European integration, while combating unemployment, slow economic growth and inflation.[59] In the summer of 1978, Schmidt and Giscard d'Estaing launched the European Monetary System (EMS) with the support of Commission President Jenkins and the Benelux countries. The EMS initiative provided Giscard d'Estaing with an opportunity to exercise political leadership in spite of the dire economic reality. Moreover, the EMS enabled France (which had struggled to limit inflation and was unable to stay within the margins of the monetary 'snake', established in 1972 to curb fluctuations between the currencies of the Member States) to align itself more closely with the German Bundesbank, which, however, did not favour closer monetary cooperation with France as this could jeopardise Germany's success in combating inflation.[60] Germany, together with the Benelux countries and Denmark, had been more successful in limiting inflation. In spite of German domestic opposition, Schmidt pursued EMS primarily in an attempt to fill the void created by the United States' abdication of leadership in transatlantic monetary affairs, which facilitated the emergence of an independent European monetary bloc.[61]

---

[57] See, for all quotations from the letter in this section, SG (78) D/12882, BAC 487/1995 26. The Commission transmitted the letter to the European Parliament and to the Council of Ministers on 10 November 1978. See, 'Removal of technical barriers to trade. Communication to the European Parliament', COM (80) 30 final, 24 January 1980 at http://aei.pitt.edu/32886/; available at https://eur-lex.europa.eu/legal-content/EN/TXT/PDF/?uri=CELEX:51980DC0030&from=EN.

[58] NP Ludlow, *Roy Jenkins and the European Commission Presidency, 1976–1980: At the Heart of Europe* (Basingstoke, Palgrave Macmillan, 2016) 176–77.

[59] See, eg, the debate in the German Bundestag, 28 September 1978, available at http://dipbt.bundestag.de/dip21/btp/08/08107.pdf.

[60] E Mourlon-Druol, *A Europe Made of Money: The Emergence of the European Monetary System* (Ithaca, NY, Cornell University Press, 2012) retrieved from https://ebookcentral.proquest.com, 266–67.

[61] ibid 278–80.

Crucially for framing the letter circulated by Commissioner Davignon in November 1978, the drive towards closer monetary cooperation engineered under Franco-German leadership and supported by the Commission was *not* accompanied by a call to reinvigorate the common market agenda. It was the Commission letter that first drew attention to the danger of protectionism by the Member States for the EU, and its repercussions for the common market agenda in particular.

The letter emphasised that while the phenomenon itself would be '[n]either new [n]or surprising', the *number* of complaints made by MEPs, national governments, professional associations, firms and individual claimants was. According to the Commission, there had been a 'considerable increase in these [protective] measures in the last three years'; the Commission was 'investigating more than four hundred dossiers on hindrances to the free movement of goods especially on Articles [34–36] of the … Treaty' – a figure that had 'more than quadrupled compared to four or five years ago'.

The four-page letter then listed examples of restrictive measures, grouped into six categories consisting of (and enumerated (a)–(f)):

(a)   Documents (including, for example, certificates of origin);
(b)   *National rules stipulating technical conditions and conditions relating to quality to which import and sale of products on the national market are subject* [emphasis added];
(c)   National rules fixing maximum or minimum prices for products;
(d)   Excessive border checks;
(e)   Systems privileging national contractors for public contracts; and finally,
(f)   Taxes having equivalent effect to customs duties.

On the crucial point (b) directly relating to the questions before the Court in *Cassis de Dijon*, the Commission acknowledged that such measures were often introduced for legitimate objectives, including, for example, health and consumer protection. The Commission stressed that these measures would discourage the imports of goods from other Member States and, consequently, partition markets and prevent the enactment of EU rules. Furthermore, the Commission condemned the 'Buy national' campaigns initiated in a number of Member States by both private associations *and* public authorities.

For our enquiry into tracing the Commission's position regarding the interpretation of Article 34, the final section of the letter is particularly important. Here, the Commission identified the economic difficulties faced by the Member States of the Community as the driving force behind the increase in protectionism, when stating that 'the risk that Member States will withdraw into themselves' would have to be seen in the context of 'the economic problems with which the [EU] is confronted'.

A final aspect of the letter of 6 November 1978 worth highlighting is that it discussed the tools available to the Commission to counteract 'the danger of re-partitioning of markets which would jeopardize the accomplishment of the internal market'. On the one hand, the Commission would continue initiating infringement procedures on the basis of Article 258 TFEU. 'On the other hand, … the Commission will not fail to initiate, when the situation so requires, global coordinated action directed at all Member States.' Finally, the Commission proposed exploring, in accordance with the new guidelines set out by the recent case law of the Court of Justice, all possibilities enabling it to ensure that the rules of the Treaty on the free movement of goods, especially Articles 34–36 TFEU, were 'strictly applied and thus to achieve a greater and more effective liberalization of intracommunity trade'.

The letter did not reference specific case law, nor did it allude to the ongoing proceedings in the *Cassis de Dijon* case. It was circulated *after* the written observations by the parties involved in the case were submitted to the Court and *before* the hearing on 28 November 1978. But the passage quoted here indicates that the Commission was keeping a close eye on the rulings concerning Articles 34–36 TFEU. Arguably, because of the unmanageable workload arising from the Member States' response to the economic challenges of the time, the Commission, and especially DG Internal Market, was waiting for a Court decision, which would enable it to address protectionism by the Member States and create the common market in goods.

Legal literature published in the aftermath of the *Cassis de Dijon* decision has drawn attention to the letter of 6 November 1978. Laurence Gormley highlighted its importance in preparing the ground for launching an attack on barriers to trade before the *Cassis de Dijon* decision was handed down in February 1979;[62] and Alan Painter even suggested the Court's judgment 'followed' the letter.[63] While Gormley's interpretation is supported by the analysis of the letter above, Painter's thesis appears a little far-fetched. If and to what extent the Court followed the letter is difficult to ascertain. It is of course possible that the Commission's message played on the minds of the judges when they deliberated the decision. But we do not have evidence to establish this for certain.

What is more interesting from a historical perspective focusing on tracing decision making and policy making is the *label* applied to the letter in the legal literature. This literature consistently referred to a 'Commission Communication' without, however, referencing this Communication. Archival research has revealed that what the legal literature called the 'Commission's Communication *Safeguarding Freedom of Trade within the Community*' was simply the abovementioned letter to the Member States, which was not even published in the *Official Journal*.[64] For a historian, this is a very interesting detail to discover, as it suggests

---

[62] L Gormley, '*Cassis de Dijon* and the Communication from the Commission' (1981) 6 *EL Rev* 454, 454.

[63] AA Painter, '*Cassis de Dijon* digested' (1981) 2 *Business Law Review* 199, 199.

[64] It has not been possible to locate records relating to the drafting of the letter of 6 November 1978, as the way the Commission records have been archived can be patchy. See, for a critical evaluation of the Commission archives, Ludlow, *Roy Jenkins* (n 58) 7.

that the Commission deliberately elevated the significance of the letter to a 'Communication'. Indeed, as we shall see, the term 'Communication' was applied only in the aftermath of the *Cassis de Dijon* decision, to provide legitimacy to the Commission's new approach.

In conclusion, when the Court pronounced the *Cassis de Dijon* judgment, the Commission's official position, expressed through the written observations by its Legal Service, suggested a view of the measures equivalent to quantitative restrictions relying on Directive 70/50. At the same time, the changing economic context, in which the Commission operated, required DG Internal Market and the Commission as a whole to start reappraising its approach to internal market liberalisation. First traces of the Commission's 'change of heart' can thus be found in the 6 November 1978 letter. The chapter will now turn to further explore the Commission's reappraisal, from its first analysis of the judgment to the Communication of 1980.

## IV. The Making of the Commission Communication of 1980

### A. Claus-Dieter Ehlermann and the Legal Service's study of *Cassis de Dijon*

The first analysis of the *Cassis de Dijon* decision by the Legal Service was authored by Heinrich Matthies and Claus-Dieter Ehlermann.[65] Dated 19 March 1979, this study was prepared for the members of the Commission. It is as important as the letter to the Member States discussed in the previous section to understanding the development of the Commission's position on Article 34 TFEU. Claus-Dieter Ehlermann, the Director-General of the Commission's Legal Service between 1977 and 1987, probably needs no introduction here.[66] Ehlermann was also involved in the Integration Through Law (ITL) Project, established by Comparative Law Professor Mauro Capelletti together with Joseph Weiler around the time of the *Cassis de Dijon* judgment at the European University Institute (EUI) in Florence.[67] The ITL project conceptualised a research programme on European legal

---

[65] JUR (79) D/00880, BAC 275/2014 196 (175), text of the German original.

[66] Claus-Dieter Ehlermann, born Scheessel (Lower Saxony), 15 June 1931; studied law in Heidelberg, Marburg and Michigan; 1954–59 Research assistant, Department of Private International Law and Foreign Law, University of Heidelberg; 1959–61; Assistant to Hans Kutscher, at the time judge at the Federal Constitutional Court, Karlsruhe; 1961 joined Commission of the EEC as legal adviser in the Legal Service; 1977–87 DG of the Legal Service; cf *Who's who in Germany*, 1996 edn.

[67] R Byberg, 'The History of the Integration through Law Project: Creating the Academic Expression of a Constitutional Legal Vision for Europe' (2017) 18(6) *German Law Journal* 1531, 1545–47, available at https://doi.org/10.1017/S2071832200022410.

integration based on a contextual and comparative approach to European law.[68] Historian Rebekka Byberg has illustrated that it was difficult for Ehlermann, as a leading Commission official, to lend support to this academic initiative attempting to institutionalise the constitutional reading of the Treaty. With his strong pro-integrationist credentials, Ehlermann was fully supportive of the project, and he was involved in the discussions at the EUI. As a representative of the Commission, however, Ehlermann was keen not to be credited with input into the project.[69]

But Ehlermann was not the only personal link between *Cassis de Dijon* and the ITL Project. Another link was provided by the Luxembourger Pierre Pescatore. According to Capelletti, Pescatore's 'philosophy of integration' provided inspiration to the project.[70] Pescatore had been intimately involved in the negotiations on the Court of Justice in the Treaty of Rome[71] and sat on the bench of the Court between 1967 and 1985. His crucial role in the creation of the 'constitutional discourse' has been well established in recent historical literature.[72] Perhaps it was no coincidence then that Pescatore was the Juge Rapporteur in *Cassis de Dijon*, given the prominent role of this judge in the writing of the judgment.

Ehlermann's involvement in developing the first assessment of *Cassis de Dijon* was crucial in providing the legal argument that underlined the Commission's approach to the judgment. Two aspects of the analysis of the judgment deserve attention here. The first aspect concerned the question of the extent to which a generalisation of the judgment was justified – a question that would be hotly contested in the political debates ensuing from the *Cassis de Dijon* decision as well as the Commission's Communication of 1980. The Legal Service's written analysis highlighted in its very first paragraph that while the decision by the Court would be expressly limited to the concrete case of fixing minimum alcohol content, 'the *reasoning* of the Court of Justice would allow for drawing general conclusions on the attitude of the Court regarding trading rules, particularly those concerning the composition or standardisation of products'.[73] The Legal Service thus indicated it would be prepared to expand the scope of the judgment.

To bolster this approach, the study drew particular attention to the second sentence of paragraph 8 of the judgment, which read:

> Obstacles to movement within the Community resulting from disparities between the national laws relating to the marketing of the products in question must be accepted in so far as those provisions may be recognized as being necessary in order to satisfy

---

[68] See, for a recent reflection on the programme and its impact, L Azoulai, '"Integration through law" and us' (2016) 14(2) *International Journal of Constitutional Law* 449, available at https://doi.org/10.1093/icon/mow024.

[69] Byberg, 'The History of the Integration through Law Project' (n 67) 1545–47.

[70] ibid 1548.

[71] A Boerger, 'Negotiating the Foundations of European Law, 1950–1957: The Legal History of the Treaties of Paris and Rome' (2012) 21(3) *Contemporary European History* 339, 351–55.

[72] A Boerger and M Rasmussen, 'Transforming European law: The establishment of the constitutional discourse from 1950 to 1993' (2014) 10(2) *European Constitutional Law Review* 199.

[73] JUR (79) D/00880, 1 (emphasis added).

mandatory requirements relating in particular to the effectiveness of fiscal supervision, the protection of public health, the fairness of commercial transactions and the defence of the consumer.[74]

In their legal study, Ehlermann and Matthies argued that this crucial section of the judgment would not explain the reasoning behind it in detail. They submitted that the reasoning could however be deduced from both Advocate General Capotorti's Opinion and a number of sections in the *Cassis de Dijon* decision itself, referencing in particular:

- – 'the essential guarantee of the fairness of commercial transactions' (included in paragraph 13 of the decision); [and]
- – 'a purpose which is in the general interest and such as to take precedence over the requirements of the free movement of goods, which constitutes one of the fundamental rules of the Community' (included in paragraph 14 of the decision).[75]

Consequently, the study proposed, 'obstacles to trade within the Community would *always* require justification, if they should not fall under the prohibition of Article [34]'. Further, for 'the *definition* of a "measure having equivalent effect"', the differentiation into distinctly and indistinctly applicable measures (Articles 2 and 3, Directive 70/50) would be rendered 'meaningless'. '*Every* measure hindering those imports … which could take place without the measure in place, would therefore constitute a measure having equivalent effect to quantitative restrictions prohibited by Article [34]'.[76] In brief, this reading of the *Cassis de Dijon* decision enabled the authors of the Legal Service's analysis to argue for an extension of the scope of the judgment beyond national rules relating to the composition of alcoholic beverages.

The second key aspect of the legal analysis followed from the considerations regarding the scope of the judgment and concerned the need to critically examine and revise the Commission's doctrine concerning trade barriers and trading regulations that were indistinctly applicable.[77] The Legal Service proposed to carry out this reassessment of measures equally applicable to domestic and imported goods together with the DG for Internal Market. The document refrained from tying this assessment to the concerns relating to the creation of the Common Market articulated in the 6 November 1978 letter. This apolitical approach should not come as a surprise – after all this was the official voice of the Commission's Legal Service speaking, and the purpose of the assessment of the Court's judgment was to provide guidance on its interpretation. Acknowledging the need to evaluate the legal consequences of the decision together with the Internal Market DG was as far as the Legal Service could go.

---

[74] JUR (79) D/00880, 6; *Cassis de Dijon* (n 1) 662.
[75] JUR (79) D/00880, 6; *Cassis de Dijon* (n 1) 664.
[76] JUR (79) D/00880, 6–7 (original emphasis).
[77] JUR (79) D/00880, 9.

To conclude, the analysis of *Cassis de Dijon* by the Legal Service provided the crucial *legal* argument for a revision of the Commission's approach to Article 34 TFEU. The analysis stressed the reasoning of the Court, which necessitated a reassessment of the measures having equivalent effect and, especially, the definition of indistinctly applicable measures. The study did not spell out the notion of equivalence, or mutual recognition, nor did it invoke the *Dassonville* formula, as the Commission Communication of 1980 would. It did, however, underline the need for the Legal Service to cooperate with the DG for Internal Market, and thus the analysis contributed to paving the way for the Commission to develop its new approach to harmonisation.

The following section will shift the focus of the chapter from the Legal Service to DG Internal Market, where the Commission's bold action programme was developed, with important input from the European Parliament and the alcohol industry over the following months.

## B.  Mattera's Coup? The Transformation of the *Cassis de Dijon* Judgment

The Legal Service refrained from promoting the potential of the *Cassis de Dijon* judgment to expand the scope beyond the subject matter of the case in its day-to-day operation. On 7 May 1979, Heinrich Matthies wrote to the DG for Internal Market referencing the Commission's decision of 21 March 1979, asking for a letter to be written to the Member States that should fulfil three objectives, namely:

-   to bring the decision to the attention of the Member States;
-   to ask Member States to inform the Commission about existing provisions in the subject matter and any measures they would consider putting into place following the judgment; and finally,
-   to ask Member States to update the Commission on hindrances they would experience when exporting their goods and resulting from established minimum alcohol contents in the countries of destination.[78]

Attached to Matthies' note was the first part of a draft letter to the Member States. In line with the interpretation developed in the Legal Service's analysis, the draft emphasised that, following the *Cassis de Dijon* judgment, national regulations stipulating the minimum alcohol content for spirits could no longer be invoked with respect to the import of beverages, lawfully produced and marketed in another Member State.[79] At the same time, the draft letter did not address the possibility of moving beyond minimum requirements for alcoholic beverages.

In another letter, Matthies even proposed that the Legal Service should advise *against* extending the purpose of the letter to other regulations and goods.

---

[78] Note Heinrich Matthies, 7 May 1979, JUR (79) D/01597; BAC 371/1991 2454.
[79] ibid.

This letter, dated 8 August 1979, was addressed to the DG for Internal Market as well as the Directorate Generals for Competition and Agriculture.[80] Ostensibly, the advice suggests that Matthies remained attached to the argument he had developed for the Commission's written submission to the Court and his preparatory notes for the oral hearing. More likely, however, Matthies backtracked from the Legal Service's endorsement of the possibility to generalise the Court's decision in the study of 19 March 1979, so as not to jeopardise any ongoing negotiations on harmonisation or new regulations.

Following the *Cassis de Dijon* judgment, the Commission began receiving correspondence from alcohol producers expressing their confusion about the repercussions of the decision, not least for the project for a common market for alcohol. Aleck Crichton, the chairman of the association representing the Community's producers, Union Européenne des Alcools, Eaux-de-vie et Spiritueux, for example, asked for clarification regarding the consequences of the Court's decision, especially the minimum strength of spirits, as this would vary greatly between the Member States.[81]

The European Parliament, too, drew attention to the pending issue of creating a common alcohol market. The liberal MEP (1973–84) and member of the German Bundestag Martin Bangemann[82] asked the Commission to clarify its approach to introducing a Regulation for a common market for alcohol against opposition from the industry concerned that would favour harmonisation under Article 115 TFEU.[83] Just like queries from the alcohol industry, Bangeman's written question shows that the *Cassis de Dijon* decision entered into an area already marked by different legal approaches to solving the problem of different requirements in the Member States. Together, the argument for revising the Commission's position vis-à-vis Article 34 TFEU, developed by its Legal Service, and the legal uncertainty created by the judgment, evidenced by queries from the alcohol industry and the European Parliament, provided the DG for Internal Market with ammunition to advance a bolder approach to removing obstacles to trade in the Community.

Against this backdrop, Alfonso Mattera authored a note on the 'contents, interpretation and implications of the *Cassis de Dijon* decision', which establishes the prominent role of the Italian official in developing the Commission's new approach beyond doubt. The note informed the structure of the first part of the 1980 Communication to the Member States[84] and provided the basis for Mattera's

---

[80] Note Heinrich Matthies, 8 August 1979, Annexe 1, JUR (79) D/02783; BAC 371/1991 2454.

[81] Telex for the attention of Roy Jenkins [28 June 1979], BAC 304/1993 110.

[82] Bangemann served as vice chairman of the Liberal and Democratic Group in the European Parliament from 1975–79, and was made chairman of that Group in 1979. CV Martin Bangemann at http://aei.pitt.edu/74666/1/BIO_-_EN_-_Bangemann.pdf.

[83] Written question with answer, No 626/79, 10 December1979, [1979] OJ C310/26-27, available at https://eur-lex.europa.eu/legal-content/EN/TXT/?uri=OJ:JOC_1979_310_R_0001_01, building on Written question 188/79, 30 July1979, [1979] OJ C192/29.

[84] This applies to the beginning of the Communication and includes part of the first 'conclusions in terms of policy'. Note, dated 17 January and circulated 22 January 1980, BAC 224/1994 4.

well-known article published in the *Revue du Marché Commun* in the same year.[85] The note also made it clear that the letter by the Commission to the Member States, initiated by Matthies, needed to be accompanied by a publicity campaign targeting industry as well as European citizens.[86] Mattera would soon go by the nickname of 'Mr Cassis' in Brussels circles.[87] Last but not least, Mattera's note referenced a (then) recent intervention in favour of exploring alternatives to harmonisation by Commissioner Davignon in a debate in the European Parliament on 22 October 1979, which is the focus of the next subsection. While Mattera's contribution was indeed crucial in shaping the Commission's new approach, his coup hinged on the politicisation of the legal issues at stake in the *Cassis de Dijon* judgment.

## C. The Politicisation of the *Cassis de Dijon* Judgment in the European Parliament

Two major developments dictated the pace for the development of the Commission's new approach to harmonisation in 1979, namely, the first direct elections of the European Parliament in May 1979 and the second oil shock, which originated in the summer of the same year when oil prices began soaring and, once again, intensified the pressure on European leaders to find solutions to dealing with the economic repercussions of the oil shock.

The elections to the European Parliament took place shortly after the notable victory of the Conservatives in the British parliamentary elections, with Margret Thatcher becoming Prime Minister on 4 May 1979. Thatcher turned her attention immediately to the pending British Budgetary Question. The Prime Minister approached the issue resulting from the system of the Community's 'own resources' – that Member States automatically transferred their contributions to the EU without requiring further approval by their governments – with a hostile attitude, especially vis-à-vis the Franco-German 'couple', Schmidt and Giscard d'Estaing. The imbalance of what Britain paid into the EU and what it got out of it was expected to tip further to its disadvantage following both the end of the transition period for the UK in 1979 and the economic downturn, which had hit Britain particularly hard.[88] Commission President Jenkins, in turn, promoted the advantages of the common market in a speech to the Confederation of British Industry at their annual dinner on 16 May 1979.[89]

In the European Parliament, newly elected British MEPs David Nicolson and Basil de Ferranti initiated a debate following up on the 1978 Commission letter on 'Safeguarding free trade within the Community' (discussed in section III.B).[90]

---

[85] Mattera, 'L'arrêt «Cassis de Dijon»' (n 50).
[86] Note, dated 17 January 1980, BAC 224/1994 4.
[87] Gormley, '*Cassis de Dijon*' (n 62) 455, fn 8.
[88] Ludlow, *Roy Jenkins* (n 58) 208–22, esp 208, 215 and 222.
[89] Roy Jenkins, Address to the CBI, 16 May 1979, available at http://aei.pitt.edu/11303/.
[90] *Official Journal of the European Communities Debates of the European Parliament*, 1979–80 Session, Report of Proceedings from 22 to 26 October 1979, available at https://op.europa.eu/en/

Nicolson and de Ferranti were members of the newly formed European Democratic Group, which at the time consisted of the UK and the Danish Conservatives.[91] Beyond his political party affiliation, Nicolson was a leading figure in the European Movement, and he served as the chairman of the London-based multinational BTR (1969–84).[92] de Ferranti, for his part, was the president of the Economic and Social Committee (1976–78) and a founding member of the 'Kangaroo Group', established in 1979 to promote the realisation of the common market as a means to advancing European integration.[93]

When he kick-started the European Parliament debate on the Commission letter on 22 October 1979, in which Commissioner Davignon crucially participated, MEP de Ferranti underlined the political nature of the highly technical details involved in harmonisation negotiations, on the one hand, and the increased accountability of the new directly elected parliament, on the other.[94] de Ferranti's collaborator in the Kangaroo Group, the German Christian Democrat MEP Karl von Wogau, elaborated on the opportunities the increased accountability for MEPs opened up in this way:

> [W]e must ... realize that in five years we must face our constituents and be able to say we have achieved something here, even if the progress has been limited. ... Non-tariff barriers to trade offer a good opportunity in this respect. We can make Europe's frontiers easier to cross. We can achieve something here, because we can use the Treaties of Rome as a lever to make real progress in this field. This is a great opportunity for us as a Parliament, and we must seize that opportunity.[95]

von Wogau thus argued that the completion of the common market for goods had potential in highlighting the benefits of European integration to citizens.

The second point made by de Ferranti in his opening statement, concerning the political nature of the free movement of goods, served as the point of departure for Nicolson, who argued:

> In the face of the growth of technical barriers and creeping protectionism, I believe we should review our organization as well as having the political will to do something about it. I think we have got to increase the horsepower behind the Commission and make it clear to them that we wish to support them in doing something in greater depth, something constructive in this area.[96]

Nicolson was clearly putting his weight behind the Commission's efforts to develop a new approach to the creation of the common market. So were other notable

---

publication-detail/-/publication/0e66931f-0265-402d-b369-aa54fecdbaf5/language-en. Nicolson and de Ferranti represented London Central and Hampshire Central, respectively.

[91] M Wagner, 'The Right in the European Parliament Since 1979' (2011) 12(1) *Perspectives on European Politics & Society* 52, 61, doi:10.1080/15705854.2011.546146.

[92] Obituary: Sir David Nicolson (1922–96), *The Independent* (29 July 1996), available at www.independent.co.uk/news/people/obituary-sir-david-nicolson-1331085.html.

[93] The Kangaroo Group was established in distinction to Altiero Spinelli's 'Crocodile Group', which promoted a constitutional treaty: see at www.kangaroogroup.de/who-we-are/kangaroo-origin/.

[94] Debate 22 October 1979, 10–12.

[95] Debate 22 October 1979, 15.

[96] Debate 22 October 1979, 21.

MEPs, including the French former Prime Minister Michel Debré.[97] Debré's support of the Commission might come as a surprise, especially as he simultaneously spearheaded a network of Gaullist jurists that openly challenged the Court's constitutional practice in France.[98] In the debate in the European Parliament, however, Debré urged that the Community should adopt 'an aggressive posture in international discussions'. According to Debré, the Common Market, built in the spirit of European cooperation, should not be guided by 'a purely commercial outlook' in order to enhance the Community's international competitiveness, not least vis-à-vis the United States and Japan.[99]

Beyond providing for the political momentum for the Commission Communication of 1980, which Mattera was preparing at the time, the debate on 22 October 1979 also turned to the *Cassis de Dijon* judgment.[100] After the Danish MEP Kai Nyborg, a member of the European Progressive Democrats, had suggested bringing new test cases before the Court to advance the free movement of goods,[101] it was the Dutch Christian Democratic MEP and long-standing member of the European Movement Elise Boot who drew attention to the judgment:

> One of the most important of the Court's judgments this spring was in the Cassis case, in which new criteria were established for measures having an effect equivalent to ... quantitative restrictions on imports. I should like to ask Mr Davignon, who referred to the possibility of new rules being announced next spring for tackling covert protectionism, what conclusions the Commission has drawn from the new criteria in what was surely a very important case before the Court of Justice. Secondly, I would ask him what the Commission plans to do now that it has drawn these conclusions.[102]

Boot's questions provided Davignon with a welcome opportunity to discuss the ideas developed by the DG for Internal Market. Although he did not use the term, the Commissioner focused on the potential of mutual recognition and stressed

---

[97] Debré was not only the principal author of the Fifth Republic's Constitution, but also its first premier (1959–62), a former member of the National Assembly (1963–68) and a former member of the cabinet (in various functions): 'Debré, Michel (-Jean-Pierre)' in *Britannica Concise Encyclopedia*, by (Encyclopaedia Britannica, Britannica Digital Learning, 2017), available at https://search.credoreference.com/content/entry/ebconcise/debre_michel_jean_pierre/0?institutionId=129.

[98] M Rasmussen and B Davies, 'From International Law to a European Rechtsgemeinschaft: Towards a New History of European Law, 1950–1979' in J Laursen (ed), *The Institutions and Dynamics of the European Community, 1973–1986* (London, Nomos/Bloomsbury, 2015) 97, 124. See, for the full story of the 'constitutional battle' in France, A Bernier, *La France et le droit Communautaire 1958–1981: Histoire d'une réception et d'une co-production* (PhD dissertation, University of Copenhagen, 2017); cf also A Bernier, 'Constructing and Legitimating: Transnational Jurist Networks and the Making of a Constitutional Practice of European Law, 1950–70' (2012) 21(3) *Contemporary European History* 399, doi:10.1017/S0960777312000264.

[99] Debate 22 October 1979, 17.

[100] Alter and Meunier-Aitsahalia, 'Judicial Politics in the European Community' (n 7) 541; E Bussière, 'Devising a strategy: the internal market and industrial policy' in E Bussière et al (eds), *The European Commission 1973–86: History and memories of an institution* (Luxembourg, Publications Office of the European Union, 2014) 263, 266–67.

[101] Debate 22 October 1979, 16.

[102] ibid 18.

it would enable the retention of regional variation in the emerging EU common market – a point emphasised time and again by Mattera.[103] According to Davignon:

> We do not want a Euro-bread or a Euro-beer, or what have you. All that the judgment of the Court did was to recognize the legitimacy of protecting at national level certain products of a special and typical nature, making the point at the same time that, to the extent that these products were legal and licensed in other [EU] countries, they should be able to move freely and without obstacle inside the [EU].[104]

The Commission followed up on the debate of 22 October 1979 in its Communication to the European Parliament, 'Removal of technical barriers to trade', on 24 January 1980.[105] Just as in the debate in the European Parliament, the point of departure of this Communication was the letter to the Member States of 6 November 1978. By now, however, the letter to the Member States had become a 'Communication',[106] indicating the Commission's intention to bolster the legitimacy of its action plan further by 'upgrading' the 1978 letter.

In its 1980 Communication to the European Parliament, the Commission made three points summarising the *Cassis de Dijon* decision. First, it mobilised the *Dassonville* formula: 'Any rules liable to hinder directly, or indirectly, immediately or in the future, intracommunity trade constitute a violation of the rules of Articles [34] et seq.'[107] Second, the Commission introduced the notion of mutual recognition by proposing that, 'As regards commercial and technical regulations more particularly, the Court stipulated that any produce legally manufactured and sold in a Member State must in principle be admitted to the market of any other Member State.' Finally, the third point stipulated the conditions under which indistinctly applicable measures would be allowed. Departing from Article 3 of Directive 70/50, and following Advocate General Capotorti, the burden of proof would be on the party trying to show that a measure restricting trade was justified.[108] The three points summarising the *Cassis de Dijon* decision were developed in Mattera's internal note and incorporated into the Commission Communication to the Member States.

The Commission Communication to the Member States of 12 September 1980 introduced the new approach to harmonisation. The Communication interpreted the *Cassis de Dijon* judgment to develop a policy programme, but this did not put an end to the political and legal debate. Far from it. One of two issues that came under immediate attack from Member State governments, including those of

---

[103] Cf Mattera, 'L'arrêt «Cassis de Dijon»' (n 50); and the reference in Oliver, 'Measures of equivalent effect' (n 50) fn 49.

[104] Debate 22 October 1979, 20.

[105] 'Removal of technical barriers to trade' (n 57).

[106] ibid 3.

[107] The *Dassonville* formula stated that 'All trading rules enacted by Member States which are capable of hindering, directly or indirectly, *actually or potentially*, intra-Community trade are to be considered as measures having an effect equivalent to quantitative restrictions.' (emphasis added to indicate a slight variation from the text of the 24 January 1980 Communication); see Dassonville (n 28) 852.

[108] Oliver, 'Measures of equivalent effect' (n 50) 230.

Germany, France and Belgium, and the Legal Service of the Council of Ministers, concerned the scope of the judgment, arguing the decision could *not* be generalised. Following this reading, *Cassis de Dijon* did not change Directive 70/50. The second issue of contention focused on the relationship between the 'new approach' and harmonisation under Article 115.[109]

The concluding section will summarise the chapter's findings and will evaluate the conclusions with regard to our understanding of the development of European (market) integration.

# V.  Conclusions and Outlook

This archive-based account of the development of the Commission position on Article 34 TFEU has shown *first* that the transformation of the *Cassis de Dijon* judgment was due to the close cooperation of the Commission's Legal Service and its DG Internal Market. The departure from Directive 70/50 and the wide interpretation of the decision is moreover associated closely with three individuals: Heinrich Matthies, Claus-Dieter Ehlermann and Alfonso Mattera.

*Second*, the Commission Communication to the Member States in September 1980 originated with the issue of an unmanageable workload for the Commission resulting from harmonisation and its enforcement. The Commission first alerted the Member States to this issue in its 1978 letter. Increasing protectionism by the Member States in the face of ongoing economic challenges aggravated this problem still further. The timing of the letter – November 1978 – also helps to explain why the Commission's submission to the Court in the *Cassis de Dijon* proceedings stayed within the framework of Directive 70/50.

Following from this evaluation, *third*, the Court indeed functioned as a 'catalyst' when it handed down *Cassis de Dijon*, as proposed by Karen Alter and Sophie Meunier in their article. Given that Judge Pescatore was the Juge Rapporteur in *Cassis de Dijon*, it is very likely that the Court assumed the function of a catalyst deliberately. As this chapter has shown for the first time, the judgment enabled Ehlermann and Matthies to develop the legal argument for revising the Commission's approach to Article 34 TFEU and for extending the scope of the decision. Legal uncertainty following the judgment, and the Legal Service's proposition to draft a letter to the Member States allowed Mattera to seize the opportunity and develop the new approach to harmonisation.

*Fourth*, the Commission's new approach was developed in the same year as the first direct elections to the European Parliament were held. Parliamentarians, acutely aware of their new role vis-à-vis the electorate, saw an opportunity to enhance their credentials by backing the Commission in its efforts to explore alternatives to harmonisation in creating the EU common market.

---

[109] Meeting Coreper, 14 November 1980, BAC 224 1994 4; see, in more detail, Alter and Meunier-Aitsahalia, 'Judicial Politics in the European Community' (n 7) 541–45.

*Finally*, the politicisation of the issues at stake in *Cassis de Dijon* focused on countering protectionism and on creating the Common Market. Beyond this, societal concerns, particularly relating to the protection of consumers, came to play an increasing role in the development of legal arguments relating to the free movement of goods. The desirability of consumer protection had already appeared in the Court's 1975 judgment regarding the labelling of Sekt and Weinbrand,[110] and it was included in the mandatory requirements of paragraph 8 of the *Cassis de Dijon* judgment.

But what do these conclusions on the European Commission and *Cassis de Dijon* mean for the development of European (market) integration? Preliminary archival research in the records relating to the lead-up to the Milan summit of the heads of state or government of the Member States of the Community in June 1985, which adopted the European Commission's White Paper on the completion of the internal market, indicated there were numerous references to 'mutual recognition'.

By the same token, there is an absence of the idea of mutual recognition in key documents associated with the Stuttgart summit two years earlier, in June 1983. The Memorandum, 'Foundations for the Future of European Industry', submitted by the European Roundtable of Industrialists to Etienne Davignon ahead of the summit in June 1983 clearly prioritises common market completion but does not address the tool of mutual recognition. The 'Solemn Declaration on European Union' the 10 heads of state or government of the member states of the (then) Community signed at Stuttgart, likewise, contains only a generic reference to the importance of completing 'the internal market in accordance with the Treaties, in particular the removal of the remaining obstacles to the free movement of goods, capital and services'.[111] The two-year window between the Stuttgart and Milan summits therefore appears to merit special attention if we want to understand the dissemination of the notion of mutual recognition, not least to pin down its likely impact on the negotiations on the Single European Act, especially on Article 114 TFEU introducing qualified majority voting on common market issues. To trace the precise links between *Cassis de Dijon* and mutual recognition and the negotiations on Article 114 TFEU requires additional archival research.

---

[110] See section III.A, *Commission v Germany*.
[111] Available at www.cvce.eu/en/obj/solemn_declaration_on_european_union_stuttgart_19_june_1983-en-a2e74239-a12b-4efc-b4ce-cd3dee9cf71d.html.

## PART II

## The Impact of a Landmark Decision

# 5

# 'Ceci n'est pas … Cassis de Dijon': Some Reflections on its Triple Regulatory Impact

INGE GOVAERE

## I. Introduction

The *Cassis de Dijon* judgment of 1979[1] and the famous oil on canvas *Ceci n'est pas une pipe* (often translated into English as *The Treachery of Images* or *This is not a Pipe*) by the Belgian surrealist painter René Magritte half a century earlier,[2] have at least two characteristics in common. First, both teach that appearances may be treacherously deceptive. At face value *Cassis de Dijon*, by introducing the principle of mutual recognition, offered an easy and ready, judge-made solution in response to EU regulatory inertia by reinstating the importance of national regulation at least of the export state. But as René Magritte warned by prominently inserting the words 'Ceci n'est pas une pipe' on his painting of a tobacco pipe, what you see is not necessarily what you get.[3] A deeper scrutiny of *Cassis de Dijon* and its consequences reveals a fundamental and direct impact on ensuing regulatory practices, even if perhaps not necessarily and originally so intended. This finding lies at the core of the reflections in this chapter on the regulatory impact of *Cassis de Dijon* at both the EU and Member State level.

---

[1] Case 12/78 *Rewe-Zentral AG v Bundesmonopolverwaltung für Branntwein (Cassis de Dijon)*, ECLI:EU:C:1979:42.

[2] *Ceci n'es pas une pipe*, oil on canvas painting, René Magritte (1929).

[3] See for instance R Pepperell, 'Artworks as dichotomous objects: implications for the scientific study of aesthetic experience' *Frontiers in human neuroscience* (9 June 2015) 295, consulted online at https://doi.org/10.3389/fnhum.2015.00295, in particular just above fig 8, where he points out that '"*The Treachery of Images*," better known as "*This is not a pipe*," is at once a bald statement of the obvious and a crafty self-denial, a patently true proposition that also undermines its own premise, a visual manifestation of the paradox wherein the statement "This statement is false" is both true and false, and a darkly humorous thesis on the indeterminacy of language and meaning. It is the "unreal" manner of its handling, as blandly illustrative, which alerts us to the dissonance between what we would expect to see in the presence of a real pipe and the pipe-like shape we actually confront.'

Second, the painting by René Magritte not only continues to puzzle many of its viewers. It also triggered a debate between the painter and the French philosopher and social theorist Michel Foucault,[4] which in itself has become a source of academic scrutiny and discussion.[5] In the same vein, *Cassis de Dijon* continues to spark discussion, puzzlement and controversy 40 years after the judgment was rendered, not merely in academia but also within the Court itself. Over time this led to an express albeit only partial reversal of *Cassis de Dijon* in the *Keck & Mithouard* judgment of 1993,[6] which in turn begged for further clarification subsequently rendered in the *Trailers* case of 2009.[7] The creator (the Court) is thus also here an active participant, rather than a mere bystander in steering the discussions about the meaning and scope of the emerging picture.

Without seeking to be exhaustive on the matter, this chapter offers some reflections on what is conceived to be the triple, yet intertwined, regulatory impact of *Cassis De Dijon*. First, attention is briefly given to its immediate impact on regulatory and democratic processes of European integration, as well as its decisive influence on shaping the new EU regulatory approach to harmonisation. This is followed by some reflections on whether, and to what extent, this 40-year-old judgment has had an impact on the new delimitation of competences between the EU and the Member States, in particular in a new post-Lisbon setting, which sought to clarify the division of competence. Lastly, but importantly, consideration

---

[4] M Foucault, *Ceci n'est pas une pipe* (Paris, Fata Morgana, 1973); M Foucault, *This Is Not a Pipe*, tr and ed James Harkness (Oakland, CA, University of California Press, 1983).

[5] See, for instance, Pepperell, Artworks as dichotomous objects' (n 3), who continues the above quote as follows: 'The philosopher Michel Foucault did his best to unravel the mystery of the painting by presenting it (not entirely convincingly, in my view) as a calligram – a word-image of the kind associated with Guillaume Apollinaire, the poet, critic and early supporter of the Cubist movement (Foucault, 1983). But like all true paradoxes, *The Treason of Images* cheerfully resists any attempt at rationalization and stubbornly asserts the fact that the shape above the words is clearly a pipe, and yet – being confected from paint – is also not a pipe.' For other academic debate on the discussions between Foucault and Magritte on this painting, see for instance S Levy, 'Foucault on Magritte on Resemblance' (1990) 85 *The Modern Language Review* 50; G Almans, 'Foucault and Magritte' (1982) 3 *History of European Ideas* 303; J Margolis, 'This is not a pipe' (1984) 43(2) *Journal of Aesthetics and Art Criticism* 224; AS Chambon and A Irving, 'They Give Reason a Responsibility Which It Simply Can't Bear: Ethics, Care of the Self, and Caring Knowledge' (2003) 24(3-4) *Journal of Medical Humanities* 265; S Levy, *Decoding Magritte* (Bristol, Sansom & Company, 2015).

[6] Joined Cases C-267/91 and C-268/91 *Keck & Mithouard*, ECLI:EU:C:1993:905, at para 16 (emphasis added): 'By contrast, *contrary to what has previously been decided*, the application to products from other Member States of national provisions restricting or prohibiting certain *selling arrangements* is not such as to hinder directly or indirectly, actually or potentially, trade between Member States within the meaning of the *Dassonville* judgment (Case 8/74 [1974] ECR 837), so long as those provisions apply to all relevant traders operating within the national territory and so long as they affect in the same manner, in law and in fact, the marketing of domestic products and of those from other Member States.' There are only very few judgments where the Court of Justice so openly reverses prior case law, the *Hag II* case is another example, see Case C-10/89, *SA CNL-SUCAL NV v HAG GF AG*, ECLI:EU:C:1990:359, at para 10, on the interpretation of the industrial and commercial property exception in Art 36 TFEU.

[7] Case C-110/05 *Commission v Italy*, ECLI:EU:C:2009:66, paras 36–37, where the Court of Justice puts forward the market access test to delineate the scope of Art 36 TFEU.

is given to the extent to which *Cassis de Dijon* has interfered with the regulatory capacity of the Member States in the absence of EU harmonisation. Three tests in particular seem to have emerged in the case law following *Cassis de Dijon*, each with potentially great impact on the Member States' discretion to legislate: the 'straitjacket test', the 'rubber-stamp exercise' and the 'balancing trick'. All too often these distinct yet stringently interrelated regulatory implications of *Cassis de Dijon* have been assessed in isolation, thereby potentially missing out on the complexity of the bigger picture.

## II.  Impact on the EU Regulatory Practice

Is it an oxymoron to link *Cassis de Dijon* to positive EU regulatory practice? This simple question is not without importance, as *Cassis de Dijon* came about precisely because of the lack of political willingness to adopt at EU level the regulatory framework needed to achieve the common market objective. As with every crisis since then, in reaction to the oil crisis of the 1970s, the emergence of nationalism and concurrent adoption of protectionist measures by individual Member States went hand in hand with provoking inertia in the EU decision-making process. It was at such historic times of 'Eurosclerosis',[8] whereby obstacles to free movement could hardly be removed through the adoption of EU harmonisation measures with its inherent democratic checks and balances, that the CJEU firmly stepped in to keep the common market objective afloat.[9]

A first and important reflection to start from is therefore that it is the very absence of EU regulatory activity that triggered the judge-made solutions in *Cassis de Dijon*, not vice versa. That being said, the impact in turn of *Cassis de Dijon* on the development of EU regulatory practice can of course hardly be overestimated; it is at least threefold and still ongoing. Immediately apparent is the intended effect of the principle of mutual recognition on the necessity, and especially the urgency, of having EU regulation at all, and the ensuing shift towards 'conditioned negative' harmonisation. Less visible but equally crucial to consider is the impact of this judge-made principle on the democratic process and democratic legitimacy of the European integration process. Finally, *Cassis de Dijon* has also been instrumental

---

[8] H Giersch, 'Eurosclerosis' (1985) 112 *Kieler Diskussionsbeiträge* 1, as consulted online in a Digitised Version at www.econstor.eu/bitstream/10419/48070/1/025296167.pdf. He coined the term as follows (ibid 4), 'The diagnosis for Europe's disease can be called Eurosclerosis.' He then proposes the following cure (ibid 12), 'For coping with Eurosclerosis I suggest we turn to citizens rather than organisations, to ordinary people rather than politicians in office.'

[9] See for instance D Kelemen, *Eurolegalism: The Transformation of Law and Regulation in the European Union* (Cambridge, MA, Harvard University Press, 2011) 156; A Awesti, 'The Myth of Eurosclerosis: European Integration in the 1970s' (2009) *L'Europe en Formation* 353; S Saurugger and F Terpan, *The Court of Justice of the European Union and The Politics of Law* (London, Palgrave Macmillan, 2016) 23 ff.

in developing a new approach to EU harmonisation, combining negative and positive harmonisation. Those three effects are necessarily linked but will be briefly
explored in turn.

## A. Shifting from 'Positive' to 'Conditioned Negative' Harmonisation

*Cassis de Dijon* exposed the fact that obstacles to free movement may arise not
only because of discriminatory national measures, whether openly so or indirectly, but simply also because the laws in force in different Member States diverge.
The normal response to counter a regulatory patchwork that thwarts the internal
market objective consists in the adoption of a political decision[10] to deregulate
at national level in favour of positive harmonisation at EU level.[11] That has been
the only solution provided for in the Treaties since their inception, now found in
Articles 114–118 TFEU. Blatant political unwillingness to harmonise, or a decision not to deregulate nationally in favour of EU harmonisation, is also a political
act that sets the regulatory framework; not just a positive decision to harmonise.
Against such a Treaty context, what then can a court do other than establish what
the existing regulatory framework is and apply it, even if it means accepting obstacles to one of the four freedoms?

Surprisingly perhaps, especially at the time,[12] the Court did not consider
this to be a rhetorical question. Instead, in *Cassis de Dijon* it formulated a truly
revolutionary answer of the same magnitude as regards EU substantive law as
the earlier *Van Gend en Loos*[13] ruling was to the autonomous EU legal order.[14]

---

[10] By the Council and the European Parliament, under the legislative procedure.
[11] Whether through directives or regulations, depending on the intended level of discretion left to the
individual Member States in implementation.
[12] To understand the importance of *Cassis de Dijon* it is crucial not to reason with hindsight, in
particular as the principle of mutual recognition today has become the norm.
[13] Case C-26/62 *Van Gend en Loos*, ECLI:EU:C:1963:1.
[14] I have argued elsewhere that *Van Gend en Loos* triggered a so-called 'Balloon dynamic', see
I Govaere, 'Interconnecting Legal Systems and the Autonomous EU Legal Order: a Balloon Dynamic'
in I Govaere and S Garben (eds), *The Interface Between EU and International Law: Contemporary
Reflections* (Oxford, Hart Publishing, 2019) 19, 19: 'The concept of the new and autonomous EU
legal order, as it emanated from the historic *Van Gend & Loos* judgment of the Court of Justice of the
European Union (CJEU), can best be pictured as an empty balloon firmly slid in-between public international law and constitutional law. At first this would sit somewhat uneasily and create some friction,
but it would not yet raise any major concerns. More important frictions with international law however
started to appear with the rapid expansion of the EU integration process both in terms of substantive
coverage and territorial scope, due to the constant transfer of competence towards the EU, coupled with
the EU enlargement process to include new Member States. The balloon imagery goes that with every
such new EU development, more air is automatically blown into the balloon. Yet strongly inflating the
EU balloon has as a direct consequence that also more and more international law (and Member States'
constitutional law) is systematically squeezed out. It is this gradual but steady EU integration process
which inevitably causes increased friction and possibly even resistance against a further expansion of
the autonomous EU legal order.'

Quite ingeniously, the Court opted to radically depart from international trade rules by simply turning them on their head, specifically for application within the common market. A simple mathematical equation lies at the basis of this move. There are manifold potential Member States of importation, but always only one Member State of exportation. Requiring compliance with the regulation in force in each State of *importation*, as is habitual in international trade, intrinsically poses problems for free movement, as a product needs to be modified accordingly whenever such legislation differs. The Court of Justice consequently ruled that, in principle, it should suffice to comply with the regulatory framework of a single Member State, namely the Member State of *exportation*. As a consequence a product can move freely between the Member States on the basis of a single regulatory framework adopted at national level, even in the absence of EU harmonisation. The principle of mutual recognition thus introduced 'negative' harmonisation, in the sense that it rendered the adoption of 'positive' harmonisation measures at EU level redundant, or at least less urgent, in order to achieve the common market objective. In that sense it interfered directly with the regulatory practice foreseen in the Treaties by shifting the burden for ensuring the four freedoms from the EU legislator back to the level of the individual Member States. As will be seen, this very exercise has not only undermined the role of the EU regulator,[15] but also concurrently led the Member States to be put in a rather tight regulatory straitjacket.[16]

At the same time, the Court of Justice anticipated in *Cassis de Dijon* the potential consequences of introducing the principle of mutual recognition in terms of provoking unwarranted regulatory competition[17] between the Member States.[18] In particular, set against the nationalist and protectionist mindset that was raging in the 1970s, an unlimited application of the principle of mutual recognition might quickly lead to a downward legislative spiral or so-called 'race-to-the-bottom' to attract business and investment, a point the German Government itself made in its submissions in *Cassis de Dijon*. As an indispensable counterweight to the principle of mutual recognition, the Court thus exceptionally allowed a Member State

[15] See section II.C.
[16] See section IV.
[17] On this concept, see for instance D Esty and D Geradin (eds), *Regulatory Competition and Economic Integration: Comparative Perspectives* (Oxford, Oxford University Press, 2001); C Radaelli, 'The Puzzle of Regulatory Competition' (2004) 24(1) *Journal of Public Policy* 1; S Deakin, 'Is regulatory competition the future for European integration?' (2006) 13 *Swedish Economic Policy Review* 71; B Gabor, *Regulatory Competition in the Internal Market* (Cheltenham, Edward Elgar Publishing, 2013); J Stark, *Law for Sale: A Philosophical Critique of Regulatory Competition* (Oxford, Oxford University Press, 2019).
[18] For a detailed analysis of the causes and solutions of regulatory competition between Member States, see I Govaere, 'L'établissement des règles des marchés nationaux ou régionaux: de l'Etat régulateur souverain aux organisations d'intégration régionale promotrices, protectrices et intermédiaires' (2003) XVII(3) *Revue internationale de droit économique* 313; S Garben and I Govaere, 'The Multifaceted Nature of Better Regulation' in S Garben and I Govaere (eds), *The EU Better Regulation Agenda: A Critical Assessment* (Oxford, Hart Publishing, 2018) 3.

to rely on its own legislation to object to the import of a good, if necessary and proportionate to protect higher objectives. Considering the underlying rationale in terms of regulatory competition, of necessity this logic could not be limited to the few derogations expressly foreseen in the Treaties, such as public health in Article 36 TFEU. Therefore the Court of Justice expressly ruled in *Cassis de Dijon* that an open-ended list of mandatory requirements, such as consumer protection or environmental protection, could additionally be invoked.

Whilst this counterweight to the principle of mutual recognition is to be much welcomed in order to avoid a race-to-the-bottom, it has also been criticised for unduly interfering with the regulatory discretion of Member States in non-economic matters[19] – which, at the time of *Cassis de Dijon*, were largely outside the realm of the economically orientated internal market rules.[20] On the one hand, it did keep the regulatory initiative for such higher objectives in the hands of the individual Member States. But on the other hand it firmly subjected the exercise of any such regulatory discretion to judicial scrutiny at EU level for compliance with the 'double' justification plus proportionality test. The rationale underlying this double test can, however, also be linked to the possible occurrence of unwarranted effects of regulatory competition triggered by the principle of mutual recognition, but now in the opposite direction. A race-to-the-top cannot, of course, in itself be totally avoided by the introduction of the justification and proportionality tests; only EU harmonisation can resolve that type of regulatory competition between the Member States. But at least it can try to ensure that a distinction is duly made between truly 'protective' measures of the Member States, which are allowed, and 'protectionist' measures, which are prohibited.[21] This then further entails that Member States are forced to take into account not only EU legal constraints but also regulatory activity across the border, because such a test is bound to fail where a higher objective is already duly taken into consideration by the Member State of exportation.[22] As such, *Cassis de Dijon* has not just provoked but also heavily conditioned 'negative' harmonisation at the level of the Member States.[23]

---

[19] See section III.

[20] See section III.B for the changing objectives and dynamics of the internal market.

[21] See, for instance, for this sometimes fine divide in relation to the precautionary principle, E Vos, 'Le principe de précaution et le droit alimentaire de l'union européenne' (2002) XVI(2) *Revue internationale de droit économique* 219.

[22] The Commission pointed to this already in its Communication from the Commission concerning the consequences of the judgment given by the Court of Justice on 20 February 1979 in Case 120/78 ('Cassis de Dijon') [1980] OJ C256/2, by stating that 'This principle implies that Member States, when drawing up commercial or technical rules liable to affect the free movement of goods, may not take an exclusively national viewpoint and take account only of requirements confined to domestic products. The proper functioning of the common market demands that each Member State also give consideration to the legitimate requirements of the other Member States …' See the 'rubber stamp exercise' in section IV.B.

[23] For further effects on the Member States in their regulator capacity, see section IV.

## B. A Slippery Slope of ' Judge-Made' Decision versus Democratic Legitimacy

In the economic and political context of the 1970s, *Cassis de Dijon* may well have been a make-or-break ruling for the internal market, which, in turn, was instrumental in maintaining peace and stability on the European continent. Seen in this broader context, this ruling and the subsequent case law is to be welcomed for relentlessly pursuing a fundamental objective of the EU Treaties, unanimously agreed upon by all the Member States and ratified in each Member State according to its constitutional rules and democratic safeguards. Paradoxically, however, precisely because of the regulatory impact of the solutions it proposes, it also raises crucial questions in terms of ongoing respect for the democratic process and democratic legitimacy. A widely discussed issue in this respect concerns how the EU's so-called 'creeping competences' have encroached on the Member States' democratic processes, which will be briefly touched upon later in this chapter.[24] Due attention should, however, also be given to the more direct and straightforward interference with the democratic processes for the adoption of binding rules by the EU institutions themselves.

The debate on over-constitutionalisation of the internal market, in particular as projected against a perceived under-democratisation of the EU, has already been elaborated upon elsewhere.[25] Suffice it to say here, the principle of mutual recognition has acquired an inherently constitutional nature. As a binding interpretation of the primary law, the Court's ruling in *Cassis de Dijon* can no longer be altered by EU secondary law even if it is precisely the absence of the latter for which it sought to compensate. The judge-made principle of EU law not only has primacy and direct effect, and thus a huge impact on the regulatory framework in force in any Member State.[26] It simultaneously dispenses with the immediate need for secondary EU law, which could have benefitted from the input of various stake holders and democratic control.[27]

As the Court derives its legitimacy directly from primary law,[28] and in *Cassis de Dijon* also interpreted Treaty provisions on the free movement of goods, only a Treaty amendment could override or alter this ruling. The flanking condition

---

[24] See section III.

[25] See S Garben, I Govaere and P Nemitz, 'Critical Reflections on Constitutional Democracy in the European Union and its Member States' in S Garben, I Govaere and P Nemitz (eds), *Critical Reflections on Constitutional Democracy in the European Union* (Oxford, Hart Publishing, 2019) 1.

[26] See section IV.

[27] But this may only be a temporary effect, so that the adoption of EU harmonisation measures may well be unavoidable in the longer term; see also the contribution to this book by Steve Weatherill, ch 6.

[28] Sacha Garben also points to the fact that 'harmonisation by stealth' through case law 'could be considered constitutionally legitimate, at least to a certain extent, since the Treaties endow the CJEU explicitly with the task and power to interpret EU law': see S Garben, 'Restating the Problem of Competence Creep, Tackling Harmonisation by Stealth and Reinstating the Legislator' in S Garben and I Govaere (eds), *The Division of Competences between the European Union and its Member States: Reflections on the Past, Present and Future* Oxford, Hart Publishing, 2017) 300, 319.

is of course that such would be unanimously agreed and enacted by the Member States as masters of the Treaties, in compliance with the procedure laid down in Article 48 TEU. A democratic remedy is thus in theory available to tackle *Cassis de Dijon*, provided that there is strong political willingness to do so. The question is whether the various Treaty modifications that took place after 1979, and which seemingly did not take issue with *Cassis de Dijon*, unlike with other judgments,[29] may then serve to underscore its legitimacy *post factum*. Even more striking is the finding that the other EU institutions, at the instigation of the Commission, openly embraced the principle of mutual recognition and quickly made it their own by adopting the 'New Approach to Harmonisation', as is reflected upon in the next section. Furthermore, indisputable proof of *post-factum* democratic legitimation was given in 2008 with the formal adoption of the EU Mutual Recognition Regulation[30] to reinforce the *Cassis De Dijon* logic in practice. The Regulation was revisited and replaced in 2019,[31] inter alia by introducing the voluntary 'mutual recognition declaration'[32] besides the 'Product Contact Points' to be established by each Member State,[33] all of which served to help enforce the *Cassis de Dijon* ruling at the level of the market participants.

## C. Triggering a New Approach to Harmonisation

In the immediate aftermath of *Cassis de Dijon*, the Commission in its 'Interpretative Communication' proactively proposed to instrumentalise the principle of mutual

---

[29] Such as, for instance, the ECOWAS ruling of the CJEU and the ensuing amendment of Art 40 TEU; see Case C-91/05 *Commission v Council*, ECLI:EU:C:2008:288. For an analysis, see P Van Elsuwege, 'On the Boundaries Between the European Union's First Pillar and Second Pillar: a Comment on the ECOWAS Judgment of the European Court of Justice' (2009) 15 *The Columbia Journal of European Law* 531.

[30] Regulation (EC) No 764/2008 of the European Parliament and of the Council of 9 July 2008 laying down procedures relating to the application of certain national technical rules to products lawfully marketed in another Member State and repealing Decision No 3052/95/EC, [2008] OJ L218/21.

[31] EU Regulation (EU) 2019/515 of the European Parliament and of the Council on the mutual recognition of goods lawfully marketed in another Member State, [2019] OJ L91/1. At point (16) of the preamble it states, 'To raise awareness on the part of national authorities and economic operators of the principle of mutual recognition, Member States should consider providing for clear and unambiguous "single market clauses" in their national technical rules with a view to facilitating the application of that principle.'

[32] Art 4(1) of Regulation 2019/515 stipulates the modalities of the Mutual Recognition Declaration: 'The producer of goods, or of goods of a given type, that are being made or are to be made available on the market in the Member State of destination may draw up a voluntary declaration of lawful marketing of goods for the purposes of mutual recognition ("mutual recognition declaration") in order to demonstrate to the competent authorities of the Member State of destination that the goods, or the goods of that type, are lawfully marketed in another Member State.'

[33] Art 9(2) of Regulation 2019/515 provides that 'Product Contact Points shall provide the following information online: (a) information on the principle of mutual recognition and the application of this Regulation in the territory of their Member State, including information on the procedure set out in Article 5; (b) the contact details, by means of which the competent authorities within that Member State may be contacted directly, including the particulars of the authorities responsible for supervising the implementation of the national technical rules applicable in the territory of their Member State; (c) the remedies and procedures available in the territory of their Member State in the event of a dispute between the competent authority and an economic operator, including the procedure set out in Article 8.'

recognition as a 'positive' regulatory tool.[34] It forcefully put forward a 'new approach', whereby negative and positive harmonisation would be successfully combined.[35] This was part of the exercise to launch the 1992 internal market objective by thoroughly revisiting EU regulatory practice, 'drawing on the lessons from the past'. In the 1985 Commission White Paper on the completion of the internal market, two important changes to enhance the efficiency of the EU regulatory framework were put on the table. Both also implied a crucial restriction on the sovereignty of the Member States, not least in their regulatory capacity.

First, the Member States had to cede sovereignty by giving up their right of veto on the adoption of internal market harmonisation measures, at least as a matter of principle. This was accepted by the Member States and firmly anchored in primary EU law by the Single European Act.[36] In so doing, the role and impact of each individual Member State in the EU regulatory process was from then on inherently weakened. Additionally direct control was lost over the enactment of laws that would become applicable in their territories.

Second, the Commission proposed to adopt a new harmonisation strategy, which was explained as follows:

–  a clear distinction needs to be drawn in future internal market initiatives between what it is essential to harmonize, and what may be left to mutual recognition of national regulations and standards; this implies that, on the occasion of each harmonisation initiative, the Commission will determine whether national regulations are excessive in relation to the mandatory requirements pursued and, thus, constitute unjustified barriers to trade according to Article 30 to 36 of the EEC Treaty;
–  legislative harmonisation (Council Directives based on Article 100) will in future be restricted to laying down essential health and safety requirements which will be obligatory in all Member States. Conformity with this will entitle a product to free movement.[37]

The ensuing new EU regulatory strategy thus implies that positive harmonisation measures will only be formulated, negotiated and decided in relation to those impediments to the internal market that are not already neutralised by the application of the principle of mutual recognition. In the new approach to harmonisation this is

---

[34] Communication from the Commission concerning the consequences of the judgment given by the Court of Justice on 20 February 1979 in Case 120/78 ('Cassis de Dijon'), [1980] OJ C256/2.

[35] 'Completing the Internal Market: White Paper from the Commission to the European Council', COM/85/0310 Final, at para 64: 'But while a strategy based purely on mutual recognition would remove barriers to trade and lead to the creation of a genuine common trading market, it might well prove inadequate for the purposes of the building up of an expanding market based on the competitiveness which a continental-scale uniform market can generate. On the other hand experience has shown that the alternative of relying on a strategy based totally on harmonization would be over-regulatory, would take a long time to implement, would be inflexible and could stifle innovation. What is needed is a strategy that combines the best of both approaches but, above all, allows for progress to be made more quickly than in the past.'

[36] See the current Art 114(1) TFEU, yet note that this is not so or the most sensitive areas (Art 114(2)) and counterbalanced by the possibility to exceptionally derogate (Art 114(4)–(6)).

[37] COM/85/0310 Final (n 35) para 65.

further combined with standardisation by standardisation bodies where possible, so that the positive harmonisation exercise through the EU decision-making process is limited to agreeing on the essential requirements in the general interest.[38]

In essence, this puts the focus of internal market harmonisation extremely narrowly and sharply, but also very firmly, on the higher objectives, such as Article 36 TFEU and the open list of mandatory requirements accepted by the Court of Justice in *Cassis de Dijon*, as the indispensable counterbalance to the principle of mutual recognition. Such a deliberate and upfront use of *Cassis de Dijon* in all its complexities clearly has a positive impact on the EU regulatory process in terms of efficacious and quick decision making. But at the same time it considerably reduces and targets the scope of positive regulatory action at EU level in a manner that provokes questions in terms of delimitation of competence, and thus also respect for Member States' regulatory competence, as conceived in the Treaties.

## III. Impact on Delimitation: EU–Member States' Regulatory Competence

Both the *Cassis de Dijon* ruling and its proactive regulatory use by virtue of the new approach to harmonisation have been heavily criticised for the unwarranted impact on the delimitation of regulatory competence as conceived in the Treaties. The higher objectives and mandatory requirements are often considered as sensitive and crucial to the Member States, so that, unsurprisingly, competence in those matters is not usually plainly conferred on the EU.[39] On the contrary, as is now firmly stated in Articles 2–6 TFEU, introduced by the Lisbon Treaty, the nature of such EU competence is mainly shared (such as for environmental protection),[40] or

---

[38] This is further combined with standardisation, see also Council Resolution 85/C 136/01 of 7 May 1985 on a new approach to technical harmonization and standards [1985] OJ C136/1, whereby four fundamental principles were established: 'legislative harmonisation is limited to essential safety requirements (or other requirements in the general interest) with which products put on the market must conform and can therefore enjoy free movement throughout the European Union; the task of drawing up technical production specifications is entrusted to organisations competent in industrial standardisation, which take the current stage of technology into account when doing so; these technical specifications are not mandatory and maintain their status of voluntary standards; the authorities are obliged to recognise that products manufactured in conformity with harmonised standards are presumed to conform to the essential requirements established by the Directive. If the producer does not manufacture in conformity with these standards, he has an obligation to prove that his products conform to the essential requirements. Two conditions have to be met in order that this system may operate: the standards must guarantee the quality of the product; the public authorities must ensure the protection of safety (or other requirements envisaged) on their territory. This is a necessary condition to establish mutual trust between Member States.' See also Regulation (EU) No 1025/2012 of 25 October 2012 on European Standardisation [2012] OJ L316/12.

[39] See Garben and Govaere (eds), *The Division of Competences* (n 28).

[40] Art 4 TFEU lists as shared competences besides the internal market, social, environment and consumer protection as well as, under (k), 'common safety concerns in public health matters, for the aspects defined in this Treaty'.

complementary to or supporting of that of the Member States (for instance public health).[41] The potential impact thereof on the regulatory capacity of the EU and the Member States respectively has, however, significantly shifted with the reformulation of the internal market objective in the Lisbon Treaty.

## A.  Pre-Lisbon Competence Creep

How can the new approach to harmonisation expressly target EU regulation of higher objectives that are not fully conferred on the EU?[42] Faced with this conundrum from the perspective of the principle of conferral, the Court of Justice elaborated the so-called *Tobacco Directive* test in a pre-Lisbon setting.[43] EU harmonisation measures may incidentally relate to such higher objectives and be adopted on the basis of Article 114 TFEU if the aim is

> to prevent the emergence of future obstacles to trade resulting from multifarious development of national laws. However, the emergence of such obstacles must be likely and the measure in question must be designed to prevent them.[44]

So this became the standard criterion to delineate the internal market-based regulatory competence of the EU. Whereas a mere finding of disparities between national rules would not do the trick, this was said to be different for an identified 'obstruction of the fundamental freedoms' or a need 'to prevent the emergence of future obstacles to trade'.[45]

---

[41] Art 6 TFEU expressly confers only supporting/complementary EU competence in relation to, for instance, protection and improvement of human health as well as culture.

[42] 'Full conferral' means that not only decision-making powers but also the countervailing democratic and judicial control mechanisms are shifted from the national to the EU level. For a typology of conferred competence and the impact thereof post-Lisbon, see I Govaere, 'To Give or to Grab: The Principle of Full, Crippled and Split Conferral of Powers Post-Lisbon' in M Cremona (ed), *Structural Principles in EU External Relations Law* (Oxford, Hart Publishing, 2018) 71.

[43] Supported by Art 114 (3) TFEU, which stipulates that 'The Commission, in its proposals envisaged in paragraph 1 concerning health, safety, environmental protection and consumer protection, will take as a base a high level of protection, taking account in particular of any new development based on scientific facts. Within their respective powers, the European Parliament and the Council will also seek to achieve this objective.'

[44] Case C-376/98, *Germany v European Parliament and Council of the European Union, Tobacco*, ECLI:EU:C:2000:544, para 86.

[45] Case C-547/14 *Philip Morris*, ECLI:EU:C:2016:325, see in particular paras 58–60: 'In that regard, while a mere finding of disparities between national rules is not sufficient to justify having recourse to Article 114 TFEU, it is otherwise where there are differences between the laws, regulations or administrative provisions of the Member States which are such as to obstruct the fundamental freedoms and thus have a direct effect on the functioning of the internal market (see, to that effect, judgments in *Germany v Parliament and Council*, C-376/98, EU:C:2000:544, paragraphs 84 and 95; *British American Tobacco (Investments) and Imperial Tobacco*, C-491/01, EU:C:2002:741, paragraphs 59 and 60; *Arnold André*, C-434/02, EU:C:2004:800, paragraph 30; *Swedish Match*, C-210/03, EU:C:2004:802, paragraph 29; *Germany v Parliament and Council*, C-380/03, EU:C:2006:772, paragraph 37; and *Vodafone and Others*, C-58/08, EU:C:2010:321, paragraph 32). … It is also settled case-law that, although recourse to Article 114 TFEU as a legal basis is possible if the aim is to prevent the emergence of future obstacles to trade as a

Already prior to the Lisbon Treaty, several authors had drawn attention to the phenomenon of 'competence creep'[46] or 'harmonization by stealth',[47] as amplified by the rulings in *Cassis de Dijon* and *Tobacco Directive*. Solutions had also been explored to contain the extent of the problem, for instance by 'restricting the restrictions' to the free movement in the aftermath of *Cassis de Dijon*.[48] The latter has famously extended the scope of application of the rules on free movement to include measures that are not discriminatory in nature, whether openly or indirectly so. It is as a direct consequence thereof that national measures regulating higher objectives came under a quasi-automatic scrutiny by the Court of Justice for compliance with the justification and proportionality tests[49] and the targeted focus of EU regulation.[50] The reasoning goes that reverting to a more restrictive reading of the internal market provisions, in particular in relation to indistinctly applicable measures, will then automatically lead to EU law's interfering less with national regulation and leaving the non-economic policy choices of the Member States in relation to such higher objectives more intact. Similar reflections most likely prompted the follow-up case law in *Keck and Mithouard* (as in turn further clarified in the *Trailers* judgment) which partially reversed *Cassis de Dijon* by expressly limiting its scope of application.[51]

## B. Post-Lisbon Untapped Potential

Underlying this whole discussion is the often unspoken but crucial issue regarding the perceived nature of the regulatory interaction in a system of multi-layered governance.[52] More often than not it is presented as dichotomous, implying that

---

result of divergences in national laws, the emergence of such obstacles must be likely and the measure in question must be designed to prevent them (judgments in *British American Tobacco (Investments) and Imperial Tobacco*, C-491/01, EU:C:2002:741, paragraph 61; *Arnold André*, C-434/02, EU:C:2004:800, paragraph 31; *Swedish Match*, C-210/03, EU:C:2004:802, paragraph 30; *Germany v Parliament and Council*, C-380/03, EU:C:2006:772, paragraph 38; and *Vodafone and Others*, C-58/08, EU:C:2010:321, paragraph 33). ... The Court has also held that, provided that the conditions for recourse to Article 114 TFEU as a legal basis are fulfilled, the EU legislature cannot be prevented from relying on that legal basis on the ground that public health protection is a decisive factor in the choices to be made (judgments in *British American Tobacco (Investments) and Imperial Tobacco*, C-491/01, EU:C:2002:741, paragraph 62; *Arnold André*, C-434/02, EU:C:2004:800, paragraph 32; *Swedish Match*, C-210/03, EU:C:2004:802, paragraph 31; and *Germany v Parliament and Council*, C-380/03, EU:C:2006:772, paragraph 39)'.

[46] S Weatherill, 'Competence Creep and Competence Control' [2004] *Yearbook of European Law* 1; S Garben, 'Competence Creep Revisited' (2017) *Journal of Common Market Studies* 1.

[47] S Garben, 'Restating The Problem of Competence Creep, Tackling Harmonisation by Stealth and Reinstating the Legislator' in Garben and Govaere (eds), *The Division of Competences* (n 28) 300.

[48] C Barnard, 'Restricting restrictions: Lessons for the EU from the US?' (2009) 68 *The Cambridge Law Journal* 575.

[49] See section II.A.

[50] See section II.C.

[51] See section I.

[52] On this concept see L Hooghe and G Marks, *Multi-level Governance and European Integration* (London, Rowman & Littlefield, 2001).

internal market integration at EU level necessarily goes at the cost of non-economic policy choices at the level of the Member States. The true challenge nonetheless lies in the opposite move towards integrating the internal market further in pursuance of such higher non-economic objectives also at EU level,[53] whilst leaving some flexibility at the level of the Member States.

It has been argued elsewhere that now, for the first time, the Lisbon Treaty allows for such a fundamental shift in approach to be firmly made, even though so far this has largely been ignored in practice.[54] Article 3(3) TEU has radically redrafted the former 'reactive' and 'instrumental' internal market objective using much more 'proactive' and 'purposeful' wording. It states:

> The Union shall establish an internal market. It shall work for the sustainable development of Europe based on balanced economic growth and price stability, a highly competitive social market economy, aiming at full employment and social progress, and a high level of protection and improvement of the quality of the environment. It shall promote scientific and technological advance.
>
> It shall combat social exclusion and discrimination, and shall promote social justice and protection, equality between women and men, solidarity between generations and protection of the rights of the child.
>
> It shall promote economic, social and territorial cohesion, and solidarity among Member States.
>
> It shall respect its rich cultural and linguistic diversity and shall ensure that Europe's cultural heritage is safeguarded and enhanced.

The Lisbon Treaty thus expressly and purposely provides that the establishment of the internal market is an objective in and of itself, and, moreover, that the Union pro-actively works to respect and promote non-economic higher objectives, such as environmental and social protection. Furthermore, the internal market rules are, of course, also subject to the provisions of general application as listed in Articles 7–13 TFEU, which are echoed in Article 3(3) TEU. As developed elsewhere,[55] the Lisbon Treaty thus provides the necessary legal framework for a

---

[53] See also G Davies, 'The Competence to Create an Internal Market: Conceptual Poverty and Unbalanced Interests' in Garben and Govaere (eds), *The Division of Competences* (n 28) 74, 85–86: 'The Union should be able to do the things necessary to create a well-functioning market, which includes creating a market-ready society – fair, tolerant, lacking opportunities for exploitation, redistributive, mutually understanding, skeptical of economics, not too materialistic, protective of its weaker members and areas, and with a job-market which allows welfare-enhancing participation in that market for all: or at least this is one mainstream European political view – and it should be able to say openly that it is doing this, and not have to always pretend that it is merely seeking to facilitate and expand trade, for that is just one tiny part of what establishing a market may be thought to entail.'

[54] See I Govaere, 'Internal Market Dynamics: On Moving Targets, Shifting Contextual Factors and the Untapped Potential of Article 3(3) TEU' in S Garben and I Govaere (eds), *Internal Market 2.0* (Oxford, Hart Publishing, 2020) 75. In particular in pt III it is, inter alia, pointed out that it is striking that the CJEU seemingly remains oblivious of these Treaty changes as it simply continues to apply the *Tobacco Directive* test post-Lisbon too.

[55] For a detailed analysis, see I Govaere, 'Modernisation of the internal market: potential clashes and crossroads with other policies' in M De Vos (ed), *European Union Internal Market and Labour Law: Friends or Foes?* (Antwerp, Intersentia, 2009) 3; for a slightly amended version, see I Govaere,

more proactive internal market that positively intertwines with other regulatory policies to be adopted at EU level.[56] Such an important legal contextual change would then also warrant a renewed appraisal of the regulatory implications of *Cassis de Dijon* in a post-Lisbon setting.

# IV.   Impact on Member States' National Regulatory Discretion

From the foregoing reflections, it is plain that, mainly through the instrumentalisation made by the Commission, *Cassis de Dijon* unwittingly had a snowball effect that heavily impacted the EU regulatory competence and process as conceived by the Member States in the Treaties. Concurrently, it has also served to greatly curtail the discretion of the Member States to formulate positive regulation, economic or non-economic, at national level. The latter regulatory consequence of *Cassis de Dijon* has received much less attention so far, but it is nonetheless actively pursued by the Commission. The paradox lies in the fact that *Cassis de Dijon* meant to upgrade the importance of national legislation in the absence of EU harmonisation but instead triggered three unwarranted yet interrelated positive law effects: the 'straitjacket test', the 'rubber-stamp exercise' and the 'balancing trick'.

The straitjacket test refers to the extent to which national positive law drafting has been influenced by the contours of the principle of mutual recognition. The rubber-stamp exercise goes a step further and denotes the 'positive' dictate to codify the principle of mutual recognition into national law. The balancing trick completes the picture of imposing the *Cassis de Dijon* logic on to the national regulator not just in relation to the principle of mutual recognition, but also as concerns the indispensable counterweight represented by the higher objectives. Although those three tests are of course interrelated, they will briefly be addressed in turn.

## A.   The Straitjacket Test: 'Pure' Negative Integration with Positive Law Implications

*Cassis de Dijon* is a prime example of 'negative' integration. As already stated, by virtue of the principle of mutual recognition, it allows for free movement of

---

'The Future Direction of the EU Internal Market: On Vested Values and Fashionable Modernism' (Winter 2009/2010) 16/1 *The Columbia Journal of European Law* 67.

[56] On the link between internal market and higher objectives, see also B De Witte, 'A competence to protect: the pursuit of non-market aims through internal market legislation' in P Syrpis (ed), *The Judiciary, the Legislature and the EU Internal Market* (Cambridge, Cambridge University Press, 2012) 25; B De Witte, 'Non-market values in internal market legislation' in N Nic Shuibhne (ed), *Regulating the Internal Market* (Cheltenham, Edward Elgar, 2006) 61.

economic commodities, also in the absence of positive measures adopted at EU level, by upgrading the importance of the regulatory framework in place in the Member State of exportation.[57] Surprisingly little attention has been paid to the cost thereof in terms of constraining regulatory freedom at the level of the Member States. A reason might be that the regulatory implications of *Cassis de Dijon*'s eating away at national regulatory discretion are not immediately apparent. As a judge-made principle of EU law with primacy over national law, it would suffice to invoke the principle of mutual recognition to restrict national laws merely in their application. National law could then, as a matter of principle, simply no longer be applied to goods produced and marketed in compliance with the regulatory framework in force in the Member State of export. In other words, there is strictly speaking no need to modify or streamline national law to achieve the internal market objective as pursued by *Cassis de Dijon*.

In practice, however, the logic of *Cassis de Dijon* has forced the Member States to carefully draft the scope of application of their national legislation in a targeted manner to keep it fully within their regulatory discretion. The premise of the principle of mutual recognition is that, in the absence of EU harmonisation measures, Member States may freely regulate both domestic and export production, provided that this is done on a truly non-discriminatory basis. The backdrop is that as soon as the limits of this regulatory discretion are trespassed upon, the internal market rules potentially kick in, requiring the national measure to survive the double justification and proportionality test. A combined reading of the *Iberian Pigs*[58] and *Emmenthal Cheese*[59] cases illustrates that this is taken to the letter and effectively limits the regulatory freedom in its expression rather than merely in its application.

The *Iberian Pigs* case concerned a Spanish decree approving quality standards for meat, ham, shoulder ham and loin, marketed under the sales designation '*ibérico de cebo*', and is proof of the fact that Member States can indeed proactively avoid competence creep, and thus potential EU interference with non-economic policy choices, by imposing the necessary self-restraint whilst exercising national regulatory discretion. In particular, a double limitation should be clearly, if perhaps not necessarily expressly, made apparent to escape the application of Articles 34 and 35 TFEU respectively: the fact that the national regulation exclusively contains local production requirements, coupled with inherently non-discriminatory export rules. If, and only if, the CJEU is satisfied that both limitations follow from the wording of the national legislation will the latter remain outside the scope of internal market rules so that no justification need be given.[60] By contrast,

---

[57] See section II.A.

[58] Case C-169/17, *Asociación Nacional de Productores de Ganado Porcino v. Administración del Estado (Iberian Pigs)*, ECLI :EU:C:2018:440.

[59] Case C-448/98, *Guimont (Emmenthal Cheese)*, ECLI:EU:C:2000:663.

[60] *Iberian Pigs* (n 58) para 28: '[I]t cannot be held that Article 34 TFEU precludes national legislation, such as that at issue in the main proceedings, which provides that the sales designation "ibérico de cebo" may be granted only to products that comply with certain conditions imposed

the *Emmenthal Cheese* case acts as a reminder that without such careful draft-ing of national laws, the internal market rules will immediately kick in to limit the regulatory discretion of the Member States, even in what at first sight seem to be purely national situations. The argument that the case concerned French regulation enforced exclusively upon a French producer, in relation to the produc-tion and sale of cheese on French soil, proved to be of no avail. Nor did the argument carry any weight that in practice this regulation was never opposed to imported products. Contrary to the Opinion of Advocate General Saggio,[61] the Court of Justice simply pointed out that this limitation was not apparent from the wording of the national law.[62] Instead, the French regulation was assessed as to its potential impediment to imports of cheese lawfully manufactured in other Member States and found to be incompatible with the internal market rules for failing the proportionality test.[63] This illustrates perfectly well that the national regulator not only has to be known to uphold the principle of mutual recogni-tion in practice, but unequivocally has to be seen to do so through its legislative activity. The national legislator is thus firmly put into the straitjacket designed by *Cassis de Dijon*.

by that legislation, since that legislation permits the importation and marketing of products from Member States other than the State that adopted the legislation at issue, under the designations they bear pursuant to the rules of the Member State of origin, even if they are similar, comparable or identical to the designations provided for in the national legislation at issue in the main proceed-ings.' And at paras 30–31: 'In the present case, it should be noted that the legislation at issue in the main proceedings does not distinguish between products destined for the domestic market and those destined for the EU market. All Spanish producers wishing to sell their Iberian pig products under the sales designations laid down in Royal Decree 4/2014 are required to comply with the requirements of that decree, regardless of the market on which they wish to sell their products. ... Accordingly, it must be held that Article 35 TFEU does not preclude national legislation such as Royal Decree 4/2014.'

[61] *Emmenthal Cheese* (n 59), Opinion of AG Saggio, ECLI:EU:C:2000:117, at points 7 and 8.

[62] ibid paras 14–17: 'On the one hand, the French Government argues that the inapplicability of Article 30 follows from the simple fact that the rule which Mr Guimont is accused of infringing is not, in practice, applied to imported products. It maintains that that rule was designed to create obligations solely for national producers and does not therefore concern intra-Community trade in any way. In its submission, the case-law of the Court of Justice, and particularly the judgment in Case 98/86 *Mathot* [1987] ECR 809, paragraphs 8 and 9, demonstrates that Article 30 of the Treaty is designed to protect only intra-Community trade. ... In response to that argument, it should be observed that Article 30 of the Treaty covers any measure of the Member States which is capable, directly or indirectly, actually or potentially, of hindering intra-Community trade (Case 8/74 *Procureur du Roi v Dassonville* [1974] ECR 837, paragraph 5). However, that article is not designed to ensure that goods of national origin enjoy the same treatment as imported goods in every case, and a difference in treatment as between goods which is not capable of restricting imports or of prejudicing the marketing of imported goods does not fall within the prohibition contained in that article (*Mathot*, paragraphs 7 and 8). ... However, as regards the national rule at issue in the main proceedings, the French Government does not deny that, according to its wording, it is applicable without distinction to both French and imported products. ... This argument of the French Government cannot therefore be accepted. The mere fact that a rule is not applied to imported products in practice does not exclude the possibility of it having effects which indi-rectly or potentially hinder intra-Community trade (see Case C-184/96 *Commission v France* [1998] ECR I-6197, paragraph 17).'

[63] *Emmenthal Cheese* (n 59) paras 25–27.

## B. The Rubber-Stamp Exercise

The straitjacket test is essentially a voluntary restraining exercise to be performed by the national regulator. It is applied on a strictly optional basis, only if and when it proactively wants to escape potentially unwarranted consequences of *Cassis de Dijon*. There is, however, no guarantee that this test will always and systematically be taken on board in practice. The fact that the national regulatory context does not properly reflect the applicable EU rules and principles applying to intra-EU trade is of course not legally problematic considering the characteristics of primacy and direct effect. It does nevertheless raise concerns in terms of transparency and legal certainty for actors in the market who may not all be EU law specialists and simply turn to national law to appraise the applicable regulatory framework.[64] Most likely, this explains why the Commission has initiated infringement proceedings to force national regulators – proactively and systematically – to write the principle of mutual recognition into their laws.

Highly important in this respect is the *Foie Gras* case, where the Court of Justice for the first time and as a matter of principle agreed with the Commission that the Member States should perform such a positive law rubber-stamp exercise of *Cassis de Dijon*.[65] The Court succinctly concluded that

> by adopting Decree No 93-999 of 9 August 1993 relating to preparations with foie gras as a base without including in it a mutual recognition clause for products coming from a Member State and complying with the rules laid down by that State, the French Republic has failed to fulfil its obligations under (now Article 34 TFEU).[66]

In other words, *Cassis de Dijon* is from then on no longer considered merely as a judge-made principle of EU law that may limit the application of national law; it is turned into a positive obligation resting on the national regulator, to duly codify the principle of mutual recognition in all relevant laws, failure to do which may in itself constitute a breach of EU law.

Furthermore, the Court in so doing also acknowledged the attribution of a preventative role to the principle of mutual recognition. The insertion in all national legislation is held to be obligatory, as a matter of principle, regardless of the specific circumstances of the case. It is interesting to note that Advocate General La Pergola had strongly argued against this suggestion of the Commission, instead calling upon the Court of Justice to simply dismiss the case, in particular having regard to the facts:[67] Foie gras is a typical French product, France did not (nor was it likely in the foreseeable future to) import foie gras, and on top of that no other Member State at that time had at all regulated the production of foie gras.

---

[64] See also the Commission interpretative communication on facilitating the access of products to the markets of other Member States: the practical application of mutual recognition [2003] OJ C265/02.

[65] Case C-184/96 *Commission v France (Foie Gras)*, ECLI :EU:C:1998:495.

[66] ibid, see conclusion.

[67] *Foie Gras* (n 65), Opinion of AG La Pergola, ECLI:EU:C:1997:495, see in particular at point 36.

The last finding in itself already poses a problem in terms of the very definition of mutual recognition. How can the principle of mutual recognition apply at all in the absence of a regulatory framework in the Member State of exportation ? As Advocate General La Pergola pointed out:

> It follows from what we have seen so far that the requirement of mutual recognition for the purposes of lawful marketing on national territory – which, according to the Commission, is incumbent on France – concerns not preparations with foie gras as a base 'lawfully produced or marketed in other Member States' (a category which is nonexistent at present), but solely goods of that type produced 'in accordance with fair and traditional practices' in the Member State of origin.[68]

Interestingly enough, the Court did not engage with this important discussion but instead expressly framed the principle of mutual recognition in its conclusion (see above) as obeying the following double test: relating to 'products coming from a Member State' and complying with 'the rules laid down by that State'. First, it is striking that the Court of Justice did not re-state that the products should be 'produced' in the Member State of exportation, thus indicating that perhaps products imported from third countries and lawfully put on the market in the Member State of exportation could benefit from the principle of mutual recognition as well.[69]

Second, the Court did seem to indicate that the existence of 'rules', and thus of a truly regulatory framework in the Member State of exportation, is required as a condition to trigger mutual recognition. A deregulated system or mere compliance with traditional practices and custom in the export State would then simply not do the trick.

The regulatory impact of the *Foie Gras* case is thus manifold, both in terms of imposing *Cassis de Dijon* terms on to the national regulator and for revisiting the role, function and definition of the principle of mutual recognition. It is also an unusually blunt ruling, in that it revisits the criss-cross relations between the EU and the Member States, as well as the judiciary and the regulator, very much like a bull in a china shop.

## C. The Balancing Trick

Not surprisingly, the *Foie Gras* case has triggered follow-up cases, with the Commission feeling strengthened in its role of enforcer of the principle of mutual recognition upon the national legislator and the latter offering great resistance thereto. In two follow-up cases, France, in particular, pushed back strongly.

In the so-called *Additives* case,[70] France forcefully argued that the *Cassis de Dijon* logic is not only about introducing the principle of mutual recognition,

---

[68] ibid point 35.
[69] See further ch 8 by Oliver in this volume.
[70] Case C-24/00 *Commission v France (Additives)*, ECLI:EU:C:2004:70.

but crucially also about accepting the indispensable counterweight to protect the higher objectives for the Member States of importation. Therefore it would make no sense – and even be deceptive – for market actors to codify the principle of mutual recognition into a national law that puts into place a system of prior authorisation for foodstuffs in order to protect consumers and public health.[71] The crux of the argument goes back to the very core and coherence of *Cassis de Dijon* in terms of avoiding regulatory competition between the Member States,[72] not eliminating national regulatory discretion altogether. This was seemingly so understood by the Court of Justice. While expressly pointing out that the national measures at stake were indeed caught by Article 34 TFEU and did not contain the principle of mutual recognition,[73] it stressed that 'national legislation which makes the addition of a nutrient to a foodstuff lawfully manufactured and/or marketed in other Member States subject to prior authorisation is not, in principle, contrary to [Union] law, provided that certain conditions are satisfied'.[74] It was only because the latter was not held to be fulfilled *in casu* that the French legislation was found to be incompatible with EU law, not because of the mere absence of the principle of mutual recognition, as had been argued by the Commission with reference to *Foie Gras*.[75]

In spite of this rather clear answer provided by the Court of Justice, the Commission nonetheless persevered and again initiated infringement proceedings against France for legislating a prior authorisation scheme for processing aids and foodstuffs without including the principle of mutual recognition. The Court finally, unequivocally rejected the argument:

> The Commission's argument in paragraph 64 of this judgment concerning the nature of the mutual recognition clause necessary in order to comply with Union law cannot be accepted.
>
> ...
>
> [T]o require in national legislation establishing a prior authorisation scheme that a mutual recognition clause be included such as that contemplated by the Commission in paragraph 64 of this judgment would go against the very rationale of such a scheme, since the Member State concerned would be obliged to allow the marketing on its territory of processing aids and foodstuffs benefiting from that clause without being able to verify the absence of genuine risks for public health.[76]

---

[71] ibid para 19.

[72] See at point 2.

[73] *Additives* (n 71) paras 23–24.

[74] ibid para 25.

[75] ibid para 17: 'Relying on the judgment in Case C-184/96 *Commission v France* [1998] ECR I-6197, the Commission argues that the absence in the French legislation of provision for mutual recognition is sufficient to demonstrate the failure to fulfil obligations.'

[76] Case C-333/08 *Commission v France (Prior Authorization Scheme)*, ECLI:EU:C:2010:44, paras 107 and 109. In para 64 it is reported that the Commission 'argues that, since other Member States must comply with the requirements, in particular, of Article 14 of Regulation No 178/2002 in relation to the rules concerning foodstuffs placed on the market, and an infringement of Community law by the latter cannot be presumed, a mutual recognition clause should be limited to providing that the provisions

In essence, in a compulsory manner this brings the full assessment of *Cassis de Dijon* down to the level of the Member States in their sovereign regulatory capacity. In line with the distinction put forward by Advocate General Mazák to reconcile the apparently contradictory outcome of the prior rulings,[77] it thus appears that where no higher objectives are targeted by the national legislation, the principle of mutual recognition should be codified in national law, and vice versa.

There is, however, a major difference. In *Cassis de Dijon* the balancing trick between the rule and the higher objective exceptions was performed by a specialised EU judiciary, *ex post*, and on a case-by-case basis. This is now transformed into an abstract exercise to be performed *ex ante* by the national regulator, who will necessarily also have to look beyond the State's own borders to take into account the regulatory framework adopted in other Member States.[78] The complexity of such a compulsory balancing exercise, to be performed at the national regulatory level, cannot be ignored. Combined with the uncertainties and controversies that have emanated from *Cassis de Dijon* – as shown in this book – this difficulty is exacerbated still further. Inevitably the national regulator then also needs to appraise and apply the follow-up case law to *Cassis de Dijon*, in particular the *Keck & Mithouard* and *Trailers* cases.[79]

# V. Conclusion

The reflections set out in this chapter serve to illustrate that what you see is thus not necessarily what you get. *Cassis de Dijon*, on the face of it, introduces a judge-made principle, with – as a counterweight – a new category of exceptions, the mandatory requirements, to further the internal market objective in the face of regulatory inertia. A closer look reveals a major and decisive impact on the making and shaping of that very regulatory framework, both at EU and Member States levels. Partly due to its instrumentalisation by the Commission, *Cassis de Dijon* blurs the lines between the respective roles of judiciary and regulator, conferred, reserved and

---

of the relevant national legislation shall not hinder the principle of the free movement of foodstuffs in the preparation of which processing aids have been used which do not comply with the provisions of that legislation but which come from other Member States of the Community where they are lawfully manufactured and/or marketed.'

[77] ibid, Opinion of AG Mazák, ECLI:EU:C:2009:523, see at para 62: 'Some uncertainties may be raised by the comparison of the judgment in Case C-184/96 *Commission v France* ... with the judgment in Case C-24/00 *Commission v France*. ... In both cases, the Commission alleged that the French Republic had failed to insert a mutual recognition clause in its legislation, so hindering the free movement of goods. Whereas, in the first case, the Court found there was a failure to fulfil obligations, in the second case it dismissed that allegation of failure to fulfil obligations. However, those cases may be distinguished by the fact that whilst, in the second case, the French Republic proved that its legislation hindering the free movement of goods was justified by the protection of public health, in the first case, no consideration relating to the protection of public health was put forward.'

[78] See section II.A.

[79] See section I.

discretionary competence, as well as EU and national regulatory prerogatives in a system of multi-layered governance.[80] As a consequence, the emerging picture of the regulatory impact of *Cassis de Dijon* is complex and subject to a changing assessment depending on the angle from which it is being studied. In that sense it presents a striking resemblance to another famous oil on canvas by the Belgian surrealist painter René Magritte, *Les mystères de l'horizon*, known in English under the befitting name *The Masterpiece* or *The Mysteries of the Horizon*.[81] To visualise this painting:

> The viewer is presented with three apparently identical men wearing bowler hats and with clearly defined outfits, placed outdoors in a dusk of indigo and black. Each upright figure has his own crescent moon hanging over him, and they all face different ways. One looks towards the white glow of the horizon, while the second shows a little of his face as he turns towards the left hand distance, and the third is seen in profile. The initial impression may be that they are sharing the same space, but they could also be inhabiting separate worlds, although it is impossible for the eye to discern where one person's sky becomes another's.

The three different angles taken here to reflect upon the regulatory impact of *Cassis de Dijon*, namely EU positive regulation, delimitation of competence, as well as Member States regulatory discretion, similarly draw on the common features of mutual recognition and mandatory requirements to reveal fundamentally different effects and horizons. Although often studied in isolation, only all those different facets of *Cassis de Dijon* taken together reveal the bigger picture of the legal masterpiece created by the Court of Justice.

---

[80] See also Hooghe and Marks, *Multi-level Governance* (n 52) esp 26–27. At 26 it is pointed out that whereas the CJEU 'rulings are pivotal in shaping European integration', it 'depends on other actors to force issues on the European political agenda and to condone its interpretations'; continuing on from there that it is the Commission that has put *Cassis de Dijon* on the 'wider agenda'.

[81] See at www.rene-magritte.com/mysteries-of-the-horizon/, last accessed 21 May 2020.

# 6

## Did *Cassis de Dijon* Make a Difference?

STEPHEN WEATHERILL*

## I. Introduction

Did the Court's ruling in *Cassis de Dijon* make a difference? On paper, yes of course it did. It transformed understanding of free movement law, and even today it is central to any explanation of the state of the law. In practice, however, the impact of the case is much harder to track. And – this is the headline finding contained in this chapter – the case would *not* today be decided in the same way as it was in 1979. This is because the regulation of blackcurrant liqueur and crème de cassis in the internal market is today the preserve of EU legislation, not the Treaty rules on free movement.

On paper, the ruling established the principle of conditional or non-absolute mutual recognition. It put in place a method for mediating the claims to exercise regulatory competence made by the home State (the State of production) and by the host State (the State of marketing). The host State may insist on compliance with its rules – provided it can show a sufficient justification for them. The point is to put trade-obstructive rules *to the test*. If they fail that test – that is, if they are not justified – they must be set aside and not applied to imports. This deregulatory impact in turn entails a reduction in the required scope of the EU's top-down programme of legislative harmonisation and instead champions consumer choice and diversity of products and of production standards within the internal market. The internal market is founded on a mix between the application of the free movement rules to obstructive national rules and EU legislative initiatives: *Cassis* extended use of the former at the expense of the latter.

However, there is *Cassis* on paper and there is *Cassis* in practice. The *Cassis* model of conditional or non-absolute mutual recognition, driven by ad hoc

* I would like to thank all the participants in the intriguing and rich discussions held in Cambridge in April 2019, both for their thoughts at the time and in immensely helpful e-mail exchanges and conversations since. I have also benefited from discussion with Stefan Enchelmaier, Kai Purnhagen, John Temple Lang and Jan Zglinski, and so too from comments gratefully received on a version of this chapter I presented at a conference held in Edinburgh in April 2019 to celebrate the Europa Institute's 50th anniversary. Given that level of learned input, there can be few mistakes left to mar the chapter, but the fault for any that have survived is mine, all mine.

litigation once trade barriers at national level are encountered, has real weaknesses as a basis for the management of non-harmonised sectors in the internal market. It tends to be opaque and hard to apply in practice. The Commission has over time increasingly confessed to this, and it has tried to supplement the Court's principle with instruments of market management such as obligations imposed on national authorities to notify it of measures that are likely to be harmful to cross-border trade and soft forms of dispute resolution such as the SOLVIT scheme. But the ready intuition is that, despite the elegance of *Cassis* in promoting diversity of products and of national regulatory regimes, harmonisation as a process of establishing common EU rules to replace diverse national rules may be a more reliable basis for managing the internal market than non-harmonisation based on conditional or non-absolute mutual recognition.

And that intuition is fully supported in the matter of blackcurrant liqueur and crème de cassis. These products are today the subject of harmonised rules adopted by the EU. They are defined by EU secondary legislation. Were the facts of the *Cassis de Dijon* case to recur today, the case would *not* be decided in the same way. Germany would have no competence even to attempt to justify its rules. The sector is fully harmonised and the EU's rules govern the matter exclusively. And a producer who wanted to market a new type of liqueur with a lower amount of alcohol by volume than is stipulated by the EU rules, in order to offer wider consumer choice backed by labelling that discloses the alcohol content, could not do so.

This appears to be little known. On its own terms it is modestly interesting, but it is what it reveals about the evolving legal structure of the internal market that is really interesting. The shift from free movement law to legislative harmonisation as the basis for trade in blackcurrant liqueur in the internal market illuminates the incentives to push for the security and clarity of harmonisation as a more reliable basis for managing the internal market than is supplied by the principle of conditional or non-absolute mutual recognition applicable in non-harmonised sectors. It shows too that there are assumptions about the market and consumer behaviour within the EU's legislative process, in particular that product composition rules rather labelling requirements are needed, that completely contradict those of the Court in *Cassis*. The bigger question is what it tells us about the viability in practice of the approach taken in *Cassis de Dijon* to the management of non-harmonised sectors in the internal market, and what it reveals about the possible risks of over-regulation in the internal market as a result of the increase in harmonised sectors at the expense of non-harmonised sectors. Behind this lies the nature of the internal market defined in Article 26 TFEU as an ambiguous concept and a dynamic process.

## II. *Cassis de Dijon*

The factual background to the litigation in the famous 'Cassis de Dijon' case – more properly, *Rewe-Zentrale AG v Bundesmonopolverwaltung für Branntwein* – is so well known that it merits only brief summary. Cassis de Dijon was a blackcurrant fruit liqueur made in France with an alcohol content of between 15 and 20 per cent.[1] It could not be sold in Germany because it did not comply with German law, which required that products of that type should have a minimum alcohol content of 25 per cent. This was not a case of discrimination against products made in France or against imports more generally. A German-made product with the same relatively low level of alcohol as the French-made product would equally have been excluded from the German market. The obstacle to trade arose because German product standards were *different* from French standards.

The Court famously based its analysis on a deft inversion of the allocation of regulatory competence between the 'home State' (here France) and the 'host State' (here Germany). Paragraph 8 of the ruling begins by stating that it is for the Member States to regulate matters on their own territory. This is a concession to 'host State' competence to set rules governing the composition of products. The Court continues in the same vein: obstacles to movement resulting from disparities between national laws 'must be accepted'. But all of a sudden the judgment bites. Acceptance of host State regulatory autonomy is conditional. The host State's obstructive rules are put to the test, and they may be applied only where necessary in order to satisfy mandatory requirements – in short, only where they are *justified*. In the absence of such justification the host State is denied the competence to apply its rules to impede imports, and in consequence the trader is allowed to penetrate the market of the host State merely by virtue of having complied with the rules of the home State. To yield to unconditional 'host State' regulatory autonomy would have allowed persisting fragmentation of the national market, pending EU legislative intervention, while to accept unconditional 'home State' regulatory autonomy would have swept aside even legitimate claims to regulate the host State market according to local preference. The Court goes to neither extreme. Neither home State nor host State control is absolute. The model is more nuanced and sophisticated. Its interpretation casts Article 34 TFEU as a provision laying down a conditional or non-absolute rule of 'mutual recognition' of the adequacy of technical standards set by the Member States. The free movement provisions create a non-absolute principle of home-country control.

Then the trade barrier was put to the test, and it failed it. The incoherent German argument that protection of public health justified banning weak alcoholic drinks but not strong ones detained the Court only briefly. Slightly more weight attached to the claim that fixing a minimum limit for alcohol content protects the consumer from unfair practices on the part of producers and distributors. After all, German consumers would, in the event that the German rule were disapplied, be exposed to alcoholic drinks of a (weak) type with which they were unfamiliar and that would not offer them the kick to which they were accustomed. In this vein the judgment notes the observation of the Commission that fixing limits may lead to

---

[1] Case 120/78 *Rewe-Zentrale AG v Bundesmonopolverwaltung für Branntwein* (*Cassis de Dijon*), ECLI:EU:C:1979:42.

standardisation of products placed on the market and of their designations, leading to greater transparency in the market.[2] This would resonate, but for EU rules not those set by Germany, and is examined further below in section V. But in its *Cassis* ruling the Court swept aside such concerns, noting instead that such anxieties could be addressed in Germany by imposing a requirement on producers to inform consumers by the display of alcohol content and origin on the packaging of the product. Mandatory minimum rules on alcohol content went too far.

The ruling is perfectly consistent with the Treaty. Article 34 TFEU prohibits barriers to inter-State trade. This favours home State control. Then Article 36 TFEU softens the prohibition by allowing the host State to show justification for its regulatory intervention. The same pattern is found in the Treaty provisions governing services: Article 56 TFEU is softened by scope for justification of trade barriers recognised by Article 52 TFEU *via* Article 62 TFEU. The Treaty assumes a model of conditional mutual recognition or non-absolute home State control – which is the same as that developed by the Court in *Cassis*. Moreover the seeds of the vocabulary used in the *Cassis de Dijon* judgment can already be found in earlier judgments.[3] So where is the novelty? The reason *Cassis* enjoys such prominence is not that it caused any radical change in the structure of the law governing free movement, but rather that it offered a more fully developed and elegant formula compared with anything that had gone before in the Treaty, in legislative texts or in the case law. The ruling elucidates a method for mediating the claims to exercise regulatory competence made by the home State (the State of production) and by the host State (the State of marketing). The host State must show 'legal empathy' towards the regulatory practices of the home State:[4] acknowledging and recognising the virtues of different practices preferred in other Member States, it may enforce its own local standards only where it is able to demonstrate that those of the home State are in some way inadequate. In this way the law of free movement serves to manage a regulatory responsibility which is shared between home and host States. Dual regulation of product and service markets is excluded in the absence of justification for host State intervention – just as in *Cassis* itself.

In truth most decided cases follow the pattern set in *Cassis* – national rules fail the test and are condemned as unjustified obstacles to inter-State trade. Some such cases are initiated by the Commission. In *Commission v Germany*, the Court was asked to examine the *Reinheitsgebot*, which imposed inflexible composition rules on any product sold in Germany as *Bier*.[5] Plainly, such rules, centuries old, had been introduced with no intent to harm the EU's internal market project, but their effect was to exclude differently made beers originating in other Member States with different brewing traditions from those prevailing in Germany, and the Court treated them as unjustified obstacles to inter-State trade. The Court took the view that the consumer could be adequately protected by labelling rules that

---

[2] ibid para 13.

[3] Especially see Case 33/74 *Van Binsbergen*, ECLI:EU:C:1974:131.

[4] K Nicolaïdis, 'Mutual Recognition: Promise and Denial, From Sapiens to Brexit' (2017) 70 *Current Legal Problems* 227, 244.

[5] Case 178/84 *Commission v Germany*, ECLI:EU:C:1987:126.

would disclose to him or her what (unfamiliar) ingredients were contained in the imported product. Many more cases have been driven by private commercial interests eager to exploit free movement law in order to slice away regulatory obstacles at national level. So, for example, in *Walter Rau*, the Court interpreted free movement law to mean that Member States could not prohibit the sale of imported margarine in cone shaped packs where local rules insisted on cube-shaped packaging.[6] Labelling would be enough to protect the consumer from any risk of confusion. Similarly in *Verein gegen Unwesen in Handel und Gewerbe Köln eV v Mars GmbH*, the Court swept aside German concern to suppress an allegedly misleading marketing practice that was permitted elsewhere on the basis that 'reasonably circumspect consumers' would suffer no detriment:[7] EU free movement law was therefore to be interpreted as precluding a German prohibition of the type in question. There are hundreds of such examples.[8]

On occasion, national measures obstructing cross-border trade escape condemnation, for example as measures designed to protect consumers vulnerable to high-pressure selling tactics[9] or consumers in particularly complex markets such as that for financial services,[10] but these instances are relatively uncommon. In general the approach taken in *Cassis de Dijon* has been immensely helpful to those seeking to challenge the thickets of regulatory intervention that have accumulated at national level over the centuries in Europe, thereby to release the competitive energy of the EU's internal market.

This, then, is the vertical implication of free movement law. Free movement law as developed in and since *Cassis* reaches beyond discrimination in the conventional sense and opens up the regulatory autonomy of each and every Member State to examination and testing, in so far as exercise of that autonomy collides with the impetus to achieve cross-border trade. But there are horizontal implications too – implications for the relationship between the judicial and the political institutions of the EU. As the Court itself makes explicitly clear in its judgment in *Cassis*, there were no common EU rules governing the matter in dispute, but there was a legislative proposal on the table, a proposal for a regulation submitted to the Council by the Commission on 7 December 1976.[11] This did not cause the Court to hesitate to apply free movement law. Instead, it showed resolute determination to propel forward the internal market by insisting on the application of the free movement rules even in the face of legislative inertia. It had done it before in *Reyners*;[12] it would do it again in *Centros*.[13] This entails a reduction in the required

---

[6] Case 261/81 *Walter Rau*, ECLI: EU:C:1982:382.
[7] Case C-470/93 *Verein gegen Unwesen in Handel und Gewerbe Köln eV v Mars GmbH*, ECLI:EU:C:1995:224.
[8] See S Weatherill, *EU Consumer Law and Policy*, 2nd edn (Cheltenham, Elgar European Law, 2013) ch 2.
[9] Case C-441/04 *A-Punkt Schmuckhandels GmbH v Claudia Schmidt*, ECLI:EU:C:2006:141.
[10] Case C-265/12 *Citroën Belux NV*, ECLI:EU:C:2013:498.
[11] *Cassis de Dijon* (n 1) para 8.
[12] Case 2/74 *Reyners*, ECLI:EU:C:1974:68.
[13] Case C-212/97 *Centros*, ECLI:EU:C:1999:126.

scope of the programme of legislative harmonisation. That reduces the burden of the legislative workload, but it also has a qualitative impact on the shape of the internal market. Preferring free movement law over legislative harmonisation is to prefer diversity of products and services and of production standards within the internal market – it is to champion consumer choice rather than the rise of legislatively mandated 'Europroducts'.

In this vein the *Cassis* judgment was quickly seized on with glee by the Commission as it plotted the development of the internal market. Its 1980 Communication, designed to explain the consequences of the 1979 *Cassis* ruling, was vividly perceptive.[14] As far as the vertical implications were concerned, it noted that 'Member States, when drawing up commercial or technical rules liable to affect the free movement of goods, may not take an exclusively national viewpoint and take account only of requirements confined to domestic products'. On the horizontal plane, it added that 'The Commission's work of harmonization will henceforth have to be directed mainly at national laws having an impact on the functioning of the common market where barriers to trade to be removed arise from national provisions which are admissible under the criteria set by the Court'. The Commission was plainly intent on taking the *Cassis* ruling beyond its own particular context and using it as a springboard to a wider restatement of its role in the shaping of the internal market. Even at the time, the ambition evident in the 1980 Communication was regarded as 'revolutionary' within the Commission.[15] Subsequent analysis has confirmed the Communication's high importance. Over a decade later, Alter and Meunier-Aitsahalia described it as 'an artful interpretation of the ruling and a bold assertion of new policy'.[16] In this book, Brigitte Leucht's chapter, 'The *Cassis de Dijon* Judgment and the European Commission' (chapter 4), presents archive-based confirmation of the Commission's astutely transformative reading of the 1979 judgment in its 1980 Communication. The Commission then embedded exactly this thematic readiness to re-focus and narrow the programme of legislative harmonisation towards measures that would survive review against the standards set by judge-driven free movement law in the agenda set by the White Paper on the completion of the internal market, which it published in June 1985.[17]

---

[14] Communication from the Commission concerning the consequences of the judgment given by the Court of Justice on 20 February 1979 in Case 120/78 ('Cassis de Dijon') [1980] OJ C256/2.

[15] I have this on the authority of Peter Oliver: he tells me that Alfonso Mattera was especially influential within the Commission and he was active outwith it too, see A Mattera, 'L'arrêt Cassis de Dijon: une nouvelle approche pour la réalisation et le bon fonctionnement du marché intérieur' (1980) 23 *Revue du Marché Commun* 505. For other contemporary comment on the Communication as an expression of the vertical and horizontal implications of *Cassis*, see L Gormley, 'Cassis de Dijon and the Communication from the Commission' (1981) 6 *EL Rev* 454; R Barents, 'New Developments in Measures having Equivalent Effect' (1981) 18 *CML Rev* 271, 296–99.

[16] K Alter and S Meunier-Aitsahalia, 'Judicial Politics in the European Community: European Integration and the Pathbreaking Cassis de Dijon Decision' (1994) 26 *Comparative Political Studies* 535, 542.

[17] COM (85) 310, esp paras 57 et seq. *Cassis* is the 'founding myth' of the single market programme: K Nicolaïdis, 'Kir Forever?' in M Maduro and L Azoulai (eds), *The Past and Future of EU Law* (Oxford, Hart Publishing, 2010) 449.

And in its 'Internal Market Strategy' of 2003, the Commission described conditional mutual recognition as 'a corner stone of the Internal Market'.[18] Three cheers for *Cassis de Dijon*!

The Court's interpretation of free movement law demonstrably affects the allocation of constitutional and institutional power within the EU. Article 26 TFEU's definition of the internal market holds that it 'shall comprise an area without internal frontiers in which the free movement of goods, persons, services and capital is ensured in accordance with the provisions of the Treaties', but nothing in those Treaties spells out what shall be the precise relationship between the free movement rules and legislative harmonisation – between courts and the political process – in achieving that aim. The shape of the internal market is not constitutionally pre-ordained; instead it has been determined by the Court's choices of interpretation and the readiness of the legislative institutions to respond.[19] The internal market is a patchwork mix of non-harmonised and harmonised sectors. *Cassis* is important for widening the scope for disciplining non-harmonised sectors according to the demands of the free movement rules applied by courts, and for consequently narrowing the required breadth of harmonisation pursued through the political process. On paper, at least: as will now be explained.

## III. Market Management

Harmonised sectors are governed by common EU rules, usually Directives. By contrast, non-harmonised sectors are marked by diverse national rules, while their capacity to apply in a way that fragments the EU's internal market along national lines is controlled by the model of conditional or non-absolute mutual recognition at the heart of free movement law. For all its appeal as a means to preserve diversity in the internal market, this model has real weaknesses as a basis for the management of non-harmonised sectors in the internal market. It tends to be opaque and inapt to generate confidence in the viability of cross-border trade because of the absence of common cross-border rules. Moreover, the free movement rules are policed by ad hoc litigation, which is pursued only once trade barriers are encountered and have caused harm.

The Commission, in its landmark 1985 White Paper on *Completing the Internal Market*, placed great faith in transformative commercial and administrative strategies inspired by the ruling in *Cassis*,[20] but it soon adopted a more cautious tone. In its *Second Biennial Report on the Application of the Principle of Mutual Recognition in the Single Market*, published in 2002, the Commission confessed that it 'has always found it very difficult to obtain … a clear and reliable picture of how the

---

[18] COM (2003) 238.

[19] See generally S Weatherill, *The Internal Market as a Legal Concept* (Oxford, Oxford University Press, 2017).

[20] COM (85) 310, esp paras 13, 65, 77.

principle of mutual recognition is actually applied in practice'; and that 'its invocation by economic operator [*sic*] remains relatively marginal'.[21]

The Commission has over time come cleaner on the deficiencies of the *Cassis* approach. In 2003 it admitted:

> The principle [applicable to the management of non-harmonized sectors] is that there are no specific procedural rules and no extra paperwork. This is its strength, but at the same time its weakness. When problems occur, there is little or no transparency, there is no commonly agreed approach to evaluating whether levels of protection are equivalent and there is no clear procedure for a company to challenge a negative decision.[22]

The scheme envisaged by *Cassis* is 'invisible' in day-to-day practice[23] – which is a strength but also a weakness. Another way to put this is to appreciate that the relatively light-touch deregulatory impact, coupled with the preservation of diversity, which is the most appealing feature of the *Cassis* model of free movement, reduces costs by diminishing the need to prepare and agree top-down homogenising measures of legislative harmonisation. However, costs of a different type emerge and are incurred at a later stage, in the shape of obstacles to smooth and predictable application of free movement law caused by stubborn retention of national rules, which might or might not after all prove to be justified despite their trade-restrictive effect but will in any event cause blockages to cross-border trade.

In 2005 the Commission noted that 'neither producers nor market surveillance authorities are sure to what extent products from one Member State can enter another Member State's market without modification', and added that according to the European Business Test Panel, 53 per cent of businesses were not even familiar with the principle of (conditional) mutual recognition.[24]

The anxiety is that *Cassis* looks delightful on paper, and on occasion it generates deregulatory litigious flashpoints, but that in practice, in the mundane operation of the internal market, national authorities doggedly insist on compliance with their own local technical standards, and many traders, especially small traders, simply knuckle under and adjust to those local standards rather than challenging them. That robs the internal market of its transformative energy.

The challenge in the internal market's non-harmonised sectors is to *manage* the regulatory diversity that persists under the principle of conditional or non-absolute mutual recognition. Litigating to attack barriers to trade once they appear is part of the required strategy, and the Commission and more significantly private parties have a long track record of doing just that, but litigation is a relatively slow and costly means of improving the functioning of the internal market.

---

[21] COM (2002) 419, paras 5.1, 5.2.

[22] COM (2003) 238, 7.

[23] J Pelkmans, 'Mutual Recognition in Goods: On Promises and Disillusions' (2007) 14 *Journal of European Public Policy* 699, 703, 708. See also, on the inadequacies of the model, C Janssens, *The Principle of Mutual Recognition in EU Law* (Oxford, Oxford University Press, 2013) esp pt I.

[24] *Commission Second Implementation Report of the Internal Market Strategy 2003–2006*, COM (2005) 11, 8.

So the Commission has wisely invested energy in promoting models that, it hopes, will dig deeper into national administrative practice in order to address problems before they erupt in litigation. This trend covers obligatory advance notification to the Commission of draft technical standards,[25] procedures to be followed by national authorities where restrictions are to be placed on products lawfully marketed in another Member State,[26] identification of designated contact points within the Member States,[27] legislative obligations to evaluate existing standards in a proactive manner[28] and services such as 'SOLVIT', which seek solutions to problems encountered in the internal market through administrative coordination without the need for litigation.[29]

These instruments of market management are well intentioned and helpful as supplements to the subjection of national practice to the discipline of free movement law through litigation. They have been made firmer, broader and clearer over time. But, as attempts to bridge the yawning gap between an EU-wide market and its regulation through national rules and national administrative infrastructure, they are unavoidably imperfect. We know, from annual reports published by the Commission, both the total number of notifications of draft technical standards made – 676 in 2017, 700 in 2016, 655 in 2014, 705 in 2013 – and also the breakdown by Member State and by sector, which reveal a broadly even pattern, with no State and no sector dominating.[30] We know too that the Court, in *CIA Security International SA v Signalson SA and Securitel Sprl*,[31] beefed up incentives to comply with the obligation to notify by ruling that that failure to comply with the procedural obligations imposed by the Notification Directive robs the offending national measure of enforceability in proceedings before national courts. But this cannot tell the full story, for it is impossible to know how many national measures should have been notified but were not. At least such notifications made pursuant to Directive 2015/1535 are easy to track: there is a dedicated website.[32] There is no equivalent applicable to the notification procedure to be followed by national authorities where restrictions are to be placed on products lawfully marketed in another Member State, today governed by Regulation 2019/515. All that is publicly available is a report prepared by the Commission on the application of

[25] Originally mandated by Directive 83/189 [1983] OJ L109/8, now Directive 2015/1535 [2015] OJ L241/1.
[26] Originally mandated by Dec 3052/95 [1995] OJ L321/1, then Regulation 764/2008 [2008] OJ L218/21, recently replaced by Regulation 2019/515 [2019] OJ L91/1.
[27] Directive 2015/1535 (n 25) Arts 9–11; also visible in sector-specific measures, eg the 'Services Directive', Directive 2006/123 [2006] OJ L376/36, Art 6.
[28] eg Directive 2006/123 (n 27) Art 39.
[29] See at http://ec.europa.eu/solvit/index_en.htm. See M Egan and MH Guimarães, 'The Single Market: Trade Barriers and Trade Remedies' (2017) 55 *Journal of Common Market Studies* 294; E Kokolia, 'Strengthening the Single Market through informal dispute resolution mechanisms in the EU: The case of SOLVIT' (2018) 25 *Maastricht Journal of European and Comparative Law* 108.
[30] For 2017 see [2018] OJ C372/3; for 2016 [2017] OJ C162/4; for 2014 [2015] OJ C174/2; for 2013 [2014] OJ C145/7; for 2012 [2013] OJ C165/5. Statistics for 2015 were not published.
[31] Case C-194/94 *CIA Security International SA v Signalson SA and Securitel Sprl*, ECLI:EU:C:1996:172.
[32] See at http://ec.europa.eu/growth/tools-databases/tris/en/.

its predecessor, Regulation 764/2008, which was published in 2012.[33] The Report states that in the period between the entry into force of the Regulation on 13 May 2009 and the end of 2011, the Commission had received 1,524 notifications. There is, however, a peculiarly uneven distribution: 1,378 of the total notifications come from one Member State and concern precious metals. This strongly suggests the Regulation is widely ignored. That suspicion is sharpened by preliminary references to and decisions of the Court, which seem to require engagement with the Regulation yet bafflingly fail even to mention it.[34] The lesson is that the Commission's attempts to improve the management of the internal market are well-intentioned but only modestly and patchily successful.

There may be an EU internal market, but EU administrative support there is not. The internal market labours under the tension caused by an assumption that national borders are economically irrelevant, while facing the very direct relevance of diverse national administrative and bureaucratic capacities and infrastructure. True, the very nature of the internal market, built on EU rules that fall to be implemented in a decentralised manner through diverse national administrative cultures, dictates that it will never be as easy to trade across borders as it is locally. As the Commission has insisted, the internal market 'is evolving, it will never be finalised'.[35] But this is particularly acutely felt in non-harmonised sectors, where even on paper there are no common EU standards on which to call in the event that an obstacle to inter-State trade is encountered. The ready intuition is that harmonisation may be a more reliable basis for managing the internal market than non-harmonisation based on conditional or non-absolute mutual recognition. And this is where the story returns to spirit drinks in general and blackcurrant liqueur and crème de cassis in particular, for in that sector exactly that shift to harmonisation has occurred.

# IV. Harmonisation – How?

Blackcurrant liqueur and crème de cassis are products that today are the subject of harmonised rules adopted by the EU. They are defined by EU law. Were the facts of the *Cassis de Dijon* case to recur today, the case would not be decided in the same way. Germany would have no competence even to attempt to justify its rules. The sector is fully harmonised and the EU's rules govern the matter exclusively. And a producer who wanted to market a new type of liqueur with a lower amount of alcohol by volume than is stipulated by the EU rules, in order to offer wider

---

[33] COM (2012) 292, available at http://eur-lex.europa.eu/legal-content/EN/TXT/HTML/?uri=CELEX: 52012DC0292&from=EN.

[34] eg Case C-672/15 *Noria Distribution* Srl EU:C:2017:310; see S Weatherill, 'The Principle of Mutual Recognition: It doesn't work, because it doesn't exist' (2018) 43 *EL Rev* 224.

[35] *A Single Market for Citizens, the interim report to the Spring 2007 European Council*, COM (2007) 60, 21 February 2007, 3, 10.

consumer choice backed by labelling that discloses the alcohol content, could not do so.

*How* this happened is the subject of this section. *Why* this happened is the subject of the next.

As already mentioned, in its ruling in *Cassis* the Court noted the existence of a legislative proposal in the field: 'a proposal for a regulation submitted to the Council by the Commission on 7 December 1976'.[36] The main issue of principle raised was that the Court, seizing the opportunity to apply what is today Article 34 TFEU to national technical standards, was not deterred by the existence of a pending legislative initiative to establish common EU rules. This was the very heart of the vibrantly significant choice made in *Cassis*. In fact, that proposal quickly died a death. It was in full an 'Amended proposal for a Council Regulation on the common organization of the market in ethyl alcohol of agricultural origin and laying down additional provisions for certain products containing ethyl alcohol',[37] but the process ran into the political sand[38] and was eventually withdrawn formally by the Commission in 1993, having lain dormant for almost a decade.[39]

But there was progress elsewhere. Ten years after *Cassis* was decided by the Court, the Council adopted Regulation 1576/89 laying down general rules on the definition, description and presentation of spirit drinks, based on Articles 43 and 100a EEC (today, after amendment, Articles 43 and 114 TFEU).[40] It was subsequently replaced by Regulation 110/2008, which harmonises rules on the definition, description, presentation, labelling and the protection of geographical indications of spirit drinks, based on Article 95 EC (today, after amendment, Article 114 TFEU). Regulation 110/2008 will in turn be replaced with effect from May 2021 by Regulation 2019/787 on the definition, description, presentation and labelling of spirit drinks, the use of the names of spirit drinks in the presentation and labelling of other foodstuffs, the protection of geographical indications for spirit drinks, the use of ethyl alcohol and distillates of agricultural origin in alcoholic beverages, based on Articles 43(2) and 114(1) TFEU.[41]

The regime has attracted most attention for its treatment of protected geographical indications applicable to spirit drinks. This matter has generated litigation under both the 1989 Regulation,[42] which pre-dated the adoption of the EU's more broadly applicable regime on protected geographical indications for agricultural products, first established in 1992 and now contained in Regulation 1151/2012, which excludes spirit drinks from its scope,[43] and its more elaborate 2008 successor.[44] But it is also the source of highly detailed common rules

---

[36] *Cassis de Dijon* (n 1) para 8.
[37] COM (1976) 274, [1976] OJ C309/2.
[38] CELEX, available at https://eur-lex.europa.eu/legal-content/EN/HIS/?uri=CELEX:51976PC0274.
[39] [1993] OJ C228/5.
[40] [1989] OJ L160/1.
[41] [2019] OJ L130/1.
[42] eg Case C-136/96 *Scotch Whisky Association*, ECLI:EU:C:1998:366.
[43] Regulation 1151/2012 [2012] OJ L323/1, Art 2(2).
[44] eg Case C-44/17 *Scotch Whisky Association*, ECLI:EU:C:2018:415.

governing spirit drinks in the EU that contradict the assumptions in favour of diversity and light-touch rule-making that surround conventional assessment of the Court's landmark ruling in *Cassis*.

Article 2(1)(c) of Regulation 110/2008 defines 'spirit drink' as an alcoholic beverage with (inter alia) a minimum alcohol strength of 15 per cent by volume. Its Annex II defines categories of spirit drinks. It covers 46 of them, from rum to honey or mead nectar, and including crème de cassis and blackcurrant liqueur, and again it defines them (inter alia) as having a minimum alcoholic strength by volume of 15 per cent. Its Article 6 adds that Member States shall not prohibit or restrict the import, sale or consumption of spirit drinks that comply with the Regulation. Regulation 1576/89 had also laid down the general 15 per cent minimum rule for spirit drinks, but was otherwise much less detailed in its prescriptions.

So this explains why, were the facts of *Cassis de Dijon* to arise today, the case would be decided differently. Whereas in 1979 the Court decided that the German rules were a restriction of cross-border trade, and then considered, and rejected, the possibility of justification, today the Court would have to decide that the drink met the requirements of the Regulation (that is, that it contained at least 15 per cent alcohol by volume) and that therefore it should not even consider the matter of justification. The EU has occupied the field by adopting secondary legislation, thereby excluding the scope for Member States even to advance justifications for stricter rules.[45] What has happened is that a matter, the achievement of the internal market, which is in principle a competence shared between the EU and its Member State,[46] has in the particular area covered by the relevant piece of secondary legislation been converted by legislative act into an area of exclusive EU competence, subject to the possibility that the EU might subsequently adjust its rules to release space once again for national choices. This is why Article 36 TFEU is disabled. Whatever interests might have motivated national rules in the areas subjected to harmonisation – public health, public morality and so on – are now dealt with exclusively by the EU. The assumption is that a Member State wanting to seek modification of the regime must pursue the matter at EU level, not unilaterally.

Harmonisation of this type is commonplace in fixing standards governing composition in goods markets. Litigation concerning Regulation 110/2008 provides an easy, if entirely trivial, example. Adding milk precludes use of the description 'egg liqueur', because Regulation 110/2008 regulates the matter exhaustively and milk is not on the list of permitted ingredients of such a beverage.[47] For cosmetics in the internal market, Regulation 1223/2009 governs the matter through its Article 9, entitled 'Free movement'.[48] This stipulates that 'Member States shall

---

[45] Cf, eg, Case 35/76 *Simmenthal*, ECLI:EU:C:1976:180; Case 190/87, *Oberkreisdirektor v Moormann*, ECLI:EU:C:1988:424; Case 148/78, *Ratti*, ECLI:EU:C:1979:110; Case 150/88 *Provide*, ECLI:EU:C: 1989:594; Case C-44/01 *Pippig Augenoptik v Hartlauer*, ECLI:EU:C:2003:205; Case 246/80 *Broekmeulen v Huisarts Registratie Commissie*, ECLI:EU:C:1981:218.

[46] Art 4(2)(a) TFEU.

[47] Case C-462/17 *Tänzer and Trasper GmbH*, ECLI:EU:C:2018:866.

[48] [2009] OJ L342/59.

not, for reasons related to the requirements laid down in this Regulation, refuse, prohibit or restrict the making available on the market of cosmetic products which comply with the requirements of this Regulation.'[49] But harmonisation of this type is not limited to product standards. Directive 2005/29 on unfair commercial practices in business-to-consumer relationships takes as its legal base Article 95 EC, which is today in amended form Article 114 TFEU.[50] The Directive requires that, in short, fair practices be permitted throughout the EU and that unfair ones be prohibited, and it includes a common EU-wide definition of unfairness. Article 4 contains its so-called *Internal market* clause: 'Member States shall neither restrict the freedom to provide services nor restrict the free movement of goods for reasons falling within the field approximated by this Directive.' The Court has had no difficulty in confirming that stricter national rules within the material scope of the Directive are *not* permitted.[51] The aim is a level regulatory playing field in the internal market within which legal and commercial certainty is enhanced, while also ensuring that the regulatory concerns that previously provoked national rules are absorbed and addressed in a uniform way at EU level, and only at EU level.

And this today is how the market for blackcurrant liqueur is regulated in the EU: not according to the model of conditional mutual recognition devised by the Court; rather, the product is instead exhaustively defined by EU law. *Cassis de Dijon* would be decided differently today! There is a 'Europroduct' defined by EU legislation! Admittedly variation is not wholly excluded. There is scope to market alcoholic drinks above the 15 per cent by volume minimum requirement – but not below it. A trader who wished to argue that consumers should have the choice to buy liqueur with only 14 per cent alcohol by volume, suitably labelled to make this clear, would be told that this is precluded in the EU.

Academic comment has long been sensitive to the intuition that the concept of conditional or non-absolute mutual recognition under *Cassis de Dijon* might generate such intransparency and uncertainty in non-harmonised sectors of the EU's internal market that it will induce a shift to the more predictable and reliable foundation of harmonisation.[52] So the *Cassis* model of market integration

---

[49] Previously Directive 76/768, which generated one of the Court's many interpretative rulings insisting on the exclusion of stricter national rules within the material scope, *Provide* (n 45).

[50] [2005] OJ L149/22.

[51] eg Case C-261/07 *VTB-VAB NV*, ECLI:EU:C:2009:244; Case C-206/11 *Georg Köck*, ECLI:EU:C:2013:14.

[52] The first comment of which I am aware to make precisely this point is J Currall, 'Some Aspects of the Relation between Articles 30–36 and Article 100 of the EEC Treaty, with a Closer Look at Optional Harmonisation' (1984) 4 *Yearbook of European Law* 169, 184–85 and 204. See also J Weiler, 'The Constitution of the Common Market Place: Text and Context in the Evolution of the Free Movement of Goods' in P Craig and G De Búrca (eds), *The Evolution of EU Law* (Oxford, Oxford University Press, 1999) ch 10, 368–69; G Davies, 'Is Mutual Recognition an Alternative to Harmonisation: Lessons on Trade and Tolerance of Diversity from the EU' in F Ortino and L Bartels (ed), *Regional Trade Agreements and the WTO* (Oxford, Oxford University Press, 2006) ch 11; W Kerber and R van den Bergh, 'Mutual Recognition Revisited: Misunderstandings, Inconsistencies, and a Suggested Reinterpretation' (2008) 61 *Kyklos* 447; Alter and Meunier-Aitsahalia, 'Judicial Politics in the European Community' (n 16) 550.

might be a trigger for harmonisation, not a substitute for it. But it seems to be little known that in relation to the very product at stake in *Cassis*, blackcurrant liqueur, exactly that shift occurred many years ago.[53] For all its elegance on paper, the *Cassis* approach to the governance of the internal market seems to have held only fragile appeal in practice.

# V.  Harmonisation – Why?

The internal market is a mix of non-harmonised and harmonised sectors. Choices need to be made. Alfonso Mattera, writing in the immediate aftermath of *Cassis*,[54] stressed that the Court's ruling meant that the harmonisation programme could be reduced in scope but did not neglect that in particular cases it might still be necessary to pursue harmonisation. The question arises as to why the shift from non-harmonisation to harmonisation as the basis on which to manage the internal market in spirit drinks occurred. The instinctive assumption would be that producers wanted the certainty of common EU rules, governing not only prized geographical indications but also product composition more generally. And although the historical record is incomplete, that explanation seems to be broadly correct.

Regulation 1579/89's Preamble asserts that common provisions governing the definition, description and presentation of spirit drinks are needed 'to assist the functioning of the common market', according to an understanding that setting quality standards is required in order to protect the product's reputation both in the EU and beyond and to exclude inferior products. Regulation 110/2008 plays the same tune, albeit in slightly more elaborate terms. It states the aim of attaining a high level of consumer protection, the prevention of deceptive practices and market transparency and fair competition. Protection of reputation both in the EU and in world markets is emphasised. Both measures also emphasise that mere information disclosure is not adequate in the spirit drinks sector. The Preamble to Regulation 1576/89 notes that 'the normal and customary means of informing the consumer is to include certain information on the label', but that 'in view of the nature of the products in question and so that the consumer may have fuller information' certain additional rules governing the products' maturation, minimum alcoholic strength and place of manufacture should be required. Regulation 110/2008 contains the same claim that measures additional to labelling requirements are required.

---

[53] I have found only one source aware of this: L Gormley, 'Free Movement of Goods and EU Legislation in the Court of Justice' in P Syrpis (ed), *The Judiciary, the Legislature and the EU Internal Market* (Cambridge, Cambridge University Press, 2012) ch 3, and even here the nugget appears only in a footnote, see ibid 55, fn 26. Albeit without referring explicitly to the relevant EU measures, the point that legislation now governs alcohol levels is also made in successive editions of D Chalmers, G Davies and G Monti, *European Union Law*, 4th edn (Cambridge, Cambridge University Press, 2019) 718.

[54] Mattera, 'L'arrêt Cassis de Dijon (n 15).

The legislative process that culminated in adoption of the first governing Regulation in 1989 began in 1982.[55] The place to go for insight into the Commission's thinking is a document issued on 9 June 1982. This is a proposal for a Council Regulation laying down general rules on the definition, description and presentation of spirituous beverages and of vermouths and other wines of fresh grapes flavoured with plants or other aromatic substances, and its sets out the thinking behind what eventually became Regulation 1576/89.[56]

The proposal begins by emphasising the economic significance of the sector. The Commission's pitch in favour of harmonising the rules that govern it, covering production and processing, and in particular those stipulating high quality and protecting traditional products, is that common rules are needed to stabilise the sector, to the advantage of both traders and consumers, and to exclude those taking advantage of consumer inability to weed out inferior products that are not made according to traditional practices. This, it is stated, should also cover some geographical ascriptions.

So, as the Commission makes clear, the proposal is 'based on common definitions of the main products in the sector'.[57] This statement is immediately followed by picking out explicitly one of the detailed rules proposed, which is 'the concept of a minimum alcoholic strength for marketing for human consumption'. This, it is explained, is needed because, without such a rule, it would be open for 'abnormally diluted products to be marketed ... under the same names as undiluted products'. The consumer, it is further explained, is accustomed to the traditional alcoholic strength of products and expects to find it when making a purchase.

But why be so prescriptive? Why not use an information-based paradigm – why not impose labelling requirements rather than mandatory composition requirements, so that consumers can see how and where a product is made, and make a choice between different types available on the market?

The Commission is dismissive of the use of labelling rules as a means to inform the consumer. It states that although some EU labelling rules have been lately adopted, 'it is likely that the consumer, who is not yet accustomed to receiving such information, will continue to attach greater importance to certain items of information than to others for some time to come'.[58] But the objection seems broader and more long-term than simply that the consumer is not *yet* ready to process information. It is added that providing information about composition in this way would make the label 'fussy' and detract from the product's trade description. Moreover, frequently consumers of alcoholic drinks do not see the bottle but rather drink by the glass in bars and hotels. So, it is concluded brusquely that 'any attempt to safeguard the consumer against misleading generic ascriptions which

---

[55] See at https://eur-lex.europa.eu/procedure/EN/1982_22.

[56] COM (82) 328 of 9 June 1982. The only online source I can find is at http://aei.pitt.edu/50894/1/A10308.pdf. Pleasingly, this is presented in the blotchy typewritten style of the time, as evocative as Betamax cassettes, The Human League and pin-stripe football shirts.

[57] ibid 5.

[58] ibid 6.

is based on labelling would lose much if not all its effectiveness'.[59] Thus the case is made for the certainty of common rules on production, not simply on labelling.

The *Cassis* ruling is not mentioned in the document, but the whole assessment of the appropriate regulatory technique contradicts it. The Commission's logic favouring legal protection of familiar products backed by suspicion that consumer confusion, not genuine choice, would follow from release on to the market of new and differently made products is in the same vein as that advanced by Germany to justify its minimum alcohol rules in *Cassis*, and rejected firmly by the Court! In *Cassis* the Court refused to accept the case for fixing minimum alcohol limits on the basis that a Member State could defend consumers from unfair practices by requiring that the product be labelled to show its origin and alcohol content. In *Commission v Germany*, the case concerning the *Reinheitsgebot*,[60] Germany had explicitly argued that German consumers treated the word *Bier* as a description exclusively used for the traditionally brewed German product. But the Court did not accept that this justified application of the law to exclude differently made imports, but rather held that labelling rules would suffice to inform the consumer. It thereby preferred an assumption of consumer adaptability and the possibility of dynamic change in the market as consumers are given the opportunity to try unfamiliar products. Rulings such as *Walter Rau*[61] and *Mars*[62] deliver the same instruction to national regulators – that they must assume consumers are alert and quick to read labels. The Commission, however, embraces the exact opposite paradigm from that embraced by the Court. The Commission's 1982 document, proposing mandatory composition requirements set at EU level, firmly rejects the consumer's capacity to absorb and adjust to information disclosed by labelling. Ignoring *Cassis*, it advances the sort of arguments about the need for mandatory rules governing composition that the German Government had put forward in *Cassis*, without success. Yet the Commission is successful in persuading the EU legislature. The ultimately adopted 1989 Regulation and its successors insist (in short) on rules, not choice, so the producer of spirit drinks containing 14 per cent alcohol by volume is excluded from the EU internal market however boldly it wishes to display that 14 per cent promise on the label.

The Commission was in fact ahead of the game. It used what we would today call behavioural insights: it believes consumers cannot or at least do not read labels. Recently, Purnhagen and van Herpen have relied on empirical studies to criticise the Court's 1995 *Mars* ruling for its over-estimation of consumers' true ability to interpret product information accurately.[63] The Commission, in refusing

---

[59] ibid.

[60] *Commission v Germany* (n 5).

[61] *Walter Rau* (n 6).

[62] *Verein gegen Unwesen in Handel und Gewerbe Köln eV v Mars GmbH* (n 7).

[63] K Purnhagen and E van Herpen, 'Can Bonus Packs mislead consumers? A demonstration of how behavioural consumer research can inform unfair commercial practices law on the example of the ECJ's Mars judgment' (2017) 40 *Journal of Consumer Policy* 217. Cf earlier in this vein H-C Von Heydebrand u d Lasa, 'Free movement of foodstuffs, consumer protection and food standards in the

to adopt the paradigm of mandatory labelling proposed by the Court in *Cassis* for the German market as a model for the wider regulation of spirit drinks at EU level, was alive as early as 1982 to this same scepticism about using the confident consumer as a basis for promoting a relatively lightly regulated market, in which ability to choose in an informed manner between different products thanks to labelling is assumed. And that is translated into harmonisation legislation setting minimum alcohol requirements. Germany cannot do that. The EU can and has.

In the *Cassis* litigation the Commission's submissions in the case about the reach of Article 34 in the absence of discrimination against imports were strikingly less bold than the Court's transformative ruling proved to be.[64] Moreover, in the *Cassis* ruling itself the Court mentioned that the Commission had observed that fixing limits may lead to standardisation of products placed on the market and of their designations, leading to greater transparency in the market.[65] This was the path the Commission quickly took in proposing EU legislation in the field. So there is a mis-match between, on the one hand, the Commission's eager embrace of *Cassis* in its 1980 Communication followed by its injection into the core of the 1985 White Paper and, on the other, what was happening elsewhere in the shaping of EU legislative proposals in the spirit drinks sector. The 1985 White Paper does not at all deny that harmonisation is sometimes needed – quite the reverse[66] – but it emphasises its reduced scope in the wake of *Cassis*.[67] The intent is a 'move away from the concept of harmonisation';[68] it enthusiastically asserts the *Cassis* approach's virtue in principle as 'an effective strategy in bringing about a common market'.[69] And even where legislative harmonisation is required, the White Paper commits to avoiding the previous practice of including detailed technical specifications.[70] And yet we now know that already, three years before the publication of the 1985 White Paper, the Commission had released plans for detailed harmonisation of the rules governing spirit drinks. The story would be enriched by discovery of contact between producers and the Commission after the *Cassis* ruling in the process of preparing the publication of the 1982 proposal. It is plausible that the Commission, having warmly embraced non-harmonisation and persisting regulatory diversity as a broadly applicable strategy for the internal market, met with resistance to reliance on such a model from producers active in

---

European Community: has the Court of Justice got it wrong?' (1991) 16 *EL Rev* 391; and see generally A-L Sibony and G Helleringer, 'European Consumer Protection through the Behavioral Lens' (2017) 23 *Columbia Journal of European Law* 607.

[64] Set out at 658–59 of the report at n 1; the Commission was 'prudent', according to AG Capotorti, ibid at 670. The Commission would have resolved the case through conventional application of the proportionality principle.

[65] ibid para 13.

[66] White Paper (n 17) esp paras 13, 61, 64, 66.

[67] ibid paras 61, 79. The same theme was advanced by Mattera in 1980 – see 'L'arrêt Cassis de Dijon' (n 15).

[68] White Paper (n 17) para 13.

[69] ibid para 66.

[70] ibid paras 67–73.

the particular sector of spirit drinks. A comprehensive account is doubtless no longer capable of excavation, but Brigitte Leucht's chapter in this book helpfully exposes some of the process, especially that running from the *Cassis* ruling in 1979 to the Commission's 1980 Communication, and she has found evidence of producer anxiety that the *Cassis* ruling would lead to diminished commitment in the Commission to pursuit of a legislative solution.[71] Writing in 1994, Alter and Meunier-Aitsahalia offer only a brief survey, but they found divergent attitudes to the judgment among producer interests and, of direct sectoral relevance, they noted that the British Food and Drink Industries' Council found *Cassis* promising as a means to promote market integration while also insisting on the supplementary role of harmonsation.[72]

The story is incomplete and it may now, 40 years on, be incapable of completion. But there plainly were incentives to push for the security and clarity of harmonisation as a more reliable basis for managing the internal market than is supplied by the principle of conditional or non-absolute mutual recognition applicable in non-harmonised sectors. And there are assumptions within the EU's legislative process about the market and consumer behaviour that completely contradict those of the Court in *Cassis* in its application of free movement law to national measures.

## VI.  Conclusion

The Court's ruling in *Cassis de Dijon* is widely hailed as a basis for mediating between the claims of the home and host country as market regulator in the EU's internal market, and as a means to maintain diversity among products and services. As explained in section II of this chapter, *Cassis* stands for an agile deregulatory model promoting consumer choice. It is widely praised for exactly this. Had the Court in *Cassis* declined to employ what is now Article 34 TFEU to address diverse but non-discriminatory national technical standards that have the effect of fragmenting the EU market along national lines, a vast amount of harmonisation would have been required to take the internal market project forward. This, as the Commission put it in its famous White Paper published in 1985, would have generated an internal market for the EU that would have been 'over-regulatory … inflexible and could stifle innovation'.[73] The Court protects the EU's internal market from this outcome by its willingness to let directly effective free movement law bite even where legislative intervention has not.

But we must not over-estimate the approach pioneered by the Court in *Cassis de Dijon*. A strategy based on confronting barriers to trade and then litigating against them is not sustainable on its own as a commercial or administrative strategy apt to realise fully the benefits of the internal market. That is why, as explained

---

[71] Leucht, ch 4 of this volume, section III.B.
[72] Alter and Meunier-Aitsahalia, 'Judicial Politics in the European Community' (n 16) 544–45.
[73] White Paper (n 17) para 64.

in section III, the Commission has expended much energy in putting in place obligations of notification imposed on national authorities considering action that will obstruct inter-State trade, thereby to achieve prevention rather than cure, and in promoting forms of problem solving that are softer and quicker than litigation, such as SOLVIT, as it has become progressively more cautious about the value and vigour of litigation-based strategies that exploit *Cassis*. Section III shows that these techniques have their benefits, but their limitations too. In general, in non-harmonised sectors governed by *Cassis*, costs are saved ex ante by setting aside the need to negotiate top-down common EU standards; but costs there are, and they emerge ex post in the difficulties in operating reliably in differently regulated national markets according to the principle of non-absolute mutual recognition. This is why harmonisation is commonly sought by producers.

Legislative practice is sobering, as revealed in section IV. In the very product sector addressed by the *Cassis* ruling, that model has long ago been abandoned as unsatisfactory and replaced by common EU rules setting mandatory standards governing composition. That has occurred because of the energetic case, explained in section V of this chapter, that was made by the Commission in favour of standardisation, deploying arguments that closely resemble those advanced by Germany in *Cassis* – yet there rejected. The Court was impressed by the virtues of information disclosure as a means to regulate the market and to enhance diversity and choice: the EU legislative process is by contrast thoroughly sceptical and prefers instead mandatory rules governing composition. So what cannot be done at national level – as seen in *Cassis* itself – is done at EU level. Thus it seems that the *Cassis* judgment drew attention to the need for EU harmonised rules, not the absence. Moreover, the 1982 proposal, like the Regulation eventually adopted in 1989, goes far beyond the issues at stake in *Cassis*. It very much looks like a story of legislative standards' being adopted under an understanding that ad hoc conditional mutual recognition under free movement law is just not adequate. It is, as Kalypso Nicolaïdis put it to me in conversation, 'the lost taste of Cassis'. It is well understood that the Commission's recent preoccupation with 'Better Regulation' is resisted by trends to regulatory density embedded with the culture of EU law making.[74] Here is a concrete example of that impulse to regulation, perhaps to over-regulation.

The big picture is provided by the nature of the internal market. The internal market is defined in Article 26 TFEU as 'an area without internal frontiers in which the free movement of goods, persons, services and capital is ensured in accordance with the provisions of the Treaties'. But this is evasive. It does not address key questions about the nature and intensity of the control exercised by free movement law over national regulatory autonomy (the vertical issue), nor does it address the respective roles of courts in applying free movement rules

---

[74] See, eg, S Garben and I Govaere (eds), *The EU Better Regulation Agenda: A Critical Assessment* (Oxford, Hart Publishing, 2018).

to obstructive national rules and of the political institutions in replacing those national rules in whole or in part with common EU rules (the horizontal issue). This is to ask about choice and diversity or centralisation and certainty; it is to ask about deregulation or re-regulation. The internal market is based on a combination of non-harmonised and harmonised sectors, but the precise contours of that relationship are neither pre-defined nor static. The story of spirit drinks in the EU is a story of re-regulation, not of deregulation. *Cassis* appears to champion the deregulatory rhythm of free movement but in fact it provoked a legislative response. So the story of blackcurrant liqueur is one of drawing attention to the need for EU harmonised rules, not the absence. This is not surprising: markets need rules, transitional markets especially need rules, often rather dense rules that, moreover, exclude the scope for diverse national rules. What is striking is how powerfully this message is delivered even in the very sector addressed by the Court's landmark ruling in *Cassis de Dijon* itself.

# 7

# EU Competition Law and the Legacy of *Cassis de Dijon*

ALBERTINA ALBORS-LLORENS*

## I. Introduction

The judgment of the Court of Justice in *Cassis de Dijon*[1] is considered one of the most iconic in the history of the Court's case law. In a few paragraphs, the Court entrenched a far-reaching ideal of free trade that would have an unprecedented impact on the interpretation of the free movement provisions and beyond. The seeds of what would afford a broad scope to negative integration as a de-regulatory technique for the achievement of the internal market had been sown in the *Dassonville*[2] decision, but *Cassis* firmly established that a vast array of national measures could come under the purview of what is today Article 34 TFEU on account of the effect that they might have on intra-Union trade. Further, *Cassis* introduced a so-called 'rule of reason' approach by permitting Member States, in the absence of harmonisation, to maintain national measures, even if these might cause obstacles to trade, so long as they are necessary[3] to satisfy mandatory

---

* I am very grateful to Bill Allan, Catherine Barnard, Brigitte Leucht and Alison Jones for their extremely helpful comments on an earlier draft.

[1] Case 120/78 *Rewe-Zentral AG v Bundesmonopolverwaltung für Branntwein (Cassis de Dijon)*, ECLI:EU:C:1979:42.

[2] Case 8/74 *Procureur du Roi v Benoît and Dassonville*, ECLI:EU:C:1974:82.

[3] The Court did not explicitly set out the application of the proportionality test in *Cassis*, though this was implied in the formula that established that the national measures should be 'necessary' to satisfy the mandatory requirements (at para 8). The Court applied it when testing the arguments based on considerations of consumer protection and fair competition advanced by the German authorities to justify the German law imposing a minimum alcohol content for fruit liqueurs (see the judgment at paras 12–13). The same approach was taken in cases decided shortly afterwards, like Case 788/89 *Gilli and Andres*, ECLI:EU:C:1980:171. Later case law specifically alluded to the proportionality stage in the analysis (see Case 261/81 *Rau Lebensmittelwerke v De Smedt*, ECLI:EU:C:1982:382, para 12 and Case 178/84 *Commission v Germany (German Beer)*, ECLI:EU:C:1987:126, para 28). The principle was articulated on the basis of the tests of suitability and necessity (see, eg, Case C-368/95 *Familiapress Zeitungsverlags- und vertriebs GmbH v Bauer Verlag*, ECLI:EU:C:1997:325, para 27 or Case C-54/05 *Commission v Finland*, ECLI:EU:C:2007:168, para 38), with recent case law developing more nuanced parameters for the application of the proportionality tests (see Case C-333/14 *Scotch Whisky Association*

requirements.[4] The judgment was ultimately propelled by what Weatherill has aptly described[5] as a *non-absolute* model of mutual recognition.[6]

What happened next has been comprehensively rehearsed in the academic literature. Despite the equal weight ostensibly attached by the judgment to the promotion of free trade, on the one hand, and to the maintenance of reasonable and justified national rules even if these had a market partitioning effect, on the other, the case law decided in the wake of *Cassis* painted a different picture. While it became easier to bring national measures under the scope of Article 34 TFEU whenever they might have a potential restrictive effect on intra-Union trade, Member States were rarely successful in invoking mandatory requirements, particularly when attempting to overcome the proportionality stage of the analysis.[7] Furthermore, national measures that applied without distinction to domestic and foreign goods and which appeared remotely connected with trade across the EU national frontiers began to be challenged before the national courts,[8] requiring the Court, in the *Keck* decision,[9] to address some of the ensuing criticism by sketching outer limits to the application of Article 34 TFEU. It did so by attempting to draw a bright line between 'product requirements' – the archetype of a *Cassis* measure that imposes a 'dual burden' on imports – which presumptively fell within the

---

*and Others v The Lord Advocate and The Advocate General for Scotland*, ECLI:EU:C:2015:845, para 55–63).

[4] Early on, Weatherill and Beaumont identified a parallel between this type of reasoning and the one that had been followed in *Van Binsbergen* (Case 33/74 *Van Binsbergen v Bestuur van de Bedrijfsvereniging voor de Metaalnijverheid*, ECLI:EU:C:1974:131), a few years earlier in the field of free movement or services. There, the Court treated a requirement of residence in the Netherlands to provide legal services as an obstacle to free movement *unless* the national rule could be 'objectively justified' (at para 14), a notion that seemed a conceptual equivalent to the mandatory requirements (S Weatherill and P Beaumont, *EC Law* (London, Penguin, 1993) 516–17). These have later been termed 'imperative requirements in the general interest' (see Case C-55/94 *Gebhard v Consiglio dell'Ordine degli Avvocati*, ECLI:EU:C:1995:411, para 37) or 'overriding reasons relating to the public interest' (Case C-288/89 *Gouda and others v Commissariaat voor de Media*, ECLI:EU:C:1991:323, para 14). In *Cassis*, the Court gave a list of four examples of mandatory requirements (at para 8), but this was an open-ended list that would continue to develop in the case law to encompass a plethora of mandatory requirements (see CS Barnard, *The Substantive Law of the EU: The Four Freedoms*, 5th edn (Oxford, Oxford University Press, 2019) 169–70).

[5] S Weatherill, *The Internal Market as a Legal Concept* (Oxford, Oxford University Press, 2017) 54–55.

[6] The so-called principle of mutual recognition emerged in the closing paragraphs of the *Cassis* judgment (see *Cassis de Dijon* (n 1) para 14), where the Court held that 'there is no valid reason why, provided that they have been lawfully produced and marketed in one of the Member States, alcoholic beverages should not be introduced into any other Member State'. As Barnard points out, the Court laid down the principle 'almost as an afterthought' (see, Barnard, *The Substantive Law of the EU* (n 4) 89). Weatherill argues that the model of mutual recognition set out in the judgment is a non-absolute one because it does not afford unconditional regulatory independence either to the host State or to the home State (Weatherill, *The Internal Market* (n 5) 54–55).

[7] There are many examples of cases where indistinctly applicable national measures failed the proportionality test. See, eg, *Rau Lebensmittelwerke v De Smedt* (n 3); Case 407/85 *3 Glocken GmbH and Kritzinger v USL Centro-Sud and Provincia autonoma di Bolzano (Durum Wheat)*, ECLI:EU:C:1988:401; Case C-12/00 *Commission v Spain (Chocolate)*, ECLI:EU:C:2003:21.

[8] See Case C-145/88 *Torfaen Borough Council v B & Q*, ECLI:EU:C:1989:593.

[9] Case C-267/91 *Criminal proceedings against Keck and Mithouard*, ECLI:EU:C:1993:905.

scope of Article 34 TFEU unless justified and proportionate, and 'selling arrangements' or 'equal burden rules', to which a presumption of legality was attached subject to specific caveats set out in paragraph 16 of *Keck*. However, new difficulties soon emerged, and an approach based on hindrance to market access[10] – at the very least applicable as a residual line of analysis[11] for national measures that did not fit the established categories in the case law – began to gain ground.[12]

The transformative effect of the *Cassis* decision on the interpretation of the provisions on free movement of goods is beyond question. However, this chapter aims to look at something different. It purports to go beyond the fundamental Treaty freedoms to identify the impact that *Cassis might* have exerted on one neighbouring area of Union competence: competition law. To this end, it begins with a background study of the connections that are immediately derived from the normative framework provided by the Treaties between competition law and the internal market provisions, as well as considering the enduring differences between the two areas. Then, it seeks to appraise the possible effects – manifested in the form of parallel substantive developments or analogous methods of legal reasoning – *Cassis* might have yielded for the development of EU competition law. It argues that there are three domains where such an impact might be identified. These are the parallels in a fundamental policy shift from a 'form-' to an 'effects-based' approach in both areas of law, the eruption of public interest considerations in the application of Article 101(1) TFEU, and the development of the notion of objective justification in the interpretation of Articles 101 and 102 TFEU. The chapter will conclude by evaluating the legacy of *Cassis* for EU competition law.

## II. *Cassis de Dijon* and the Interpretation of the EU Competition Rules: Setting Out an Analytical Framework

Leading scholars in the field have identified the existence, and have argued for the desirability, of a limited degree of convergence between the competition and free movement rules.[13] Others have counselled against it,[14] or provided alternative

---

[10] Case C-110/05 *Commission v Italy (Trailers)*, ECLI:EU:C:2009:66.

[11] Case C-456/10 *Asociación Nacional de Expendedores de Tabaco y Timbre (ANETT) v Administración del Estado*, ECLI:EU:C:2012:241.

[12] S Prechal and S de Vries, 'Seamless Web of Judicial Protection in the Internal Market?' (2009) 34 *EL Rev* 5, 8.

[13] See the seminal work by K Mortelmans, 'Towards Convergence in the Application of the Rules on Free Movement and on Competition' (2001) 38 *CML Rev* 613, 645–49, which supported a limited convergence but cautioned against any trend towards full convergence. See further Prechal and de Vries, 'Seamless Web' (n 12) 6 and 23–24, who approached the issue of convergence not only in terms of scope of application or substantive convergence but also from the perspective of convergence in the field of judicial protection.

[14] See Gormley, who argued that the functions of the competition and free movement rules were distinct and that competition law analysis should not be applied to the analysis of free movement

proposals to regulate a potential overlap between the two areas of law.[15] On many occasions, the Court has been asked to consider the combined or alternative application of these two sets of rules[16] and, as we shall see, the Court of Justice has emphasised their complementary nature on account of their shared single market rationale. However, it has tended to treat them as separate[17] because of the important differences that exist between them regarding their aims, their addressees, their scope of application and the analyses deployed in their application.[18] Within the context of that broad debate, this chapter has a much narrower purpose and seeks to explore not the overall convergence or separation between these two areas of law but evidence of any specific impact that the *Cassis de Dijon* decision might have yielded on the interpretation of the EU competition rules. Two themes will be addressed: first, the goal of market integration as a common value held by the competition and free movement provisions; and, second, the fundamental differences and 'false parallels' between the two sets of rules. The first theme will lay down the foundations to discover whether the single market ideal, not only in the abstract but also the type of single market envisioned in *Cassis*, may have somewhat pervaded the application of the EU competition provisions. The second will provide an awareness of the limitations on any spillover effect. It is argued in this chapter that these two issues mark, respectively, and at opposite ends of the spectrum, the points of intersection and of divergence between the two sets of rules. Between them lies the realm of influence that we are seeking to ascertain.

## A. Competition Law and the Single Market

In order to appreciate fully the potential effect of the *Cassis* decision on the interpretation of the TFEU competition provisions (Articles 101–109 TFEU), it is necessary to go back to basics and to look at the connection between these rules and the single market. Competition law has developed into a major and very successful area of Union competence – a process facilitated by the alignment of national

---

rules (LW Gormley, 'Competition and Free Movement: Is the Internal Market the Same as a Common Market?' (2002) 13 *European Business Law Review* 517, 520).

[15] See the exhaustive study carried out by Mislav, which concludes by supporting a solution where overlap between the two areas should be possible in a limited number of cases, while generally arguing that the separation between the two areas should be maintained (M Mislav, *Private Regulation and the Internal Market* (Oxford, Oxford University Press, 2016) 114–56).

[16] See, for some examples, amongst many others, *Dassonville* (n 2); Case 229/83 *Leclerc and others v SARL 'Au blé vert'*, ECLI:EU:C:1985:1; Case C-415/93 *Union royale belge des sociétés de football association v Bosman*, ECLI:EU:C:1995:463; Cases C-94/04 and C-202/04 *Cipolla and others*, ECLI:EU:C:2006:758.

[17] For an early example, see Joined Cases 177 & 178/82 *Criminal proceedings against van de Haar and de Meern*, ECLI:EU:C:1984:144, paras 11–14. See also Case C-65/86 *Bayer v Süllhöfer*, ECLI:EU:C:1988:448, paras 11–13.

[18] See, for a detailed examination, Mislav, *Private Regulation* (n 15) 124, 126 and 136–50; and section II.B of this chapter.

antitrust regimes with Articles 101 and 102 TFEU – with the EU Commission becoming one of the leading and most powerful enforcement agencies in the world. It is tempting to argue, when we behold the sheer scale and intricacy of EU competition legislation, guidance documents and case law, or the technicality of some aspects of competition law analysis, that EU competition law is a vast but ultimately self-contained, even esoteric, branch of EU law.[19] However, the single market imperative that justified the inclusion of these provisions in the Treaties has always been the vitally important bridge that connects EU competition law to the free movement rules. Neither of these two areas of EU law can therefore be wholly appraised without an understanding of the workings and the potential influence of the other.[20]

The primary link between the competition rules and the internal market provisions is evident in the Treaties themselves. The Treaty of Lisbon may have removed the reference to competition law as one of the activities of the EU 'necessary to ensure the functioning of the internal market',[21] and relegated it to the Protocol on the Internal Market and Competition, but the unbreakable bond between the two sets of provisions remains.[22] Thus, Article 3(1)(b) TFEU refers to the exclusive competence of the EU to establish competition rules 'necessary for the functioning of the internal market'. Anti-competitive agreements (in Article 101 TFEU), abuses of dominant position (in Article 102 TFEU) and State aids (in Article 107(1) TFEU) are all, in principle, prohibited 'as incompatible with the internal market'. Although the pursuit of aims such as the maintenance of effective competition[23] or the achievement of efficiencies and consumer welfare[24] are ingrained in the genetic code of EU competition law,[25] the wording of those provisions suggests that they were always meant to be interpreted and applied so as *also* to serve

---

[19] For an account of the reasons why competition policy might have been perceived a separate area of Union (Community) policy earlier in the history of EU law, see I Mahler, 'Competition Law Modernization: An Evolutionary Tale?' in P Craig and G de Búrca (eds), *The Evolution of EU Law*, 2nd edn (Oxford, Oxford University Press, 2011) 717, 718.

[20] In 1992, Ehlermann had already considered the mutual influence exerted between these two areas of law, see C-D Ehlermann, 'The Contribution of EC Competition Policy to the Single Market' (1992) 29 *CML Rev* 257, 257–61 and 264ff.

[21] This was present in old Art 4(1) EC. In contrast, see now Art 3 TEU, which enumerates the activities of the EU.

[22] See Case C-496/09 *Commission v Italy*, ECLI:EU:C:2011:740, para 60.

[23] *van de Haar and de Meern* (n 17) para 11; Case C-8/08 *T-Mobile Netherlands and Others*, ECLI:EU:C:2009:343, para 38; Case C-280/08 P *Deutsche Telekom v Commission*, ECLI:EU:C:2010:603, para 176.

[24] See the Commission Notice *Guidelines on the Application of Article 81(3)* [now 101(3)] *of the Treaty* [2004] OJ C101/08, para 13, which provide that the objective of Art 101 TFEU is 'to protect competition on the market as a means of enhancing consumer welfare and ensuring an efficient allocation of resources'. See also *Guidance on the Commission's enforcement priorities in applying Article 82 of the EC Treaty* [now Article 102 TFEU] *to abusive exclusionary conduct by dominant undertakings* [2009] OJ C47/7, para 5, where the Commission explains that it 'will direct its enforcement to ensuring that markets function properly and that consumers benefit from the efficiency and productivity which result from effective competition between undertakings'.

[25] For the role played by other core objectives such as economic freedom, see G Monti, 'Article 81 EC and Public Policy' (2002) 39 *CML Rev* 1057, 1059–62.

the specific goal of market integration. Consequently, even post-Modernisation and after the Commission espoused a move towards a more 'economics-based' approach[26] and the elevation of consumer welfare to the rank of key objective of EU competition law[27] – a view not unconditionally supported by the Court[28] – the ideal of market integration has continued to occupy a prominent place in the analysis of anti-competitive practices deployed by the Union judicature.[29] The core Treaty provisions on competition, all of which take the form of prohibitions on anti-competitive behaviour, require for these to be activated both the element of a restriction or distortion of competition[30] – which responds to the achievement of the general goals of competition law mentioned above – *and* the existence of an effect on intra-Union trade. As we shall see, the latter element may well be predominantly a jurisdictional threshold but is also, to an extent, a requirement connected with internal market objectives. From the outset, the single market narrative gave EU competition law a distinctive complexion that would always condition not only any comparison between it and other systems of competition law, but also the range of its analysis.

Early case law explained *why* the inclusion of the competition rules in the Treaty was necessary to secure a single market. Thus, in the landmark decision in *Consten and Grundig*,[31] when justifying that a market-partitioning vertical agreement should come within the prohibition in Article 101(1) TFEU, the Court gave as one reason that 'the Treaty, whose preamble and content aim at abolishing the barriers between States, and which in several provisions gives evidence of a stern attitude with regard to their reappearance, could not allow undertakings to reconstruct such barriers'.[32] This reasoning was therefore grounded on the complementarity of the

---

[26] See, inter alia, the Commission Communication on the application of EU competition rules to vertical restraints [1998] OJ C365/3, section I.2, where the Commission had set out the need to follow a more economics-based approach relying on effects on the market to remedy the shortcomings of the old system of Block Exemption Regulations, and, now, the current *Commission Guidelines on Vertical Restraints* [2010] OJ C130/01. See also the *Guidance on the Commission's enforcement priorities in applying Article 82 of the EC Treaty* [now Article 102 TFEU] (n 24) para 6.

[27] See the landmark speech of the (then) Competition Commissioner and Vice-President of the EU Commission, Joaquin Almunia, 'Competition – what's in it for consumers?', delivered in Poznan on 24 November 2011, available at http://europa.eu/rapid/press-release_SPEECH-11-803_en.htm, where he said that 'Consumer welfare is not just a catchy phrase. It is the cornerstone, the guiding principle of EU competition policy.' However, in the same speech, he also emphasised that 'Competition policy is also a key instrument to protect and deepen our Single Market.'

[28] See Case C-52/09 *Konkurrensverket v TeliaSonera Sverige*, ECLI:EU:C:2011:83, paras 21–22.

[29] See Joined Cases C-468/06 to C-478/06 *Sot Lélos kai Sia and Others*, ECLI:EU:C:2008:504, para 65; Case C-501/06P *GlaxoSmithKline Services and Others v Commission and Others*, ECLI:EU:C:2009:610, paras 59–60; and Case C-403/08 *Football Association Premier League Ltd and Others v QC Leisure and Others*, ECLI:EU:C:2011:631, para 139.

[30] This requirement is explicitly set out in the letter of Arts 101(1) and 107(1) TFEU. In the case of Art 102 TFEU, the requirement of 'abuse' encompasses the distortion of competition. See the definition of (exclusionary) abuse given by the Court in Case 85/76 *Hoffmann-La Roche v Commission*, ECLI:EU:C:1979:36, para 91, which refers to a type of unilateral behaviour by an undertaking as a result of which competition in a market is 'weakened'.

[31] Joined Cases 56/64 & 58/64 *Consten and Grundig v Commission*, ECLI:EU:C:1966:41.

[32] ibid 340. See also Case 32/65 *Italy v Commission*, ECLI:EU:C:1966:42, 408. See further, SM Ramírez Pérez and S van de Scheur, 'The Evolution of the Law on Articles 85 and 86 EEC

competition provisions – which together with the common policies constitute the remaining pieces in the common market jigsaw – and the free movement rules.[33] It underlined that both sets of rules supplemented one another in the achievement of the single market.[34] In his seminal work, Baquero Cruz already referred to the complementary character of competition and free movement of goods, and highlighted what could be described as the negative and positive dimensions of this relationship of complementarity.[35] The former reflects the approach taken in *Consten and Grundig*, and refers to the function of the competition provisions in *preventing* the rebuilding of barriers to trade following the removal of barriers put in place by Member States.[36] The latter promotes the joint role of the competition and free movement provisions when *building* a competitive single market.[37] Correspondingly, the Commission has also seen the internal market objectives as supplementing the natural objectives of EU competition law to which we referred above.[38] More recently, the Court has emphasised not only the supporting but also the *independent* role that the competition provisions play in the functioning of the single market,[39] awarding them the rank of provisions of public

[Articles 101 and 102 TFEU]' in KK Patel and H Schweitzer (eds), *The Historical Foundations of EU Competition Law* (Oxford, Oxford University Press, 2013) 39.

[33] This complementarity has also been invoked to underscore the classic distinction drawn between the vertical direct effect of the free movement provisions and the horizontal direct effect of the competition rules. See the Opinion of AG Poiares Maduro in Case C-438/05 *International Transport Workers' Federation and Finnish Seamen's Union v Viking Line*, ECLI:EU:C:2007:292, para 34. See further Barnard, *The Substantive Law of the EU* (n 4) 73–75.

[34] In this respect, see *Leclerc* (n 16) para 9 (emphasis added), where the Court emphasised this common aim by stating that 'Articles 2 and 3 of the Treaty set out to establish a market characterized by the free movement of goods where the terms of competition are not distorted. That objective is secured inter alia by Article 30 et seq [now Article 34 TFEU] prohibiting restrictions on intra Community trade, to which reference was made during the proceedings before the Court, *and* by Article 85 et seq [now Article 101 TFEU] on the rules on competition.' For evidence of an implicit relationship of complementarity, see the Commission Decision concerning the ticket distribution for the 1998 Football World Cup (Commission Decision of 20 July 1999 relating to a proceeding under Article 82 of the EC Treaty and Article 54 of the EEA Agreement [2000] OJ L5/55), where the Commission found that the Comité Français d'organisation de la Coupe du Monde de football 1998 (CFO) had abused its position of dominance when selling tickets to the general public. In particular, CFO's behaviour amounted to the imposition of unfair trading practices that indirectly discriminated against consumers outside France on the basis of nationality, by limiting the allocation of tickets to consumers who were able to provide a postal address in France. The Commission observed that 'such conduct represents a breach of fundamental Community principles'(at para 122).

[35] See J Baquero Cruz, *Competition and Free Movement* (Oxford, Hart Publishing, 2002) 86.

[36] ibid. On the evolution of this process of negative integration following the accrual of new areas of competence by the EU, see CU Schmid, 'Diagonal Competence Conflicts between European Competition Law and National Regulation – A Conflict of Laws Reconstruction of the Dispute on Book Price Fixing' (2000) 8 *European Review of Private Law* 155, 156 –57.

[37] In this vein, see also the *Guidance on the Commission's enforcement priorities in applying Article 82 of the EC Treaty* [now Article 102 TFEU] *to abusive exclusionary conduct by dominant undertakings* (n 24) para 1.

[38] See the *Commission Guidelines on Vertical Restraints* (n 26) para 7, where the Commission explains that 'market integration enhances competition in the European Union'; and the Commission *Guidelines on the Application of Article 81(3)* [now 101(3)] *of the Treaty* (n 24) para 13.

[39] See *Konkurrensverket v TeliaSonera Sverige* (n 28) paras 21–22.

policy[40] and referring to the effective implementation of Articles 101 and 102 as a matter of 'general interest'.[41]

The single market imperative has therefore played a crucial – and occasionally controversial – role in the application of the EU competition rules. The treatments dispensed to vertical restraints conferring absolute territorial protection,[42] to export bans,[43] to geographical price discrimination[44] and to restrictions on parallel importation[45] – to cite but a few examples – have earned the Commission and the Court criticism from within and outwith the EU on what was perceived as their primary alignment with the single market objectives instead of with purely economic efficiency criteria.[46] However, and despite a degree of evolution post-Modernisation,[47] the red lines drawn by the single market objective still remain and are likely to remain.[48] Within the parameters set out above – which reflect the complementary nature of free movement law and competition law in the EU and the adoption of the single market imperative as a common goal – an important question is whether the vision of the single market that reverberates through the *Cassis* judgment or the type of legal reasoning used in that decision can be seen reflected in the interpretation and application of the EU competition provisions.

## B.  Differences and 'False Parallels'

Before we attempt to identify any transversal effect of the *Cassis* decision on competition law, there are two pre-emptive issues that need to be addressed. First, the market integration common lineage notwithstanding, it must be recognised

---

[40] See Case C-126/97 *Eco Swiss China Time Ltd v Benetton*, ECLI:EU:C:1999:269, paras 36 and 39; and Case C-08/08 *T-Mobile Netherlands v Raad van bestuur van de Nederlandse Mededingingsautoriteit*, ECLI:EU:C:2009:343), para 49.

[41] See Case C-360/09 *Pfleiderer v Bundeskartellamt*, ECLI:EU:C:2011:389, para 19.

[42] See *Consten* (n 31) and the *Commission Guidelines on Vertical Restraints* (n 26) para 100. See further, Monti, 'Article 81 EC and Public Policy' (n 25) 1065.

[43] Case 19/77 *Miller International Schallplatten v Commission*, ECLI:EU:C:1978:19, para 7.

[44] Case 27/76 *United Brands v Commission*, ECLI:EU:C:1978:22, paras 232–233.

[45] *Sot Lélos kai Sia and Others* (n 29), para 66.

[46] See for instance, the influential work (pre-Modernisation) by BE Hawk, 'System Falure: Vertical Restraints and EC Competition Law' (1995) 32 *CML Rev* 973, 981, as a critique of the previous approach to vertical restraints of competition.

[47] Following the Modernisation process, the influence of a more economics-based approach has, for instance, tempered some of the formalism applicable to the treatment of vertical restraints, which was partly attributed to the endorsement of single market objectives. See the *Commission Guidelines on Vertical Restraints* (n 26) paras 60–64, which recognise individual cases where hardcore restraints such as export bans may be objectively necessary for certain agreements and therefore may fall outside the scope of Art 101(1) TFEU. A reference to what may read as a dilution of the single market rationale permeating the Modernisation reforms can be seen in the Executive Summary of the Commission 1999 *White Paper on Modernisation of the Rules Implementing Articles 85 and 86 of the EC Treaty* [1999] OJ C132/1, para 8.

[48] See A Jones, B Sufrin and N Dunne, *EU Competition Law*, 7th edn (Oxford, Oxford University Press, 2019) 43–44; R Whish and D Bailey, *Competition Law*, 9th edn (Oxford, Oxford University Press, 2018) 639; see also, writing in 2002, Monti, 'Article 81 EC and Public Policy' (n 25) 1092.

that the free movement and the competition rules present significant differences that necessarily have an impact on the way they are applied,[49] and which correspondingly limit the potential for a spillover effect. Second, while similar terms appear in both areas of law, a close scrutiny of these terms is necessary to determine whether they are really substantively similar or whether they constitute what we could term 'false parallels'. If the latter, caution must be exercised when arguing for any extension of a '*Cassis* effect'. This chapter will provide only a summary taxonomy of those differences and false parallels, given that a body of academic literature has already examined some of them in considerable detail.

At an early stage, O'Keefe and Bavasso explored the broader dimension of the internal market and considered the synergies between the free movement principles and the competition rules.[50] While acknowledging the shared single market objective, they also highlighted a fundamental difference between the two areas. In particular, they pointed out that, in the case of the free movement rules, the free circulation of goods, persons or services constituted the 'value protected' and the 'very means to attain that objective'.[51] By contrast, as we saw in section II.A, reinforcing the single market principles – and in particular free movement – is certainly an important objective of the competition rules – but not the *only* one. This fundamental difference was bound to have an impact on the interpretation of both sets of rules. Baquero Cruz began to sketch a number of more specific differences between the two areas.[52] These included the extraterritorial character of the competition rules – *versus* the intra-Union scope of the free movement rules[53] – the absence of a *de minimis* threshold in the application of the free movement provisions and the fact that, in principle, the competition rules apply to undertakings whereas the free movement rules apply to Member States[54] – a distinction that has been somewhat blurred in some instances in the case law.[55] Even the body

---

[49] See Weatherill, *The Internal Market* (n 5) 57–58.

[50] See D O'Keefe and AF Bavasso, 'Four Freedoms, one Market and National Competence: In Search of a Diving Line' in D O'Keefe and AF Bavasso (eds), *Judicial Review in European Union Law (Liber Amicorum in honour of Lord Slynn of Hadley)*, vol I (Alphen aan den Rijn, Kluwer, 2000) 541, 554.

[51] ibid 554.

[52] See Baquero Cruz, *Competition and Free Movement* (n 35) 86–87.

[53] See Joined Cases C-89/85 and others *Ahlström Osakeyhtiö and others v Commission (Woodpulp I)*, ECLI:EU:C:1988:447, paras 16–18; and Case T-102/96 *Gencor v Commission*, ECLI:EU:T:1999:65, para 90. In a sense, it could be argued that the main difference stems from the identity of the parties to whom the respective provisions are addressed. Whereas the competition laws are addressed to undertakings, which are plainly capable of entirely extraterritorial conduct that may affect intra-EU trade, the free movement laws are (primarily at least) addressed to the Member States, whose conduct must invariably be capable of having a domestic link even if the effect on intra-Union trade must be, of course, also satisfied.

[54] See *van de Haar and de Meern* (n 17) para 11.

[55] See, ie, Case C-281/98 *Angonese v Cassa di Risparmio di Bolzano*, ECLI:EU:C:2000:296, para 36, which recognised the horizontal direct effect of what is today Art 45 TFEU; or cases where the State has been made responsible for actions carried out by private parties that created obstacles to the free movement of goods (Case C-265/95 *Commission v France*, ECLI:EU:C:1997:595, paras 30–32); or the line of competition cases where the Court has taken the view that, although the competition rules are concerned with the activities of undertakings, in conjunction with Art 4(3) TEU, they also 'require the

of literature supporting a limited degree of convergence between competition and free movement has argued that the significant differences between the two sets of provisions should not be overlooked.[56] One of the most systematic and interesting studies has been recently carried out by Mislav, who divided the differences between the two sets of rules into a tripartite classification of foundational, doctrinal and institutional differences.[57] For this author, the foundational differences between these rules refer to the role of economic analysis in those areas of law and the way in which their aims are conceived.[58] The doctrinal differences lie in the dissimilar conceptions of the notion of 'economic activity', the contrasting definitions and evidentiary hurdles applicable in the analysis of the concepts of 'restrictions of competition' and 'obstacles to free movement', and the markedly different character of the justifications and exceptions that are used in free movement on the one hand and competition on the other.[59] Finally, Mislav remarks on the significantly dissimilar institutional framework and remedial landscape that underpins competition and free movement enforcement.[60]

Alongside these differences, we can also identify some similar expressions used in both areas of law. The question here is whether they are truly and intrinsically similar or whether they constitute 'false parallels'. Of these, two merit particular attention: the requirement of an *effect on intra Union trade* and the use of the expression *rule of reason* to label analytical approaches discussed both in the context of free movement of goods and in the field of competition law.

In relation to the first, the Treaty provides that both anti-trust prohibitions – in Articles 101 (1) and 102 TFEU – will apply only if the relevant behaviour 'may affect trade between Member States'. In turn, the famous *Dassonville*[61] definition of measures having an equivalent effect to quantitative restrictions refers to the need for a hindrance to intra-Union trade for national measures to come within the scope of Article 34 TFEU. The cases that first interpreted the constituent element of effect on intra-Union trade in the Treaty anti-trust prohibitions established three important parameters. First, they categorised this condition, in the abstract, as a jurisdictional boundary that delimited the application of EU and national competition law.[62] Second, when providing criteria to determine when this threshold would be crossed in practice, they initially linked these to the realisation of

Member States not to introduce or maintain in force measures, even of a legislative nature, which may render ineffective the competition rules applicable to undertakings' (Case C-267/86 *Van Eycke v ASPA*, ECLI:EU:C:1988:427, para 16).

[56] See Mortelmans, 'Towards Convergence' (n 13) 624, 632–36.
[57] See Mislav, *Private Regulation* (n 15) 136–50.
[58] ibid 136–40.
[59] ibid 140–46.
[60] ibid 146–50.
[61] *Dassonville* (n 2).
[62] See *Consten and Grundig* (n 31) 341; and Joined Cases 6/73 & 7/73 *Istituto Chemioterapico Italiano and Commercial Solvents Corporation v Commission*, ECLI:EU:C:1974:18, para 31. This requirement also appears in the wording of the prohibition on State aid in Art 107(1) TFEU. There, however, the nature of this requirement is different: it does not seem to operate as a jurisdictional criterion but as a condition 'inextricably linked' to one of the other constituents elements in the Art 107(1) TFEU

the single market objective of the Treaty. The classic formula dispensed in *Société Technique Minière v Maschinenbau Ulm* stated that the requirement would be fulfilled when 'the agreement in question may have an influence, direct or indirect, actual or potential, on the pattern of trade between Member States',[63] and this appeared to be closely connected with the single market objective. Thus, this case referred to this requirement as being met when 'there is a possibility that the realization of a single market between Member States might be impeded'.[64] Today, however, the *Commission Guidelines on the Effect on Trade Concept* state that the impact of an agreement on the single market objective is '*a* factor which can be taken into account',[65] and the implication seems to be that while this criterion is certainly associated with the single market imperative, it is not entirely dependent on it. Finally, first the case law[66] and now the Guidelines have established that the threshold for the engagement of the antitrust prohibitions will only be crossed if the effect on trade is 'appreciable'.[67] In other words, a *de minimis* rule applies to this requirement.[68]

By contrast, the existence of an effect on trade between the Member States is not explicitly laid down in the wording of the provisions on free movement of goods. When interpreting the concept of 'measures having equivalent effect' to quantitative restrictions in Article 34 TFEU, the *Dassonville* decision held that these are 'all trading rules enacted by Member States which are capable of hindering, directly or indirectly, actually or potentially, intra-Community trade'.[69]

---

prohibition, namely, the existence of a restrictive effect on competition. In this respect, see Case T-298/97 *Alzetta v Commission*, ECLI:EU:T:2000:151, para 81, where the General Court observed that, in that context, 'when State financial aid strengthens the position of an undertaking compared with other undertakings competing in intra-Community trade, the latter must be regarded as affected by that aid'. This position is also now reflected in the Commission Notice on the notion of State aid [2016] OJ C262/1, paras 186 and 190–198.

[63] Case 56/65 *Société Technique Minière v Maschinenbau Ulm*, ECLI:EU:C:1966:38, 249.

[64] ibid. In *Consten and Grundig* (n 31) 341, the Court held that 'what is particularly important is whether the agreement is capable of constituting a threat, either direct or indirect, actual or potential, to freedom of trade between Member States in a manner which might harm the attainment of the objectives of a single market between States'. For other cases where such a direct connection can be found, see Case 23/67 *Brasserie de Haecht v Consorts Wilkin-Janssen*, ECLI:EU:C:1967:54, 415, where the Court held that for this requirement to be met, a practice may appear to be capable 'of being conducive to a partitioning of the common market and of hampering the economic interpenetration sought by the Treaty'; Case T-62/98 *Volkswagen v Commission*, ECLI:EU:T:2000:180, para 179; and Case T-24/93 *Compagnie Maritime Belge Transports v Commission*, ECLI:EU:T:1996:139, para 201.

[65] See the *Commission Notice on the Guidelines on the Effect on Trade concept contained in Articles 81 and 82 of the Treaty [now Articles 101 and 102 TFEU]* [2004] OJ C101/81, para 23, fn 16.

[66] Case 22/71 *Béguelin Import v SAGL Import Export*, ECLI:EU:C:1971:113, para 16; Case C-306/96 *Javico v Yves Saint Laurent Parfums*, ECLI:EU:C:1998:173, para 17.

[67] See the *Commission Guidelines on the effect on trade concept* (n 65), paras 13 and 44–57, for the concept of appreciability and the criteria to quantify it in relation to the element of the effect on intra-Union trade.

[68] In the application of Art 101(1) TFEU, the element of restriction of competition – another of the three constituent elements in that prohibition – is also subject to a *de minimis* rule (see Case 5/69 *Völk v Vervaecke*, ECLI:EU:C:1969:35, para 7; and the current Commission Notice on Agreements of Minor Importance [2014] OJ C291/01).

[69] *Dassonville* (n 2) para 5.

As several commentators have observed,[70] the striking similarity between the form of words used in *Dassonville* and the formula for the effect on intra-Union trade criterion provided several years earlier in the competition cases[71] is difficult to miss.

However, does this required 'direct or indirect', 'actual or potential' effect on intra-Union trade respond to the same guiding principles in both areas? It is true that the single market objective clearly determines the application of this concept in the area of free movement and, as we have seen, *may* also inform the application of the competition rules. Furthermore, in both situations remote or purely hypothetical effects on trade are excluded.[72] There is nonetheless still a fundamental difference in the deployment of this term in these two areas – apart from the Court's well-documented, and to a limited extent ostensible,[73] rejection of the adoption of a *de minimis* rule in the context of free movement. This refers to the *neutrality* of this element in the context of the anti-trust prohibitions against the active requirement of the need of a *hindrance* to intra-Union trade in the framework of free movement.[74] Thus, first the case law[75] and then the *Commission Guidelines on the Effect on Trade Concept* have explained that the influence on the patterns of trade between the Member States is 'not a condition that trade be restricted or reduced'.[76] In fact, the Notice recognises that 'patterns of trade can be affected when an agreement causes an *increase* in trade'.[77] The determinant consideration is whether trade between the Member States would develop – to an appreciable extent – differently in the absence of the agreement or practice. In other words, the 'effect on trade' criterion seems entrenched as a jurisdictional criterion that carries substantive neutrality.[78] By contrast, in the context of free movement, the (direct

---

[70] See Baquero Cruz, *Competition and Free Movement* (n 35) 89; and Weatherill, *The Internal Market* (n 5) 58.

[71] See *Société Technique Minière* (n 63) and *Consten and Grundig* (n 31).

[72] See, for competition law, the *Commission Guidelines on the effect on trade concept* (n 65) para 43; and for free movement of goods, see Case C-69/88 *Krantz*, ECLI:EU:C:1990:97, para 11.

[73] See, for the rejection of a *de minimis* rule in free movement, *van de Haar and de Meern* (n 17) para 13. See also the judgment of the Court in Case C-412/93 *Leclerc-Siplec v TF1*, ECLI:EU:C:1995:26, where the Court did not follow the suggestion from AG Jacobs to adopt a *de minimis* threshold to gauge the required impact on intra-Union trade to engage the application of Art 34 TFEU. However, more recent cases following the *Trailers* decision (n 10) can be interpreted as moving towards the adoption of a certain (and problematic) *de minimis* requirement when determining a hindrance to market access. See, more generally, Barnard, *The Substantive Law of the EU* (n 4) 136–37.

[74] *Commission Guidelines on the effect on trade concept* (n 65) para 34.

[75] See the seminal decision in *Consten and Grundig* (n 31) 341–42. More recently, see Case T-65/89 *BPB Industries v Commission*, ECLI:EU:T:1993:31, para 135.

[76] *Commission Guidelines on the effect on trade concept* (n 65) para 34.

[77] ibid (emphasis added).

[78] This approach also transcends the so-called 'wholly internal situations', because agreements or practices limited to the territory of one Member State – or even part of a Member State – may *still* influence the patterns of intra-Union trade (see Case 8/72 *Vereeniging van Cementhandelaren v Commission*, ECLI:EU:C:1972:84, para 29; and the *Commission Guidelines on the effect on trade concept* (n 65) paras 77–99). By contrast, in free movement, 'purely internal situations' are prima facie excluded from the application of the free movement rules because an inter-State element is necessary to trigger the application of these provisions (see Case 175/78 *The Queen v Saunders*, ECLI:EU:C:1979:88, paras 10–11).

or indirect, actual or potential) 'hindrance' to trade between Member States is a substantively charged requirement for this condition to be borne out. There, we are not looking simply for an appreciable influence (of any kind) on cross-border activity as a jurisdictional trigger for the application of EU Law but for the exist-ence of an actual or potential *obstacle* to free movement or to market access. This element therefore does not draw the boundary between the application of national and EU law but is the substantive reason for the application of free movement EU rules – which, as we know, is to protect freedom of trade or movement – across the Member States as a *core* value. In sum, while determining an *effect* on intra-Union trade is an essential part of the process of application of both the competition and the free movement provisions, the philosophy underlining that application is considerably different.

A second 'false parallel' might be the usage of a *rule-of-reason* approach in the context of the cases on free movement and in the framework of US anti-trust law. We consider it here because, for a time, there was a lively debate as to whether a US-style *rule-of-reason* approach had been endorsed in the case law of the CJEU in the interpretation of Art 101(1) TFEU. In the field of US anti-trust law, as is well known, this principle of interpretation was coined in the case law of the US Supreme Court in an effort to inject some flexibility to the rigid prohibition on contracts in restraint of trade laid down in Section 1 of the Sherman Act, which, if applied literally, would render illegal many contracts relating to trade.[79] In that context, it reflects an analytical mechanism that – except for those specific practices that are deemed to be so harmful to competition per se that they are instantaneously prohibited[80] – consists of weighing the pro- and anti-competitive effects of an agreement, with the aim of prohibiting only *unreasonable* restraints in competition.[81] The discussion as to whether evidence of such reasoning could be found in EU cases applying Article 101(1) TFEU was particularly intense in the early years of the Union.[82] Some leading commentators warned then that the differences between US and EU competition law – particularly the absence of an exception rule akin to that found in Article 101(3) TFEU in US anti-trust law through which potential efficiencies could be considered – were too signifi-cant, urging caution on the importation of this method of reasoning into EU

---

[79] See *Standard Oil Co of New Jersey v US* 221 (US) 502, 517 (1911); *Chicago Board of Trade v US* 246 (US) 231, 238 (1918). See further, H Hovenkamp, 'The Rule of Reason' *University of Pennsylvania Legal Repository* (2018), available at https://scholarship.law.upenn.edu/faculty_scholarship/1778, 83–166.

[80] These would be the case for example for horizontal agreements to fix prices (see, eg, *United States v Socony-Vacuum Oil Co*, 310 (US) 150, 210, 218 (1940).

[81] See *Continental TV, Inc v GTE Sylvania, Inc*, 433 (US) 36, 49 (1977).

[82] Decisions like the ones in *Société Technique Minière* (n 63) and *Metro SB-Großmärkte v Commission*, Case 26/76, ECLI:EU:C:1977:167, esp para 27, were cited as possible examples of an approach based on a US-style rule-of-reason approach in the application of Art 101(1) TFEU. See further R Joliet, *The Rule of Reason in Antitrust Law, American, German and Common Market Law in Comparative Perspective* (The Hague, Faculté de Droit, Liège and Martinus Nijhoff, 1967) and the Opinion of AG Lèger in Case C-309/99 *Wouters v Algemene Raad van de Nederlandse Orde van Advocaten*, ECLI:EU:C:2001:390, para 103.

competition law.[83] However, for a time, there was some ambiguity as to whether case law interpreting Article 101(1) TFEU occasionally supported this mechanism. Following the introduction of a fully decentralised system of enforcement by Regulation 1/2003,[84] which gave national courts the power to apply the conditions in Article 101(3) TFEU, the debate lost some traction. This was mainly because one of the most significant procedural advantages that could be yielded by transposing a US-style rule of reason to the interpretation of Article 101(1) TFEU became redundant. Furthermore, around that time, the General Court asserted in a series of cases that it was doubtful that the rule of reason (in the pure US anti-trust sense) applied in relation to the analysis of cases under Article 101(1) TFEU.[85]

In the field of free movement of goods, as seen, the expression *rule of reason* is normally connected to the *Cassis* judgment and to the reasoning that uses mandatory requirements to justify national rules that in principle create obstacles to trade – so long as the rules are proportionate. Advocate General Van Themaat, in his Opinion in *Oosthoek*,[86] already remarked on the one basic parallelism that arises between the approach followed in US antitrust law and that derived from *Cassis*.[87] This is that in both cases, this principle of interpretation is based on 'reasonableness' and used to mitigate the rigour of strict prohibitions.[88] In both instances, therefore, a balance of considerations to assess the reasonableness or unreasonableness of the rule or practice is undertaken. Beyond that common

[83] See R Whish and B Sufrin, 'Article 85 and the Rule of Reason' (1987) 7 *Yearbook of European Law* 1, 36. More recently, see P Manzini, 'The European Rule of Reason crossing the sea of doubt' [2002] *European Competition Law Review*, 392, 394–97.

[84] See in particular Art 1 of Council Regulation (EC) No 1/2003 of 16 December 2002 on the implementation of the rules on competition laid down in Articles 81 and 82 of the Treaty [2003] OJ L1/1 and Recital [4] in the Preamble to the Regulation.

[85] See Case T-112/99 *Métropole télévision (M6) v Commission*, ECLI:EU:T:2001:215, paras 75–77; Case T-65/98 *Van den Bergh Foods v Commission*, ECLI:EU:T:2003:281, paras 101–102; and Case T 328/03, *O2 (Germany) v Commission*, ECLI:EU:T:2006:116, para 69. There might be some recent signs, however, that Modernisation process might have rekindled the embers of that debate. This seems to be case despite the fact that the Commission, in one of its leading preparatory documents to the adoption of Regulation 1/2003, considered and rejected the idea of the adoption of a 'rule-of-reason' approach in the context of Art 101(1) TFEU, see *White Paper on Modernisation of the Rules Implementing Articles 81 and 82 EC* [1999] OJ C132/1, para 57, reaffirming the traditional division of functions between Arts 101(1) and (3) TFEU. Yet following the introduction of a more economic approach spearheaded by the Modernisation process, some commentators have recognised the application of this method of anti-trust analysis in recent cases concerning the application of the prohibition in Art 102 TFEU (see, eg, in relation to exclusivity rebates, N Petit, 'The Judgment of the EU Court of Justice in *Intel* and the Rule of Reason in Abuse of Dominance Cases' (2018) 43 *EL Rev* 728). Others have highlighted its relevance in relation to traditional restrictions of competition by object in EU law, like resale price maintenance in the context of vertical restraints. This is the case as regards Callery, who carries out an interesting study following the decision of the US Supreme Court in *Leegin* 551 (US) 877 (2007) – which overturned earlier case law that that labelled resale price maintenance as a per se restriction of competition and subjected it to a 'rule-of-reason' approach (see C Callery, 'Should the European Union Embrace or Exorcise Leegin's "rule of reason"?' [2011] *European Competition Law Review* 42).

[86] Case 286/81 *Oosthoek*, ECLI:EU:C:1982:302. AG Van Themaat referred to para 6 of the decision in *Dassonville* (n 2) as first introducing a 'rule of reasonableness' which was then carried through and developed by *Cassis* (n 1) 4592. See further B Leucht, (2018) 24 *European Law Journal* 191.

[87] See n 3 and accompanying text.

[88] See n 79.

theme, however, it is submitted that the nature of the elements balanced – *effects* in US anti-trust cases (pro- and anti-competitive effects) and *interests* (free trade and imperative national interests) in *Cassis* – and the type of *balance* applied – fundamentally economic in anti-trust law and non-economic in free movement[89] – are different.

For the purposes of this chapter, we can conclude that despite the existence of an intrinsic comparability in using a 'reasonableness' – and hence balancing – approach, the expression *rule of reason* conveys the deployment of substantially dissimilar analytical components in these two areas when this expression is understood in the US anti-trust sense. However, there is one strand of EU competition law cases that seems to have developed what one commentator has aptly described as a '*European* rule of reason approach',[90] where anti-competitive effects seem to have been balanced against public policy considerations in the application of Article 101(1) TFEU. There, greater analogy between the *Cassis* rule of reason and the methodology followed in those competition cases can be discerned. This is the *Wouters*[91] line of case law, which will be considered in detail in the next section.

## III. EU Competition Law and the Spell of *Cassis*: Influence, Spillover Effect or Comparable Approach?

In the preceding sections we established the general parameters for our examination. On the one hand, the single market link between competition and free movement determines that these two sets of provisions should be interpreted harmoniously in the light of this ideal. This may promote a certain degree of alignment between the two areas. On the other, the significant differences between them mean that any suggestion of substantive or procedural convergence needs to be treated with caution. We can now narrow down our examination to the specific impact of the *Cassis de Dijon* decision on the interpretation of the EU competition provisions, particularly Articles 101 and 102 TFEU. The existence of a conclusive *influence* is, of course, impossible to prove in the absence of an express recognition by the Court. However, it is possible to observe what could be defined, more neutrally, as either a spillover effect of the decision or, at least, the role of *Cassis* as a harbinger for the adoption of some comparable legal analyses in competition and free movement. This is not an argument supporting convergence but one that simply identifies homologous approaches and their consequences.

---

[89] The Court has repeatedly held that the mandatory requirements or imperative requirements in the public interest cannot be used to serve economic ends (see, eg, *Bond van Adverteerders and Others*, ECLI:EU:C:1988:196, para 34; Case C-288/89 *Gouda*, ECLI:EU:C:1991:323, para 11. See further, P Oliver, 'When, if ever, can restrictions on free movement be justified on economic grounds?' (2016) 41 *EL Rev* 147, 174.

[90] See Monti, 'Article 81 EC and Public Policy' (n 25) 1086.

[91] Case C-309/99 *Wouters v Algemene Raad van de Nederlandse Orde van Advocaten*, ECLI:EU:C:2002:98.

This chapter identifies three domains where it might be possible to highlight trends in the application of the anti-trust provisions that display an affinity with the approach pioneered by *Cassis de Dijon* – even if adapted to the particular goals and complexion of competition law. These are the policy shift from a 'form-' to an 'effects-based' approach in both areas of law, the emergence of public interest considerations in the application of Article 101(1) TFEU, and the development of the notion of objective justification in the interpretation of Articles 101 and 102 TFEU; and each will be considered in turn.

## A.  A Fundamental Policy Shift – From 'Form' to 'Effects'

At the levels of general policy and of a particular vision of the single market, we have seen that *Cassis* openly acknowledged the importance of the *effect* of a national measure on trade – instead of concentrating solely on the distinctly applicable nature of national measures. The fundamental shift from focusing on the *form* of national measures to also considering the *effect* that they could have on trade – regardless of their form – then resonated across the four freedoms and moulded the single market by giving an unprecedentedly broad scope of application to the Treaty provisions.

In the context of competition law, the Modernisation process – which began some 20 years after the *Cassis* decision was delivered – brought about, inter alia, a move from a formalistic approach to anti-competitive practices to an 'effects-based' approach that would prohibit anti-competitive practices only where it could be determined that these were liable to have an appreciably harmful *effect* on competition and were not redeemed by efficiencies or objectively justified. The impact of this process was felt in the analysis of vertical and horizontal agreements and of the behaviour of dominant companies,[92] and in the adoption of a new substantive test for the assessment of proposed concentrations.[93] Significantly, this approach placed greater emphasis on economic analysis than on a pure examination of the *form* adopted by the anti-competitive conduct – which would *assume* the existence of an anti-competitive effect in the market, particularly in the context of the application of Article 102 TFEU, without the need to determine it or even to show its likelihood. Leaving aside the controversies surrounding that shift,[94] it can be argued that a certain parallelism might be discerned between this trend and that heralded by *Cassis* in the field of free movement in promoting a move from a formalistic approach to one that considers the impact of practices or rules on competition and on trade, respectively. In that very broad sense, we can identify a degree of comparability between the type of single market envisioned in *Cassis* and

---

[92] See n 47.
[93] See Art 2 of Council Regulation (EC) No 139/2004 of 20 January 2004 on the control of concentrations between undertakings (the EC Merger Regulation) [2004] OJ L24/1.
[94] See, further Jones, Sufrin and Dunne, *EU Competition Law* (n 48) 293–99, 375–78.

the (post-Modernisation) non-formalistic philosophy propelling the application of the EU anti-trust rules.

As a counterargument, it could be posited that there are other factors that might undermine the existence of a strong causal connection between these comparable developments in the fields of free movement and competition law. For instance, in the intervening period of 20 years between the delivery of the decision in *Cassis* and the beginning of the Modernisation process, a strong formalistic and economically detached approach continued to pervade some areas of competition law, notably the old system of block exemption regulations.[95] Furthermore, other elements, such as the external influence from seminal US anti-trust decisions like the one in *Sylvania*[96] and internal influences such as that of the newly established Merger Task Force and the creation of the (then) Court of First Instance, might have also decisively contributed to direct EU competition law towards a more economic, effects-based, approach, particularly in the field of vertical restraints. However, it is submitted that these arguments do not necessarily exclude the potential influence of the *Cassis* model. Rather, the conclusion might be that, at a time when EU competition law was looking for a new approach to address challenges within its substantive and enforcement systems, the *Cassis* decision might have provided a useful model or source of inspiration to meet these challenges.

There are also important differences in the complexion of this shift in these two areas of law that cannot be overlooked. Thus, from an analytical perspective, the type of effects examined is significantly different in nature. In the context of competition law, we are referring to a move towards the scrutiny of economic efficiencies and harms; whereas in free movement we are looking at an analysis that has a broad economic foundation but really focuses on the existence of a *hindrance* to free movement or access to the common market, and which weighs non-economic considerations against restrictions to free movement. From a normative point of view, it could even be said that this analytical shift from form to effects triggers an opposite dynamic in those two areas. In free movement it results in the broadening of the scope of the Treaty prohibitions, because the nebulous underpinnings of the concept of hindrance to intra-Union trade push the outer limits of the free movement provisions. By contrast, in competition law, that shift has the effect of ultimately restricting the scope of the Articles 101 and 102 TFEU prohibitions, because the form of an agreement or practice is no longer sufficient to trigger their application and a concrete and specific effect on competition based on tangible economic criteria needs to be demonstrated.

---

[95] See, eg, the old Block Exemption Regulation on exclusive distribution agreements (Commission Regulation (EEC) No 1983/83 of 22 June 1983 on the application of Article 85(3) of the Treaty to categories of exclusive distribution agreements [1983] OJ L173/1) or the old Block Exemption Regulation on exclusive purchasing agreements (Commission Regulation (EEC) No 1984/83 of 22 june 1983 on the application of Article 85(3) of the Treaty to categories of exclusive purchasing agreements [1983] OJ L173/6).

[96] *Continental TV, Inc v GTE Sylvania, Inc*, 433 US 36 (1977).

Even in points of ostensible intersection, the evaluated effects are clearly dissimilar. This is the case, for example, when we compare the weighing of the efficiencies received by consumers against the anti-competitive effects of an agreement in the application of Article 101(3) TFEU with the balancing of the protection of the interests of consumers against the restriction of trade in the *Cassis* line of case law.[97] Further, in free movement, the *Cassis* approach that considers the effect on trade of national measures is superimposed on the analysis based on the discriminatory character of national measures, giving rise to possible lines of reasoning depending on whether a national measure is distinctly or indistinctly applicable, a selling arrangements or a residual type of measure that hinders market access.[98] By contrast, in competition law analysis, the form adopted by anti-competitive practices still remains important in the narrow situation of particularly harmful types of anti-competitive agreements that are considered to be restrictive of competition by object – and prohibited by Article 101(1) TFEU without its being necessary to prove that they produce any anti-competitive effects[99] – but the implication is that an 'effects-based' approach should, on the whole, *supersede* a formalistic one.[100]

## B. Public Interest Considerations in the Framework of Competition Law

Perhaps the clearest indication of a spillover effect, or at least of a comparable approach, which has already been remarked upon by several commentators,[101] is the one emanating from the line of case law inaugurated in the *Wouters* decision.[102]

---

[97] This is more so when considering that the foundational definition of 'consumer' in competition law (see Commission *Guidelines on the Application of Article 81(3)* [now 101(3)] *of the Treaty* (n 24) para 84) is different from the one used in the *Cassis* line of case law (see Case 210/96 *Gut Springenheide v Oberkreisdirektor des Kreises Steinfurt*, ECLI:EU:C:1998:369, para 31).

[98] See further Barnard, *The Substantive Law of the EU* (n 4) 133.

[99] This has been a long-entrenched line of the case law of the CJEU (see, for a recent and clear statement, Case C-67/13 *Groupement des cartes bancaires (CB) v Commission*, ECLI:EU:C:2014:2204, paras 49–51) and covers, inter alia, horizontal price-fixing and market-sharing agreements. Such practices are even excluded from the application of the Commission Notice on Agreements of Minor Importance (see n 68, para 13), and can only be saved, if at all, by Art 101(3) TFEU. However, even within this category, this form-based assessment is justified by an underlying effects-based assessment that these restrictions exhibit a high probability of having an anti-competitive effect.

[100] There are other, more specific, aspects of competition law that also endorse a non-formalistic approach to potentially anti-competitive conduct and focus on the effect of the conduct on the market and on competition. For an example, see the line of case law elucidating the meaning of the notion of 'agreement' (see Case T-41/96 *Bayer v Commission*, ECLI:EU:T:2000:242, para 69; and Cases C-204/00P *Aalborg Portland v Commission*, ECLI:EU:C:2004:6, paras 81–86) in the context of Art 101(1) TFEU.

[101] See, inter alia, Monti, 'Article 81 EC and Public Policy' (n 25) 1087; Jones, Sufrin and Dunne, *EU Competition Law* (n 48) 255; IS Forrester, 'Where Law Meets Competition: Is *Wouters* like a *Cassis de Dijon* or a Platypus' in C-D Ehlermann and I Atanasiu (eds), *European Competition Law Annual 2004: The Relationship Between Competition Law and the Liberal Professions* (Oxford, Hart Publishing, 2006) 271, 286–90. In very clear terms, see R O'Loughlin, 'EC Competition Rules and Free Movement Rules: An Examination of the Parallels and their furtherance by the ECJ *Wouters* decision' (2003) 24 *European Competition Law Review* 62, 68–69.

[102] *Wouters* (n 91).

The facts of the case are well known and concerned the compatibility of regulations adopted by the Dutch Bar, prohibiting partnerships between lawyers and accountants (multi-disciplinary partnerships), with EU competition law. The pattern of reasoning followed by the Court initially took the form of a classic and systematic application of the constituent elements in Article 101(1) TFEU. The Court first decided that the Netherlands Bar Association was acting as an association of undertakings for the purposes of Article 101(1) TFEU – rather than fulfilling a social function or exercising powers connected with the exercise of public authority, which would have excluded the application of that provision.[103] Therefore, the rules fell, in principle, within the scope of Article 101(1) TFEU. The regulations constituted a form of cooperation within the meaning of Article 101(1) TFEU,[104] were liable to have an adverse effect on competition by potentially limiting production or technical development[105] and were also found to have an effect on intra-Union trade.[106] It seemed therefore to follow that the prohibition in Article 101(1) TFEU did apply – and that any efficiencies or pro-competitive effects should then be considered within the context of Article 101(3) TFEU.

However, it was at this point in the judgment that the reasoning of the Court took an unexpected – and interesting – turn. Not only did the Court not mention Article 101(3) TFEU,[107] but it took the interpretation of Article 101(1) TFEU along a novel path of reasoning. It placed the regulations of the Bar Association within the *context* within which they were supposed to take effect, and highlighted that their objectives were to provide a regulatory framework to ensure the integrity of the legal profession, the protection of consumers of legal services and the sound administration of justice.[108] Then the Court held that it had to be considered whether 'the consequential effects restrictive of competition [were] *inherent* in the pursuit of those objectives'.[109] In doing so, it therefore introduced a balancing exercise between the potential anti-competitive effects of the regulations and those *public interest* objectives – a notion that evokes the concept of mandatory requirements – within the very scope of Article 101(1) TFEU. From then onwards, the judgment used an approach strongly reminiscent of the *Cassis* decision. First it referred to the freedom of the Member States to regulate the legal profession in the absence of harmonisation, and to the unavoidable regulatory diversity that

---

[103] ibid paras 56–71.

[104] ibid para 64.

[105] ibid paras 87–90.

[106] ibid paras 95–96.

[107] However, there might have been good reasons for the failure to allude to Art 101(3) TFEU. As Jones pointed out, national courts did not have then the power to apply Art 101(3) TFEU, and hence the referring court would have been obliged to conclude that the restrictive rules were void. Furthermore, at that time, no individual exemptions could be granted by the Commission without previous notification, and the Dutch Bar Council regulations had not been notified to the Commission (see A Jones, 'Regulating the Legal Profession: Article 81, the Public Interest and the ECJ's judgment in *Wouters*' (2008) 19 *European Business Law Review* 1079, 1011).

[108] *Wouters* (n 91) para 97.

[109] ibid (emphasis added).

this created.[110] This seemed to echo the principle of regulatory independence that emerged in the opening paragraphs of *Cassis*, which had also recognised the obstacles – to trade rather than competition – that could arise in the absence of common EU rules as a result of diverse national rules.[111] Second, it went on to consider whether the restriction of competition created by the regulations was proportionate to the achievement of the identified public interest objectives. The Court ultimately concluded that the effects restrictive of competition created by the regulations did not go beyond what was necessary to ensure the proper practice of the legal profession.[112] Again, there were salient similarities between this reasoning and the *Cassis de Dijon* rule-of-reason interpretative technique. Ultimately, with an analysis facilitated by the open texture of Treaty provisions and entirely conducted within the parameters of Article 101(1) TFEU – just like the *Cassis* reasoning was developed wholly within the parameters of Article 34 TFEU – the Court found that the Bar regulations were not contrary to Article 101(1) TFEU.

From a competition perspective, the most significant dimension of this decision is the uncommon use of public interest objectives as a balancing tool within a competition law analysis and, more specifically, within the application of Article 101(1) TFEU. The debate as to whether considerations aside from purely efficiency-based gains have a place in EU competition law analysis to act as counterweight to competition harms has mainly referred to the application of the conditions in Article 101(3) TFEU and is intensely controversial in that context.[113] The decision in *Wouters* takes this debate a step further, because it appears to place this exercise within the scope of Article 101(1) TFEU, ostensibly introducing public interest considerations as a variable in the application of that provision.

Is such a reasoning alien to competition law, and more particularly to the determination of the existence of a restriction of competition? The *Wouters* approach, despite being conducted within the confines of Article 101(1) TFEU, does not

---

[110] ibid para 99. The regulatory freedom of the Member States also influenced the analysis of the proportionality test. Thus, the Court explained, later in the judgment (para 108), that the fact that other Member States had less strict rules did not automatically mean that the Dutch rules were disproportionate. See also the Opinion of AG Mischo in Case C-496/01 *Commission v France*, ECLI:EU:C:2003:382, para 83, who applied this rationale in *Wouters* to the analysis of a justification to a free movement of services restriction.

[111] See section I.

[112] *Wouters* (n 91) paras 106–110.

[113] See, for instance, the divergent views of C Townley, *Article 81 and Public Policy* (Oxford, Hart Publishing, 2009) and O Odudu, 'The Wider Concerns of Competition Law' (2010) 30 *OJLS* 599, 612–13. Despite earlier examples of Commission decisions that appeared to take account, within the analytical framework of Art 101(3) TFEU, of goals such as environmental or employment considerations (see the Commission decision in Case IV.F.1/36.718 *CECED* [2000] OJ L187/47, paras 47–57 and the Commission decision in Case IV/33.814 *Ford/Volkswagen* [1993] OJ L20/14, para 36, respectively), the current *Guidelines on the Application of Article 81(3)* [now 101(3)] *of the Treaty* (n 24) take a very narrow approach to the application of the conditions in Art 101(3) TFEU and confine these to economic efficiency considerations (see the *Guidelines*, paras 11 and 42; the latter paragraph refers obliquely to 'other goals' as being capable of consideration, 'only to the extent that they can be subsumed under the four conditions of Article 101(3) TFEU'). Surprisingly, there is no allusion to *Wouters* in the section of the *Guidelines* that describes the analytical framework of Art 101(1) TFEU, even though the judgment was handed down two years before these *Guidelines* were adopted.

seem analogous to a *US-style* anti-trust rule-of-reason approach[114] because it does not seem to involve a balance of pro- and anti-competitive effects but the weighing of harms to competition against public interest considerations.[115] However, some leading competition law scholars have explained *Wouters* as an unprecedented case, albeit one that can be still located within the parameters of a competition law analysis, by using the notion of 'ancillary restraints', developed by the CJEU in competition cases.[116] This concept covers 'any alleged restriction of competition which is directly related and *necessary* to the implementation of a main non-restrictive transaction and proportionate to it'.[117] The pure doctrine of ancillary restraints thus infuses the application of Article 101(1) TFEU with flexibility and looks at the overall context of an agreement in order to enable the implementation of commercial transactions that are overall non-restrictive of competition. Those authors note a resemblance between this doctrine and the approach in *Wouters*, with the main difference being that, in this decision, the restraint of competition was necessary to facilitate the application of a *regulatory* obligation instead of a *commercial* one, which had been the orthodox rationale in competition cases thus far.[118] Seen in this light, the reasoning in *Wouters* could be understood as a progression of the competition case law.

The burning issue was whether the *Wouters* decision would inaugurate a self-contained and specific line of case law, or whether it would extend to suggest a broader interpretative alignment between the competition and free movement case law. Later cases have entrenched the *Wouters* line of reasoning, but have also demonstrated its relatively narrow range of application. Thus the clear public-interest-based approach in *Wouters* seems so far confined to enabling regulatory obligations.[119] All subsequent cases where the Court has considered the application of the *Wouters* formula, like *Meca-Medina*,[120] *OTOC*,[121] *CNG*,[122] *API*[123] and

---

[114] See further section II.B.

[115] In this respect, see the Opinion of AG Léger in *Wouters* (n 82) paras 104, 105.

[116] See Whish and Bailey, *Competition Law* (n 48) 138–41.

[117] See the *Guidelines on the Application of Article 81(3)* [now 101(3)] *of the Treaty* (n 24) para 29 and the case law where this doctrine emerged (ie Case 42/82 *Remia v Commission*, ECLI:EU:C:1985:327, paras 18–20; *Métropole télévision (M6)* (n 85) paras 104–106).

[118] See Whish and Bailey, *Competition Law* (n 48) 139–40; and A Ezrachi, *EU Competition Law*, 6th edn (Oxford, Hart Publishing, 2018) 125. See also the Opinion of AG Trstenjak in Case C-209/07 *Competition Authority v Beef Industry Development Society*, ECLI:EU:C:2008:4670, para 54 for a similar view; and for an endorsement of this approach by the General Court, see the more recent judgment in Case T- 680/14 *Lupin v Commission*, ECLI:EU:T:2018:908, para 143).

[119] Indeed, in cases where a body has been found to no have regulatory power, the Court has declined to extend the *Wouters* reasoning (see Case T-90/11 *Ordre national des pharmaciens (ONP) and Others v Commission*, ECLI:EU:T:2014:1049, paras 40 and 343–348). However, see section III.C.

[120] Case C-519/04 *Meca-Medina and Majcen v Commission*, ECLI:EU:C:2006:492.

[121] Case C-1/12 *Ordem dos Técnicos Oficiais de Contas (OTOC) v Autoridade da Concorrência*, ECLI:EU:C:2013:127.

[122] Case C-136/12 *Consiglio nazionale dei geologi (CNG) v Autorità garante della concorrenza e del mercato and Autorità garante della concorrenza e del mercato*, ECLI:EU:C:2013:489.

[123] Case C-184/13 *Anonima Petroli Italiana (API) and Others v Ministero delle Infrastrutture e dei Trasporti*, ECLI:EU:C:2014:2147.

*CHEZ Elektro*,[124] have involved the applicability of the competition rules to the decisions of regulatory bodies such as sporting[125] or professional associations. The case law post-*Wouters* does not therefore support an expansive use of public interest objectives or other legitimate goals as a balancing tool in the application of the constituent elements in Article 101(1) TFEU. It continues to be the case that, outside the realm of the justification of regulatory obligations, only the application of the conditions in Article 101(3) TFEU can save an agreement that falls, in principle, within the scope of the Article 101(1) TFEU.[126] This can be supported by using as an argument the traditional boundaries between the competition and the free movement rules. The mandatory requirements developed in *Cassis* are principally tailored to the justification of measures adopted by public authorities. Therefore, the use of public interest objectives in a competition analysis might fit much more naturally in relation to the decisions of entities that, while constituting associations of undertakings for the purposes of competition law, have a rule-making function than within the traditional analysis of anti-competitive agreements concluded between private parties.[127] Moreover, these decisions have illuminated the versatility of interpretation offered by *Wouters*, by strongly emphasising that the analytical pattern set in that decision relies on the *context* in which the relevant regulations are issued and the objectives they pursue, and on the fact that the realisation of such goals *inherently* carries potential effects restrictive of competition. Therefore, *Wouters* and its progeny would be broadly explicable within the parameters of the contextually based competition law analysis[128] previously described.

However, if we adopt a panoramic view of EU law – instead of a self-contained perspective of EU competition law – we cannot fail to appreciate the comparability with the *Cassis de Dijon* reasoning in terms of the use of imperative requirements in the public interest as potential justifications for a restriction, subject to the application of a proportionality test.[129] If we strip the reasoning to its kernel, what we

---

[124] Case C-427/16 *CHEZ Elektro Bulgaria AD v Kotsev*, ECLI:EU:C:2017:890.

[125] In *Meca-Medina*, the General Court had ruled out the application of the *Wouters* formula to anti-doping rules adopted by the International Olympic Committee (IOC) on the basis that these sporting rules could not be likened to market conduct and hence fell altogether outside the scope of Arts 101 and 102 TFEU (Case T-313/02 *Meca-Medina and Majcen v Commission*, ECLI:EU:T:2004:282, para 65). However, the Court of Justice, on appeal, set aside the judgment of the General Court and confirmed the applicability, in principle, of the competition provisions to these rules and the suitability of the *Wouters* reasoning as a mechanism to elucidate whether ostensible restrictions of competition created by these rules can nevertheless be justified by legitimate objectives – such as the promotion of fairness in competitive sport (Case C-519/04 *Meca-Medina* (n 120), paras 22–34) For a very interesting discussion of this particular aspect of the judgment and the wider implications that it carried in relation to the applicability of the competition rules to sport, see S Weatherill, 'Anti-Doping revisited – the Demise of the rule of "purely sporting interest"' (2006) 27 *European Competition Law Review* 645.

[126] However, see the cases discussed in section III.C in relation to selective distribution agreements.

[127] See, eg, Case T-49/02 *Brasserie nationale v Commission*, ECLI:EU:T:2005:298, where the General Court rejected attempts by the applicants, using both *Cassis* and *Wouters*, to justify a horizontal agreement restrictive of competition by object on the basis of alleged legitimate objectives such as (in that case) the preservation of commercial loyalty (para 85).

[128] For an illustration of this, see the Opinion of AG Wahl in Case C-67/13 *Groupement des cartes bancaires* (CB) *v Commission*, ECLI:EU:C:2014:1958, para 44, where he explains the effect of the contextual approach in *Wouters* as neutralising the anti-competitive effects of the practice in question.

[129] See further, O'Loughlin, 'EC Competition Rules' (n 101) 68–69.

are saying in both cases is that a restriction (of trade in *Cassis* and/or competition in *Wouters*) may be considered compatible with EU law if it is necessary to pursue a recognised public interest objective. As we shall see, the devil is in the detail in both cases too, because the application of the proportionality test has acted a barrier for the dilution of the Treaty prohibition of restraints on competition in the post-*Wouters* line of case law, just as the application of the proportionality test has determined the ultimate incompatibility with EU law of many national measures in the wake of *Cassis*.[130] Monti's appraisal of *Wouters* as representing the emergence of a '*European* rule of reason' approach in the landscape of EU competition law seems therefore very suitable to highlight this strong similarity.[131]

The theme of this chapter is the search for the potential legacy of the *Casssis* decision to EU competition law. It is argued here that even if it is possible to frame *Wouters* within a competition analytical framework, it is also undeniable from what we have seen that this particular decision draws inspiration in more ways than one from the path of reasoning illuminated by *Cassis* and adapts it to a competition law framework. In doing so, the Court has broadened the parameters of competition law analysis.

It is also suggested that this exercise has yielded further similarities in these two areas, as demonstrated in the cases that have followed *Wouters*. Thus, while in *Wouters* and *Meca-Medina* the restrictions of competition inherent in the decisions by the regulatory bodies were found to be justified and proportionate, it is significant that all subsequent measures adopted by regulatory bodies examined through the lens of the *Wouters* formula either have failed the proportionality test or the final decision has been devolved to the referring national court.[132] The impact of the proportionality test reveals parallels with the post-*Cassis* case law, where many national measures were found to be disproportionate even though the mandatory requirements invoked seemed to be prima facie respected by the Court as legitimate choices made by Member States in the absence of harmonisation.[133]

---

[130] See section I.

[131] See n 90. Nazzini presented a persuasive view that simultaneously rooted the *Wouters* formula in a competition law analysis and recognised its *methodological* parallels with the *Cassis* case law (R Nazzini, 'Article 81 EC Between Time Present and Time Past: A Normative Critique of "Restriction of Competition" in EU law' (2006) 43 *CML Rev* 497, 521–30). He suggested that the Court applied a bi-dimensional test that added a new layer to the application of Art 101(1) TFEU in cases involving regulatory obligations. He argued that, in *Wouters*, the weighing-up exercise performed by the Court was not simply between anti-competitive effects and public interest considerations but between the former and *both* pro-competitive effects and public interest considerations (ibid 525–27). This allowed him to place the *Wouters* formula within the traditional analytical framework of competition law analysis – because only public interest objectives that *also* carried welfare-enhancing effects would be applicable in a *Wouters* context (ibid 527) – while at the same time acknowledging the methodological similarities with a free movement rule-of-reason approach.

[132] See, eg, *Consiglio nazionale dei geologi* (n 122), where the Court held that rules adopted by National Association of Geologists in Italy encouraging its members to apply a scale of professional fees were liable to produce restrictive effects on competition in the internal market but left the actual determination of these effects and of the proportionality of this restriction to ensure the offering of appropriate guarantees to consumers to the national court (paras 53–57). Similarly, see *CHEZ Elektro* (n 124) paras 55–58.

[133] See section I.

Thus, in *OTOC*,[134] the Court scrutinised the compatibility of a quality control regulation adopted by the Portuguese Chamber of Chartered Accountants with Article 101 TFEU. After deciding that the regulation was liable to have a restrictive effect on competition, the Court applied the *Wouters* formula and went on to hold that these restrictions – which concerned the compulsory training of accountants – went 'beyond what is necessary to guarantee the quality of the services offered by chartered accountants'.[135] In other words, the legitimacy of the objective was not contested; what determined the incompatibility with EU law was the lack of proportionality of the restriction of competition. Even more strikingly, in *API*,[136] the key issue was whether rules adopted by an Italian body – set up by law but composed principally of representatives of professional associations of carriers and customers – that laid down minimum operating costs for the road haulage sector, fell within the prohibition in Article 101(1) TFEU. After establishing that this body was acting as an association of undertakings and not in the exercise of public power, the Court applied the *Wouters* formula.[137] While the Court recognised that the justification invoked for these rules – protecting road safety – might constitute a legitimate interest,[138] it found that the fixing of minimum operating costs was neither *appropriate* nor *necessary* to achieve this objective.[139] The articulation of the proportionality test there seemed closer to that found in the *Cassis* case law[140] than, for example, to a classic Article 101(3) TFEU analysis of proportionality, where the *necessity* of a restriction generally appears as the central consideration.[141]

## C. The Development of the Notion of Objective Justification in Articles 101 and 102 TFEU

This chapter will explore as a final dimension of comparability between the decision of the Court in *Cassis* and the evolution of EU competition law, the development of the notion of objective justification in the interpretation of Articles 101(1) and 102 TFEU. It will be argued that the analytical structure given to this concept by

---

[134] *OTOC* (n 121).
[135] ibid para 100.
[136] *API* (n 123).
[137] ibid para 47.
[138] ibid para 51.
[139] ibid paras 52 –58.
[140] In fact, it is very interesting that the Court in *API* (n 123) used free movement cases to support its analysis of proportionality (paras 53–55).
[141] Thus, in the application of the third condition in Art 101(3) TFEU, the Commission explains in its *Guidelines* on the application of that provision (n 24, para 73) that 'this condition implies a two-fold test. First the restrictive agreement as such must be reasonably necessary in order to achieve the efficiencies. Secondly, the individual restrictions of competition that flow from the agreement must also be reasonably necessary for the attainment of the efficiencies.'

the Court presents important methodological similarities to the objective justification mechanism pioneered in *Cassis* in the shape of the notion of mandatory requirements, particularly in certain subcategories of cases.

In the context of Article 101(1) TFEU, a relevant line of case law is that dealing with selective distribution agreements. Until the Modernisation of competition law and the adoption of a new style of umbrella block exemption regulations,[142] the analysis of this type of vertical agreement was entirely developed by the case law and, in particular, the seminal decision in *Metro I*,[143] delivered two years before the *Cassis* decision. There – and in later cases – the Court held that some restrictions of competition found in a selective distribution agreement would not come under the scope of the Article 101(1) TFEU prohibition, provided that certain conditions were satisfied. These were: that the nature of the product in question required selective distribution; that the distributors were chosen on the basis of objective qualitative criteria that were applied in a uniform and non-discriminatory way; and that these criteria did not go beyond what was necessary for the product in question.[144] The analysis that emerged in this line of case law is, in some ways, analogous to an objective justification approach because, despite the fact that some clauses in these agreements may evidently affect competition, it is understood that, as the Court explains, they serve a legitimate goal – that is, maintenance of specialist trade, after-sales services for highly technical goods – that may improve competition in relation to non-price factors.[145] The achievement of this legitimate goal, subject to the conditions set out in *Metro* – which, as we have seen, include a proportionality test – ultimately justifies the overall conclusion that there has not been a breach of the basic prohibition in Article 101(1) TFEU. This formula is still valid today, and a selective distribution agreement whose clauses fulfil these criteria will be considered as objectively justified and hence fall outside the scope of Article 101(1) TFEU, without the need to engage the application of the Block Exemption Regulation on Vertical Agreements.[146] For the purposes of this chapter, we can discern a methodological parallelism in the justification pattern utilised in *Cassis*. Yet while the legal technique employed is very similar, the two analyses appear to involve the consideration of different factors at a substantive level – that is, public interest factors in free movement versus non-price related competition considerations.

---

[142] See the current Block Exemption Regulation on Vertical Agreements (Commission Regulation 330/2010 of 20 April 2010 on the application of Article 101(3) of the Treaty on the Functioning of the European Union to categories of vertical agreements and concerted practices [2010] OJ L102/1) and its immediate predecessor, Commission Regulation (EC) No 2790/1999 of 22 December 1999 on the application of Article 81(3) of the Treaty to categories of vertical agreements and concerted practices [1999] OJ L336/21, which was the first umbrella Block Exemption Regulation adopted post-Modernisation.

[143] Case 26/76 *Metro SB-Großmärkte v Commission*, ECLI:EU:C:1977:167.

[144] ibid para 20; Case 31/80 *L'Oréal v PVBA*, ECLI:EU:C:1980:289, paras 15–16; and Case C-439/09 *Pierre Fabre Dermo-Cosmétique v Président de l'Autorité de la concurrence and Ministre de l'Économie, de l'Industrie et de l'Emploi*, ECLI:EU:C:2011:649, para 41.

[145] See *Pierre Fabre* (n 144) para 40. See further Jones, Sufrin and Dunne, *EU Competition Law* (n 48) 781.

[146] See the current *Commission Guidelines on Vertical Restraints* (n 26) para 175.

However, in more recent cases concerning selective distribution agreements – in particular, those involving bans on internet selling – that closeness has also been accentuated at a substantive level, with the Court explicitly borrowing strands of reasoning from free movement cases in order to determine what constitutes a legitimate aim that could objectively justify a clause restrictive of competition within a selective distribution agreement. For instance, in *Pierre Fabre*,[147] there was a clause in the system of selective distribution operated by a supplier of cosmetics that required that its products could only be sold by retailers and distributors in a physical space and with a qualified pharmacist present. This effectively amounted to a de facto comprehensive ban on internet selling, which the supplier had attempted to justify during the administrative proceedings led by the French Competition Authority, inter alia,[148] on grounds of consumer well-being (ie the dangers to the consumer that could derive from an incorrect use of the products).[149] The Court alluded to this in its judgment and rejected this suggestion, referring to the reasoning that it had used in the cases on free movement, like *Ker Optica*[150] and *Doc Morris*,[151] where it had given short shrift to arguments invoking the need to provide individual guidance to consumers, which sought to justify de facto bans on the online selling of contact lenses[152] and non-prescription medicines[153] respectively.[154] Even though, as Monti argues, in the free movement cases it was the disproportionate nature of the national measures rather than the legitimacy of the goal that ultimately determined their incompatibility with EU law,[155] the approach of the Court was, for our purposes, significant on two counts. First because it appeared at least to consider a model of objective justification based on public interest requirements within the parameters of Article 101(1) TFEU in a context different from that found in *Wouters*[156] and, second, because it provided a rare example of express cross-fertilisation in the use of justifications in competition and free movement.[157]

Turning to Article 102 TFEU, this provision has a more open-ended texture than Article 101 TFEU and contains only a prohibition on abuses of dominant position and a list of examples of abusive practices. In particular, there is no

---

[147] *Pierre Fabre* (n 144).

[148] The supplier also argued that the restrictions of competition were objectively justified by another legitimate goal, this time a competition related one, namely the need to maintain the prestigious image of the products at issue (see ibid para 45).

[149] ibid para 24.

[150] Case C-108/09 *Ker-Optika v ÀNTSZ*, ECLI:EU:C:2010:725.

[151] Case C-322/01 *Deutscher Apothekerverband v DocMorris*, ECLI:EU:C:2003:664.

[152] *Ker-Optika* (n 150) para 76.

[153] *Deutscher Apothekerverband* (n 151) paras 112–113.

[154] See *Pierre Fabre* (n 144) para 44.

[155] See G Monti, 'Restraints on Selective Distribution' (2013) 36 *World Competition* 489, 502.

[156] In this respect, see the Opinion of AG Mazak in *Pierre Fabre* (ECLI:EU:C:2011:113), where he uses the *Wouters* case by analogy to support the exceptional possibility that restrictions on online selling could be justified by legitimate objectives of a public nature (para 35).

[157] Monti regards this transposition of the reasoning from the internal market case law as frustrating the economics-based approach brought about by the Modernisation of EU competition law ('Restraints' (n 155) 502).

provision equivalent to Article 101(3) TFEU, or in other words, of a Treaty-based structure for the consideration of potential efficiencies that may justify ostensibly abusive behaviour and take it outside the prohibition in Article 102 TFEU. In the absence of such an express mechanism, the CJEU developed, through the inter-pretation of Article 102 TFEU, the possibility that apparently abusive behaviour could be justified and hence ultimately fall outside the scope of that prohibition. This approach first appeared in *United Brands*,[158] where the applicants sought to justify their refusal to supply bananas to a longstanding customer on the basis of the protection of their commercial interests. In that decision, delivered a year before the *Cassis* decision, the Court recognised that it was necessary to examine whether the refusal to supply was justified[159] and proportionate.[160] In later cases, the Court broadened the scope of this notion; implicitly to encompass public interest objectives such as health and safety[161] and explicitly to include efficien-cies that also benefitted consumers and that might outweigh the potential harm to competition.[162] The systematisation of these threads of the case law was achieved by the *Commission Guidance Paper on Enforcement Priorities in the Application of Article 82 EC (now Article 102 TFEU)*.[163] There, the Commission divided possible justifications into two categories: *objective necessity*[164] and *efficiencies*.[165] In rela-tion to the first, the *Guidance Paper* consolidates existing case law and explains that the determination of whether conduct is objectively necessary and propor-tionate is based on factors external to a dominant undertaking. It uses as an example considerations of health and safety, and emphasises that, when trying to invoke these, it must be borne in mind that is *normally* the task of the public authorities – and not of the dominant undertaking – to set and enforce public health and safety standards.[166] In relation to the second, it sets out a four-limbed test to determine whether the efficiencies yielded by ostensibly abusive behaviour

---

[158] Case 27/76 *United Brands v Commission*, ECLI:EU:C:1978:22.

[159] ibid para 184.

[160] ibid paras 190–196. In more recent high-profile cases like Case T-219/99 *British Airways v Commission*, ECLI:EU:T:2003:343, the Court developed this notion further to clarify that for the protec-tion of the competitive position of a dominant undertaking to be lawful, it should be based on criteria of economic efficiency (para 280). In carrying out this fuller examination, the Court also embedded a proportionality type of analysis. For example, in that case, the Court essentially reached the conclu-sion (paras 279–292) that the incentives provided by British Airways were not economically justifiable because they did not seem to be appropriate to achieve cost savings or efficiency gains, and because the *real* motivation behind their fidelity-building nature seemed to be ousting rival outlines (see also n 177 and accompanying text). In other words, the Court intimated that the dominant company had an ulterior motivation for its practices.

[161] See Case T-30/89 *Hilti v Commission*, ECLI:EU:T:1991:70, paras 115–119; and Case T-83/91 *Tetra Pak International v Commission (Tetra Pak II)*, ECLI:EU:T:1994:246, paras 138–140.

[162] Case C-95/04 *British Airways v Commission*, ECLI:EU:C:2007:166, paras 69 and 86.

[163] See n 26.

[164] The Court had alluded to the notion of objective justification much earlier in the case law (see Case 311/84 *Centre belge d'études de marché – Télémarketing (CBEM) v Compagnie luxembourgeoise de télédiffusion (CLT)*, ECLI:EU:C:1985:394, para 27.

[165] See the *Commission Guidance Paper* (n 26) para 28.

[166] ibid para 29.

justify conduct that leads to the foreclosure of competitors and hence determine that, overall, there is no breach of Article 102 TFEU.[167] This classification has been subsequently endorsed by the CJEU,[168] but both heads of justification are notably difficult to prove in practice.

Of the two categories of justification, the consideration of efficiencies fits neatly into a classical competition law analysis because it seeks to determine whether the exclusionary effect created by potentially abusive conduct can be counterbalanced or outweighed by efficiencies that also benefit consumers.[169] It embodies a traditional – if intricate – balance between harms and benefits generated to the competitive process and consumers conditioned by a proportionality test that we encounter in the context of the two other pillars of EU competition law, that is, in Article 101 TFEU, where such a balance is enshrined in the Treaty itself[170] and in the field of merger control.[171] However, a dimension of the objective necessity justification that bears a closer affinity to a *Cassis*-type of reasoning is the use of health and safety considerations – developed first in the case law and then used as an example by the *Commission Guidance Paper* to illustrate that concept.[172] Although there is evidence in the case law that the notion of objective necessity is broader and may refer to other external factors, such as commercial or technical considerations[173] – which are more removed in nature from overriding requirements in the public interest – the theoretical possibility that ostensibly abusive behaviour might be justified by health and safety reasons is much closer to the line of analysis offered by the *Cassis* mandatory requirements.

Thus, in the *Hilti* case,[174] the first case in which health and safety considerations were argued, a dominant company that manufactured nail guns, nails and cartridge strips attempted to justify the tie of the sale of its cartridges to the purchase of its own nails on the basis that the nails manufactured by two of their competitors were of inferior quality and could result in injury to the users. The General Court rejected this argument on the grounds that Hilti had made no attempt to approach the public authorities for a ruling that the competing nails were dangerous, and that, given the existence of national laws on product liability, it was for the public authorities to enforce these laws and not for undertakings to take steps individually to eradicate products they regarded as dangerous.[175] In other words, the Court seemed to recognise that a justification on grounds of health and safety

---

[167] ibid para 30.

[168] Case C-209/10 *Post Danmark v Konkurrencerådet (Post Danmark I)*, ECLI:EU:C:2012:172, paras 40–41; and Case T-286/09 *Intel v Commission*, ECLI:EU:T:2014:547, para 94.

[169] See the *Commission Guidance Paper* (n 26) para 30.

[170] See similarity with the analysis carried out in the context of Art 101(3) TFEU.

[171] See the *Guidelines on the assessment of horizontal mergers under the Council Regulation on the control of concentrations between undertakings* [2004] OJ C 31/5, paras 76–88.

[172] See section I.

[173] See *CBEM* (n 164) paras 26–27; and Case C-457/10P *AstraZeneca v Commission*, ECLI:EU:C:2012:7, para 135.

[174] *Hilti* (n 161).

[175] ibid paras 115–119.

was conceivable in an Article 102 TFEU context but that it was not borne out by the facts, because the actions of the undertaking ultimately suggested that its *real* motivation was the exclusion of competing nails and therefore the protection of the company's commercial position.[176] The approach of the General Court there is reminiscent of cases in the wake of *Cassis*, where the Court implicitly unmasked the latent protectionist purpose of Member States that outwardly pleaded requirements in the public interest.[177] One salient difference between the two is that, in the free movement cases, such exposure was less obvious and the ultimate incompatibility of the relevant national measures with EU law was channelled through the application of the proportionality test, whereas in the *Hilti* case, the Court took a less deferential and more direct approach to the actions of the dominant company without having to make recourse to the consideration of the suitability and necessity of the measure, which would have been the final step in the analysis of the justification. The proportionality test was, however, briefly applied in *Tetra Pak II*,[178] where the General Court held, in another case in which a dominant company attempted to justify the tie of two of its products – filling machines and cartons – on grounds of public health, that the protection of public health could be guaranteed by less restrictive means,[179] before reaffirming the *Hilti* principle that the remedy should normally lie in public health regulations and not in rules individually set out by undertakings.[180]

# IV.  Conclusions

This chapter has sought to analyse the impact of *Cassis de Dijon* beyond its natural realm of free movement to encompass some aspects of the interpretation of the EU anti-trust provisions. The analysis has been framed, at opposite ends, by the shared common aim of the competition and free movement provisions to build the single market and prevent the erection of barriers that could undermine it, and by the significant differences between them. An extensive body of academic literature has discussed the desirability of a convergence between these two areas of law. This chapter has not argued in favour or against this convergence but has examined

---

[176] In this respect, see also the arguments of the Commission in that case, ibid paras 108–111.

[177] This can be seen, eg, in cases where Member States tried to invoke mandatory requirements to justify rules that did not serve the objective for which they were supposedly intended but appeared to serve disguised protectionist or over-regulatory goals. See, eg, in the field of free movement of goods, *Rau Lebensmittelwerke v De Smedt* (n 3) paras 14–17, or Case C-220/98 *Estée Lauder Cosmetics v Lancaster*, ECLI:EU:C:2000:8, paras 25–31; and in the field of free movement of services and workers, respectively, Case C-42/02 *Lindman*, ECLI:EU:C:2003:613, paras 20–27 and Case C-185/04 *Öberg v Försäkringskassan*, ECLI:EU:C:2006:107, paras 19–26.

[178] *Tetra Pak II* (n 161).

[179] ibid para 84. The proportionality test has also been applied in other cases where the justification of objective necessity has been invoked outside the realm of health and safety considerations (see the Commission Decision in *OPCOM/Romanian Power Exchange* (summary) [2014] OJ C314/7, para 18).

[180] *Tetra Pak II* (n 161) para 84.

a different and narrower issue. It has searched for evidence of the effect that the ruling in *Cassis* might have had in the application of the Treaty competition provisions. While in the absence of direct references to it, it may not be possible to prove with pellucid certainty that the decision in *Cassis de Dijon* has influenced the development of EU competition law, it has posited that it is nonetheless possible to acknowledge the footprints of that ruling and recognise its vast reach in some of the interpretative dimensions of Articles 101 and 102 TFEU.

Three potential domains where the effect of *Cassis* might have been felt have been identified. First, and in terms of general policy, the Modernisation of EU competition law heralded a fundamental policy shift from a formalistic to an effects-based approach in a similar manner to that in which *Cassis* moved the interpretation of the free movement provisions from a formalistic approach to one that looked at the effect of national measures on intra-Union trade. There are very significant differences in the nature of the effects examined in both areas – in *Cassis*, this was an endorsement of a particular vision of the single market, whereas in competition law, it meant embracing an economics-based approach. However, it can still be argued that an essential parallelism in the direction of travel – from form to effect – arises in these two areas of law. Second, much more specifically, the line of case law inaugurated by the Court in *Wouters* offers perhaps the clearest example of the impact of a *Cassis* rule-of-reason approach on EU competition law from both a substantive and a methodological perspective. At a substantive level, because it brings public interest considerations to the application of Article 101(1) TFEU, or in other words, considerations that are much closer to the mandatory requirements than to efficiency concerns. At a methodological level, because after applying a conventional competition law analysis to determine the potential existence of a restriction of competition, it then considers a legitimate objective that could objectively justify the restriction and the proportionality of the latter. Third, the development of the notion of objective justification, particularly in the context of Article 102 TFEU, but also in some aspects of the interpretation of selective distribution agreements in Article 101(1) TFEU, presents interesting analytical similarities with the justification model embodied by *Cassis*.

The decision in *Cassis de Dijon* represented a turning point in the development of the single market, a revolution that broadened the scope of application of the free movement provisions and fashioned the analysis that would apply to indistinctly applicable measures entirely through the interpretation of the basic prohibition on measures having equivalent effect set out in Article 34 TFEU. In the context of EU competition law, an examination of those areas where this chapter has argued for the existence of parallelisms with the *Cassis* analytical approach and rationale suggests that the result might have been the broadening of the parameters of competition law analysis and the injection of a degree of flexibility in the application of the two basic anti-trust provisions. Thus, the structure of Article 101 TFEU suggests that only the factors contemplated in Article 101(3) TFEU can save agreements that fulfil all the elements of the prohibition in Article 101(1) TFEU. Yet the *Wouters* line of case law and some of the decisions concerning selective distribution agreements illustrate an interpretative exercise conducted wholly within the scope of Article 101(1) TFEU that is reminiscent of the *Cassis* approach. In particular, the *Wouters* approach allows, in principle, for the net of EU competition law to be cast more widely – just like *Cassis* did in relation to the application of Article 34 TFEU – while allowing the justification of proportionate regulatory obligations and therefore their ultimate compatibility with EU law. Finally, the emergence of the objective necessity justification in the context of the prohibition of abuses of dominant position in Article 102 TFEU also expands the analytical possibilities applicable to that provision, even if in practice such justification seems almost impossible to prove. These might indeed be discrete lines of case law, but they make the legacy of *Cassis* for EU competition law difficult to ignore.

# 8

## Mutual Recognition: Addressing Some Outstanding Conundrums

PETER OLIVER*

## I. Introduction

Not only was it a great pleasure for me to participate in the workshop in Cambridge to mark the 40th anniversary of *Cassis de Dijon*, but it was also a trip down memory lane. I had the great fortune to start work in 1978 in the Legal Service of the Commission in the field that most interested me, namely the free movement of goods; and it was the most exciting time to be there. My first day was 1 November (which happens to be a public holiday in Belgium and in the Commission), just four weeks before the hearing, at which the institution was represented by my Director, Heinrich Matthies, a brilliant and forbidding German official of the old school.[1] Then the Opinion of Advocate General Capotorti followed on 16 January 1979 and finally, just over a month later, the seminal ruling of the Court,[2] which prompted an outburst of intellectual and professional exhilaration such as I have rarely experienced since then.

At the tender age of 25 years and six days, and with less than four months' career in the Commission behind me, I can only claim to have been a foot-soldier in this historic (and fortunately peaceful) event. Little did I realise then that I would be devoting a significant part of my professional life to this epoch-making judgment and its abundant progeny.

As the reader will be well aware, after finding that the German measure constituted a measure of equivalent effect within the meaning of what is now Article 34

* My thanks go to Robert Schütze, Thomas van Rijn and Stephen Weatherill for their very helpful comments on an earlier draft of this chapter. But responsibility for any errors is mine alone.
[1] Those who have never experienced the travails of attempting to decipher old-fashioned German handwriting could not imagine how I struggled with his hand-written notes on my draft legal opinions. The first step was always to establish whether the message was in French or German; and that could take several minutes. The message was never in English, a language that – like most of his generation of Commission officials – he never really mastered.
[2] Case 120/78 *Rewe-Zentral AG v Bundesmonopolverwaltung für Branntwein (Cassis de Dijon)*, ECLI:EU:C:1979:42.

TFEU, the Court made the following pronouncement in paragraph 14 of its ruling in *Cassis*:

> There is … no valid reason why, provided that they have been lawfully produced and marketed in one of the Member States, alcoholic beverages should not be introduced into any other Member State; the sale of such products may not be subject to a legal prohibition on the marketing of beverages with an alcohol content lower than the limit set by the national rules.[3]

Thus was born the mutual recognition principle (MRP), sometimes known as the principle of equivalence, which has since spread to countless other areas of Union law,[4] reaching its apogee in *Opinion 2/13*,[5] where the Court described the legal structure of the Union as being

> based on the fundamental premiss that each Member State shares with all the other Member States, and recognises that they share with it, a set of common values on which the EU is founded, as stated in Article 2 TEU. That premiss implies and justifies the existence of mutual trust between the Member States that those values will be recognised and, therefore, that the law of the EU that implements them will be respected.[6]

In a later passage of *Opinion 2/13*, the Court added that

> the principle of mutual trust between the Member States is of fundamental importance in EU law, given that it allows an area without internal borders to be created and maintained. That principle requires, particularly with regard to the area of freedom, security and justice, each of those States, save in exceptional circumstances, to consider all the other Member States to be complying with EU law and particularly with the fundamental rights recognised by EU law.[7]

In part, the development of the MRP was due to the Commission's Communication on the ruling published in October 1980,[8] which significantly raised the profile of the judgment and the MRP in particular, thereby playing a major role in boosting economic integration within the EU. At that time, the publication of a formal

---

[3] According to Catherine Barnard, this passage reads 'almost as an afterthought' (C Barnard, *The Substantive Law of the EU – The Four Freedoms*, 5th edn (Oxford, Oxford University Press, 2016) 93. It comes at the very end of the judgment – after the Court had established that the contested German measure was not justified. But see n 20.

[4] See eg M Möstl, 'Preconditions and Limits of Mutual Recognition' (2010) 47 *CML Rev* 405 and W-H Roth, 'Mutual Recognition' in P Koutrakos and J Snell (eds), *Research Handbook on the Law of the EU's Internal Market* (Cheltenham, Edward Elgar, 2017) 427.

[5] *Opinion 2/13*, ECLI:EU:C:2014:2454.

[6] ibid para 168. Subsequently, President Lenaerts described mutual recognition as a constitutional principle of the Union: '*La Vie après l'Avis*: Exploring the Principle of Mutual (Yet not Blind) Trust' (2017) 54 *CML Rev* 805, 806.

[7] *Opinion 2/13* (n 5) para 191. This wording appears to cover all areas of EU law, whether or not fundamental rights are at stake: C Timmermans 'How Trustworthy is Mutual Trust? Opinion 2/13 Revisited' in K Lenaerts et al (eds), *An Ever-Changing Union – Perspectives on the Future of EU Law in Honour of Allan Rosas* (Oxford, Hart Publishing, 2019) 21, 27.

[8] Communication from the Commission concerning the consequences of the judgment given by the Court of Justice on 20 February 1979 in Case 120/78 ('Cassis de Dijon') [1980] OJ C256/2. See K Alter and S Meunier-Aitsahalia, 'Judicial Politics in the European Community: European Integration and the Pathbreaking Cassis de Dijon Decision' (1994) 26 *Comparative Political Studies* 535, 541, and Brigitte Leucht's contribution to this volume (ch 4).

Communication by the Commission on a single judgment was extremely rare, if not unprecedented. The credit for this masterly step must go to Alfonso Mattera.[9]

In any case, even if a product has been 'lawfully produced and marketed' elsewhere in the EU, the Member State of importation may of course impose a stricter measure so long as it can show that is objectively justified under Article 36 TFEU or, to use the language of *Cassis*, the mandatory requirements.[10]

Furthermore, as the Court held in *Denkavit Futtermittel v Minister of Agriculture*, decided shortly before *Cassis*, the Member State claiming that a restriction caught by Article 34 is justified bears the burden of proving that proposition.[11] This amounts to a rebuttable presumption that a restriction is not justified. Where the MRP applies, the presumption is that the standard of the Member State of production is equivalent to that of the Member State of the final destination.

In this chapter, I will concentrate on four major issues raised by the MRP test, namely:

(a)  what is meant by 'lawfully produced and marketed' in a Member State (section II);
(b)  how the principle applies to goods originating in third countries (section III);
(c)  why the principle does not apply when public morality is at stake (section V); and
(d)  what happens when mutual recognition breaks down (section VI).

Bizarrely, after 40 years and despite a wealth of literature on this case law, it is still not possible to give a straightforward answer to these questions.

## II. 'Lawfully Produced and Marketed'

### A.  Does 'and' Mean 'or' in this Context ?

As we saw, paragraph 14 of *Cassis* refers to goods 'lawfully produced and marketed in one of the Member States'. However, Advocate General La Pergola took the view in *Commission v France (Foie Gras)* that it suffices for goods to be lawfully produced *or* marketed in another Member State.[12] However, apart from relying

---

[9] Alfonso Mattera Ricigliano devoted his whole career to the single market, and the free movement of goods in particular, as an official in the Directorate-General of the Commission now known as DG Grow. At the time of the ruling in *Cassis de Dijon*, he was the Head of Unit responsible for that sector. He rose to become Deputy Director-General of that DG, and even after his retirement he continued to act as an Special Advisor to successive Commissioners responsible for that DG. He was also a distinguished academic and wrote very widely in this field.

[10] *Cassis de Dijon* (n 2) paras 9–13, and countless subsequent judgments.

[11] Case 251/78 *Denkavit Futtermittel v Minister of Agriculture*, ECLI:EU:C:1979:252. This ruling has been confirmed on innumerable occasions, as in Cases C-297/05 *Commission v Netherlands (Vehicle Identification)*, ECLI:EU:C:2007:531, paras 78–79 and C-265/06 *Commission v Portugal (Tinted Film)*, ECLI:EU:C:2008:210, para 39.

[12] Case C-l84/96 *Commission v France (Foie Gras)*, ECLI:EU:C:1998:495, para 28.

on two judgments that – with great respect – do not appear to support his case,[13] the Advocate General failed to set out any reasoning in support of this conclusion. Subsequently, in *Canal Satélite Digital*, the Court stated that the principle applied to 'goods lawfully marketed in one Member State',[14] while maintaining that this is what it had ruled in *Cassis de Dijon*! However, since the Court did not elaborate on this point at all in *Canal Satélite Digital*, this may have been no more than an oversight.

What is more, in its famous Communication of 2003 on the practical application of mutual recognition, the Commission also adopted the same position as Advocate General La Pergola;[15] but in this passage[16] the Commission developed this point at some length, so that this clearly cannot be regarded as an 'accidental' endorsement of the Advocate General's Opinion.

Laurence Gormley was more forthright when he wrote that the above-quoted paragraph of *Cassis de Dijon* 'makes the famous mistake of using the term "lawfully produced and marketed" instead of "lawfully produced *or* marketed" that the scheme of the free movement within the European Union requires'.[17]

The fact is that there is no inherent reason why the test should be cumulative, and in practice the Court does not require that, even if it regularly repeats the paragraph 14 mantra which it first spelt out in *Cassis*. That is why, in the past, I have also subscribed to the approach followed by the Advocate General and the Commission.[18]

On second thoughts, however, the situation appears to be a little more complicated. First of all, very few rules relating to production are relevant; marketing rules (especially those relating to the composition of products) are of far greater

---

[13] Cases 59/82 *Schutzverband gegen Unwesen in der Wirtschaft v Weinvertriebs GmBH*, ECLI:EU:C:1983:101, para 12 and C-131/93 *Commission v Germany (Crayfish)*, ECLI:EU:C:1994:290, para 10. In *Schutzverband*, the the MRP was not relevant (see section II.D), and in the latter case, in finding against the defendant Member State, the Court inexplicably appeared to take no cognisance of the MRP.

[14] Case C-390/99 *Canal Satélite Digital v Administration General del Estado*, ECLI:EU:C:2002:34, para 37.

[15] Commission Interpretative Communication on Facilitating the Access of Products to the Markets of Other Member States: The Practical Application of Mutual Recognition [2003] OJ C265/2. See L Gormley, *Prohibiting Restrictions on Trade within the EEC* (Amsterdam, North Holland, 1985) 48; and A Mattera, 'L'article 30 du Traité CEE la jurisprudence "Cassis de Dijon" et le principe de la reconnaissance mutuelle' (1992) *Revue du Marché unique européen* 13, 46. For some reason, the Communication uses the word 'manufactured' as opposed to 'produced' (the term employed in para 14 of the judgment in *Cassis*). The same applies to the French version of the Communication, which uses '*fabriqué*', whereas in *Cassis* the adjective '*produits*' appears. The words 'manufactured' and '*fabriqués*' scarcely seem appropriate where raw materials such as agricultural products are concerned; and yet the principle of mutual recognition applies equally to them. In any case, nothing turns on this anomaly; and in German the same word ('*hergestellt*') is used in both texts.

[16] Communication (n 15) para 2.2.

[17] L Gormley, 'Free Movement of Goods and their Use: what is the Use of it?' (2011) 33 *Fordham International Law Journal* 1589, 1611.

[18] S Enchelmaier in P Oliver (ed), *Oliver on Free Movement of Goods in the European Union*, 5th edn (Oxford, Hart Publishing, 2010) 231–32. (Although this work was written by six co-authors as well as myself, the views expressed there are also mine.) In part because of the recent ruling in Case C-525/14 *Commission v Czech Republic (Hallmarking)*, ECLI:EU:C:2016:714 (discussed in section III.E), the position advocated here differs in some respects from the view expressed in that passage of the book.

importance in this context. Second, what if the Member State of origin exempts goods intended for export from its national rules on production and the goods are never marketed there?[19] It is quite likely that the product is subject to stringent marketing rules in the same Member State, especially if it is intended for human consumption. This particular conundrum will be addressed in section II.E.(c); but first it is appropriate to consider the role of EU harmonisation and then the meaning of 'lawfully produced' and 'lawfully marketed' in this context.

## B.  Union Legislation

In paragraph 8 of its ruling in *Cassis de Dijon*, the Court emphasised that the problem concerned arose because there was an 'absence of common rules relating to the production and marketing of alcohol'.[20] Not all EU legislation precludes the application of MRP: only EU measures that establish 'common rules' for a product (ie harmonising legislation) have this effect.[21] Moreover, where the Union legislation only entails minimum harmonisation and the Member State of final destination has gone beyond that, then of course MRP comes into play. In addition, the MRP is sometimes enshrined in EU legislation; but that falls outside the scope of this chapter.[22]

## C.  What is Meant by 'Lawfully Produced'?

There appears to be a dearth of authority as to what is meant by 'lawfully produced' in a Member State. In essence, we are concerned here with process and production methods (PPMs). While standards of hygiene relating to the processing of foodstuffs and rules concerning their ingredients are relevant, it is not clear what other rules of production, such as those relating to the work environment, should be taken into account.

For instance, what if the manufacturer has flouted national labour laws in the Member State of production? What if the staff had not been paid the national minimum wage in that Member State?[23] To take another example, what if the

---

[19] That situation occurred in *Schutzverband* (n 13), as explained in section II.D.

[20] This statement, which is to be found in an early part of the judgment, sets the backdrop against which the MRP was laid down. Arguably, the fact that the MRP features in a later passage of the decision, which might at first sight appear to be unconnected to para 8, is therefore of little significance.

[21] For instance, the General Safety Directive (Directive 2001/95 [2001] OJ L11/4, as amended) does not harmonise national measures; see section II.C. What is more, a very substantial body of EU legislation itself requires the Member States to recognise one another's standards. Indeed, Art 53(1) TFEU constitutes the legal base for Directives on 'the mutual recognition of diplomas, certificates and other evidence of formal qualifications'; see Roth, 'Mutual Recognition' (n 4).

[22] However, see section VI.

[23] This is entirely a matter for the Member States. By virtue of Art 153(4), no EU legislation designed to harmonise and improve working conditions may be adopted pursuant to Art 153.

producer had relied on child labour contrary to national law?[24] Even though such breaches of the law are manifestly reprehensible, it is not obvious that such considerations are pertinent, since the link between them and the arrival of the finished product in another Member State is so remote.[25]

Planning laws are a more extreme example of this phenomenon. Conceivably, it could be argued that if goods have been produced in a factory that has been unlawfully built without planning permission, those goods have not been lawfully produced there. However, this seems fanciful and far-fetched, since the causal link between such legislation and the finished product is extremely remote.

Are we back to the distinction between 'product-bound' measures and other rules, which has caused such controversy in relation to *Keck*[26] over the years? Perhaps! In practice, however, this prospect – a nightmare for many – may not arise in practice, for the reasons set out below.

At all events, even where rules are relevant, trivial transgressions (eg where workers only wash their hands once, and not twice as required, before handling foodstuffs) should not count. Even though the Court has rightly decided that measures cannot escape the scope of Article 34 on the grounds that they are *de minimis*,[27] the *de minimis* principle ought to have a place in this very different context.

## D.  What is Meant by 'Lawfully Marketed'?

A search for a definition of 'lawfully marketed' in the case law would be a wild goose chase. Indeed, it is not clear that the Court has ever defined this term in the context of *Cassis de Dijon* and its progeny, although it is clear that this condition relates primarily to the rules relating to the composition of products. Nor was it defined in Regulation 764/2008 of the European Parliament and the Council, the

---

[24] Council Directive 94/33 on the protection of young people at work [1994] OJ L216/12, as amended, lays down requirements in this regard. In particular, the minimum working or employment age must not be lower than 'the minimum age at which compulsory full-time schooling as imposed by national law ends or 15 years in any event' (Art 1). However, given that these are only minimum standards, this Directive leaves room for national law to impose more stringent rules. See P Watson, *European Social and Employment Law*, 2nd edn (Oxford, Oxford University Press, 2014) ch 18.

[25] Quite apart from that, restrictions on free movement can never be justified on purely economic grounds: Case 7/61 *Commission v Italy (Pork)*, ECLI:EU:C:1961:31, confirmed in numerous cases including Case C-254/98 *Schutzverband gegen unlauteren Wettbewerb v TK-Heimdienst Sass*, ECLI:EU:C:2000:12, para 33 and Case C-398/98 *Commission v Greece (Petroleum Products)*, ECLI:EU:C:2001:565, para 30. See P Oliver, 'When, if Ever, Can Restrictions on Free Movement be Justified on Economic Grounds?' (2016) 41 *EL Rev* 147 and W-H Roth, 'Economic Justifications and the Internal Market' in M Bulterman et al (eds), *Views of European Law from the Mountain* (Alphen aan den Rijn, Kluwer, 2009) 73. Consequently, measures falling under Art 34 cannot be justified by the manufacturer's failure to abide by the national minimum wage in the Member State of production.

[26] Case C-267/91 *Keck*, ECLI:EU:C:1993:905.

[27] Cases 177/82 *Van de Haar*, ECLI:EU:C:1984:144 and C-67/97 *Bluhme*, ECLI:EU:C:1998:584.

initial Mutual Recognition Regulation,[28] which laid down procedures relating to the application of certain national technical rules to products lawfully marketed in another Member State.

However, the Commission has produced a Guidance Document on the concept of 'lawfully marketed' goods in this Regulation.[29] The Commission takes as its starting-point Regulation 765/2008 of the European Parliament and the Council setting out the requirements for accreditation and market surveillance relating to the marketing of products.[30]

Although the latter Regulation is not directly in point, the Commission in its Guidance Document regards two of the definitions set out in Article 2(1) as being of assistance in this context. This provision defines 'making available on the market' to 'mean any supply of a product for distribution, consumption or use on the Community market in the course of a commercial activity, whether in return for payment or free of charge'. Furthermore, with rather questionable English, Article 2(1) defines 'placing on the market' to mean 'the first making available of a product on the Community market'. From these definitions, the Commission deduces that, for products subject to the Mutual Recognition Regulation, 'marketing' means

> any supply of a product for distribution, consumption or use in another Member State …, in the course of a commercial activity, whether in return for payment or free of charge.[31]

Still according to the Guidance Document, to be lawful the supply of the product must conform both to national legislation and to the General Safety Directive.[32] This Directive only lays down procedures for ensuring safety and rules of a very general nature; it does not apply where products are subject to specific requirements laid down by Union legislation. Consequently, it differs fundamentally from Union harmonisation legislation.

---

[28] Regulation (EC) No 764/2008 of the European Parliament and of the Council of 9 July 2008 laying down procedures relating to the application of certain national technical rules to products lawfully marketed in another Member State and repealing Decision No 3052/95/EC [2008] OJ L218/21. This Regulation was enacted to overcome the problems encountered by traders who found that the authorities of the Member States were slow to apply the MRP. See Barnard, *The Substantive Law of the EU* (n 3) esp 96 and 197–99; and S Weatherill in *Oliver* (n 18), paras 13.115 et seq.

[29] COM(2013)592 final. This and other relevant documents can be found on the Commission's website at https://ec.europa.eu/growth/single-market/goods/free-movement-sectors/mutual-recognition_en.

[30] Regulation (EC) No 765/2008 of the European Parliament and of the Council of 9 July 2008 setting out the requirements for accreditation and market surveillance relating to the marketing of products and repealing Regulation (EEC) No 339/93 [2008] OJ L218/30. In 2021, this Regulation will be amended and partially replaced by Regulation 2019/1020 [2019] OJ 169/1.

[31] Guidance Document (n 29) 5. The omitted words concern goods originating from the European Free Trade Association (EFTA) countries that are also party to the European Economic Area (EEA). Imports from those third countries are the subject of a separate chapter in this book by Georges Baur (see ch 9).

[32] See n 21.

With effect from 19 April 2020, the old Mutual Recognition Regulation (Regulation 764/2008) was replaced by Regulation 2019/515 of the European Parliament and the Council, which does contain a definition of 'lawfully marketed in another Member State'.[33] The definition of this term is set out in Article 3(1), which reads as follows:

> 'lawfully marketed in another Member State' means that goods or goods of that type comply with the relevant rules applicable in that Member State or are not subject to any such rules in that Member State, and are made available to end users in that Member State.

The words 'goods or goods of that type' are puzzling. Why does this definition not simply refer to 'the goods'? At all events, this provision is supplemented by Article 3(2) of Regulation 2019/515, which provides that 'making available on the market' means 'any supply of goods for distribution, consumption or use on the market within the territory of a Member State in the course of a commercial activity, whether in return for payment or free of charge'.

The language of the new Article 3(1) and (2) corresponds closely to the provisions of Regulation 765/2004, which have been quoted above. From a reading of the new Article 3(1) and (2) together it follows that a product is marketed in a Member State where it is 'made available to end users in that Member State' – even if the purchaser immediately transports them to a second Member State with a view to selling them there.

On a different note, it is striking that the Regulation does not specify what types of rule are 'relevant' for the purpose of Article 3(1). However, at the very least it is surely irrelevant whether goods have been sold in the 'other' Member State in breach of Sunday trading laws or rules requiring certain goods to be sold in specialised shops. For the purposes of the MRP, only the inherent characteristics of the product concerned appear to be relevant.

Manifestly, it will not suffice for goods to comply with the marketing rules laid down in the 'other' Member State; the goods must actually be marketed there. That is plain from the final limb of Article 3(1) ('and are made available to end users in that Member State') and from Article 3(2).

Needless to say, when applying Articles 34 and 36 TFEU themselves, the Court need not take into account the Commission's Guidance Document, which is not even binding. By the same token, the Court is not bound to apply Article 3(1) and (2) of Regulation 2019/515 by analogy to Articles 34 and 36 TFEU – although it might of course choose to do so.

---

[33] Regulation (EU) 2019/515 of the European Parliament and of the Council of 19 March 2019 on the mutual recognition of goods lawfully marketed in another Member State and repealing Regulation (EC) No 764/2008 [2019] OJ L91/1. Art 1(2) of the new Regulation spells out the link with Arts 34 and 36 TFEU in greater detail than the corresponding provision in the earlier Regulation. Art 1(2) reads: 'This Regulation lays down rules and procedures concerning the application by Member States of the principle of mutual recognition in individual cases in relation to goods which are subject to Article 34 TFEU and which are lawfully marketed in another Member State, having regard to Article 36 TFEU and the case-law of the Court of Justice of the European Union.'

## E.  Some Hypothetical Cases

At this juncture, it is helpful to consider the following range of possible scenarios:

(a)   Let us suppose that a widget is lawfully produced in France, then lawfully sold on the French market before reaching Germany.

In this case, the MRP clearly applies.

(b)   What if the same situation occurs, but the widget is never placed on the French market, although it complies with French marketing standards and is exported to Germany, its final destination?

Logically, the MRP must apply: as long as the goods meet French marketing standards, there is no reason why the goods should actually have been marketed in France. After all, the report of the facts in *Cassis de Dijon* itself does not reveal whether the goods were ever marketed in France before they reached Germany: they may well have been sold directly to Rewe or another company based there. However, this understanding of the MRP has never been confirmed by the Court, and it is not covered by Regulation 2019/515.

(c)   What if a widget is lawfully produced in France but does not meet French marketing standards, and is then exported directly to Germany?

If the MRP is really meant to apply to goods that are lawfully produced *or* marketed in 'another' Member State then clearly there is no problem. But this has not been clearly established in the case law.

The issue becomes more delicate where the goods have been produced in a Member State that exempts goods intended for export from its rules on production, especially if it also lays down stringent marketing rules for the same goods.

In that case, as indicated in section II.A, if the goods are produced in that Member State for export and are never marketed there, the standards laid down there for goods sold in that territory have effectively been circumvented, albeit with the support – some might say connivance – of that Member State. Accordingly, it is submitted that in these circumstances, the MRP should not be applicable.

At first sight, this position might appear to run counter to the judgment in *Schutzverband*;[34] but on closer examination that is not so. That case concerned vermouth produced in Italy. Had it been marketed there, it would have had to contain 16 per cent alcohol in accordance with Italian law. However, the Italian Decree-Law waived this rule with respect to vermouth intended for export, provided that the law of the country of destination was observed. The consignment concerned was exported directly to Germany – which required

[34] See n 13.

such drinks to comply with the marketing rules of the country of production. At the same time, German vermouth was not subject to any such rules at all. Accordingly, the Court found that the German measure fell foul of Article 34, since it discriminated against exports on its face. Surely, that conclusion must be correct: since Germany had no relevant marketing rules, the MRP had no bearing on the case. In any case, the approach I am proposing is perfectly compatible with this judgment.

(d)  Let us take the case of a widget that is produced in France but in breach of the relevant French production rules, and which does not meet French market-ing standards either. The widget is then lawfully placed on the Belgian market before reaching Germany, its final destination. Does the fact that this prod-uct has been lawfully marketed in Belgium cure the 'defects' that occurred in France?

In the light of the considerations set out in section II.A, it is submitted that the answer must be in the affirmative. Naturally, in these circumstances, French production and marketing standards do not come into the picture. Rather, Germany is in principle required to recognise the Belgian marketing standards.

(e)  Finally, what if the situation is the same as in case (d) above, but the goods are not marketed in Belgium (although they comply with Belgian marketing standards) or any other Member State before reaching their final destination in Germany?

In these circumstances, the product will not have been lawfully produced or marketed in any Member State before it arrives in Germany. Consequently, the MRP does not apply.

Readers might find all this somewhat laborious – all the more so because the Court has so rarely confronted these issues, in part because the national courts appear not to be concerned by them or are unwilling to raise them in preliminary references. However, this passage is the prelude to the proposal to reformulate the 'lawfully produced and marketed rule', which is set out in section IV of this chapter.

## III.  Goods Originating in Third Countries

### A.  General

Read literally, the wording of paragraph 14 of the ruling in *Cassis de Dijon* (quoted at the outset) excludes goods originating from third countries from the benefits of the MRP. However, that is not the end of the matter. For a start, it is quite likely that the Court simply did not have them in mind: in the instant case the product concerned had originated in a Member State. The same applies to its numerous progeny, in which the Court has repeated the phrase 'lawfully produced and marketed in a Member State'.[35] Moreover, as explained immediately below, two other considerations come into play.[36]

Only in 2016 was the Court called upon to confront this issue squarely. For that reason, after discussing the relevant provisions and the Commission's position, it is appropriate to follow the unusual course of considering the (very sparse) literature before examining the case law.

## B.  The Relevant Provisions

As is well known, Article 28(1) TFEU provides that the Union 'shall comprise a customs union which shall cover all trade in goods', while Article 28(2) states that Articles 30 and 34 to 37 'shall apply to products originating in Member States and to products coming from third countries which are in free circulation in Member States'. More specifically, Article 29 reads as follows:

> Products coming from a third country shall be considered to be in free circulation in a Member State if the import formalities have been complied with and any customs duties or charges having equivalent effect which are payable have been levied in that Member State, and if they have not benefited from a total or partial drawback of such duties or charges.

In its seminal judgment in *Donckerwolcke*, the Court stated:

> It appears from Article [28] that, as regards free circulation of goods within the Community, products entitled to 'free circulation' are definitively and wholly assimilated to products originating in Member States.

> The result of this assimilation is that the provisions of Article [34] concerning the elimination of quantitative restrictions and all measures having equivalent effect are applicable without distinction to products originating in the Community and to those which were put into free circulation in any one of the Member States, irrespective of the actual origin of the products.[37]

---

[35] Equally, in *Opinion 2/13* (n 5), the Court rejected the Agreement on the accession of the EU to the European Convention on Human Rights (ECHR) inter alia on the grounds that the mutual trust inherent in the MRP applies exclusively between the Member States because they all subscribe to the values enshrined in Art 2 TEU (n 6). Yet the EU has extended the entire Schengen *acquis* to Iceland, Liechtenstein, Norway and Switzerland on the basis of mutual trust; and it seems virtually inconceivable that, in taking this step, the Council acted unlawfully: C Ladenburger, 'The Principle of Mutual Trust in the Area of Freedom, Security and Justice' in Lenaerts et al (eds), *An Ever-Changing Union* (n 7), 163, 173.

[36] The status of goods originating in Iceland, Liechtenstein or Norway (which are parties to the Agreement establishing the EEA) or Turkey (which is in a customs union with the EU covering some goods) will not be considered here. Both are mentioned in pt 2.2 of the Commission's Communication of 2003 (n 15). In any case, as already mentioned, the EEA is the subject of Georges Baur's contribution to this volume (ch 9). Equally, Emilija Leinarte and Catherine Barnard's chapter in this book (ch 10) is devoted to goods covered by Free Trade Agreements with third countries.

[37] Case 41/76 *Donckerwolcke*, ECLI:EU:C:1976:182, paras 17–18, confirmed in Cases 125/88 *Nijman*, ECLI:EU:C:1989:401 and C-216/01 *Budějovický Budvar*, ECLI:EU:C:2003:618, para 95.

A particularly clear illustration of this principle is to be found in *Commission v Ireland*, where it was held that the defendant State had infringed what is now Article 34 by imposing an import licensing system for potatoes originating in Cyprus but in free circulation in the United Kingdom (UK).[38] At that time, the UK was in the EEC but Cyprus was not.[39]

For completeness, it should be mentioned that the EU's membership of the World Trade Organisation (WTO) may require the EU to grant such goods the benefit of the MRP. Lorand Bartels maintains that that is the case in certain circumstances.[40] This aspect cannot be considered in greater depth here.

## C. The Position of the Commission and the EU Legislator

In its Communication of 2003,[41] the Commission stated that the MRP applies to goods from third countries that are in free circulation in the EU.[42] It deduced this from what is now Article 28(2) and from the passage of the judgment in *Canal Satélite Digital* quoted in section II.A.[43] Similarly, in its Guidance Document on the concept of 'lawfully marketed' goods in the Mutual Recognition Regulation,[44] the Commission said that goods originating in a third country must be lawfully marketed in a Member State before they can benefit from free circulation.[45]

In keeping with these Commission documents, the two successive Mutual Recognition Regulations provide for mutual recognition of goods lawfully marketed in a Member State without regard to the place of production.[46] Consequently, they do not apply where goods have been lawfully produced in France and comply with French marketing standards but have never been placed on the market there before being exported to Germany, their final destination (case (b) in section II.E).[47]

---

[38] Case 288/83 *Commission v Ireland*, ECLI:EU:C:1985:251; see J Usher, 'The Single Market and Goods Imported from Third Countries' (1986) 6 *Yearbook of European Law* 159, 179. For a more recent example, see also Case C-291/09 *Guanieri v Vandevelde*, ECLI:EU:C:2011:217, para 14.

[39] By the time this volume appears, that situation will have been reversed.

[40] L Bartels, 'The Legality of the EU Mutual Recognition Clause under WTO Law' (2005) 8(3) *Journal of International Economic Law* 691. On this issue, see also L Ankersmit, 'What if Cassis de Dijon were Cassis du Québec? The Assimilation of Goods of Third Country Origin in the Internal Market' (2013) 50 *CML Rev* 1387, 1407–08.

[41] See n 15.

[42] Endnote 21 to the Communication.

[43] See n 14.

[44] See n 29.

[45] Guidance Document, ibid 6.

[46] Art 1(2) of Regulation 764/2008 (n 28) and Art 2(1) of Regulation 2019/515 (n 33).

[47] In that event, they will not have been lawfully 'marketed' in France according to the definition in Art 3(1) of Regulation 2019/515 (n 33), as they will not have been 'made available to end users' there.

## D. The Literature Prior to the Czech *Hallmarking* Case

The restrictive interpretation was propounded by Eric White in his seminal article published in 1989.[48] In his view, there is no need to construe Article 34 read with Article 28(2) as prohibiting the application of 'indistinctly applicable measures of the *Cassis de D*ijon kind to products imported from third countries via other Member States'.[49] Such an interpretation, he reasoned, would allow third country goods to enter the Union via the Member States with the most lax rules, and the goods from those Member States would not even gain any reciprocal advantage from the third countries concerned.

My own long-standing view is that, regardless of the position under in WTO law, Articles 28 and 29 TFEU require the EU to apply the MRP to goods originating in third countries;[50] and Piet Eeckhout's view is essentially the same.[51] In addition to the above-mentioned cases relating to those provisions, authority for that position may be found in *Co-Frutta*, a judgment relating to what is now Article 110 TFEU.[52] That provision prohibits internal taxation which discriminates against 'products of other Member States'. Nevertheless, on the basis of the articles just mentioned, the Court reached the conclusion that goods originating in third countries also benefit from Article 110, if they have been put into free circulation in another Member State.

Laurens Ankersmit shared this view, while also contending that a product originating in a third country need only be 'marketable' in a Member State (without necessarily being actually marketed there) before it arrives in the Member State of its final destination (eg Germany).[53] In other words, he maintained that the MRP applies even where the product is not actually marketed in any Member State before it reaches Germany.

## E. The Case Law

The ruling in *Nijman*[54] touched on the application of the MRP to third country goods without really addressing it. The accused in the main case had been charged

---

[48] E White, 'In Search of the Limits to Article 30 of the EEC Treaty' (1989) 26 *CML Rev* 235. For a very helpful summary of the views expressed by various authors, see R Schütze, *From International to Federal Market – the Changing Structure of European Law* (Oxford, Oxford University Press, 2017) 194ff.

[49] White, 'In Search of the Limits' (n 48) 263.

[50] See Enchelmaier (and Oliver et al) in *Oliver* (n 18) 233. In effect, this has been my position since 1982 (P Oliver, *Free Movement of Goods in the EEC* (London, European Law Centre, 1982) 78–79).

[51] P Eeckhout, *The European Internal Market and International Trade: a Legal Analysis* (Oxford, Clarendon Press, 1994) 272.

[52] Case 193/85 *Co-Frutta*, ECLI:EU:C:1987:210.

[53] Ankersmit, 'What if Cassis de Dijon were Cassis du Québec?' (n 40).

[54] *Nijman* (n 37).

with contravening Dutch legislation by selling in the Netherlands a plant protection product without obtaining an authorisation under that legislation. The product had been imported from Sweden, which was then a third country. Repeating the essence of its ruling in *Donckerwolcke*, the Court stated that what are now Articles 34 and 36 'apply without distinction to products originating in the Community and to those admitted into free circulation in any of the Member States, whatever the real origin of such products'.[55] From this the Court drew the following conclusion:

> In the present case, the prohibition, enforced by penalties in criminal law, of selling, storing or using any plant-protection product not authorised by a national law is capable of affecting imports from other Member States where the same product is admitted wholly or in part and thus of constituting a barrier to intra-Community trade. Such rules therefore constitute a measure having an effect equivalent to a quantitative restriction.[56]

This ruling is puzzling, since both the Court and the Advocate General, who reached the same conclusion, failed to set out any reasoning to support the statements quoted here.

In contrast, in *Commission v France (Foie Gras)*, Advocate General La Pergola stated in a footnote that goods from third countries cannot benefit from the MRP.[57] However, this assertion is not supported by any reasoning either.

Not until 2016 did the Court fully engage with this issue, in *Commission v Czech Republic (Hallmarking)*.[58] The Czech authorities had refused to recognise hallmarks stamped by WaarborgHolland, an independent assay office based in the Netherlands and accredited there, whether the hallmarking was carried out in that Member State or in third countries (China and Thailand). That was despite the fact that all those hallmarks were recognised in the Netherlands and the items containing certain precious metals bearing them had been put into free circulation in the EU. This meant that, before those artefacts could be sold in the Czech Republic as being authentic, they had to be stamped with an additional, Czech hallmark. Hallmarking is one of the sectors for which the EU has not adopted any harmonising legislation.

The Commission endorsed Ankersmit's particularly liberal approach. Indeed, the Commission argued that, once they had been put into free circulation, goods hallmarked by WaarborgHolland in a third country were in precisely the same situation as those hallmarked by the same organisation in the Netherlands. In line with Advocate General Campos Sanchez-Bordona's Opinion, the Grand Chamber found that the defendant had infringed Article 34 TFEU, while rejecting this part of the Commission's case.

---

[55] ibid para 11.
[56] ibid para 12.
[57] *Foie Gras* (n 12). The statement in question is to be found in fn 26 to the Opinion.
[58] *Hallmarking* (n 18); see the case note by Anne-Lise Sibony in (2017) *Revue Trimestrielle de Droit européen* 831.

After referring to Article 28(2) and its judgment in *Donckerwolcke*, the Court then confirmed other rulings to the effect that goods put into free circulation in the Union could not necessarily be placed on the market of any Member State.[59] The Court deduced from this that, contrary to the Commission's contention, it did not suffice for the goods to comply with the hallmarking rules in a Member State before they were imported into the Czech Republic: for the MRP to apply, those goods must actually have been placed on the market in the first Member State.[60] That proposition seems logical, as explained in section II.F (case (d)).

Finally, the Court found that, with regard to artefacts that fulfilled all these conditions, the refusal of the Czech authorities to recognise the hallmarking carried out in third countries was not justified.[61]

The ruling in the Czech *Hallmarking* case deserves a warm welcome, but inevitably it did not and could not address all the hypothetical situations that might arise. We shall now direct our attention to those situations.

## F.  Some Hypothetical Cases

At this juncture, it is necessary to consider a range of possible circumstances that could arise in relation to a widget originating in Uruguay:

(a)   What if a widget is directly imported from Uruguay into Germany without being put into free circulation in another Member State first?

In these circumstances, Articles 34 to 36 are manifestly not engaged.

(b)   What if the same widget has been put into free circulation in France and lawfully sold on the French market in compliance with domestic law before reaching Germany?

In this case, the MRP applies, as the Czech *Hallmarking* case shows.

(c)   What if the widget from Uruguay is put into free circulation in France but not marketed there, and is then lawfully marketed in Belgium before reaching Germany?

In these circumstances, the MRP also applies.[62]

---

[59] *Hallmarking* (n 18) para 38, referring to Cases C-296/00 *Expo Casa Manta*, ECLI:EU:C:2002:316, paras 31–32 and C-154/04 *Alliance for Natural Health*, ECLI:EU:C:2005:449, para 95.

[60] *Hallmarking* (n 18) para 39.

[61] ibid paras 44–68. In fact, the Court went further, rejecting the Czech Republic's contention that it was unable to distinguish between those two categories of goods on the one hand and on the other those that had been hallmarked by WaarborgHolland in a third country and put into free circulation in the EU but *not* lawfully marketed in another Member State. Since the defendant could have required imports to be accompanied by certificates specifying their precise status, the Court found that its blanket ban was contrary to the principle of proportionality and therefore unjustified in its entirety. However, that is not relevant here.

[62] See *Hallmarking* (n 18) para 39.

(d)   Let us imagine that the Uruguayan widget is put into free circulation in France but is never lawfully marketed there or in any other Member State before it reaches Germany (its final destination).

In that event, the MRP does not apply, even if it complies with the marketing requirements of another Member State.[63] This is entirely logical, since it corresponds to case (e) in section II.E. There is no reason why goods that have neither been lawfully produced nor lawfully marketed in a Member State should be more favourably treated if they originate in a third country rather than within the EU. That would be reverse discrimination.

# IV.  A Proposed Solution to the Problems Discussed in Sections II and III

In the light of the considerations set out in sections II and III, it is surely time to replace the term 'lawfully produced and marketed in a Member State' with language that corresponds to the realities. Indeed, since the ruling in the Czech *Hallmarking* case, this test has become unsustainable. Three points are of note here:

(a)   With the ruling in *Commission v Czech Republic* the term 'lawfully produced and marketed in a Member State' has become manifestly obsolete. By definition, third country goods are not produced in a Member State; and, as already mentioned, to require goods originating in the Union to meet that test when those originating outside it need only be lawfully marketed in a Member State would amount to reverse discrimination.
(b)   As explained above in section II.E (case (b)), logic suggests that the MRP must apply where a product is produced in France but is never placed on the French market, even though it complies with French marketing standards and is exported directly to Germany.
(c)   The phrase 'lawfully produced *or* marketed in a Member State' does not fit the bill, as it would allow goods produced in a Member State to benefit from the MRP even if that Member State exempts goods intended for export from its national rules on production and the goods are never marketed there.[64]

In view of the third consideration, it cannot be right to replace the term 'lawfully produced and marketed in a Member State' with 'lawfully produced *or* marketed in a Member State'. Instead, I would propose wording along the following lines: 'produced in a Member State in accordance with its marketing rules or lawfully marketed in a Member State'.

---

[63] Judgment in *Hallmarking* case (n 18) para 39; see also para 50, point (b) of the AG's Opinion in the same case.
[64] See section II.A.

# V.  Where Mutual Recognition Never Applies

So far we have focused on the classic language of 'lawfully produced and marketed'; we turn now to a situation where the MRP never applies, namely public morality.

*Dynamic Medien*[65] concerned Japanese cartoons in DVD or video cassette format that had been imported into the UK before being shipped to Germany. The British authorities classified these films as suitable for viewers aged 15 years and over. The Court accepted that such restrictions might be justified for the protection of young people, an objective that is 'linked to public morality and public policy';[66] but it held that it was for the national court to decide whether the national rules in issue were designed to protect children against information and materials injurious to their well-being.

For present purposes, the Court's most important finding was that, despite the British measure, Germany was entitled to ban the sale of the DVDs and video cassettes by mail order unless and until its authorities had authorised the films concerned. Crucially, the Court did not suggest that the German authorities were required even to take cognisance of the British measure. However, it did state (paraphrasing somewhat) that Member States might not have a shared conception of the level of protection required,[67] and that each Member State therefore enjoyed a 'definite margin of discretion'.[68] While the word 'definite' is puzzling, the reality is that the Court showed a higher degree of deference to the national decision-maker than is usually the case.[69] Questions of public morality are essentially subjective, and therefore do not lend themselves to the MRP.

While it would clearly have been preferable for the Court to acknowledge and provide reasoning for its departure from the MRP, the result is entirely logical in view of the inherently subjective nature of public morality. Given the impossibility of establishing an objective yardstick in this area, the Court in effect acknowledged that mutual recognition has no role to play there.

However, it by no means follows that the Member States enjoy unbridled powers in this regard: the Court was at pains to stress that their authorities must exercise their discretion within the bounds set by the confines of the recognised

---

[65] Case C-244/06 *Dynamic Medien*, ECLI:EU:C:2008:85.

[66] ibid para 36. Neither the AG nor the Court alluded to the fact that the DVDs and video cassettes originated in a third country, namely Japan.

[67] ibid para 44, where the Court referred to, and applied by analogy, para 37 of its judgment in Case C-36/02 *Omega Spielhallen v Bonn*, ECLI:EU:C:2004:614. That case concerned a 'game' involving simulated homicide, committed by participants' 'shooting' one another with laser guns. The question before the Court was whether a ban on this economic activity, which it regarded as the provision of services enshrined in what is now Art 56 TFEU, could be justified on the grounds of the protection of human dignity in accordance with Art 1 of the *Grundgesetz* (German Constitution). The Court found that such a ban was justified under the public policy exception 'by reason the fact that that activity is an affront to human dignity' (para 41).

[68] *Dynamic Medien* (n 65) para 44.

[69] D Doukas, 'Morality, Free Movement and Judicial Restraint at the European Court of Justice' in P Koutrakos, N Nic Shuibhne and P Syrpis, *Exceptions from EU Free Movement Law* (Oxford, Hart Publishing, 2016) 143, 161.

rules of EU law.[70] If need be, the Court would no doubt have regard to the case law of its counterpart in Strasbourg, which has far greater experience of deciding cases involving public morality.[71]

In relation to services and establishment, the Court followed the same approach in *Stoß*,[72] which concerned games of chance, another sector that has not been subject to EU harmonisation. In a preliminary ruling, the Court held that the holder of a gambling licence in one Member State did not automatically enjoy the right to carry on the same economic activity in another Member State.

The Court confirmed its earlier case law to the effect that

> moral, religious or cultural factors, as well as the morally and financially harmful consequences for the individual and for society associated with betting and gaming, may serve to justify a margin of discretion for the national authorities, sufficient to enable them to determine, in accordance with their own scale of values, what is required in order to ensure consumer protection and the preservation of public order ...[73]

The Court then added:

> Having regard to that margin of discretion and the absence of any Community harmonisation in the matter, a duty mutually to recognise authorisations issued by the various Member States cannot exist having regard to the current state of EU law.[74]

The fact that – unlike in *Dynamic Medien* – the Court acknowledged that it was departing from the MRP deserves a warm welcome. However, if taken at face value, the sentence just quoted is hard to accept: the decision not to apply the MRP cannot be explained by the absence of harmonisation at EU level since, as explained in section II.B, in relation to the free movement provisions of the Treaty the MRP only comes into play in these circumstances.[75] Surely, the true reason can only be that the margin of discretion is particularly wide where public morality (sometimes characterised by the Court as public policy)[76] is in issue.

Another case that deserves a mention here is *Commission v Poland*.[77] What initially appeared to be a run-of-the-mill case on the failure to implement a Directive came close to giving rise to a ruling of major constitutional importance.

---

[70] *Dynamic Medien* (n 65) paras 45 *et seq.*

[71] eg *Handyside v United Kingdom* App no 5493/72 (ECtHR, 7 December 1976), finding the ban on the *Little Red Schoolbook* for obscenity contrary to Art 10 ECHR; *Otto-Preminger Institute v Austria* App no 13470/87 (ECtHR, 20 September 1994), upholding the seizure of a film offensive to Catholics; and *Murphy v Ireland* App no 44179/98 (ECtHR, 10 July 2003), upholding the ban on religious advertising on television.

[72] Case C-316/07 *Stoß*, ECLI:EU:C:2010:504.

[73] ibid para 76, to which para 111 refers.

[74] ibid para 112. See also Case C-347/09 *Dickinger*, ECLI:EU:C:2011:582, para 96.

[75] See G Anagnostaras, 'Les Jeux sont Faits? Mutual Recognition and the Specificities of Online Gambling' (2012) 37 *EL Rev* 191, 194.

[76] As noticed above, in *Omega* (n 67) the Court relied on the public policy exception alone, whereas in *Dynamic Medien* it referred to both exceptions. Arguably, public morality is the more appropriate exception, but nothing turns on this. Wisely, the Court has generally refrained from establishing rigid distinctions between the various grounds of justification.

[77] Case C-165/08 *Commission v Poland*, ECLI:EU:C:2009:473.

The Commission's charge was that Poland prohibited certain genetically modified organisms (GMOs) in breach of an EU Directive. Rather than dispute this charge, Poland claimed that its ban was justified on ethical or religious grounds. For the Court to accept that a Member State could refuse to implement or apply EU legislation on such grounds would have been unprecedented. In the event, this awkward argument was rejected on the basis that Poland had failed to substantiate it.[78]

Von Bogdandy and Schill point out that it would have been otherwise if the values invoked by Poland had been part of its national identity, which the Union is required to respect in accordance with Article 4(2) TEU – provided that 'non-compliance with the EU Directive was proportionate in view of the conflicting principles'.[79] Those authors appear to acknowledge that if Poland had argued that (i) the teachings of the Catholic Church were part of its national identity and (ii) GMOs were incompatible with those teachings, no doubt it would still have had to substantiate those propositions – which in relation to the second one would be no more self-evident than it was in the case discussed here. While Article 4(2) has the potential to open a substantial breach in the uniformity of Union law, the Court has been robust in scrutinising arguments based on that provision.

## VI.  Where Mutual Trust Breaks Down

It is axiomatic that mutual recognition is founded on mutual trust.[80] Where that trust breaks down, mutual recognition cannot apply. As the reader will be aware, the Court has recently had to grapple with several major cases relating to the Council Framework Decision on the European arrest warrant,[81] where the executing judicial authority expressed grave doubts as to whether the Member State seeking the extradition of an individual ('the issuing Member State') respected the conditions laid down in that Decision and the Charter of Fundamental Rights. For instance, in *Aranyosi* the Court interpreted the relevant provisions to mean that

> where there is objective, reliable, specific and properly updated evidence with respect to detention conditions in the issuing Member State that demonstrates that there are deficiencies, which may be systemic or generalised, or which may affect certain groups of people, or which may affect certain places of detention, the executing judicial authority must determine, specifically and precisely, whether there are substantial grounds to believe that the individual concerned by a European arrest warrant, issued for the

---

[78] ibid para 52.

[79] A von Bogdandy and S Schill, 'Overcoming Absolute Primacy: Respect for National Identity under the Lisbon Treaty' (2011) 48 *CML Rev* 1417, 1445.

[80] Thus in *Opinion 2/13* (n 5) the Court used the phrase 'mutual trust' rather than 'mutual recognition' (eg in para 168, quoted in the text accompanying n 6). See also the article on the Opinion by President Lenaerts (n 6).

[81] Decision 2002/584/JHA [2002] OJ L190/1, as amended.

purposes of conducting a criminal prosecution or executing a custodial sentence, will be exposed, because of the conditions for his detention in the issuing Member State, to a real risk of inhuman or degrading treatment, within the meaning of Article 4 of the Charter, in the event of his surrender to that Member State.[82]

Furthermore, the Court held that the executing judicial authority was required to investigate this evidence and, if the existence of the risk could not be discounted within a reasonable time, to decline to execute the warrant.[83]

Precisely the same situation could arise in relation to free movement. For instance, let us suppose that Member State A's rules relating to the marketing of widgets are equivalent to those of Member State B, but that Member State A is turning a blind eye to – or is even complicit in – systemic breaches of its own rules. In these circumstances, Member State B must be in a position to withhold recognition of the rules of Member State A, if there is strong evidence that the goods concerned are likely to be affected by this deficiency. In that event, Member State B must be entitled to take steps that would otherwise be unlawful, such as carrying out controls on the widgets to ensure that they do indeed comply with Member State A's norms. This could of course have deleterious consequences for the latter's exports.

Admittedly, while the cases concerning the European Arrest Warrant necessarily involve the courts of both Member States, that would not usually be the case with regard to the free movement of goods: other national authorities would probably be involved instead. However, nothing turns on this, as administrative bodies are just as qualified as courts to withhold mutual recognition.

# VII.  Conclusion

What is surprising is that such a basic question as the precise meaning of 'lawfully produced and marketed in one of the Member States' has scarcely been addressed in the case law – let alone elucidated – after 40 years. With hindsight, it is plain that this phrase never meant what is said; and since the ruling in *Commission v Czech Republic* it has even become unsustainable. Accordingly, a thorough reappraisal and a search for a new form of words that reflects the realities is overdue. For the reasons set out in section IV, I would propose the following: 'produced in a Member State in accordance with its marketing rules or lawfully marketed in a Member State'.

---

[82] Case C-404/15 PPU *Aranyosi*, ECLI:EU:C:2016:198, para 104, noted by G Anagnostaras, 'Mutual confidence is not blind trust! Fundamental rights protection and the execution of the European Arrest Warrant: *Aranyosi* and *Caldararu*' (2016) 53 *CML Rev* 1675; see also Case C-216/18 PPU *LM*, ECLI:EU:C:2018:586. Similarly, with respect to asylum, see Case C-297/17 *Bashar Ibrahim*, ECLI:EU:C:2019:219. See also Ladenburger, 'The Principle of Mutual Trust' (n 35).
[83] *Aranyosi* (n 83).

Supposing that my assessment of the situation is correct, it follows that there is an unfortunate gap in the Mutual Recognition Regulation: it does not apply where a widget has been lawfully produced in France and complies with French marketing standards but is never placed on the market there before being exported to Germany, its final destination (case (b) in section II.E). It may well be that in *Cassis de Dijon* itself the goods were never marketed in France before being sold to Rewe or another buyer based in Germany, which makes this gap in the Regulation all the more poignant.

The fact that other issues have begun to emerge in the meantime is less surprising. The issue discussed in section V has already arisen, while the problem explored in section VI is likely to arise in the near future. And what will the next 40 years bring?

# 9

## Mutual Recognition and EFTA

GEORGES BAUR

## I. Introduction

The decision in *Cassis de Dijon*[1] has had a profound effect on the advent of the EU's single market. But has the effect spilled over to the EU's closest neighbour, namely, to Member States of the European Free Trade Association (EFTA) – Iceland, Liechtenstein, Norway and Switzerland? These four States are, now next to the United Kingdom (UK), economically and politically the EU's closest partners. They participate in, or have at least partial access to, the EU's internal market.[2] Hence, the EFTA States have also been influenced by EU law, both legislation and jurisprudence.

While mutual recognition has gained a lot of academic attention in the EU, its application in the context of the EFTA States has not attracted much interest. Either it is simply seen as a 'given', or, in the case of Switzerland, scholarship concentrates on the specific Swiss situation.

This chapter seeks to argue that the *Cassis de Dijon* story does not stop at the EU's borders. It has had a significant effect in all States of the European Economic Area (EEA), including the three participating EFTA States, which may not be surprising given their level of integration with the EU. More surprising is the dramatic effect of the *Cassis* ruling in Switzerland,[3] internally, with the EU and in respect of external trade more generally. Yet so far little EU attention has been paid to this story. This lack of interest coincides with the ignorance of other models of European integration, such as EFTA.

---

[1] Case 120/78 *Rewe-Zentral AG v Bundesmonopolverwaltung für Branntwein (Cassis de Dijon)*, ECLI:EU:C:1979:42. See also the Communication from the Commission concerning the consequences of the judgment given by the Court of Justice on 20 February 1979 in case 120/78 ('Cassis de Dijon') [1980] OJ C256/2.

[2] G Baur, 'Privileged partnerships – The partner countries' (institutional) perspectives' in S Gstöhl and D Phinnemore (eds), *The Proliferation of Privileged Partnerships between the European Union and its Neighbours* (London, Routledge, 2020) 23, 24–25.

[3] Acknowledged in the UK Internal Market White Paper, available at https://assets.publishing.service. gov.uk/government/uploads/system/uploads/attachment_data/file/901225/uk-internal-market-white-paper.pdf, 99–100.

This contribution will first look at what EFTA is and how its Member States relate to the EU's internal market legislation and jurisprudence. Then it will look at how mutual recognition and the *Cassis de Dijon* principle are respectively applied, if at all. The position of Switzerland, given its special form of association with the EU's internal market with regard to the free movement of goods, and indeed the partial lack of a link with the EU regarding other freedoms, will be of particular interest in this context. We will, however, focus on the free movement of goods and only consider the other freedoms occasionally. The chapter will conclude with a set of final observations.

## II. The European Free Trade Association

EFTA is an intergovernmental organisation founded in 1960 by those Western European countries that did not share the belief of other Western European countries in an economic community, with a customs union, that would gradually evolve into a political community, or, as it happened, Union.[4] These countries had unsuccessfully advocated a large Western European free trade area prior to the inception of the European Economic Community (EEC) in 1957.[5] They still preferred to form a free trade zone among themselves, without surrendering much of their sovereignty or adopting the aim of deepening political integration.[6] The signatories to the EFTA Convention[7] were Austria, Denmark, Norway, Portugal, Sweden, Switzerland and the UK. Finland joined later as an associate member, a special status that was necessary to enable it to accommodate its membership with the EU with its policies to the then Soviet Union.[8] Iceland joined in 1970, and Liechtenstein, which had been covered from the beginning through a protocol due to its regional union with Switzerland, formally joined in its own right in 1991. There were also successive withdrawals from EFTA by Denmark and the UK on 1 January 1973; Portugal on 1 January 1986; and Austria, Finland and Sweden on 1 January 1995. These countries all joined what became the EU.

---

[4] See, eg, V Curzon-Price, The essentials of Economic Integration (Basingstoke, Macmillan, 1974) 31, describing the sceptical attitude of the UK in view of the 'plans for a comprehensive customs union including not only industrial trade, but also agricultural production and a host of other common transport, social and services policies'.

[5] See B Hurni, 'The failure to establish the large free trade area' in P du Bois and B Hurni (eds), *L'AELE d'hier à demain/EFTA from Yesterday to Tomorrow* (Geneva, EFTA, 1987) 27.

[6] See generally L Rye, 'Integration from the outside' in HA Ikonomou, A Andry and R Byberg (eds), *European Enlargement across Rounds and Beyond Borders* (Abingdon, Routledge, 2017) 194.

[7] Convention Establishing the European Free Trade Association signed in Stockholm on 4 January 1960 ('Stockholm Convention').

[8] Finland had managed, with difficulty and bravery, to remain independent after 1945, but at the price of not daring to antagonise the Soviet Union. On the one hand, it thus had to remain neutral, in a sense that fully joining EFTA was difficult in the light of the UK's being its driving force and at the same time one of the Soviet Union's major antagonists; see G Baur, *The European Free Trade Association* (Cambridge, Intersentia, 2020) 66.

Since its foundation EFTA has had two major aims: first, the introduction of free trade of industrial goods and several processed agricultural and fisheries products between its Member States; and, second, the creation of a free trade area comprising both the seven members of EFTA and the six (now 27) EEC Member States. Later, a third aim was added, namely concluding free trade agreements (FTAs) with third parties other than the EU.

The EFTA States entered a new era altogether when they signed, in 1992, the Agreement on the EEA. By signing that, the EFTA States were effectively to join the European Community's (EC) internal market and to be treated with regard to it as if they were EC Member States.[9] Switzerland, however, did not ratify the EEA Agreement. After some more years of negotiations, the EU and Switzerland agreed on essentially two sets of 'Bilateral [sectoral] Agreements' to gain access to the internal market, at least in some important areas.[10]

# A. Free Trade Areas

Achieving the first aim mentioned in the EFTA Convention meant establishing a free trade area among the EFTA States, while the second aim meant extending that free trade area to the then EEC, establishing free trade between the EFTA States and the EU. We will deal with each in turn.

## i. *The Free Trade Area between the EFTA States*

The original purpose of establishing a free trade zone between its Members is still the basic aim of the EFTA Convention. Initially, the objectives were:

(a) the promotion of continued and balanced strengthening of trade and economic relations;
(b) free trade in goods.

The aim of establishing a free trade area between the EFTA States themselves was achieved – with the exception of Portugal, which benefited from a certain 'development bonus' – by 31 December 1966, when all tariffs were lowered to zero.

In the wake of the conclusion of the first batch of Bilateral Agreements between the EU and Switzerland in 1999, which gave the latter certain amount of access to the EU's internal market, the four EFTA States agreed to revise the EFTA Convention[11] so as to achieve a sufficient basis to also mutually grant one another the rights conferred to the EU by the EEA Agreement and the Bilateral Agreements respectively. The EFTA Convention's objectives, which essentially consisted in

---

[9] See section III.A.
[10] See section III.B.
[11] The revised EFTA Convention ('Vaduz Convention') was signed on 21 June 2001 and entered into force on 1 June 2002.

establishing free trade in goods, were thus supplemented by the following additional objectives:

(c)   the progressive liberalisation of the free movement of persons;
(d)   the progressive liberalisation of trade in services, and of investment;
(e)   fair conditions of competition affecting trade between the Member States;
(f)   the deepening of the public procurement markets of the Member States; and
(g)   appropriate protection of intellectual property rights.

In practice, the four EFTA countries integrate internal market legislation autonomously into the annexes to the EFTA Convention, making EFTA law vastly similar to EU law – or EEA law for that matter – as far as it is applicable. EFTA thus becomes a 'free trade area with internal market elements'.[12] Therefore, this can be seen as a triangle of mutual rights and duties between (i) the EU and the EEA EFTA States, (ii) the EU and Switzerland, and (iii) Switzerland and the three other EFTA States, Iceland, Liechtenstein and Norway.

As the Bilateral Agreements between the EU and Switzerland grant – compared to the EEA – the lowest degree of mutual rights, this was agreed to be the common denominator for liberalisation among the four EFTA countries. Take the free movement of persons as an example: with regard to that freedom, Iceland, Liechtenstein and Norway have essentially the same level of integration as the EU, especially given the incorporation of the so-called 'Union Citizenship Directive'[13] into the EEA Agreement, as amended according to the scope of that Agreement.[14] This Directive has not yet, however, been made part of the Agreement on the Free Movement of Persons (AFMP) between the EU and Switzerland. It has therefore not been incorporated into the EFTA Convention either.

## ii. *The Free Trade Agreements between the EEC States and the EFTA States*

With the accession of Denmark, Ireland and the UK to the (then) EEC, links also became closer between the EEC and the remaining EFTA countries (Austria, Finland, Iceland, Norway, Portugal, Sweden and Switzerland with Liechtenstein).

---

[12] See Baur, *The European Free Trade Association* (n 8) 8, 78.

[13] European Parliament and Council Directive (EC) 2004/38 of 29 April 2004 on the right of citizens of the Union and their family members to move and reside freely within the territory of the Member States amending Regulation (EEC) No 1612/68 and repealing Directives 64/221/EEC, 68/360/EEC, 72/194/EEC, 73/148/EEC, 75/34/EEC, 75/35/EEC, 90/364/EEC, 90/365/EEC and 93/96/EEC [2004] OJ L158/77.

[14] Decision of the EEA Joint Committee No 158/2007 of 7 December 2007 amending Annex V (Free movement of workers) and Annex VIII (Right of establishment) to the EEA Agreement, [2004] OJ L 158/77, 'whereas … (8) The concept of 'Union Citizenship' is not included in the Agreement. (9) Immigration policy is not part of the Agreement. (10) The Agreement does not apply to third country nationals. Family members within the meaning of the Directive having third country nationality shall nevertheless enjoy certain derived rights such as those foreseen in Articles 12(2), 13(2) and 18 when entering or moving to the host country.'

The EU-Swiss FTA is the last of a series of standardised FTAs the (then) EEC had concluded in 1972 and 1973 with each of those EFTA States that, unlike the UK and Denmark, had not chosen to join the EEC or, as in the case of Norway, could not do so because of a negative referendum on EEC membership. Interestingly, it was the UK that wanted the EEC to negotiate these FTAs, in order to maintain its trade relations with its former EFTA partners upon joining the EEC.

The main objective of the EEC-EFTA FTAs was the dismantling of tariff barriers. On 1 July 1977, after a transitional period of four and a half years, the last tariff barriers, except for certain sensitive products, between the (by then) EC and the EFTA states had been removed. And as from 1 January 1984, the last remaining tariffs were abolished. By that time, a large Western European free trade area ('internal trading area'), with a population of over 300 million people and encompassing 17 countries, had been created.[15] The 'large Western European free trade area' came into being 27 years after it had initially failed.

A second objective of the EEC-EFTA FTAs was the abolition of quantitative restrictions (ie quotas) that occurred in bilateral trade when the agreements entered into force. Some EFTA countries did, however, retain a small number of quantitative restrictions.

Apart from the agreement with Iceland, where tariff concessions were granted for certain fish products, no liberalisation of primary agricultural trade was provided for in the FTAs.

Since the free trade zone was not a customs union, it was necessary to establish rules to define clearly which goods were eligible for duty-free treatment (rules of origin).[16] By this, goods could be prevented from entering the free trade area through the country with the lowest customs tariff.

An FTA cannot be a surrogate for trade in goods that otherwise would constitute free movement of goods as, for example, in the EEA Agreement. The FTA is an international law agreement that clearly falls outside of the scope of an association agreement as mentioned in Article 217 of the Treaty on the Functioning of the European Union (TFEU). Rather it is a trade agreement in accordance with Article 207 TFEU.

As a consequence, there is no direct effect of EU law or corresponding interpretation of the case law of the Court of Justice in the EFTA States. This was made clear through jurisprudence in some of the EFTA States. In contrast to the EU's position, which foresees the direct effect of FTAs,[17] the direct effect of the FTAs' provisions was mostly denied by national courts of the EFTA States. This was the case even in Switzerland and Austria, which have a monistic international law system and a generally international law-friendly attitude. Sticking

---

[15] N Faustenhammer, 'Introduction' in HG Koppensteiner (ed), *Rechtsfragen der Freihandelsabkommen der Europäischen Wirtschaftsgemeinschaft mit den EFTA-Staaten* (Vienna, Orac, 1987) 1, 13.

[16] Put simply, in order to assess whether goods qualify for tariff waivers or reductions, and also whether these can be imported quota-free, it has to be assessed where these goods originate.

[17] Case 104/81 *Hauptzollamt Mainz v CA Kupferberg & Cie KG aA*, ECLI:EU:C:1982:362.

with Switzerland, the case *Stanley Adams*[18] was an important example: the Swiss Federal Court said that an individual who had 'blown the whistle' on his employer for illicit business practices, could not rely on Article 23 FTA (competition and state aid) because it did not lay down concrete duties for private parties. It only stated what practices were not compatible with the provisions of the FTA, without prohibiting these. Another such case, clearly deviating from the Court of Justice's practice, was *OMO*:[19] the Court of Justice allows the holder of an intellectual property right (eg a trademark) to block the placing of the product on the market by a competitor, but only for so long as the trademark owner has not placed the product on the relevant market (here, the EU) for the first time. However, in *OMO*, the Swiss Federal Tribunal refused to apply the same approach in the context of the FTA: Articles 13 (quantitative restrictions on imports) and 22 (principle of sincere cooperation) FTA were subject to an autonomous interpretation. The Swiss court held that there was nothing that would allow for a corresponding application of the Court of Justice's jurisprudence, despite the same or similar wording. Hence, the trademark owner could forbid parallel imports at all times. There were more cases confirming that view.

The Court of Justice retaliated in its famous landmark decision *Polydor*,[20] a case concerning the importation into the UK of gramophone records from Portugal. The Court of Justice held that despite 'the similarity between the terms of Articles 14(2) and 23 of the FTA – here between the EEC and Portugal – on the one hand and those of Articles 30 and 36 of the EEC Treaty on the other,' this was 'not a sufficient reason for transposing to the Agreement the [Court of Justice's] aforementioned case law.'[21] It saw such a distinction as being necessary because the scope of that case law had to be determined in the light of 'the [Union's] objectives and activities', that is merging 'national markets into a internal market having the characteristics of a domestic market'.[22] This was not so with the FTA, however, which has a different objective, namely to establish a free trade area and to eliminate all obstacles to the Member States' trade in accordance with GATT rules.[23] This argument was taken up by the Swiss Federal Court again in its decision in *Physiogel*.[24] The case was about imported products that were advertised as having a healing effect. These products were not registered as medicinal products, however, and were therefore considered to be cosmetics. For cosmetics, though, promotions of any kind that would indicate healing, soothing or preventative effects were prohibited. Promotions such as 'in collaboration with dermatologists', 'for itchy skin prone to allergies' or 'for the care of neurodermatitis, diabetes, psoriasis'

[18] BGE/ATF 104 IV 175.
[19] BGE/ATF 105 II 49.
[20] Case 270/80 *Polydor Limited and RSO Records Inc v Harlequin Records Shops Limited and Simons Records Limited*, ECLI:EU:C:1982:43.
[21] ibid para 15.
[22] ibid para 18.
[23] ibid para 10.
[24] Swiss Federal Court, 6 September 2006, 2A.593/2005.

contradicted the provisions of food legislation. Hence, imports were forbidden by the competent administrative body and ultimately confirmed by the Swiss Federal Court. The latter reverted to the argument that Article 13 FTA, although essentially identical in wording with Article 34 TFEU, could not be interpreted in the same way, as the objectives of the two treaties were different. Furthermore, Switzerland had not agreed to directly apply the *Cassis de Dijon* principle, nor was there (at the time) anything in internal legislation to that effect.[25] This example is to show that as a – probably unintended – consequence[26] of the Swiss Federal Court's rather rigid interpretation of the FTA, it could not be used as a basis to apply the *Cassis de Dijon* principle. Had the Swiss Federal Court set the course of jurisprudence in another direction at the time, that is in the same way as the Court of Justice later did in *Kupferberg*,[27] which was absolutely possible, the FTA might well have been a sufficient basis for applying the *Cassis de Dijon* principle between the EU and Switzerland as well.

Although all four EFTA States are now linked to the EU by either the EEA Agreement or the Swiss-EU Bilateral Agreements, the EEC-EFTA FTAs are still partly in force. Mainly for Iceland and Norway, provisions on imports of fish and fisheries products into the EU are laid down in additional protocols to the respective FTA with the EU. These protocols are re-opened regularly when importation quotas are raised as a trade-off for an increase in payments into the Financial Mechanisms (cohesion funds of the EEA EFTA States and of Norway 'bilaterally') following EEA Enlargement. The EEC-Switzerland FTA still provides the legal basis for trade in goods between Switzerland and the EU. And the Agreement between the EU and Switzerland on mutual recognition in relation to conformity assessment (Mutual Recognition Agreement (MRA)[28]), one of the Bilateral Agreements of the first package, also refers to the EEC-Switzerland FTA. The picture is thus more than complex.

# III. The Relationship of the EFTA States with the EU and in Particular its Internal Market

Section IV will look at mutual recognition and *Cassis de Dijon* in the context of the EEA and of the Swiss-EU relationship respectively. Before that, this section will

---

[25] N Diebold and M Ludin, 'Das *Cassis de Dijon*-Prinzip in Praxis und Politik' in *Schweizerisches Jahrbuch für Europarecht/Annuaire Suisse de droit européen 2016/2017* (Bern, Stämpfli, 2017) 373.

[26] Unintended consequence is an important concept of historical institutionalism. It tries to explain why gaps emerge between the initial intentions and later developments. Factors that are likely to create such gaps include autonomous actions of actors or institutions, their restricted time horizons, including the discounting of long-term consequences and actors' changing preferences over time; see S Gstöhl and D Phinnemore, 'Introduction: Privileged Partnerships between the European Union and Third States' in Gstöhl and Phinnemore (eds), *The Proliferation of Privileged Partnerships* (n 2) 1, 7.

[27] *Hauptzollamt Mainz v CA Kupferberg & Cie KG aA* (n 17).

[28] See further ch 10 by Leinarte and Barnard in this volume.

introduce the two concepts of accessing the EU's internal market and participating in it.

## A.  Iceland, Liechtenstein and Norway's Participation in the EEA as the EU's Enlarged Internal Market

When the EEC embarked on the creation of an internal (common) market in the mid-to-late 1980s, the EFTA States were interested in participating in it. In 1992, all EFTA States, with the exception of Switzerland, ratified the EEA Agreement. It has therefore become the comprehensive basis for cooperation between the EU and the three EEA EFTA States, Iceland, Liechtenstein and Norway.

The aim of the EEA Agreement is to promote a continuous and balanced strengthening of trade and economic relations between the EEA States, with equal conditions of competition and respect for the same rules. Experience confirms that the EEA Agreement is functioning well and generally to the satisfaction of the EEA States. All relevant EU legislation in the field of the internal market has been integrated into the EEA Agreement, and implementation rates of this legislation in the EEA EFTA States are comparable with those of the EU Member States. The internal market is governed by the same basic rules, enabling goods, services, capital and persons to move freely about the EEA.

Participating in the EEA does not, however, entail membership of the Customs Union, thereby permitting EEA/EFTA States to make their own FTAs with third countries, which they have done extensively. It also excludes EU agricultural and fisheries policies. With respect to the internal market rules, all four freedoms on which the EU is based are to be applied, in principle, in the same way as in the EU.[29]

In order to make the EEA work without the EFTA States' encroaching on the EU's autonomy, a two-pillar-structure was established. The EU instititutions, such as the Commission or the Court of Justice, were mirrored by respective EFTA institutions: the EFTA Surveillance Authority and the EFTA Court. The two pillars are bridged either by common institutions or by a system that ensures close cooperation and homogeneous decision making.

The internal market rules ensure that goods can move freely across the borders of all (now) 30 countries in the EEA on the basis of equal conditions of competition. Buyers and sellers of goods do not have to pay customs duties when trading in most products. Prior to the internal market, there were many different national technical regulations and standards, which stipulated that products needed to be manufactured and tested in specific ways or that the products had to have certain properties. Through the mutual recognition or harmonisation of national technical

---

[29] See generally C Frommelt, 'The European Economic Area: a flexible but highly complex two-pillar system' in Gstöhl and Phinnemore (eds), *The Proliferation of Privileged Partnerships* (n 2) 46.

standards, and through the mutual recognition of testing procedures, these technical barriers to trade (TBTs) are being removed.

## B. Swiss-EU Relationship

The relationship between Switzerland and the EU, unlike the EEA Agreement, is not a coherent set of rules set out in one agreement. Its two main features, which will be considered in the context of this contribution, are (i) Switzerland's selective ('sectoral') access to the internal market, and (ii) the autonomous adaptation of Swiss law following the EU's legal development.

### i. Selective Access to the Internal Market

Switzerland, having rejected accession to the EEA in 1992, needed several years to negotiate sectoral agreements ('Bilateral Agreements') giving it access to the EU's internal market in some areas of mutual interest. A first batch of Bilateral Agreements included free movement of persons, mutual recognition in relation to conformity assessment, public procurement, agriculture, land transport, civil aviation and research. These agreements were signed in 1999 and entered into force in 2002, 10 years after the EEA Agreement had been rejected in a referendum.

A second batch of Bilateral Agreements, signed in 2004, included membership of Schengen/Dublin, the automatic exchange of information (former taxation of savings agreement), the combating of fraud, processed agricultural products, the environment, statistics, participation in the MEDIA Programme (Creative Europe), pensions and education. These agreements entered into force between 2005 and 2009. Few additional agreements have been concluded since.[30]

The approach taken in the EU-Swiss relationship with regard to the four freedoms is thus, unlike the EEA Agreement, piecemeal. The free movement of goods does not in itself follow the comprehensive approach laid down in the EEA Agreement in Articles 8–27. The FTA of 1972 continues to be the basis for the free movement of goods between the two parties, but is now supplemented by the Agreement on the Elimination of Technical Barriers to Trade (also known as the Mutual Recognition Agreement (MRA)).[31] It regulates the recognition, compliance and examination of many industrial products traded between Switzerland and the EU. This is done on the basis of harmonisation of the law and equivalence of product requirements. Thus, placing on the market is facilitated reciprocally in almost 20 sectors, in particular for machinery, motor vehicles, medical devices, electrical equipment and telecommunication equipment. The last of these helps in integrating Switzerland into the EU's telecommunications market.

---

[30] See generally M Oesch, *Switzerland and the European Union* (Zurich, Dike, 2018).
[31] Agreement of 21 June 1999 between the Swiss Confederation and the European Community on mutual recognition in conformity assessment [2002] OJ L114/369.

With regard to the other freedoms, only the free movement of persons is close to the level of integration found in that of the EEA EFTA States. The Agreement on the Free Movement of Persons (AFMP)[32] is fairly comprehensive. It lacks, however, the dynamic element of the EEA Agreement that would guarantee that Agreement to reflect the level of integration in the EU or the EEA for that matter. This explains why, for example, the Citizens' Rights Directive 2004/38[33] is not covered by the AFMP. As to services, only a is minimum covered by the Bilateral Agreements, such as cross-border services in the AFMP or land and air transport in the respective agreements.[34]

The EU always saw these Bilateral Agreements as a transitional arrangement that would ultimately be replaced by a more comprehensive agreement, and it insisted on adding an institutional framework to the existing Bilateral Agreements. The requirement for an overarching institutional or governance framework was triggered by the refusal of the Swiss to update the AFMP. Formal negotiations began five years ago, and around the same time that the (first) Withdrawal Agreement (2018) between the EU and the UK was published, a draft Institutional Framework Agreement (IFA) between the EU and Switzerland was made available to the public.[35] Although the situation is not quite comparable in substance, reactions to the draft text, political discussions and reactions to wishes for renegotiation by the EU have been very similar on both the British and Swiss political scene.

## ii. *Autonomous Adaptation of Swiss Law*

In order to understand the discussion in the next section on *Cassis de Dijon* in Swiss law, the Swiss concept of autonomous adaptation ('*autonomer Nachvollzug*', '*reprise autonome*')[36] needs to be introduced. Historically, Swiss law has been influenced by European law since the early days of the EEC. This is obvious, given Switzerland's geographical situation at the centre of the continent, surrounded by EU Member States. This became government policy in 1988, shortly before negotiations on the EEA Agreement began:

> Our goal has to be to secure the greatest compatibility of our legislation with the legislation of our European partners in the areas of cross-border significance (and only there).

---

[32] Agreement between the European Community and its Member States, of the one part, and the Swiss Confederation, of the other, on the free movement of persons [2002] OJ L114/6.

[33] See n 13.

[34] See n 32 and the Agreement between the European Community and the Swiss Confederation on the Carriage of Goods and Passengers by Rail and Road [2002] OJ L114/91, as well as the Agreement between the European Community and the Swiss Confederation on Air Transport [2002] OJ L114/73.

[35] Available at www.eda.admin.ch/dam/dea/fr/documents/abkommen/Acccord-inst-Projet-de-tex te_fr.pdf; see generally C Kaddous, 'Switzerland and the EU – Current issues and new challenges under the Draft Institutional Framework Agreement' in Gstöhl and Phinnemore (eds), *The Proliferation of Privileged Partnerships* (n 2) 68.

[36] See generally F Maiani, 'Legal Europeanization as Legal Transformation: Some Insights from Swiss "Outer Europe"' in F Maiani, R Petrov and E Mouliarova (eds), *European Integration Without EU Membership: Models, Experiences, Perspectives* (Max Weber Programme (MWP)) (Florence, EUI, 2009/10) 4–9; Oesch, *Switzerland and the European Union* (n 30) 139–53.

… This pursuit of parallelism is not motivated by the introduction of an automatism to adopt European law, but by the prevention of unwanted and unnecessary legal differences, which hamper the aspired mutual recognition of legislation on a European level.[37]

This policy of rendering Swiss law 'euro-compatible' by autonomous adaptation was then set in law: all new laws or amendments of old ones had to be 'systematically examined as to their compatibility with EU law'.[38]

When EU law is adopted without the existence of a legal obligation to do so, there is, of course, a wide variety of ways to do this. Authors write of 'autonomous adaptation' when the EU model is adopted more or less unchanged. European law can, however, also influence Swiss law in a more general and informal way, for example by adoption of its principles or a general spirit, that does not differ fundamentally from the influence of other preparatory work, for example on a bill.[39] Of course, if the adjustment is based not on economic incentives but on pressure, there can no longer be any talk of an 'autonomous' process. This is the case, for example, when compatibility with EU law is a prerequisite for access to the EU's internal market.[40]

In the first half of the 1990s, the Swiss economy was characterised by a marked weakness in growth. The causes seemed to be not only the strong currency, but also – due to the absence of any form of integration with the internal market – the protectionist character of the Swiss economy combined with a low level of competition. After Swiss voters had refused to contemplate membership of the EEA, there was a call for a revitalisation of the Swiss economy. Basic reforms laid the ground nationally for the Bilateral Agreements. While these Agreements opened the markets in important areas, the autonomous adaptation of Swiss commercial law was crucial for intensifying competition in the domestic market. In 1995, three important laws in key regulatory areas were passed on the same day: the Federal Act on Technical Barriers to Trade,[41] which removed non-tariff barriers; the Internal Market Act,[42] which broke down inter-cantonal boundaries; and the new Cartel Act,[43] which introduced effective rules for competition.

---

[37] Swiss Federal Council, *Report on Switzerland's position in the European integration process*, BBl 1988 III 249, 380 (German) / FF 1988 III 233, 365 (French); translation by Oesch, *Switzerland and the European Union* (n 30) 140.

[38] Oesch, *Switzerland and the European Union* (n 30) 140; Federal Act on the Federal Assembly [Parliament], SR/RS 171.0, Art 141(2)(a).

[39] For terminology that alternates between 'autonomous adaptation' and 'inspiration', see Swiss Federal Council, *Europe Report 2006*, BBl/FF (Federal Gazette) 2006, 6815, 6831–33 (German). As a criterion for choosing the form of adaptation see ibid 6831 (translation by the author): 'The so-called autonomous adaptation is sought wherever economic interests (competitiveness) require or justify it.'

[40] A Heinemann, 'Rechtliche Transplantate zwischen Europäischer Union und der Schweiz' in L Fahrländer et al (eds), *Europäisierung der schweizerischen Rechtsordnung* (Zürich, Dike, 2013) 20.

[41] Bundesgesetz über die technischen Handelshemmnisse (THG)/Loi fédérale sur les entraves techniques au commerce (LETC), 6 October 1995, SR/RS 946.51.

[42] Referring to the Swiss domestic internal market; Bundesgesetz über den Binnenmarkt (BGBM)/ Loi fédérale sur le marché intérieur (LMI), 6 October 1995, SR/RS 943.02.

[43] Bundesgesetz über Kartelle und andere Wettbewerbsbeschränkungen (Kartellgesetz, KG)/Loi fédérale sur les cartels et autres restrictions à la concurrence (Loi sur les cartels, LCart), 6 October 1995, SR/RS 251.

The alignment with EU trade law provided a stimulus for growth: greater freedom was given to entrepreneurship, while tightening the antitrust law was meant to rein in the anticompetitive behaviour of undertakings. The economic advantages of the autonomous adaptation of Switzerland's trade law can thus be summarised as follows: (i) cost reductions resulted from the Europe-wide standardisation of legal requirements; (ii) the markets were opened; (iii) competition was intensified by legal imports that were induced by an economic interest on the legislator's part.[44]

# IV. Mutual Recognition and *Cassis de Dijon*

## A. The Enlarged Internal Market

In the Introduction, I briefly sketched the structure of free movement of goods in the EU:[45] essentially, there is either (i) harmonisation, or (ii) in the non-harmonised area, mutual recognition under the terms of the *Cassis de Dijon* jurisprudence.

To put it simply, under the EEA Agreement, the three EFTA States – Iceland, Liechtenstein and Norway (EEA EFTA States) – were granted treatment, 'as if they were EU Member States'.[46] This means that the EU's approach applies to the EEA EFTA States. The provisions on free movement of goods are set out in Part II of the EEA Agreement. The chapter on the basic principles includes product coverage,[47] provisions relating to the rules of origin,[48] rules concerning customs duties and charges having equivalent effect,[49] quantitative restrictions and measures having equivalent effect,[50] discriminatory internal taxation[51] and rules on State monopolies of a commercial character.[52] These rules 'reproduce the wording of the corresponding provisions in the EEC Treaty' and, therefore, with a few exceptions, following from the fact that the EEA Agreement does not create a customs union, 'the EEA Agreement ensures the free movement of goods to the same extent as the EEC Treaty'.[53]

The Agreement aims at creating 'a dynamic and homogeneous European Economic Area'.[54] From this it follows that the EEA Agreement (ie its Annexes) is

---

[44] Heinemann, 'Rechtliche Transplantate' (n 40) 19.
[45] See section I.
[46] M Emerson, 'Which Model for Brexit?', *CEPS Special Report 147* (Brussels, Centre of European Policy Studies, 2016) 3.
[47] Art 8 EEA.
[48] Art 9 EEA.
[49] Art 10 EEA.
[50] Arts 11–13 EEA.
[51] Arts 14 and 15 EEA.
[52] Art 16 EEA.
[53] S Norberg et al, *EEA Law – A Commentary on the EEA Agreement* (Stockholm, Fritzes, 1993) 314–15.
[54] Preamble to the EEA Agreement, fourth recital.

constantly updated, 'as closely as possible to the adoption by Union of the corresponding new Union legislation with a view to permitting a simultaneous application of the latter as well as the amendments of the Annexes to the Agreement'.[55]

In order to guarantee homogeneity, this must also be reflected in the jurisprudence. However, the EEA Agreement refers only to 'the relevant rulings of the Court of Justice of the European Communities given prior to the date of signature of this Agreement'.[56] The Agreement between the EFTA States on the Establishment of a Surveillance Authority and a Court of Justice (Surveillance and Court Agreement (SCA)),[57] however, also sets out rules for future jurisprudence of the Court of Justice, in as much as

> the EFTA Surveillance Authority and the EFTA Court shall pay due account to the principles laid down by the relevant rulings by the Court of Justice of the European Communities given after the date of signature of the EEA Agreement …[58]

Nonetheless, in practice, this distinction was not greatly pondered by the EFTA Court, which from the very beginning interpreted EEA law in conformity with the jurisprudence of the Court of Justice, irrespective of whether such rulings were handed down prior to or after the date of signature of the EEA Agreement.[59] It was therefore also clear that the three EEA EFTA States could not be affected by the *Polydor* jurisprudence,[60] at least with regard to policies falling within the scope of the EEA Agreement.

Hence, the set-up in the EEA with regard to the free movement of goods from a legislative point of view was the same as in the EU: a harmonised area, including the relevant secondary legislation of the EU, and the non-harmonised area where mutual recognition applies. With regard to the rules that apply to the latter, the scope of the *Cassis de Dijon* principle was extended to the EEA EFTA countries as the Court of Justice's jurisprudence was applicable under the EEA Agreement as well.

## B. Switzerland

In order to mitigate the consequences of not participating in the internal market, Switzerland autonomously[61] introduced *Cassis de Dijon* into its domestic law. This was done in two ways: first, *Cassis de Dijon* was used as a means to liberalise the

---

[55] Art 102(1) EEA.
[56] Art 6 EEA.
[57] [1994] OJ L344/3.
[58] Art 3(2) SCA.
[59] Case E-1/94 *Restamark* [1994-1995] EFTA Ct Rep 15; P Wennerås, 'Commentary to Article 6 EEA' in F Arnesen et al (eds), *Agreement on the European Economic Area – A Commentary* (Baden-Baden, Nomos, 2018) fnn 8–9.
[60] See n 20; S Norberg. 'The European Economic Area' in P Oliver (ed), *Oliver on Free Movement of Goods in the European Union*, 5th edn (Oxford, Hart Publishing, 2010) 493.
[61] See section II.B.ii.

domestic market (see section IV.B.i); second, and more interestingly in the context of this chapter, it was introduced to facilitate external trade (see sections IV.B.ii–v). There is, however, no direct link, by international agreement or otherwise, that formally connects these Swiss forms of *Cassis de Dijon* to the principle of EU law. Nor is there any duty to apply the Court of Justice's jurisprudence in that respect. Therefore, each form of the Swiss '*Cassis de Dijon* principle' is to be interpreted autonomously in its respective context. It thus rather becomes '*Cassis de Berne*'.[62]

## *i. Federalism and the Notion of* Cassis de Dijon

Switzerland is a federal state. Federalism is, next to direct democracy and neutrality, seen as one of the pillars of the Swiss Constitution.[63] The position of the cantons is very strong and, to cut a long story short, they normally hold those legislative rights that have not been expressly handed to the Confederation, that is, the national level.[64] Hence, many laws regulating the market, for example on lawyers' access to the bar, or conditions for submitting offers for local construction projects or even rules regarding the efficiency of boilers, were (and to some extent still are) cantonal. This led to a closed domestic market and high prices for goods and services. Much of this would have been remedied by the legislative programme, 'Eurolex', which would have opened up the national market when Switzerland prepared for joining the EEA in 1992. *Cassis de Dijon* would have had the same meaning in Switzerland as in the EU, as is the case in the other EFTA States, Iceland, Liechtenstein and Norway.

However, when EEA accession was rejected in a referendum by the Swiss electorate, the Government in 1993 proposed transposing most of its 'Eurolex' Bill into its subsequent 'Swisslex' Bill. One of the laws contained in that package was the so-called Internal Market Act (IMA).[65] The central provision of that IMA reads as follows:

> Any person has the right to offer goods, services and work throughout the territory of Switzerland, provided that the exercise of the relevant gainful activity is permitted in the canton or commune in which [s]he is established or domiciled.[66]

In its explanatory message, the Swiss Government expressly referred to 'the *Cassis de Dijon* principle' to explain its intention behind the IMA.[67]

---

[62] T Cottier and D Herren, 'Das Äquivalenzprinzip im schweizerischen Aussenwirtschaftsrecht: von Cassis de Dijon zu Cassis de Berne' in *Schweizerisches Jahrbuch für Europarecht/Annuaire Suisse de droit européen 2016/2017* (Bern, Stämpfli, 2009) 249.

[63] See, eg, O Nicole-Berva, *Swiss direct democracy: a brief history and current debates* (2016) available at www.demokratiezentrum.org/fileadmin/media/pdf/Direkte%20Demokratie/Swiss_direct_democracy_OpheliaNicoleBerva.pdf.

[64] Art 3 Swiss Constitution.

[65] See n 412.

[66] Art 2(1) IMA (author's own translation).

[67] BBl_1995 I_1213, 1263 (German), FF 1995 I 1193, 1243 (French).

So, as if it were a magic wand to solve all problems, the term '*Cassis de Dijon* principle' entered the arena. Given that there is no formal link with *Cassis de Dijon* (for example, there was no agreement introducing the *Cassis de Dijon* principle as it is understood in the EU into Swiss law), that term, in the Swiss domestic context, started to have a life of its own. It is not fully identical with that in the EU.

On the one hand, there are clearly common features. For example, Swiss law follows EU law in its central point; the central provision of the IMA quoted above, ie free movement of goods services and labour, if lawful under the cantonal or local legislation of origin, was directly inspired by the EU principle and is therefore often seen as the central *Cassis de Dijon* principle ('*Cassis de Dijon*-Grundsatz *per se*').[68] The recognition of professional qualifications (diploma) as in Article 4 IMA is seen as derived from EU law as well.[69] Further, Swiss law recognises mandatory requirements. The original version of the law mentioned, for example, the protection of public health, the fairness of commercial transactions, the protection of the environment, consumer protection, social and energy policy, safeguarding a sufficient level of education with regard to professional qualifications subject to licensing.[70] It thus copied some elements from the Court of Justice's decision in *Cassis de Dijon*[71] and added some more that were not exhaustive. These mandatory requirements were subject to a proportionality test. The law also stated in which cases such mandatory requirements were seen as proportional. This was, however, not enough to break up protectionist practices at sub-federal level. Therefore, in 2006, these provisions were amended. According to the amended law, there are no longer any explicit mandatory requirements. Rather, the aforementioned list was replaced by a provision that foresaw under what conditions mandatory requirements were *not* to be seen as being proportional.[72] An example would be that a mandatory requirement would a priori not withstand the proportionality test if the protection of public interests could be achieved by provisions of the place of origin.[73]

On the other hand, there are differences between the Swiss approach and that of the EU: for instance, the IMA covers only restrictions to free movement originating from public authorities; in the EU, as the decision in *Bosman*[74] shows, EU law applies to a wider range of regulatory activities. However, *Cassis* in its Swiss domestic version applies in a broader manner and covers all four freedoms.[75]

---

[68] D Herren, 'Das Cassis de Dijon-Prinzip im schweizerischen Recht' in T Cottier (ed), *Die Europakompatibilität des schweizerischen Wirtschaftsrechts: Konvergenz und Divergenz* (Basel, Helbing Lichtenhahn, 2012) 59, 66.

[69] See D Herren, 'Das Cassis de Dijon-Prinzip' (Berne, Stämpfli 2014) 227; C Janssens, The Principle of Mutual Recognition in EU Law (Oxford, Oxford University Press, 2013) 15.

[70] Article 3(2) IMA of 1994.

[71] *Cassis de Dijon* (n 1) para 8.

[72] Art 3(2) IMA.

[73] Art 3(2)(a) IMA.

[74] Case C-415/93 *Bosman*, ECLI:EU:C:1995:463.

[75] T Cottier and B Merkt, 'La fonction fédérative de la liberté du commerce et de l'industrie et la loi sur le marché intérieur suisse: l'influence du droit européen et du droit intérnational économique' in

Furthermore, the notion of *Cassis de Dijon* in the Swiss domestic context provides for a statutory a priori equivalence of the different cantonal regulations.[76]

## ii.  *Unilateral rather than Mutual Recognition?*

The blurring did not end there. As will be shown, Switzerland unilaterally introduced 'the *Cassis de Dijon* principle' into its legislation regulating international trade.[77] Because Switzerland did not join the EEA in 1992, the 1972 FTA with the EU remained the basis for bilateral trade in industrial products. As mentioned before, the Swiss Federal Court refused to adopt the case law of the Court of Justice on the free movement of goods on that basis. This was notably the case[78] with regard to the decisions in *Dassonville*,[79] *Cassis de Dijon*[80] and *Keck*.[81]

Switzerland does not therefore benefit from the *Cassis de Dijon* principle of mutual recognition, as is the case in the EEA, and numerous technical barriers to trade remained in place that contribute, for instance, to very high prices in Switzerland. It proved, however, not possible to overcome this unsatisfactory situation by negotiating a bilateral agreement with the EU introducing the *Cassis de Dijon* principles, or at least mutual recognition. This was due, on the one hand, to the difficulties in domestic politics as far as the relations between Switzerland and the EU are concerned. On the other hand, there was no interest on the EU's part to enter into further sectoral agreements, especially such that would benefit only Switzerland. Therefore, the Swiss legislator decided to introduce the *Cassis-de-Dijon* principle of mutual recognition autonomously and apply it unilaterally to products from the EEA.[82] This was done by amending the Federal TBT Act.[83] The respective amendments entered into force on 1 July 2010. The introduction of the *Cassis de Dijon* principle was expected to lead to lower prices for consumers, facilitating trade with the EEA States and thus saving well over CHF 2 billion annually.[84]

This newly introduced concept of *Cassis de Dijon* in the Swiss external trade context is not fully identical with that used in the Swiss domestic context.[85]

---

P Zen Ruffinen and A Auer (eds), *De la constitution. Etudes en l'honneur de Jean-François Aubert* (Basel, Helbing, 1996) 467.

[76] Art 2(5) IMA.

[77] M Oesch, 'Die Europäisierung des schweizerischen Rechts' in T Cottier (ed), *Die Europakompatibilität des schweizerischen Wirtschaftsrechts: Konvergenz und Divergenz* (Basel, Helbing Lichtenhahn, 2012) 13, 36.

[78] Swiss Federal Court (n 24) consideration 6.

[79] Case C-8/74 *Procureur du Roi v Benoît and Gustave Dassonville*, ECLI:EU:C:1974:82.

[80] See n 1.

[81] Cases C-267/91 and C-268/91 *Keck and Mithouard*, ECLI:EU:C:1993:905.

[82] See generally Oesch, *Switzerland and the European Union* (n 30) 149–51.

[83] See n 41.

[84] C Perritaz and N Wallart, 'Les conséquences économiques de la révision de la loi sur les entraves techniques au commerce' in *Die Volkswirtschaft/La Vie économique 10–2008*, 23.

[85] Oesch, 'Die Europäisierung des schweizerischen Rechts' (n 77) 36.

It suffices to mention the example of the mandatory requirements, equally fore-seen in the external trade context.[86] In contrast to the amended version of the IMA, these are, however, explicitly stated in the TBT Act. Public interests that may constitute mandatory requirements may be the protection of public order and security, the protection of public health, the protection of the environment, security at work, consumer protection and fairness of commercial transactions, protection of the cultural heritage and the protection of property. These elements are, unlike those in the original version of the IMA, exhaustive.[87] A test of propor-tionality is to be applied here as well.[88]

And, again, the term '*Cassis de Dijon*' was not to be understood as identical with EU law. The recognition of the principle of mutual recognition in the Swiss measure differs in two ways from the *Cassis de Dijon* principle of mutual recogni-tion that applies in the EEA:

– On the one hand, the Swiss version covers both products that are lawfully marketed based on Union product regulations and products that – in the case of incomplete or missing harmonisation in the EU – correspond to the techni-cal regulations of an EEA Member State. Since the revision of the TBT Act, the *Cassis de Dijon* principle therefore applies to all products that are legally sold in the EEA.

– On the other hand, the autonomous introduction of that principle means that easier market access is one-sided, that is, in favour of products imported from the EEA. Conversely, Swiss products and their manufacturers in Switzerland do not benefit from easier market access in the EEA; it is a one-way street.[89] Even if such a procedure contradicts the fundamental principle of reciprocity, the legislator consciously accepts this disadvantage, since the mere unilateral application also appears to be economically advantageous for Switzerland.[90]

Prior to the legislative amendment, some academics were of the opinion that there was no need for legislative intervention in order to apply the *Cassis de Dijon* prin-ciple to products from the EU. These voices argued that it would be quite possible to interpret Article 13 of the FTA between Switzerland and the EU accordingly, and thereby introduce the *Cassis de Dijon* principle of mutual recognition through jurisprudence, at least for industrial goods.[91] However, as mentioned before, the Swiss Federal Court had hitherto shown little willingness to interpret the FTA

---

[86] Art 4(4) TBT Act.

[87] Botschaft [explanatory message by the government] zur Teilrevision des Bundesgesetzes über die technischen Handelshemmnisse vom 25. Juni 2008, BBl 2008 7275, 7309.

[88] Art 4(3)(c) TBT Act.

[89] C Tobler, 'Cassis de Dijon für die Schweiz: Pur oder on the Rocks' (2005) *Swiss Review of International and European Law* 567, 568.

[90] Explanatory message (n 87) 7299.

[91] In this vein see Tobler, 'Cassis de Dijon für die Schweiz' (n 89) 569–70; or A Kellerhals and T Baumgartner, 'Das "Cassis-de-Dijon" – Prinzip und die Schweiz' (2006) 102 *Schweizerische Juristenzeitung* 321, 326.

accordingly, and it did not show any signs that it would change its attitude significantly. Furthermore, it would be questionable anyway whether the Swiss Federal Court could manage such a far-reaching interpretation of the FTA, even if it were willing to adapt its jurisprudence. Compared to the integrative, pioneering role played by the Court of Justice in completing the internal market, the Swiss Federal Court's function in interpreting the FTA has been quite a different, and much more self-restrained.[92]

## *iii. Main Features of the New Regulation*

Since the amendment of the TBT Act in 2010, products that have been manufactured and legally placed on the market in accordance with the relevant provisions of EU law in the harmonised area, or of the EEA country of origin in the non-harmonised area, can also be imported and sold in Switzerland without further testing.[93] There is, however, a caveat with respect to product information. There, the principle applies that the product information must be written in at least one of the official Swiss languages.[94] Exceptions are permitted if product information in another language provides sufficient and unequivocal information about the product. This applies, for example, to Spanish or Greek wine, which is already labelled in a foreign language in Switzerland and can thus be sold.[95] Cosmetics, textiles and clothing, food and home furnishings, for example, all benefit from the unilateral introduction of the *Cassis de Dijon* principle of mutual recognition. These are products that do not comply – or do not comply fully – with Swiss technical regulations and whose free circulation between the EEA and Switzerland is not guaranteed by an international agreement either.[96]

There are, however, a few exceptional cases subject to special regulation to which the *Cassis de Dijon* principle does not apply.[97] This is the case with regard to products:

– that are subject to approval or registration. This primarily includes medicinal products based on the Medicinal Products Act,[98] as well as substances that are subject to legislation on chemicals;

– that require a prior import permit or are subject to a general ban on imports. This applies, for example, to products whose import is subject to authorisation

---

[92] M Oesch, 'Die einseitige Einführung des Cassis-de-Dijon-Prinzips' (2009) 11-12 *Anwalts Revue de l'Avocat* 520; as to the Swiss Federal Court's self-restrained attitude, see BGE/ATF 105 II 49 (n 19) consideration 3.

[93] Art 16a TBT Act.

[94] Arts 4a and 16e TBT Act.

[95] Explanatory message (n 87) 7312.

[96] ibid 7357.

[97] Art 16a(2) TBT Act.

[98] Bundesgesetz über Arzneimittel und Medizinprodukte (Heilmittelgesetz, HMG)/Loi fédérale sur les médicaments et les dispositifs médicaux (Loi sur les produits thérapeutiques, LPTh), 15.12. 2000, SR/RS 812.21.

based on the War Material Act[99] or the Goods Control Act,[100] as well as for products from countries against which Switzerland has issued an embargo based on the Embargo Act;[101]

– whose privileged import would be against overriding public interests. With regard to such products the Federal Council (Government) can issue an express exception.[102] It laid down certain exceptions in the executive ordinance. Such exceptions include alcopops, detergents and eggs from prohibited cage farming, where the respective legislation as to declaration of content is stricter than according to EU legislation.[103]

Products that have no access to the Swiss market for these reasons are listed on a special negative list available on the website of the State Secretariat for Economic Affairs (SECO).[104]

## iv. Special Regulation for Food

Food is subject to special regulation. Accordingly, foodstuffs that have been legally placed on the market in the EEA but do not meet the relevant provisions of Swiss food legislation require a special permit for marketing in Switzerland.[105] The Federal Office of Public Health is the licensing authority. Authorisation is granted if the food product:

– meets the product regulations in the EU or – in the event of lacking or incomplete harmonisation of EU law – the regulations of an EEA State and has been lawfully marketed;

– complies with the general level of Swiss health protection; and

– meets the requirements for product information.

---

[99] Bundesgesetz über das Kriegsmaterial (Kriegsmaterialgesetz, KMG)/Loi fédérale sur le matériel de guerre (LFMG), 13.12.1996, SR/RS 514.51.

[100] Bundesgesetz über die Kontrolle zivil und militärisch verwendbarer Güter, besonderer militärischer Güter sowie strategischer Güter (Güterkontrollgesetz, GKG)/Loi fédérale sur le contrôle des biens utilisables à des fins civiles et militaires, des biens militaires spécifiques et des biens stratégiques (Loi sur le contrôle des biens, LCB), 13.12.1996, SR/RS 946.202.

[101] Bundesgesetz über die Durchsetzung von internationalen Sanktionen (Embargogesetz, EmbG)/ Loi fédérale sur l'application de sanctions internationales (Loi sur les embargos, LEmb), 22.3.2002. SR/ RS 946.231.

[102] Art 16a(2)(e) TBT Act.

[103] Art 2 TBT Ordinance (Verordnung über das Inverkehrbringen von nach ausländischen technischen Vorschriften hergestellten Produkten und über deren Überwachung auf dem Markt, VIPaV/ Ordonnance réglant la mise sur le marché de produits fabriqués selon des prescriptions techniques étrangères et la surveillance du marché de ceux-ci, OPPEtr; SR/RS 946.513.8).

[104] At www.seco.admin.ch/dam/seco/en/dokumente/Aussenwirtschaft/Wirtschaftsbeziehungen/ Technische%20Handelshemmnisse/Negativliste/negativliste.pdf.download.pdf/Liste_N%C3%A9 gative_fr_20191120.pdf (French), www.seco.admin.ch/dam/seco/de/dokumente/Aussenwirtschaft/ Wirtschaftsbeziehungen/Technische%20Handelshemmnisse/Negativliste/negativliste.pdf.download. pdf/Negativliste_de_20191120.pdf (German).

[105] Arts 16c and 16d TBT Act.

The permit is issued in the form of a general ruling and also applies to similar food products.[106] If a similar food product complies with the product regulations on which the general ruling is based, it can be sold on the Swiss market without further testing and approval. Swiss producers can also rely on such a ruling if they want to manufacture and distribute food based on the provisions of such a ruling. There are, however, reservations with regard to the Swiss provisions on labour standards and animal protection.[107]

In practical terms, despite these special regulations, the *Cassis de Dijon* principle is equally applied in the area of food. The most important divergence from its application to other products is the need for prior approval for the first import. Nonetheless, this special regulation makes law enforcement easier in the food sector. The control effort is only to be incurred during the approval process prior to the first import. Thereafter, corresponding controls and clarifications are no longer necessary as part of market surveillance. This relieves the burden in particular on the cantons, which are traditionally responsible for enforcing food legislation.[108]

## v. Some Drawbacks: Discrimination against National Products and Sovereignty Concerns

The unilateral introduction of the *Cassis de Dijon* principle may result in domestic producers' being disadvantaged compared to their European competitors if a product from the EEA has to comply with less stringent product regulations than under Swiss law for producing the same product in Switzerland. Unsurprisingly, the problem of such national discrimination was discussed throughout the legislative process when the TBT Act was amended.[109]

In order to mitigate discriminatory effects, Swiss producers who produce only for the domestic market may also manufacture and market their products in accordance with technical regulations of the EU or – if there is no harmonisation – an EEA State.[110] Swiss producers can therefore freely choose whether they want to manufacture their products based on the Swiss product regulations, or based on the relevant provisions of EU law or of an EEA State.

Swiss academics take a rather positive view of Switzerland's having unilaterally introduced the *Cassis de Dijon* principle, as the chosen regulation consistently eliminates any form of possible disadvantage for domestic producers compared to competitors from the EEA. In their view it is the most liberal of all possible solutions, failing a respective agreement with the EU, and goes far beyond the approval procedure for hardship cases originally proposed by the Swiss Government. At the same time, there remains a certain level of discomfort. On the one hand, and

---

[106] Art 16d(2) TBT Act.
[107] Explanatory message (n 87) 7325.
[108] Oesch, 'Die einseitige Einführung des Cassis-de-Dijon-Prinzips' (n 92) 521.
[109] ibid 522.
[110] Art 16b TBT Act.

as a result of the unilateral approach, this system works only for imports, not for Swiss exports into the internal market. On the other hand, Swiss product regulations are quasi optional: the free choice of law in the area of product regulations is difficult to reconcile with a traditional understanding of sovereignty, as it prevails in Switzerland.[111]

In 2013, SECO published a report assessing the consequences of the introduction of the unilateral application of the *Cassis de Dijon* principle.[112] While the general effect is seen as positive, the assessment is more cautious in detail. It concludes that the direct benefits of the unilateral introduction of the *Cassis de Dijon* principle are rather modest. It was, in particular, difficult to assess the benefits in concrete monetary terms. Indirect effects, however, such as greater competitiveness – for example through increased parallel imports – are seen to be more important. Furthermore, less regulatory activity, thus liberating enterprises from bureaucracy, could also be observed. Overall, the unilateral introduction of the *Cassis de Dijon* principle in Switzerland seems to yield some benefits. However, it obviously does not create a situation similar to that in the EEA. And in comparison with the surrounding EU countries, prices for consumers in Switzerland still remain very high.

# V.  Conclusion

By its landmark decision in *Cassis de Dijon*, including further jurisprudence in the same context, the Court of Justice, and in its wake the Commission with its respective Communication, set the framework for what EU Member States may – and may not – do with regard to mutual recognition in the non-harmonised area of free movement of goods. This jurisprudence gradually developed into a principle and spread. On the one hand, it is being applied to the other freedoms as well. On the other, through the EEA Agreement, that jurisprudence is also applied in the three EFTA States: Iceland, Liechtenstein and Norway. With respect to their participation in the EU's internal market, *Cassis de Dijon* hence applies in the same way as within the EU. The fourth EFTA State, Switzerland, however, does not fully benefit from the *Cassis de Dijon* principle, as its trade link with the EU is a much weaker one than that of the other EFTA States. With regard to free movement of goods, it still rests on the provisions of the bilateral FTA from 1972. And despite similar wording in both the FTA and the EEC Treaty, respective jurisprudence led to a situation where *Cassis de Dijon* could not be applied to free movement of goods between the EU and Switzerland. Hence, there was no mutual recognition

---

[111] Oesch, 'Die einseitige Einführung des Cassis-de-Dijon-Prinzips' (n 92) 522; Heinemann, 'Rechtliche Transplantate' (n 40) 23.

[112] *Report of the (Swiss) State Secretariat of Commerce on on the effects of the introduction of the "'Cassis de Dijon"-principle' in Switzerland* (2013) available at www.newsd.admin.ch/newsd/message/attachments/ 30420.pdf (German).

similar to the EEA. Yet, as we have seen, *Cassis de Dijon* has had a profound effect on the Swiss system: first, as an adapted statutory rule to open the domestic market; then as an autonomous adaptation of Swiss law. This time the purpose was to mitigate negative foreign trade effects failing an agreement with the EU granting mutual recognition outside the scope of the TBT Agreement. The term 'Cassis de Dijon' is used neither in an identical manner as in EU law, nor coherently. In Switzerland, 'the *Cassis de Dijon* principle' sometimes means the '*Cassis de Dijon* principles', according to the Court of Justice jurisprudence of the Court of Justice and as adapted to its use in Swiss law; sometimes it is rather used as a *pars pro toto* for mutual recognition alone.

The motivation for introducing 'the *Cassis de Dijon* principle' was essentially economic: prices for consumers should be lowered and trade with the EEA States facilitated. This was expected to lead to important annual savings for the Swiss economy. There are doubts, however, as to whether these expectations are being met.

Given the unilateral approach, this principle applies only to imports, not to exports, irrespective of whether they correspond to the applicable EU regulations[113] In this respect, harmonisation coordinated with the EU would of course be preferable.[114] Nonetheless, the unilateral introduction of the *Cassis de Dijon* principle also has some advantages. The waiver of harmonisation coordinated with the EU is simple and quick: no negotiations are needed, counterclaims can therefore not be made and Switzerland remains the mistress of the exceptions.[115]

It should also be noted that the introduction of the *Cassis de Dijon* principle has a strong dynamic component.[116] The recognition of foreign technical regulations refers not only to the present but also to the future. The free movement of goods thus becomes an experimental field in which experience with dynamic legal adjustments can be gained.

The unilateral introduction of the *Cassis de Dijon* principle by Switzerland can be seen as a lesson in Swiss integration policy. The Swiss legislator has once again had to make a concession to the fact that being outside of the internal market is associated with considerable disadvantages, mainly given the fact that the EU is Switzerland's major trading partner by far, and the country, geographically, is situated in its midst. At the same time, the EU is visibly less willing to take Swiss

---

[113] C Baudenbacher, 'Swiss Economic Law Facing the Challenges of International and European Law' (2012) 131 *Zeitschrift für Schweizerisches Recht II* 612: 'To be sure, autonomous implementation does not produce reciprocal rights and therefore no right to access to the EU's internal market for Swiss citizens and economic actors.'

[114] See the Swiss Government's position in *Europe Report 2006* (n 389) 6832: 'The enactment of law that is compatible with European law can alleviate discrimination in relation to the EU countries, but not eliminate it. The gap [between remaining discrimination and mutual recognition] can only be bridged by means of an agreement which would ensure that facilitations for the exchange of goods and services and for the movement of people are mutually granted. This means in particular that wherever possible, adaptation to Community law should not be done autonomously, but contractually.' (Translation by the author as closely as possible to the German original text.)

[115] Heinemann, 'Rechtliche Transplantate' (n 40) 23.

[116] Oesch, 'Die Europäisierung des schweizerischen Rechts' (n 77) 13, 38.

peculiarities into account and to provide tailor-made solutions for Switzerland. This attitude has increased with Brexit and the UK now acting, vis-à-vis the EU, from a similar position as Switzerland. Hence, Switzerland is left with the option either to participate in the internal market within the agreements offered by the EU, or not to participate. In the latter case, there are only autonomous options for Switzerland to minimise – at least to a certain degree – the economically most obvious disadvantages of staying outside. Ultimately, this is the price that Switzerland has to pay for its political independence.[117]

---

[117] In the same vein, Oesch, 'Die einseitige Einführung des Cassis-de-Dijon-Prinzips' (n 92) 522.

# 10

# Negotiating Mutual Recognition Agreements: Challenges and Techniques

EMILIJA LEINARTE AND CATHERINE BARNARD*

## I. Introduction

In recent years, multilateral economic institutions have come under threat from the states that helped create them. Cuts to US funding for UN agencies and programmes, the blocking by the US of the appointment of new judges to the Appellate Body of the World Trade Organisation (WTO) and the UK's withdrawal from the European Union (EU), are just some of the examples of how long-lasting criticism over competence creep has led some countries to take a step back from multilateralism in the name of sovereignty. On the other hand, bilateral economic relationships are flourishing. In addition to the many new-generation free trade agreements (FTAs) that have been concluded in the past decade, other forms of economic cooperation are also becoming increasingly popular. One such instrument is mutual recognition agreements (MRAs), which help facilitate inter-state trade by eliminating duplicate product safety testing. These MRAs, however, have received considerably little attention from legal scholars, as compared to, for example, FTAs or bilateral investment protection treaties. Apart from a handful of comprehensive studies,[1] little is known about the nuances of MRA treaty-making.

In this chapter we should like to offer some insights into the challenges in the negotiation of MRAs (section IV) and some of the techniques that have been employed by MRA negotiators to address them (section V). Before we engage in our analysis on these two questions, section II provides a brief overview of the

* We are grateful to Giacomo Mattino, the Head of Unit, SME Internationalisation Unit, DG Internal Market, Industry, Entrepreneurship and SMEs of European Commission for a very helpful discussion. All views and errors expressed in this chapter remain ours.

[1] eg A Correia de Brito, C Kauffmann and J Pelkmans, 'The Contribution of Mutual Recognition to International Regulatory Co-operation', *OECD Regulatory Policy Working Paper No 2* (Paris, OECD Publishing, 2016) available at http://dx.doi.org/10.1787/5jm56fqsfxmx-en, last accessed 15 May 2020 (hereinafter 'OECD Report 2016'); C Devereaux, RZ Lawrence and MD Watkins, 'International Trade Meets Domestic Regulation: Negotiating the US-EU Mutual Recognition Agreements' (Case Programme at the Kennedy School of Governance, Case study, Kennedy School of Governance) (hereinafter 'KSG Case Study'); K Nicolaidis and G Shaffer, 'Transnational Mutual Recognition Regimes: Governance Without Global Government' (2005) 68 *Law and Contemporary Problems* 263.

nature and different types of MRAs, while section III discusses some of the incentives for concluding such agreements. We will argue that despite the existence of strong incentives for mutual recognition, past experience shows that negotiating MRAs is a complex and sensitive process, which requires a high degree of trust between the parties. However, while achieving trust is not easy, various trust-building techniques may facilitate the process of negotiation of and then subsequent implementation of MRAs.

We should like to make one preliminary point. Some of the earliest MRAs date back to the 1900s and mainly covered mutual recognition of academic qualifications.[2] Inter-governmental (bilateral and in some limited cases multilateral) MRAs on product safety were mostly concluded in the 1990s, and more recently with the new wave of FTAs. In this chapter we will focus exclusively on these post-1990 MRAs.[3] We do not touch upon the mutual recognition regime under the EU internal market law, which is discussed in detail in other chapters of this volume. One should not, however, perceive the EU's internal market mutual recognition regime and intergovernmental MRAs as unrelated. Some of the MRAs concluded in the 1990s have been inspired by the European *Cassis de Dijon* idea. For example, the drafters of the Commonwealth's Mutual Recognition Act 1992 did consider (but ultimately did not model itself on) the European mutual recognition case law.[4] The definition of mutual recognition enshrined in the 1998 Trans-Tasman Mutual Recognition Arrangement (TTMRA) has been modeled on the *Cassis de Dijon* case.[5] Some have suggested that the US negotiators of the EU-US MRA of 1998 were driven by the success and the resulting competitive advantage of the EU internal market under the *Cassis de Dijon* mutual recognition principle.[6] This chapter thus demonstrates how mutual recognition has an important international life outside the world of the EU's internal market.

# II. The Typology of Mutual Recognition Agreements

Mutual recognition agreements are a form of international regulatory cooperation (IRC).[7] The purpose of MRAs is to facilitate market access by reducing the effects

---

[2] One study suggests that one of the earliest MRAs was signed in 1892, between representatives from the colonies of New South Wales, Victoria, Queensland, South Australia, Western Australia and New Zealand, and covered certificates of competency for surveyors: D Rannveig Mendoza et al, 'Reinventing Mutual Recognition Agreements: Lessons from International Experiences and Insights for the ASEAN Region' (Asian Development Bank, 2017) 3, available at www.adb.org/sites/default/files/publication/224071/reinventing-mras-asean.pdf, last accessed 16 May 2020.

[3] See section II.D.iii.

[4] Industry Commission (Office of Regulation Review), 'Impact of Mutual Recognition on Regulations in Australia: A Preliminary Assessment' (Information Paper, January 1997) 3, available at www.pc.gov.au/research/supporting/mutual-recognition/mutrec.pdf, last accessed 16 May 2020.

[5] OECD Report (n 1) 20.

[6] See section III.D.

[7] OECD identified 11 IRCs in total, and MRAs as one of the four forms of IRCs employing hard law; see OECD, *International Regulatory Co-operation – Addressing Global Challenges* (Paris,

of technical barriers to trade (TBT), which arise due to divergencies in national technical regulations. They allow a product produced and certified in State A to be exported to State B without undergoing additional testing in State B. States parties to an MRA recognise the competence of a designated testing body in the export country to perform the assessment on the basis of technical requirements of the import country, and vice versa. Thus MRAs avoid duplicate testing in global trade without the need for the states to harmonise their technical requirements.

This form of IRC is thus limited in scope but binding, and is typically not subject to derogations. Mutual recognition may be part of a trade agreement[8] (integrated in the text of a (regional) FTA or as a separate agreement[9]), or may constitute a stand-alone MRA (the preferred option in majority of cases). According to 2016 data of the OECD, more than 130 MRAs have been concluded globally, most during the past several decades.[10]

Most MRAs cover only conformity assessment, that is, they provide for the recognition of the competence of testing laboratories of State A (the export state) to issue certificates of compliance with State B's (the import state) technical regulations and standards. This type of MRAs, often referred to as 'traditional' MRAs of conformity assessment, do not provide for harmonisation of technical rules or recognition of each other's rules as equivalent. In some limited cases, however, states negotiate 'enhanced' MRAs, which are based on equivalence or alignment of technical requirements. In this case, testing laboratories in State A approve products that meet State A's requirements, and State B recognises State A's requirements as equivalent (or, in case of regulatory alignment, State A and State B follow one same set of rules). In the sections below we will address the different types of MRAs in more detail.

## A.  Conformity Assessment

Conformity assessment may take various forms, including inspection, testing, certification and licensing. While efforts are being made to internationalise accreditation and certification processes, international harmonisation of technical regulations is, however, limited.[11] Conformity assessment is in most cases conducted on the basis of compulsory national technical regulations and

---

OECD Publishing, 2013) available at www.oecd.org/env/international-regulatory-co-operation-978 9264200463-en.htm, last accessed 15 May 2020.

[8] An OECD study of 99 RTAs reveals that 41.4 % of the sampled agreements require or promote mutual recognition of conformity assessment, while six incorporate an MRA (Japan-Philippines, Japan-Thailand, Japan-Singapore, Korea-Singapore, New Zealand-China and New Zealand-Singapore FTAs); see OECD Report 2016 (n 1) 46.

[9] eg an upgraded New-Zealand Closer Economic Partnership, which entered into force on 1 January 2020.

[10] OECD Report 2016 (n 1) 10.

[11] International standardisation efforts are led by ISO and IEC, which are non-governmental bodies that develop and publish fully consensus-based International Standards. One other example of international standards is the International Maritime Organisation's requirements for maritime equipment.

non-compulsory standards that are aimed at preventing safety, environmental and health risks. Mutual recognition agreements are thus typically bilateral.

Conformity assessment may or may not require third-party intervention. In the case of the former, conformity is conducted by conformity assessment bodies (CABs), which are various test laboratories and certification entities. Alternatively, for some products[12] states may allow the Supplier Declaration of Conformity (SDoC) regime, which is a written assurance by the supplier of a product of conformity with the applicable technical regulations of the import country.[13] Under the SDoC regime, intervention of CABs is not necessary.

Conformity assessment may be centralised (eg the US Food and Drug Administration) or decentralised (eg in the EU, CABs are private testing bodies). CABs must be accredited by accreditation bodies (ABs) which may be public[14] or private.[15] Typically, in the absence of an MRA, product assessment is as follows:

(a)   state A's regulatory agency designates an AB in state A;
(b)   it accredits a CAB in state A;
(c)   the CAB certifies a product in accordance with state A's technical requirements.

An MRA between state A and state B allows state A's CABs to certify a product in accordance with state B's technical requirements for the purpose of import to state B. For example, under the 1998 EU-US MRA in the telecommunications sector, the National Institute of Standards and Technology, which is a body recognised by the US Federal Communications Commission, designates ABs, which then accredit Telecommunication Certification Bodies (ie CABs) to perform conformity assessment in accordance with the EU's technical requirements for imports to the EU; similarly, in the EU, Member States designate Notified Bodies (NBs) to accredit CABs to perform conformity assessment in accordance with US requirements.

Mutual recognition agreements usually consist of a framework agreement and sectoral annexes that are considered an integral part of the MRA. The framework agreement addresses questions such as the process and institutional arrangements for the implementation of the agreement (usually a joint committee),[16] a transition period, confidentiality and other questions. Sectoral annexes define the scope and coverage of the respective MRA. Intergovernmental MRAs are typically multi-sectoral, but there may exist single-sector MRAs, such as the 1997

---

[12] eg under EU law, low-voltage electrical products are subject to SDoC; see Directive 2014/35/EU of the European Parliament and of the Council of 26 February 2014 on the harmonisation of the laws of the Member States relating to the making available on the market of electrical equipment designed for use within certain voltage limits [2014] OJ L96/357.

[13] B Fliess, F Gonzales and R Schonfeld, 'Technical Barriers to Trade: Evaluating the Trade Effects of Supplier's Declaration of Conformity', *OECD Trade Policy Papers, 2008, No 78* (Paris, OECD Publishing, 2008) available at http://dx.doi.org/10.1787/235814036326, last accessed 15 May 2020.

[14] eg the FDA.

[15] eg the Accreditation Commission for Conformity Assessment Bodies in India.

[16] Usually MRAs are implemented through a joint committee, eg the 1998 EU-US MRA.

telecommunications-only MRA between Canada and Korea, or the 2004 EU-US MRA on marine equipment. The Comprehensive Economic and Trade Agreement between Canada and the EU (CETA) is an MRA with the broadest sectoral coverage to date.

## B. Enhanced MRAs

Typically, MRAs of conformity assessment[17] do not require harmonisation of states' technical standards and regulations, nor do they require that the parties to an MRA recognise each other's requirements as equivalent – they are limited to the recognition of the competence of the partner's CABs to conduct conformity assessment. However, in some limited cases governments may conclude a more ambitious MRA on alignment of technical regulations.[18] The two types of MRAs are sometimes referred to as 'traditional' MRAs (conformity assessment only) and 'enhanced' MRAs (conformity assessment based on aligned regulations).[19] Apart from the most notable 'enhanced' MRA regime – the internal market of the EU – other examples of mutual recognition of rules include the 2004 EU-US MRA on marine equipment, which is based on International Maritime Organisation rules, the 1998 Trans-Tasman Mutual Recognition Arrangement between Australia and New Zealand (TTMRA) and the 2002 EU-Swiss MRA. In all cases, 'enhanced' MRAs are concluded either on the basis of a broad and deep regulatory alignment that stems from a unique and close relationship between the two partners (eg the EU internal market and the TTMRA) or international standards (EU-US MRA on marine equipment).

The New-Zealand Closer Economic Partnership is an example of mutual recognition of both conformity assessment[20] and equivalence of mandatory technical requirements.[21] It is generally considered that the above noted 'enhanced' MRAs are functioning well, which may be explained by the fact that they are concluded by trading partners that have a close social and economic relationship and share deep historical and cultural ties.

---

[17] For the purposes of this chapter, our reference to 'MRA' means MRA of conformity assessment, not mutual recognition of rules.

[18] There may be a further distinction between mutual recognition of equivalence of technical regulations and mutual recognition of technical regulations. In the case of the former, technical regulations may be different but must adequately fulfil the same objective; while in case of the latter, parties cannot require that their regulations are equivalent: see OECD Report 2016 (n 1) 43.

[19] This terminology was first employed by the European Commission, see Commission, 'Priorities Bilateral/Regional trade related activities in the field of Mutual Recognition Agreements for industrial products and related technical dialogue', Commission Staff Working Paper, SEC(2004)1072.

[20] Art 35(2)(b) of the Agreement.

[21] Art 35(2)(a) of the Agreement provides that the Parties accept 'the mandatory requirements of the other Party as producing outcomes equivalent to those produced by its own corresponding mandatory requirements ie mutual recognition of equivalence of mandatory requirements'.

## C. Other Arrangements

### i. Voluntary Multilateral Recognition Arrangements

In addition to the typical inter-state MRAs, there may exist multilateral recognition arrangements (MLAs) between CABs or ABs that are located in different countries. These are non-governmental voluntary arrangements, either bilateral or multilateral, by which the parties recognise the quality of each other's testing, certification and/or accreditation procedures. For example, the International Accreditation Forum (IAF) MLA requires member ABs to recognise the certificates issued by CABs accredited by all other signatories of the IAF MLA. Another notable example is the MRA concluded under the International Laboratory Accreditation Cooperation (ILAC) forum between ABs. Under the ILAC MRA, the ABs, which are evaluated in accordance with the requirements of ISO/IEC 17011, accept the results of each other's accredited CABs. While MLAs do not bind governments, they facilitate testing activities. In addition to multilateral agreements between CABs/ABs, there may exist private cooperation arrangements between CABs in different countries, for example the IECEE-CB scheme on safety of electrical and electronic products.[22]

### ii. Sector-Specific Intergovernmental Arrangements

There may also be sector-specific intergovernmental arrangements that differ from the typical MRAs in their voluntary and multilateral nature. Several examples of this type of arrangement exist between the members of the Asia-Pacific Economic Cooperation (APEC): the MRA for Conformity Assessment of Telecommunications Equipment (the APEC TEL MRA); and the MRA for Electrical and Electronic Safety (the APEC EE MRA). What is unique about this type of arrangements is that its implementation follows a phased approach: APEC countries interested in implementing either of the MRAs between them must declare their will to do so before being actually bound by the agreement.[23] While the APEC TEL MRA has proved to be functioning well, this is not the case regarding the APEC EE MRA.[24] A similarly non-binding intergovernmental arrangement is the Association of Southeast Asian Nations (ASEAN) Framework Agreement on Mutual Recognition, which serves as a common basis for developing and implementing bilateral MRAs between the ASEAN Member States.

---

[22] The IECEE-CB scheme connects 57 testing bodies that are members of the International Electrotechnical Commission. Under the arrangement, conformity assessment results of a member CAB are accepted by all participating CABs.

[23] OECD Report 2016 (n 21) 33.

[24] One of the reasons, according to the OECD, is that neither the US nor Canada has expressed interest in the implementation of the APEC EE MRA; see OECD Report 2016 (n 1) 34.

## iii.  EU MRAs

Mutual recognition agreements concluded by the EU offer yet another dense branch in the network of different types of MRAs. Unlike the US, the EU does not follow a single model MRA and instead negotiates different types of MRAs depending on its relationship with the trading partner in question. The first two categories are Protocols to the European Agreements on Conformity Assessment (PECAs) and Agreements on Conformity Assessment and Acceptance of Industrial Products (ACAAs). Both PECAs and ACAAs are 'enhanced' bilateral MRAs based on alignment rules.

### a.  PECAs and ACAAs

The PECAs are typically concluded with candidate countries with which the EU has association agreements, and constitutes a step in the accession process.[25] The purpose of PECAs is to align the technical rules of a candidate country with those of the EU in the preparation of membership of the EU, which renders these type of MRAs temporary in nature.[26] They provide for the recognition of conformity assessment of industrial products when the legislation of the candidate countries is aligned to that of the EU, and establish the system of CE (*Conformité Européenne*) marking to attest compliance in the candidate country in the same way as in the EU. Similarly to typical MRAs, PECAs consist of a framework agreement and sectoral annexes, which are defined in accordance with the level of implementation of the EU technical legislation by the candidate country.

An example of an ACAA with a neighbouring country is the 2013 EU-Israel MRA, a single-sector ACAA of good manufacturing practices (GMP) for pharmaceutical products, which is based on the alignment of the legislative system and infrastructure of Israel with those of the EU.[27]

### b.  Special Cases

Two special cases must be mentioned. First, Turkey. Turkey does not (yet) have an MRA with the EU, primarily because there is no practical need for one. Turkey, a candidate country since 1999, is part of the EU-Turkey Customs Union,[28] which

---

[25] Typically, the EU's association agreements provide for the conclusion of ACAAs, eg Art 51(2)(ii) of the EU-Ukraine Association Agreement.

[26] A commitment to conclude an ACAA has been included in association agreements with the candidate countries but there are currently no formal ongoing negotiations; see Commission, 'Technical Barriers to Trade: Mutual Recognition Agreements and Agreements on Conformity Assessment and Acceptance of Industrial Products' (hereinafter 'Newsletter No 10') February 2018, available at https://trade.ec.europa.eu/doclib/docs/2018/february/tradoc_156599.pdf, last accessed 15 May 2020.

[27] ACAAs currently under consideration include those with Algeria, Egypt, Jordan, Lebanon, Morocco, Palestine and Tunisia.

[28] The EU-Turkey Customs Union was established on 1 January 1996 by Council Decision No 1/95 of the EC-Turkey Association Council of 22 December 1995 on implementing the final phase of the Customs Union, 96/142/EC [1996] OJ L35/1.

removed tariffs and quantitative restrictions in bilateral trade between Turkey and EU Member States and sets a single tariff for imports from third countries.[29] While there has been little progress in accession talks,[30] Turkey is progressively aligning its laws with the EU *acquis* in order to remove technical barriers.[31] Furthermore, since 2011 the Turkish Standards Institution has been a full member of European standardisation organisations CEN and CENELEX. Testing results of Turkish-notified CABs are mutually recognised in the EU (and vice versa).[32]

The second special case is Switzerland. The 2002 EU-Swiss 'enhanced' MRA is considered the broadest MRA ever to have been concluded. While Switzerland is neither a candidate country, nor part of the European Economic Area (EEA), it nevertheless has a very close relationship with the EU.[33]

It has yet to be seen whether the future trade relationship between the EU and the UK will provide yet another special MRA. It is unlikely, however, that the UK and the EU will negotiate an 'enhanced' MRA based on regulatory alignment. Given that the UK Government has rejected on numerous occasions the EU's call for regulatory convergence, the limited 'traditional' MRAs of conformity assessment will likely be the only feasible option. As the time of writing this chapter, however, the European Commission has rejected mutual recognition of conformity assessment conducted by British testing laboratories, leaving it uncertain whether any type of MRA will be negotiated in the future if the UK does not agree to regulatory alignment with EU rules.[34]

## c. MRAs under New-Generation FTAs

Finally, in the 1990s the EU concluded a number of MRAs with third countries, including those with Australia, Canada, Japan, New Zealand and the US. These are traditional MRAs of conformity assessment and typically include pharmaceutical good manufacturing practice (GMP), medical devices telecommunications and electrical safety. While some of the sectoral annexes have been working well

---

[29] C Barnard and E Leinarte, 'EU-Turkey Customs Union', *UK in a Changing Europe* (8 June 2018) available at https://ukandeu.ac.uk/explainers/eu-turkey-customs-union/, last accessed 15 May 2020.

[30] The last meeting of the Accession Conference with Turkey at ministerial level was held on 30 June 2016.

[31] The list of EU instruments relating to the removal of technical barriers to trade that Turkey must implement are listed in Council Decision No 2/97 of the EU-Turkey Association Council of 4 June 1997 establishing the list of Community instruments relating to the removal of technical barriers to trade and the conditions and arrangements governing their implementation by Turkey, 97/438/EC [1997] OJ L191/1.

[32] Art 2(3) of the Council Decision No 1/2006 of the EC-Turkey Association Council of 15 May 2006 on the implementation of Article 9 of Decision No 1/95 of the EC-Turkey Association Council on implementing the final phase of the Customs Union, 2006/654/EC [2006] OJ L265/18.

[33] For an in-depth analysis of the EU-Swiss MRA, see ch 9, 'Mutual Recognition and EFTA', by Georges Baur.

[34] James Crisp, 'European Commission rejects call for UK testing labs to certify products for export to EU market' *The Telegraph* (14 May 2020) available at www.telegraph.co.uk/news/2020/05/14/european-commission-rejects-call-uk-testing-labs-certify-products/, last accessed 16 May 2020.

(eg telecommunications), others are not operational (eg electrical safety, medical devices, pharmaceutical GMP, recreational craft) due to various reasons, some of which we address in the following sections.[35] In its 2004 Working Paper the European Commission concluded that 'traditional' MRAs have proved difficult to negotiate and even more difficult to implement, which renders them not worth pursuing in the future.[36] However, while the European Commission has suggested that only 'enhanced' type MRAs, which are based on alignment of the partner's regulatory regime with that of the EU, are capable of offering the best prospects of implementation and trade facilitation, its recently concluded new-generation FTAs with third countries reveal a U-turn in the European Commission's approach.

The newly concluded FTAs provide for the conclusion of 'traditional' MRAs of conformity assessment in the future, both in the goods and services sectors.[37] For example, Article 4.6 and Article 7.21(4) of the EU-Korea FTA foresee the negotiation of 'traditional' mutual recognition regimes for goods and services respectively. In addition, the EU and the US have recently renegotiated the 1998 Pharmaceutical GMP Annex – a 'traditional' MRA that has proved to be unsuccessful for the reasons we address in section IV.C (the new MRA came into force in 2017).[38] Significantly, under the 2017 EU-US Pharmaceutical GMP MRA, the parties are relieved from batch-testing[39] human medicines covered by the MRA, provided these controls have been carried out in the US for products manufactured in, and imported from, the US. Waiving the batch-testing requirement when importing medicinal products from the US will relieve the so-called Qualified Persons (QPs) of the European pharmaceutical companies of their responsibilities for carrying out the controls laid down in Article 22(1)(b) of Council Directive 75/319/EEC,[40] which requires each production batch coming from third countries to undergo full testing in accordance with the requirements of the marketing authorisation (provided that each batch is accompanied by a batch certificate issued by the manufacturer and signed by the person responsible for releasing the batch). Given how complex and time-consuming batch-manufacturing processes

---

[35] Newsletter No 10 (n 26).

[36] Commission, 'Priorities for Bilateral/Regional trade related activities in the field of Mutual Recognition Agreements for industrial products and related technical dialogue', Staff Working Paper, SEC(2004)1072.

[37] While Art 4.6 refers to 'exchange of information' on a number of different forms for acceptance of each other's conformity assessment results, including voluntary agreements between CABs/ABs, Art 7.21(4) establishes an obligation to negotiate a bilateral MRA.

[38] The MRA has been fully operational for human medicines as of 11 July 2019, following a transition phase.

[39] Batch testing is the main manufacturing approach in the pharmaceutical sector. In batch production, manufacturing is divided into multiple steps – there are stops at the end of each step before moving to the next step. This may be time-consuming, especially as materials are shipped to a different location between steps. An alternative method of production is continuous manufacturing, where products are produced in one continuous process, in one facility, without hold times.

[40] Second Council Directive of 20 May 1975 on the approximation of provisions laid down by law, regulation or administrative action relating to proprietary medicinal products, 75/319/EEC [1975] OJ L147/13.

are, the batch-testing waiver will greatly reduce the regulatory burden for drug-importing companies. The waiver will allow both the US and the EU to reallocate resources towards the inspection of drug-manufacturing facilities with potentially higher risks across the globe.

In this context CETA stands out from the other new-generation FTAs, in that instead of calling the parties to negotiate MRAs in the future, it actually contains MRAs of conformity assessment for a number of products. CETA's Protocol on the mutual acceptance of the results of conformity assessment (CETA CA Protocol) obliges the parties to accept conformity assessment results in a wide range of sectors,[41] and envisages an expansion of sectoral coverage in other priority sectors.[42] In addition, CETA contains the Protocol on the mutual recognition of the compliance and enforcement programme regarding good manufacturing practices for pharmaceutical products (CETA Pharmaceutical GMP), which provides for mutual recognition of certificates of GMP compliance. It should be noted, however, that while the mutual recognition regime under CETA provides for broad sectoral coverage, it is limited to recognition of conformity assessment results, not of technical requirements, that is, CETA does not provide for the conclusion of 'enhanced' MRAs.

Finally, Chapter 11 of CETA establishes guidelines for negotiating MRAs for professional qualifications. Chapter 11 is largely modelled on the approach and experience of the 2008 Québec-France Agreement on the mutual recognition of the qualifications of skilled workers. The guidelines are aimed at the relevant authorities or professional bodies within EU/Canada, which are called to submit joint recommendations for MRAs in specific professions. While the Chapter 11 guidelines are non-binding, they must be considered as good practice in the field. The only recommendation submitted thus far is the draft Mutual Recognition Agreement of Professional Qualifications between the Architects' Council of Europe and the Canadian Architectural Licensing Authorities.[43] The draft MRA was considered in the first meeting[44] of CETA's Joint Committee on Mutual Recognition of Professional Qualifications.[45]

## iv. Preliminary Conclusions

So far in this chapter we have considered the different types of MRAs that have been negotiated to date. It is noticeable how far short these MRAs are from the

---

[41] Annex 1 of the CA Protocol lists the following sectors: electrical and electronic equipment, telecommunications, electromagnetic compatibility, toys, construction products, machinery, measuring instruments, hot-water boilers, ATEX equipment, outdoors equipment and recreational craft.

[42] Annex 2 of the CA Protocol lists the priority categories, including medical devices.

[43] The text of the draft agreements is available at www.ace-cae.eu/fileadmin/New_Upload/_14_International/MOUs/ACE-CALA_MRA__180409_v16_FINAL.pdf, last accessed 15 May 2020.

[44] The meeting took place in Brussels on 16 April 2019.

[45] Established under Art 26.2.1(b) of CETA.

*Cassis de Dijon* model underpinning the EU's internal market. Nevertheless, they are clearly better than nothing (although as section III will show, their economic benefits are difficult to quantify). In the following sections of this chapter we shall address some of the challenges that arise during the negotiations of MRAs (section IV) and some of the trust-building techniques that have been adopted by trade negotiators to address them (section V). Our analysis is based on two primary case studies: the 1998 EU-US MRA and the CA Protocol under CETA. The two MRAs show the changing approach to MRA negotiations, and thus offer a number of valuable lessons for MRA treaty-making.

One final note by way of introduction. A question has arisen as to whether MRAs are compatible with WTO law. The issue has been addressed in detail elsewhere and thus will not be covered in this chapter.[46] Suffice it to say that Bartels has suggested that technical regulations that contain the mutual recognition regimes applicable to products from specific countries ipso facto violate the most-favoured-nation obligation under Article I:1 GATT 1994, and may violate the national treatment and most-favoured-nation obligation under Articles 2.1 and 6.1 of the Agreement on Technical Barriers to Trade (TBT Agreement), unless participation in such regimes, while conditional, is nevertheless open to all WTO members.[47]

# III.  Incentives to Negotiate MRAs

## A.  Economic Benefits

So why are MRAs negotiated? The obvious answer is cost saving. However, somewhat surprisingly, given their importance, the exact effects of MRAs on trade flows are not known.[48] One of the factors that prevent the collection of empirical data is that many countries do not have registers collating the number of testing reports issued under MRAs.[49] Furthermore, impact assessments prior to negotiation of an

---

[46] eg L Bartels, 'The Legality of the EC Mutual Recognition Clause under the WTO Law' (2005) 8 *Journal of International Economic Law* 691; JP Trachtman, 'Embedding Mutual Recognition at the WTO' (2007) 14 *Journal of European Public Policy* 780; Joel P Trachtman, 'Regulatory Jurisdiction and the WTO' (2007) 10 *Journal of International Economic Law* 631; Joshua A Zell, 'Just Between You and Me: Mutual Recognition Agreements and the Most-Favoured Nation Principle' (2016) 1 *World Trade Review* 3; Robert Howse, 'Regulatory Cooperation, Regional Trade Agreements, and World Trade Law: Conflict or Complementarity?' (2015) 78 *Law and Contemporary Problems* 137.

[47] Bartels, 'The Legality of the EC Mutual Recognition Clause' (n 46).

[48] The most notable survey of empirical literature on the impact of MRAs has been conducted by M Vancauteren, 'Trade Effects of Approaches Intended to Facilitate Acceptance of Results of Conformity Assessment: What is the evidence?', Paper presented at the 2009 Workshop and Policy Dialogue on Technical Barriers to Trade: Promoting Good Practices in Support of Open Markets, OECD Headquarters, Paris, 5–6 October 2009, available at www.researchgate.net/publication/237832028_Trade_effects_of_approaches_intended_to_facilitate_acceptance_of_results_of_conformity_assessment_What_is_the_evidence, last accessed 15 May 2020.

[49] World Trade Organisation, 'Japan's Experience Concerning Cross-border Designation System' (Committee on Technical Barriers to Trade, 2007) Doc G/TBT/W/277.

MRA are not always carried out or do not include a comparison with alternative international regulatory cooperation mechanisms.[50] Nevertheless, while the value of the role of MRAs in trade liberalisation can be questioned, given that most costs of TBTs are attributed to regulatory divergence that is not (directly) affected by traditional MRAs, studies do suggest that MRAs have a positive effect on the initial decision to export,[51] as well as on trade flows.[52]

This explains why expectation of economic gains is the primary incentive for MRAs. For example, the US Commerce Department had estimated that the 1998 EU-US MRA would save US industries more than $1 billion annually in testing and certification costs.[53] In the electronics sector alone, double testing and certification cost $70 million to the US exporters to Europe each year.[54] On the US side, the strongest support for the EU-US MRA came from the telecommunications industry, which, at the time of the start of negotiations of the MRA in 1994, exported to Europe more than twice the value of telecommunications equipment exported by the EU to the US,[55] prompting Art Wall, MRA negotiator on behalf of the US Federal Communications Commission, to say the Telecom Industry Association was the major force driving the EU-US MRA in the United States.[56] The Europeans, too, were motivated by economic benefits. The EU was determined to include the pharmaceuticals and medical devices sectors – no surprise given that in 1990s the EU was the world's largest producer and exporter of pharmaceutical products.[57]

Relatedly, past MRA negotiation experience shows that strong demand for mutual recognition in particular sectors has often led to sectoral bargaining. For example, during the negotiations of the 1998 EU-US MRA, both sides had clear sectoral preferences. As has been mentioned, the US sought to include the telecommunications sector, an offer that was met with little enthusiasm from the EU. As a trade-off, the EU officials came forward with a number of sectors they wanted to include, primarily pharmaceuticals, medical devices and electrical safety.[58]

---

[50] OECD Report 2016 (n 1) 38.

[51] S Baller, 'Trade Effects of Regional Standards Liberalisation: a Heterogeneous Firms Approach', *World Bank Policy Research Paper, WPS4124* (2007) available at http://documents.worldbank.org/curated/en/620221468337797645/pdf/WP04124.pdf, last accessed 15 May 2020.

[52] G Orefice, R Piermartini and N Rocha, 'Harmonization and mutual recognition: What are the effects on trade?', Paper presented at the 15th Annual Conference on Global Economic Analysis, Geneva, 2012, available at www.gtap.agecon.purdue.edu/resources/download/5808.pdf, last accessed 15 May 2020.

[53] KSG Case Study (n 1), referring to Charles Ludolph, Deputy Assistant Secretary for Europe, US Department of Commerce, hearing before the House Subcommittee on Oversight and Investigations of the Committee on Commerce, 'Imported Drugs: US-EU Mutual Recognition Agreement on Drug Inspections' (105th Congress, 2nd session, 2 October 1998).

[54] Editorial, 'The Strength of Dialogue' *The Journal of Commerce* (5 June 1997) 6A.

[55] KSG Case Study (n 1) 7.

[56] ibid.

[57] M Perez Pugatch, The International Political Economy of Intellectual Property Rights (Cheltenham, Edward Elgar 2004) 83.

[58] KSG Case Study (n 1) 8.

The two partners had a different approach to sectoral negotiations – the EU sought to negotiate the MRAs as a package, with the selection of sectors based on economic interests, whereas the US promoted unbundling, that is, separating out the sectors.[59] Following the EU's firm position that it would not negotiate agreements in the other sectors unless pharmaceutical GMP was included, the US agreed to cover the latter.[60]

## B. Dealing with Regulatory Divergence

Mutual recognition agreements are more likely in those sectors subject to high regulatory divergence.[61] This is particularly so with respect to those industries in which there is a conscious choice not to change or reform domestic regulation.[62] A good example in this regard is the telecommunications sector, which is included in the majority of existing MRAs and where mutual recognition has proved to be functioning well.[63] In the telecoms equipment and electronic goods sectors, where regulatory divergence is a major trade obstacle, mutual recognition is a particularly attractive instrument, because there is a need for compatibility and interoperability of equipment, which also explains the demand for the development of international standards (IEC) in this sector.[64] Other heavily regulated sectors include high-risk medical devices, medicines, cars and trucks, chemicals and metrology. It should be noted, however, that MRAs in heavily regulated sectors are only possible once a considerable degree of alignment has taken place, a point we address in more detail in section IV.

## C. Testing Requirements

Another incentive that plays an important role in determining the scope of MRAs is testing requirements. Mutual recognition agreements are limited to those sectors that are subject to mandatory conformity assessment by a third party prior to products'

---

[59] ibid 20.

[60] Trade talks broke down in March 1996 when European negotiators rejected a US proposal to delink and drop pharmaceuticals and medical devices sectors from the negotiations due to slow progress in these two sectors: KSG Case Study (n 1)19.

[61] MRAs usually do not apply to harmonised regulatory regimes, see ASEAN, *Guidelines for the Development of Mutual Recognition Arrangements*, 2nd edn (ASEAN Consultative Committee on Standards & Quality, 20 May 2016) Annex 2, 20, available at https://asean.org/storage/2012/05/Guidelines-for-the-Development-of-Mutual-Recognition-Arrangements.pdf, last accessed 15 May 2020.

[62] OECD Report 2016 (n 1) 58.

[63] eg the European Commission has stated that, in general, the Telecommunications Annex under the 1998 EU-US MRA is working satisfactorily, see Commission, 'Technical Barriers to Trade: Mutual Recognition Agreements and Agreements on Conformity Assessment and Acceptance of Industrial Products' (Newsletter No 9) October 2015 (hereinafter 'Newsletter No 9').

[64] OECD Report 2016 (n 1) 38.

being placed on the market.[65] Accordingly, goods that are subject to the SDoC usually fall outside the scope of MRAs – given that the SDoC regime allows supplies to self-declare the conformity of a product with the applicable technical regulations of the import country, the parties do not have an interest in mutual recognition of conformity assessment. In some cases, an MRA may include a product that is subject to third-party certification in one state while a supplier's declaration is sufficient in the other. In such situations an MRA would be operative one way only (ie for products imported to the state party that does not require assessment by CABs).[66] Past experience has shown, however, such MRAs are not successful. A good example in this regard is low voltage electrical equipment, which under EU law is subject to the SDoC regime and does not involve assessment by CABs.[67]

Electrical safety MRAs have been included in the 1998 EU-Canada MRA, the 2002 EU-Japan MRA, the 1998 EU-US MRA, the 1999 EU-Australia and the 1999 EU-New Zealand MRA but are not operational (ie those sectoral MRAs have been concluded but have not been used in practice) under any of the agreements.[68] Furthermore, there being no requirement for third-party assessment may reduce the bargaining power during MRA negotiations, which proved to be the experience of EU negotiators during the 1998 EU-US MRA talks. According to Giacomo Mattinò, an MRA negotiator from the European Commission's Directorate-General for Enterprise, the EU had no leverage in electrical safety because the US manufacturers already had full market access as they could certify themselves.[69] Recreational craft provides another example of a sector that has been included in a number of MRAs but has typically proved to be not operational, precisely because it is not subject to mandatory third-party testing (eg the 1999 EU-Canada MRA, the 1998 EU-US MRA).

## D. Other Matters

Other incentives may also motivate MRA treaty-making. For example, the OECD identified several principal drivers for international cooperation in the field of chemical safety, which covers, inter alia, industrial chemicals, pharmaceuticals, pesticides, food and cosmetics. In addition to economic reasons (the cost for a pesticide company to test one new active ingredient for health and environmental effects is approximately €17 million[70]), MRAs assist states in creating an

[65] ibid 17.

[66] eg while electrical installations and appliances are included in CETA, some of these products do not require third-party conformity assessment and are subject to self-declaration, see Directive 2014/35/EU (n 12).

[67] Directive 2006/95/EC of 12 December 2006 on the harmonisation of the laws of Member States relating to electrical equipment designed for use within certain voltage limits does not require third-party certification [2006] OJ L374/10.

[68] Newsletter No 10 (n 26).

[69] KSG Case Study (n 1) 25.

[70] OECD, Joint Meeting of the Chemicals Committee and Working Party on Chemicals, Pesticides and Biotechnology Report, *Cutting Costs in Chemicals Management: How OECD Helps Governments*

international comprehensive risk management scheme, ensuring more effective assessments based on international cooperation, which is vital in the chemical safety sector due to its high risk of cross-border environmental damage.

There may, in some cases, be political or strategic reasons for negotiating an MRA. For example, it has been suggested that the US pharmaceutical industry saw the 1998 EU-US MRA negotiations as an opportunity to encourage reforms in the US Food and Drug Administration (FDA).[71] At the time of the trade talks there was, especially within the medical device industry, a certain frustration with the FDA's market approval process, which some business actors perceived as slow and complex. In the pharmaceuticals sector, too, there was a wish to streamline testing procedures that were considered costly, time-consuming and slow. The MRA would allow pharmaceutical companies to choose to work with either the FDA or a private EU testing body, depending on which one was more efficient, since it would allow EU agencies to inspect a US manufacturers' product to verify that it met US requirements. The US industry considered the new European medical device regulation system, which was based on a public-private partnership in which the private NBs approved products based on the set standards, to be more modern, efficient and highly developed than that of the FDA.

Finally, it has been suggested that the US Government was motivated to negotiate an MRA with the EU because of the US's concerns that the EU's pursuit of the single market threatened to drive out US exports by imposing EU-wide trade barriers.[72] Europeans, on the other hand, may have seen the MRA as an opportunity to create a consensus-based system that would counteract the more argumentative approach of the US, experienced under the GATT system.[73]

Despite the parties' incentives for bilateral mutual recognition regimes, past experience shows that the process of MRA negotiation has often been complex. In the next section we address some of the key challenges to the negotiation of mutual recognition agreements.

# IV.  Challenges to the Negotiation of Mutual Recognition Agreements

## A.  Introduction

Given that the essence of MRAs is delegation of product testing functions to foreign entities, these agreements require a high and sustained degree of trust between the parties in each other's regulatory regimes for accreditation and

---

*and Industry*, (Paris, OECD Publishing, 2010) available at www.oecd.org/env/ehs/47813784.pdf, last accessed 15 May 2020.
[71] KSG Case Study (n 1) 13.
[72] ibid 6.
[73] ibid 19.

conformity assessment. While trust is usually not an issue in the case of 'enhanced' MRAs, which are based on aligned technical requirements, parties to traditional MRAs must trust that a CAB in the production state is well aware of the rules and procedures of the importing state and will be able to effectively implement these regulations. The OECD suggests that a lack of trust can be costly; it may undermine the cooperative attitude of partners and derail the MRA scheme.[74] This may explain why the vast majority of MRAs have been concluded between developed countries.[75]

Mutual trust, however, is not an easy goal to achieve. Evidence of past experience in negotiating MRAs suggests that there are two main challenges that prevent parties to an MRA from trusting each other's capacity to ensure that imported products meet their standards and technical regulations: first, differences in the nature and competences of the parties' regulatory bodies; and, second, differences in the technical requirements for accreditation and product testing.

In this section we address the two noted challenges by referring to the experience of negotiating the Pharmaceutical GMP Annex and Medical Devices Annex under the 1998 EU-US MRA as a case study. The two sectoral annexes provide a valuable illustration of how regulatory and institutional differences between the EU and US regimes made it difficult for the parties to reach a common understanding over mutual recognition. The 1998 EU-US MRA negotiations, which were first of their kind, took years of on-off discussions (pre-discussions commenced in 1992 but were not fruitful) and were marred by differences in approach to the sectoral coverage, the role of business lobbying, the function of regulatory bodies and many other aspects of mutual recognition. Negotiations of the Pharmaceutical GMP Annex were particularly complicated, primarily because, according to Lydgale and Winters, the differences in drug approval procedures were difficult to overcome, and the US was reluctant to concede that EU producers could meet its safety standards.[76]

## B. Institutional Differences

One of the biggest challenges to trust between the parties during the negotiations of the 1998 EU-US Pharmaceutical GMP Annex stemmed from the fundamentally different nature of US and European regulators. Before we address some of these differences in more detail, we should like to give a brief overview of the relevant regulatory agencies.

The US adopts a centralised system, in which clinical trials and market approval of new drugs are conducted at the federal level by a single regulatory body, the FDA.

---

[74] OECD Report 2016 (n 1) 12.

[75] The OECD identifies two MRAs concluded with developing countries – those between Japan and the Philippines and Taiwan: ibid 38.

[76] E Lydgale and AL Winters, 'Deep and Not Comprehensive? What the WTO Rules Permit for a UK-EU FTA' (2019) 18 *World Trade Review* 463.

In the EU, the position is more complicated. Clinical trial applications are approved at the Member State level,[77] whereas marketing authorisation applications may follow one of four routes: centralised, national, mutual recognition and decentralised authorisation procedures.[78] The centralised procedure is compulsory for certain groups of medicines (eg those derived from any biotechnological processes or intended for the treatment of cancer or autoimmune diseases, as well as medicines used for rare diseases).[79] Under the centralised procedure, a drug is tested by the European Medicines Agency (EMA), which recommends it to the European Commission for final approval.[80] A centralised procedure allows pharmaceutical companies to obtain a single marketing authorisation, which is valid in all Member States as well as in the EEA.

Medicines that do not fall under the mandatory centralised procedure category (this includes most generic medicines and medicines available without a prescription) are assessed by the Member States following the national authorisation procedure. Each Member State designates accredited NBs to conduct conformity assessments. A manufacturer can place a CE mark on a medical device once it has passed conformity assessment. The national procedure allows the producer to market a product in the Member State where the CE was issued. If a manufacturer wishes to obtain an authorisation in several EU Member States for a medicine that is outside the scope of the centralised procedure, it may follow a mutual recognition regime that allows for an authorisation granted in one Member State to be recognised in other EU countries, or, alternatively, a decentralised procedure, whereby a medicine that has not yet been authorised in the EU can be simultaneously authorised in several EU Member States. The European multi-route system synchronises regulations of the Member States in order to eliminate duplication of institutional work when parallel submissions for approvals are made to individual Member States.[81]

Accordingly, one of the significant differences between the regulatory set-up in the EU and the US, which became apparent during negotiations of the 1998 EU-US Pharmaceutical GMP Annex, was that the US regulator – the FDA – is directly involved in the conformity assessment process and is responsible for issuing approvals, whereas in the EU the public authority is not directly certifying

---

[77] Clinical trials are regulated by Regulation (EU) No 536/2014 of the European Parliament and of the Council of 16 April 2014 on clinical trials on medicinal products for human use, and repealing Directive 2001/20/EC [2014] OJ L158/1.

[78] Competence for marketing approval was transferred from the Member States to the EU in 1993 with the adoption of the Maastricht Treaty – before that, each country had its own approach to device evaluation.

[79] UN Kashyap, V Gupta, HV Raghunandan, 'Comparison of Drug Approval Process in United States & Europe' (2013) 5 *Journal of Pharmaceutical Sciences & Research* 133.

[80] Note that under EU law, EMA has no authority to actually permit marketing in the different EU countries.

[81] MH Allchurch et al, 'Fifty Years of the European Medicines Regulatory Network: Reflections for Strengthening Intraregional Cooperation in the Region of the Americas' (2016) 39 *Revista Panamericana. De Salud Pública* 288.

products but instead delegates this function to third parties, each of which follows its own processes.[82] Such differences, according to Van Norman, mean that while the EU process may provide for more flexibility, its complex network of institutions and responsibilities for oversight make the EU system more difficult to define.[83] Therefore, in the early stages of negotiations these complex systemic arrangements required additional time for, to use Karl Falkenberg's phrase, 'mutual education', and the first two years of negotiations were mainly devoted to information sharing in order for partners to become familiar with each other's conformity assessment procedures.[84]

Another fundamental institutional aspect that made negotiations of the 1998 Pharmaceutical GMP and Medical Devices Annexes more challenging relates to the differences in the *nature* of the FDA and the European medicines regulatory network. Though both European and US regulatory bodies perform similar functions, the underlying foundation of these institutions differs significantly, and these differences lie primarily in their historical origins. Van Norman suggests that the FDA was established as a central answer to the problem of the increasing marketing of health products that were harmful, or for which benefits were unproven or minimal.[85] The Federal Food, Drug and Cosmetics Act of 1938 invested the agency with competence to oversee that drugs are not only effective, but also safe.[86] Product safety concerns were (and remain) at the core of the FDA's mandate.[87] By contrast, the EMA, which was founded in 1995, was charged with harmonisation tasks aimed at reducing annual costs to drug companies, as well as the elimination of competition-restricting regulations, while at the same time preserving national autonomy.[88] Similarly, the European system of NBs was developed out of initiatives to foster innovation and commercial policies, not as public health or consumer protection bodies.[89] This 'trade v safety standards' mission of the regulatory agencies posed a number of challenges during the negotiations of the 1998 EU-US MRA.

One of the issues that became apparent during the negotiations was that due to its consumer-protection orientated nature, the FDA's experience in trade-related negotiations was scarce, save for its limited involvement in the Uruguay Round of discussions in the 1990s.[90] Walter Batts, the FDA's director of international relations

---

[82] KSG Case Study (n 1) 14.

[83] GA Van Norman, 'Drugs and Devices: Comparison of European and US Approval Processes' (2016) 1 *JACC Basic to Translational Science* 399.

[84] KSG Case Study (n 1)14.

[85] GA Van Norman, 'Drugs, Devices, and the FDA: Part 1: An Overview of Approval Processes' (2016) 1 *JACC Basic to Translational Science* 170.

[86] US Food and Drug Administration, 'Milestones in US Food and Drug Law History', available at www.fda.gov/about-fda/fdas-evolving-regulatory-powers/milestones-us-food-and-drug-law-history, last accessed 15 May 2020.

[87] The 1976 Medical Device Amendments to the 1938 Federal Food Drug and Cosmetic Act gave the FDA power to regulate medical devices.

[88] Van Norman, 'Drugs and Devices' (n 83) 400.

[89] ibid 403.

[90] KSG Case Study (n 1) 10.

who represented the regulator in the MRA negotiations, noted that the FDA is not a trade agency. According to him, 'until very recently, there hasn't been anything in our legislation that indicates we should be involved in these kind of things … But at the same time, because we regulate such a wide range of products, we obviously have impact on trade'.[91] In the meantime, the Office of the United States Trade Representative (USTR) and the Department of Commerce, which were part of the inter-agency negotiating group that also involved sectoral regulators,[92] perceived the negotiations of the EU-US MRA from a trade perspective. Meanwhile, the FDA was adamant that mutual recognition of conformity assessment had to be negotiated as a regulatory matter.[93] This mismatch in priorities put the FDA in a contradictory situation. One the one hand, despite its lack of experience in trade discussions, it became a key negotiator (alongside the USTR and the Department of Commerce) of the Pharmaceutical GMP Annex. At the same time, it was reluctant to participate in the negotiations of an agreement primarily aimed at trade liberalisation.[94]

The FDA's concerns that trade priorities may take over safety standards stemmed not only from its mistrust of the trade orientated nature of its co-negotiators. The commercial aspects of the European system of certification, too, were a cause of mistrust. In particular, the CE mark is an indication of compliance with EU requirements. It is not in itself a guarantor of quality, at least from an external perspective. This can be seen by the 2014 report on the approval process for medical devices in the EU prepared by the Global Legal Research Center, which noted that 'The legal value of the CE marking lies in its proof that the medical device concerned is in full compliance with applicable legislation. On the other hand, the CE marking does not represent quality'.[95]

The European system of issuing CE marks, too, did not exactly reflect the regulatory approach of the FDA. Notified Bodies, which are assigned by the Member States to conduct CE marking, are private for-profit companies that collect fees from manufacturers for issuing CE certificates that allow a product to be marketed in an EU Member State.[96] Though, from a legal perspective, producers can apply to only one NB at a time, in practice they often approach several NBs before deciding which one is more likely to approve their products, and some suggest that NBs are often on the side of the manufacturer and their products, not on the side of patients.[97] Notified Bodies follow different standards, which allows

---

[91] ibid 5.

[92] Among the agencies involved in the inter-agency negotiating group were the Federal Communications Commission, the Environmental Protection Agency and the Federal Aviation Agency.

[93] KSG Case Study (n 1) 21.

[94] ibid 3.

[95] Global Legal Research Center, 'Approval of Medical Devices' (the Law Library of Congress, September 2014) available at www.loc.gov/law/help/medical-devices/index.php, last accessed 15 May 2020.

[96] AJM Boulton, 'Registration and Regulation of Medical Devices Used in Diabetes in Europe: Need for Radical Reform (2013) 1 *Lancet Diabetes Endocrinol* 270.

[97] D Cohen, 'How a Fake Hip Showed Up Failings in the European Device Regulation' (2012) 345 (7880) *British Medical Journal* 19.

device manufacturers to select an NB with the least stringent requirements.[98] The Bodies may thus be disincentivised to disapprove devices, as this may decrease the number of subsequent applications. Furthermore, given that NBs are private companies that enter into contracts with manufacturers, the data reviewed by these bodies, the tests they require of applicants and the results of these tests are subject to commercial confidentiality, which is contrary to the FDA's policies.[99]

A related institutional aspect that became a challenge during the negotiations of the 1998 EU-US MRA was the question of agency monopoly. When negotiations of the 1998 EU-US MRA officially commenced in 1994, both parties formed their negotiating teams. Work on the US side was led by an inter-agency group consisting of the USTR, the Department of Commerce and sectoral agencies.[100] From Europe, the talks were conducted by the European Commission's DG Trade, with representatives from DG Enterprise also participating. One of the essential institutional differences, noted by the lead EU negotiator Karl Falkenberg of the DG Trade, was allocation of authority: while the USTR and sectoral regulators, like the FDA, acted independently of one another, the European Commission is a collective entity composed of various Directors-General, who have different responsibilities.[101] Accordingly, the FDA enjoys a regulatory monopoly and, according to the OECD, what for the EU boils down to merely following the spirit of the MRA, may signify regulatory reform and sense of 'loss' of control for an agency so accustomed to a full say on a matter.[102] Accordingly, such agencies might wish to protect their full remit, but also claim that any change would possibly jeopardise health and safety.[103] Karl Falkenberg seconds this view by suggesting that regulatory authorities

> believe that the only safe products are those tested by the agency itself – every foreign body is unfit. That attitude existed in Europe as it exists in the US, or anywhere else. In Europe, the New Approach to recognition within the EU basically broke this monopoly. Member States were forced to recognize what their Portuguese, Spanish, British, Swedish, French, or other colleagues were doing. In the US, we were still up against a complete monopoly. There was only the FDA.[104]

It should not be suggested, however, that tendency to retain authority during the negotiations of the MRA was a characteristic exclusive to the US agencies. For example, it has been suggested by one US negotiator that the reason for the DG Trade's push for a framework agreement that would overarch

---

[98] Van Norman, 'Drugs and Devices' (n 83) 403.

[99] P McCulloch, 'The EU's System for Regulating Medical Devices: Now is the Time for Radical Change' (2012) 345 (7880) *British Medical Journal* 10.

[100] Among the participating agencies were the Federal Communications Commission, the Federal Aviation Agency, the Environmental Protection Agency, the Occupational Safety and Health Administration, the US Department of Agriculture.

[101] KSG Case Study (n 1) 14.

[102] OECD Report 2016 (n 1) 27.

[103] ibid.

[104] KSG Case Study (n 1) 21.

sectoral MRAs – an idea the US negotiators considered unnecessary and overly burdensome – may have been motivated by the DG Trade's quest to stay in charge of all other Directors-General that were responsible for their respective sectors.[105]

Institutional differences were one of the key challenges that prevented the parties from reaching a consensus during the negotiations of the 1998 EU-US MRA. Another major obstacle was regulatory divergence, due to which negotiations have repeatedly ground to a halt.

## C. Regulatory Divergence

We suggested in section III that regulatory divergence serves as an incentive for mutual recognition regimes: different testing procedures and requirements constitute a barrier to trade that can be mitigated by MRAs. There is, however, a paradox. While regulatory divergence is a driver for MRAs, it may also pose serious challenges for the successful negotiation and functioning of this type of agreements. This is especially so in heavily regulated sectors, such as the automobile industry, which is one of the reasons why there are no MRAs in this sector, except for the Automotive Products Annex under the 1999 EU-Australia MRA[106] and the successor 2019 UK-Australia MRA (these MRAs cover automotive components, not whole cars).

The OECD suggests that MRAs in heavily regulated markets are only possible once a considerable degree of regulatory alignment has taken place.[107] This explains why one of the most successfully functioning bilateral MRAs to date is the TTMRA, an MRA between Australia and New Zealand. The two partners have a unique relationship based on closely aligned regulatory regimes. Furthermore, New Zealand is part of the Council of Australian Government for the purposes of the MRA, which has resulted in both states enacting laws for the legal implementation and enforcement of the TTMRA.[108]

Another example of a successful MRA is the 2004 EU-US MRA on marine equipment, which is based on International Maritime Organisation (IMO) rules. The OECD's Mutual Acceptance of Data (MAD) system under the Environment, Health and Safety Programme for OECD-wide acceptance of testing results for chemical safety provides an example of a well-functioning multilateral mutual recognition regime based on aligned quality requirements for tests.[109] On the

---

[105] ibid 30.
[106] The Annex, however, is not operational.
[107] OECD Report 2016 (n 1) 27.
[108] ibid 20.
[109] The MAD system is based on the OECD Test Guidelines and GMP, see OECD, *International Regulatory Co-operation: Case Studies*, vol 1: *Chemicals, Consumer Products, Tax and Competition* (Paris, OECD Publishing, 2013) 12–14, available at www.oecd.org/regreform/regulatory-policy/international-regulatory-co-operation-case-studies-vol-1-9789264200487-en.htm, last accessed 15 May 2020.

side of the spectrum is the 1998 EU-US MRA, which illustrates the unwillingness of the parties to engage in regulatory alignment, despite the limited scope of the MRA (it does not cover high-risk medical devices and is limited to pharmaceutical GMP). In this section we address some of the differences between the US and EU technical regulations in the pharmaceuticals and medical devices sectors, which impeded the progress of MRA negotiations. The following discussion does not aim to provide a comprehensive comparison of the two regimes and only selected regulatory aspects will be addressed.

Overall, drug approval processes in the EU and the US share many similarities. In the EU, harmonisation of drug approval dates back to 1965 when Directive 65/65/EEC,[110] which established consistent guidelines on the information that had to be submitted for drug approval, was adopted. According to Van Norman, these guidelines mirrored US regulations regarding new drug approval applications.[111] Both EU and US systems mandate pre-clinical testing, three phases of clinical trials and a final approval procedure as part of the drug development process.[112] There are, however, significant regulatory differences, which made it more difficult for the parties to reach a consensus during the MRA negotiations.

One of the reasons for the lack of trust between the parties during the 1998 Pharmaceutical GMP Annex negotiations concerned differences in the level of scrutiny of new medicines. The US regulations call for some of the strictest standards for approving new drugs worldwide. The FDA's guidelines regarding the development and valuation of patient-reported outcomes are more stringent than those of the EMA, although both agencies note the role and value of these measures in bringing the patient's perspective to the assessment of therapeutics.[113] One of the differences, for example, is that while the EMA focuses on global assessments of patient-reported quality of life, the FDA focuses on symptom-specific measures, and requires early planning and cooperation with patient groups to determine the most important symptom concerns.[114] With respect to approval of medical devices, too, the US requirements are more difficult to meet than those of the EU. For example, before approval in the US, a medical device must be shown not only

---

[110] Council Directive 65/65/EEC of 26 January 1965 on the approximation of provisions laid down by Law, Regulation or Administrative Action relating to proprietary medicinal products [1965] OJ L22/369. Repealed by Directive 2001/83/EC of the European Parliament and of the Council of 6 November 2001 on the Community code relating to medicinal products for human use [2001] OJ L311/67.

[111] Van Norman, 'Drugs and Devices' (n 83) 400.

[112] MM Sifuentes and A Giuffrida, 'Drug Review Differences Across the United States and the European Union' (2015) 4 *Pharmaceutical Regulatory Affairs* 4, available at www.hilarispublisher.com/open-access/drug-review-differences-across-the-united-states-and-the-european-union-2167-7689-1000e156.pdf, last accessed 15 May 2020.

[113] LJ Howie, BR Hirsch and AP Abernethy, 'A Comparison of FDA and EMA Drug Approval: Implications for Drug Development and Cost of Care' (2013) 27 *Oncology Journal, Practice & Policy* 12, available at www.cancernetwork.com/oncology-journal/comparison-fda-and-ema-drug-approval-implications-drug-development-and-cost-care, last accessed 15 May 2020.

[114] Sifuentes and Giuffrida, 'Drug Review Differences' (n 112) 1.

to be safe, but also efficacious.[115] The EU, on the other hand, requires only that the producer demonstrate safety and performance, that is that the device performs as designed and that potential benefits outweigh potential risks.[116] Differences in approval standards lead to varying approvals results. One study finds that despite the submission of identical clinical data supporting the same drug, the EMA and the FDA can come to different evaluations and conclusions. Between 1995 and 2008, 20 per cent of oncological pharmaceuticals were approved by either the FDA or the EMA, but not both, and 28 per cent of approved drugs had significant variations in the label wording.[117]

Relatedly, the two systems reveal differences in the speed and rate of approval of new drugs and devices due to the different level of scrutiny over safety and efficacy issues. One study reveals that of the drug applications submitted to EMA and the FDA from 1995 to the end of 2007, the EMA rejected 26 applications that were approved by the FDA, and the FDA rejected 14 application that were approved by the EMA.[118] The agencies' reasons for rejection differed – for the EMA it was the lack of additional data, where the FDA's rejections were primarily due to safety and efficacy issues.

Differences in the agencies' acceptance of specific types of studies were also notable. With respect to the speed of approvals, studies reveal that the FDA typically approves drugs more quickly than the EMA.[119] One study investigating 289 applications for novel therapeutic agents approved from 2001 through to 2010 revealed that 63.7 per cent were first approved in the US as compared to the EU.[120] One of the reasons for the slower processes by the EMA may relate to the fact that market approval in the EU is subject to additional regulations adopted by some Member States, which are the ultimate arbiters of which specific drugs will be marketed under the decentralised procedure.[121]

Another notable difference between the US and EU regimes related to procedures for market surveillance. In the US, physicians, manufacturers and patients have the ability to report adverse effects of marketed drugs and medical devices directly to the FDA, which can withdraw the marketing of an unsafe product. The EU, on the other hand, has adopted a decentralised market surveillance system, where adverse effects are reported to the Member States in which the CE mark was

---

[115] DB Kramer, MD, Shuai Xu, MSc, and AS Kesselheim, 'Regulation of Medical Devices in the United States and European Union' (2012) 366 *The New England Journal of Medicine* 848.

[116] Van Norman, 'Drugs and Devices' (n 83) 404.

[117] F Trotta et al, 'Evaluation of Oncology Drugs at the European Medicines Agency and US Food and Drug Administration: When Differences Have an Impact on Clinical Practice' (2011) 29 *Journal of Clinical Oncology* 2266.

[118] P Huckle, Are Today's Regulatory Submissions Flawed? An Industry Viewpoint. Workshop Report: Predictable Outcomes – Why do Potential Winners Fail? (CMR International Institute for Regulatory Science, 2008), 21.

[119] eg SA Roberts, JD Allen, and EV Sigal, 'Despite Criticism Of The FDA Review Process, New Cancer Drugs Reach Patients Sooner In The United States Than In Europe' (2011) 30 *Health Aff* 1375.

[120] NS Downing et al, 'Regulatory Review of Novel Therapeutics – Comparison of Three Regulatory Agencies' (2012) 366 *The New England Journal of Medicine* 2284.

[121] Sifuentes and Giuffrida, 'Drug Review Differences' (n 112) 1.

obtained. It is the responsibility of the Member States to restrict or withdraw the device. Van Norman suggests that the complexity of bringing a case in the maze of agencies, offices, distributers and manufacturers in the decentralised system of the EU is daunting.[122] This may perhaps explain why product liability lawsuits are less common in Europe than in the US.

Another regulatory difference that complicated the negotiations of the 1998 EU-US MRA was the timing of inspections of manufacturing processes. The US negotiators maintained that negotiations should focus on post-approval (ie once the product is on the market) and not the pre-approval stage (ie when a pharmaceutical company is about to launch a new medicine), whereas the EU side considered that both stages should be covered by the agreement.[123] Despite support of the industry for the European approach, the FDA resisted an agreement that addressed pre-approval processes.[124] Finally, however, the FDA agreed to include the pre-approval stage in exchange for acceptance of its demand for a longer transition period to determine which EU inspection processes would be deemed equivalent to its own.[125]

The parties disagreed not only about the timing of inspections, but also about their publication. The US Food, Drug and Cosmetics Act requires disclosure of inspection reports to the public.[126] The EU negotiators, however, believed that certain documents should not be made public.[127] Furthermore, the EU and the US had different views regarding publication of data, which is generated for drug approval but not submitted for peer review. While the FDA makes available online non-published data included in new drug applications,[128] in the EU such data is considered 'commercially sensitive' and thus not publicly available.[129] Differences in data disclosure policies posed a significant disagreement during the MRA negotiations. While the European Commission declared that it would not support public disclosure of plant inspection reports, it was clear that the US industry and the FDA were not going to seek modifications to the Food, Drugs and Cosmetics Act because changes would require a lot of time.[130] In the end, with the endorsement of European businesses,[131] the European Commission conceded on the disclosure of inspection reports, allowing for the negotiations to proceed.[132]

---

[122] Van Norman, 'Drugs and Devices' (n 83) 409.

[123] KSG Case Study (n 1) 23.

[124] ibid 28.

[125] ibid 34.

[126] § 537 of the US Food, Drug and Cosmetics Act.

[127] KSG Case Study (n 1) 23.

[128] US Food and Drug Administration, 'Drugs@FDA: FDA-Approved Drugs', available at www. accessdata.fda.gov/scripts/cder/drugsatfda/, last accessed 15 May 2020.

[129] Van Norman, 'Drugs and Devices' (n 83) 402.

[130] KSG Case Study (n 1) 23.

[131] Reportedly, the European CEOs of SmithKline Beecham and Glaxo Wellcome insisted that the European pharmaceutical industry is not sensitive regarding the public disclosure of inspection reports, see ibid 28.

[132] K Gopal, 'Discordant Voices' (1997) 17 *Pharmaceutical Executive* 40.

This time it was the FDA that made a concession in return by agreeing to carry out second inspections of EU drug imports only in special circumstances.[133]

Finally, the negotiating parties had different views on the inclusion of rules of origin. Rules of origin allow governments to determine where goods originate, which is relevant when identifying which customs duties to apply to an imported product.[134] In the context of MRAs, these rules impede products with their origin in other countries from benefitting from the MRA. In fact, a study by Chen and Mattoo finds that MRAs tend to be trade promoting unless they contain restrictive rules of origin.[135] While the majority of MRAs do not contain rules of origin,[136] the EU sought to include origin requirements in the 1998 EU-US MRA. The US negotiators, however, saw in this position a protectionist goal, which was to encourage more manufacturing in Europe by limiting trade flows from third countries.[137] Finally, following strong resistance from the US Government as well as US business representatives, especially those in the telecom industry, the European Commission agreed to leave rules of origin out of the agreement.[138]

The EU's insistence on the inclusion of rules of origin was not unique to the EU-US trade talks and was reflective of the EU's general policy for MRA negotiations in the 1990s. For example, rules of origin were initially included in the EU-Australia and the EU-New Zealand MRAs. There has, however, been a change in the EU's position as it aims to introduce greater flexibility in the MRAs. Both the EU's MRA with Australia and the MRA with New Zealand have been modified to remove rules of origin.[139] The latest evidence of the EU's more flexible approach to rules of origin is Article 10(3) of the CA Protocol under CETA, which provides that no regard will be given to the country of origin of the product for which the conformity assessment activities were performed. Accordingly, a conformity assessment body can test or certify equipment manufactured anywhere in the world, as long as it has gone through the appropriate designation and recognition process in Canada or in the EU.

In conclusion, challenges to treaty-making as seen in the EU-US MRA relate to MRAs that were negotiated in the 1990s. There was at the time a lack of experience in negotiating this type of agreements because they were the first of their kind.

---

[133] ibid.

[134] C Barnard and E Leinarte, 'Rules of Origin: Can the EU-UK Trade Be Frictionless?' *UK in a Changing Europe* (5 June 2018) available at https://ukandeu.ac.uk/explainers/rules-of-origin-can-the-eu-uk-trade-be-frictionless/, last accessed 15 May 2020.

[135] MX Chen and A Mattoo, 'Regionalism in standards: good or bad for trade?' (2008) 41 *Canadian Journal of Economics* 3.

[136] OECD Report 2016 (n 1) 23.

[137] KSG Case Study (n 1) 26.

[138] ibid.

[139] Art 2 of the Agreement between the European Union and Australia amending the Agreement on mutual recognition in relation to conformity assessment, certificates and markings between the European Community and Australia [2012] OJ L359/02; Art 2 of the Agreement between the European Union and New Zealand amending the Agreement on mutual recognition in relation to conformity assessment between the European Community and New Zealand [2012] OJ L356/02.

Therefore, it is more appropriate to consider the issues that impeded the progress of negotiations (and later implementation) of the EU-US MRA as part of the learning process rather than as failures. The past experience may have informed the new millennium MRA negotiators of the various trust-building techniques that were employed in the negotiations of the new-generation MRAs. The following section will address these techniques in more detail.

# V. Trust-Building Techniques

Given the challenges that arise from a lack of trust between the trading parties over each other's ability to ensure product safety, a number of trust-building techniques have been employed in the negotiations of the second-wave MRAs[140] in order to enhance information sharing, communication and collaboration. The OECD suggests that much can be done to earn trust, including a co-operative attitude in committees and the allowance of time to build up trust between regulators or CABs.[141] In fact, a number of MRAs, for example the 2012 Canada-Mexico and the 2011 US-Mexico MRA[142] in telecommunications, provide for a transition period after the date of signing the MRA, during which a number of trust-building activities are to take place.[143] Furthermore, in some cases, for example the 2013 Canada-Israel MRA in telecommunications, the implementation of an MRA is divided into several phases, with Phase I implementation providing for the mutual recognition of testing laboratories while Phase II is to be agreed at a later stage. While trust-building techniques are many, and it is not possible to discuss them all in this chapter,[144] we will address the following methods that were adopted by the negotiators of the CETA CA Protocol and the 2017 EU-US Pharmaceutical GMP MRA: (i) the conclusion of a special agreement between the regulators that calls for inter-agency cooperation; (ii) the making of the necessary legislative changes; and (iii) the use of pilot projects. In addition, we will refer to the 1998 EU-US MRA in order to illustrate the role of industry in MRA treaty-making.

---

[140] Our reference to the 'second wave' is not based on any official categorisation but is instead intended to distinguish between the first MRAs concluded in the 1990s and MRAs concluded post-2000.

[141] OECD Report 2016 (n 1) 59.

[142] The Agreement was signed on 26 May 2011 and was implemented (by the US) on 26 September 2017.

[143] Arts 17 of both MRAs, which are entitled 'Confidence Building Work Program and Transition Period', list a number of possible trust-building actions, including joint meetings between designating authorities, regulatory authorities and accreditation bodies; facilitation of technical cooperation activities; and joint training courses and seminars for testing laboratories, manufacturers and accreditation bodies, and others.

[144] Some of the examples include training of CABs in the partner's regulatory requirements, organisation of joint inspections, conduct of inspections of manufacturers located in the partner's territory, and others.

## A.  Inter-agency Cooperation

An agreement between the regulatory bodies aimed at enhancing information sharing and communication under the CETA CA Protocol is an example of a technique to build trust between the parties to an MRA. The Bilateral Cooperation Agreement (BCA) was signed on 10 July 2016 between the Standards Council of Canada (SCC) and the European cooperation for Accreditation (EA), a regional accreditation body formally appointed by the European Commission[145] that brings together, on the basis of a multilateral agreement of mutual recognition (the EA MLA), the national accreditation bodies in Europe.[146] The EA's partner institution on the Canadian side – the SCC – is a Crown corporation established to accredit organisations that perform conformity assessment.[147]

The purpose of the BCA is to facilitate the recognition of CABs, allowing for the mutual acceptance by Canada and the EU of test results and product certifications delivered by each other's recognised bodies.[148] The Agreement enables exchange of information on the applicable standards and assessment procedures, the setting up of an assessor pool, and observation of experts from the EA/the SCC of each other's performance of assessment of CABs in accordance with its legislation. Importantly, mutual recognition of accreditation will only occur once the SCC and the EA consider both parties to be ready.[149] It has been agreed that products subject to assessment will be selected and implemented, upon consultation with CABs, on a schedule mutually agreed on by regulators.[150] According to the EA and the SCC, the regulators have collaborated to build confidence in each other's accreditation systems by exchanging relevant information on matters regarding the CA Protocol (standards, technical regulations and procedures), as well as exchanging experts for on-site assessments to CABs and mutual information on the progress of work related to activities and the development in the cooperation.[151]

---

[145] The EA was established under Regulation (EC) No 765/2008 of the European Parliament and of the Council of 9 July 2008 setting out the requirements for accreditation and market surveillance relating to the marketing of products and repealing Regulation (EEC) No 339/93 [2008] OJ L218/30.

[146] CABs are evaluated on the basis of Regulation (EC) No 765/2008, the international standard ISO/IEC 17011 and other relevant standards.

[147] The SCC accredits six types of organisations: testing and calibration laboratories, management systems registration bodies, personnel certification bodies, product certification bodies, inspection bodies and auditor course providers.

[148] It is expected that the BCA will support the elimination of import duties and technical obstacles to trade, enabling European exporters to save around €500 million a year.

[149] Standards Council of Canada, 'Summary of the Standards Council of Canada's Information Session on the Conformity Assessment Protocol of the Canada-EU Comprehensive Economic and Trade Agreement' (10 May 2017) 1, available at www.scc.ca/sites/default/files/file_attach/SSEB_RPT_CETA-Event-Summary_v2_2017-05-03_2.pdf, last accessed 15 May 2020.

[150] ibid.

[151] European Accreditation, 'CETA Agreement and Conformity Assessment: Accreditation, a Tool to Enhance Trade Between the European Union and Canada' available at https://portail-qualite.public.lu/dam-assets/fr/publications/accreditation-notification/publications-olas/ceta-agreement.pdf, last accessed 15 May 2020.

An earlier example of an inter-agency cooperation is a 2005 agreement signed by the FDA, the EMA and the European Commission, which introduced seven initiatives aimed at increasing transparency and an understanding of each agency's viewpoint regarding drug regulation.[152] Among the initiatives are monthly teleconferences to share information on pending regulatory decisions, reviews, requests for discontinuing clinical trials, and any significant changes in statistical analyses. One other example of inter-agency cooperation is the 17 June 2008 Transatlantic Administrative Simplification Action Plan agreed by the FDA and the European Commission DG Enterprise and Industry. The aim of the document is to introduce a number of administrative simplification projects, including joint FDA/EMA inspections of manufacturers (in the EU/US as well as third countries) and convergence of risk management formats.[153]

## B.  Legislative Flexibility

The inter-agency cooperation initiatives addressed in section V.A are not aimed at, and do not lead to, legislative changes.[154] As mentioned in the preceding section, however, one of the key challenges to the negotiation of MRAs is significant differences in the regulatory regimes of the parties. Inability or unwillingness to make legislative changes that would help bring both sides to a mutual understanding and increase trust in each other's ability to assess products has caused significant problems during MRA treaty-making. In its 2013 study, the OECD listed regulatory specificity and lack of flexibility as major challenges to international regulatory cooperation.[155]

The 1998 EU-US MRA experience serves as an example of how the inability to effect legislative changes may prevent mutual recognition. One of the difficulties that arose during the negotiations of the 1998 Pharmaceutical GMP Annex was a statutory requirement for the FDA to review and approve products before they are marketed. The US Food, Drug and Cosmetics Act did not allow delegation of this

---

[152] 'FDA Launches 7 Initiatives With European Drug Regulators' (2006) 15 *Cancer Network* 1, available at www.cancernetwork.com/articles/fda-launches-7-initiatives-european-drug-regulators, last accessed 15 May 2020.

[153] Directorate-General for Health and Consumers, European Medicines Agency and US Food and Drug Administration, 'Transatlantic Administrative Simplification Action Plan – Final Report on Implementation' (26 July 2011) EMA/440869/2011, available at www.ema.europa.eu/en/documents/report/transatlantic-administrative-simplification-action-plan-final-report-implementation_en.pdf, last accessed 15 May 2020.

[154] The 2008 Transatlantic Administrative Simplification Action Plan expressly states that the implementation of instrument does not require changes to legislation: European Medicines Agency, European Commission and the US Food and Drug Administration, 'Medicines Regulation: Transatlantic Administrative Simplification Action Plan' (17 June 2008) available at https://ec.europa.eu/health//sites/health/files/files/international/doc/eu_fda_action_plan_200806_en.pdf, last accessed 15 May 2020. Similarly, the seven initiatives under the 2005 agreement between the FDA and the EMA are not intended to mandate unanimity of regulatory decisions: 'FDA Launches 7 Initiatives' (n 151).

[155] OECD, *International Regulatory Co-operation* (n 7) 76.

authority, especially to a foreign government. The underlying principle of an MRA, however, is that testing bodies of one party inspect a product to another party's standards, and vice versa. One EU negotiator noted that the FDA's unwillingness to make changes to its own procedures, assuming instead that Europe should simply recognise US certification procedures without any changes to US legislation, was a major problem during the trade talks.[156] It is likely that the lack of legislative flexibility was one of the reasons why the Pharmaceutical GMP Annex, which nominally entered into operation in 2001, was never implemented in practice.[157] Similarly, the Medical Devices Annex under the 1998 EU-Canada MRA did not become operational because, according to the European Commission, the Canadian regulators, citing primacy of their domestic responsibilities, required control over approval of CABs, which in the EU's opinion was not compatible with the essence of mutual recognition.[158]

At the same time, past MRA experience suggests that making necessary legislative changes may serve as a strong catalyst during MRA negotiations. The EU-US Pharmaceutical GMP MRA saga yet again offers a useful illustration. In 2012, the US Congress passed the Food and Drug Safety and Innovation Act that, inter alia, explicitly authorises the FDA to enter into written agreements with foreign governments to recognise the inspection of foreign drug establishments. The Act allows the US regulator to accept findings of a foreign inspector if the FDA determines that those authorities are 'capable' of meeting US requirements (§ 712). The adoption of the Act gave a new impetus to renegotiate the 1998 MRA in the pharmaceuticals sector, which, as has been mentioned, was not operational. Accordingly, from May 2014 the FDA and the EU conducted a number of collaborative projects in order to evaluate whether mutual recognition could be achieved in practice.[159] The revised MRA entered into force on 1 March 2017. In June 2017, the European Commission confirmed that the FDA has the capability, capacity and procedures in place to carry out GMP inspections at a level equivalent to the EU. Accordingly, the EU Member States and the EMA may rely on inspection results from the FDA. With the recognition in July 2019 by the FDA of the last remaining Member State – Slovakia – the EU and the United States have now fully implemented the MRA for inspections of manufacturing sites for certain human medicines in their respective territories.[160]

---

[156] KSG Case Study (n 1) 21.

[157] One of the reasons why the Pharmaceutical GMB Annex was nevertheless concluded was the passing of the US Food and Drug Administration Modernisation Act of 1997, which (§ 410) obliged the FDA to support the USTR, in consultation with the Secretary of Commerce, in efforts to move toward the acceptance of mutual recognition agreements.

[158] Commission, Newsletter No 9 (n 63) 7.

[159] eg the FDA was invited to observe the EU's Joint Audit Program in which two EU Member States audit a regulatory agency of a third Member State.

[160] European Medicines Agency, 'One Additional Country to Benefit from EU-US Mutual Recognition Agreement for Inspections' (News, 27 June 2019) available at www.ema.europa.eu/en/news/one-additional-country-benefit-eu-us-mutual-recognition-agreement-inspections, last accessed 15 May 2020.

CETA, too, illustrates the point. Making a U-turn from the inflexible approach of Canadian regulators with respect to the Medical Devices Annex under the 1998 EU-Canada MRA,[161] the SCC has suggested that some changes to regulations may be needed in order to implement the CETA CA Protocol. In particular, the SCC has noted that where the regulation states that producers are to be certified by a CAB accredited by SCC, the text may need to be revised to accommodate EU national accreditation bodies, recognised by the SCC, to be able to accredit to Canadian requirements.[162]

In addition to the direct legislative changes through the adoption of the US Food and Drug Safety and Innovation Act, the negotiations of the 2017 EU-US Pharmaceutical GMP MRA have also been facilitated by increasing concordance of the FDA/EMA marketing approvals. Studies on product approvals by the FDA and the EMA point to a growing correlation between the agencies' initial decisions on marketing approvals. One study on regulatory outcomes between 2006 and 2008 found that 64 per cent of applications were approved by both the DFA and the EMA.[163] A study by Kashoki et al shows that in the period 2014–16, concordance in the agencies' initial decisions on marketing approval reached 91 per cent.[164] According to Kashoki at al, while the primary reason for different outcomes was differing conclusions about efficacy, mainly due to differences in judgment, the second most common root for divergent outcomes was differences in clinical data submitted in support of an application.[165] This may indicate an increasing convergence of the parties' requirements for the submission of market approval applications.

## C. Pilot Projects

The BCA between the EA and the SCC addressed in section V.A provides for a pilot project, the aim of which is to allow the parties to the CA Protocol to assess regulations and observe each other's accreditation assessments. The pilot project constitutes the first step of trust-building activities under the BCA. The results of the pilot project will be used to build a common understanding between the SCC

---

[161] It should be noted, however, that in 1990s Canada did show regulatory flexibility in the telecommunications sector by modifying the Telecom Regulations and Radiocomm Regulations in order to allow the Minister of Industry to delegate the authority of issuing certificates to recognised certification bodies, as was required for the implementation of Phase II of its MRAs: Government of Canada, 'About MRAs', available at www.ic.gc.ca/eic/site/mra-arm.nsf/eng/h_nj00048.html, last accessed 15 May 2020.

[162] Standards Council of Canada, 'Summary of the Standards Council of Canada's 2nd Information Session on the Conformity Assessment Protocol of the Canada-EU Comprehensive Economic and Trade Agreement (CETA)' (31 January 2018) available at www.scc.ca/sites/default/files/file_attach/Summary_of_the_2nd_Information_Session_on_the_Conformity_Assessment_Protocol_of_CETA.pdf, last accessed 15 May 2020.

[163] JK Jenkins, *New Drug Review: 2008 Update*, FDA/CMS Summit, Washington, DC (2008).

[164] M Kashoki et al, 'A Comparison of EMA and FDA Decisions for New Drug Marketing Applications 2014–2016: Concordance, Discordance, and Why' (2020) 107 *Clinical Pharmacology & Therapeutics* 199.

[165] ibid 199.

and the EA to define what model is most effective to implement mutual recognition of other products.[166] The idea behind the pilot project is for the SCC and the EA to undertake observation visits to CABs in each other's jurisdiction to better understand their respective system.[167] According to the SCC, the project is for information and confidence-building only and will not result in mutual recognition.[168]

The project has been divided into two phases. The first phase of the pilot project was developed on the ATEX[169] (Europe) and HAZLOC[170] (Canada) systems, which govern equipment allowed in an explosive atmosphere. The product was chosen due its regulatory similarity in the EU and Canada.[171] During Phase I of the project, the SCC observed the national accreditation body of France, CORFAC (*Comité français d'accréditation*), perform conformity assessment on the basis of ISO/IEC 17065 and ATEX. The EA conducted corresponding observations of SCC's testing activities. According to the SCC, the project revealed many similarities in how assessments were conducted by both regulators. Some of the differences identified included additional accreditation requirements arising from specific national rules and EU law requirements, and expression of accreditation scopes. Given the successful conclusion of the first phase of the project, the project moved to its second phase, which focused on defining mechanisms for ensuring the competence of the accreditation body's assessors to evaluate the other party's requirements.[172] The pilot project was concluded by the end of 2017 and assessments EU-wide were commenced.

The ATEX/HAZLOC project under CETA's CA Protocol is not the first pilot programme designed to streamline and synchronise inter-state regulation in the context of pharmaceuticals approvals. In 2011, the FDA and the EMA launched a pilot programme to jointly assess risks of pharmaceuticals development and ensure product quality. While the design of this programme differed considerably from the CETA's ATEX/HAZLOC project,[173] they share similar goals of knowledge sharing and harmonisation of regulatory decisions to the greatest extent possible,

---

[166] Standards Council of Canada, 'Summary of the Standards Council of Canada's Information Session' (n 149) 1.

[167] ibid 4.

[168] ibid.

[169] Directive 2014/34/EU of the European Parliament and of the Council of 26 February 2014 on the harmonisation of the laws of the Member States relating to equipment and protective systems intended for use in potentially explosive atmospheres [2014] OJ L96/309.

[170] Installation of equipment intended for use in hazardous locations (haz loc) is covered in Part I of the Canadian Electric Code.

[171] The SCC has suggested, however, that non-safety-related products should be chosen for the start of the implementation of the CA Protocol: see Standards Council of Canada, 'Summary of the Standards Council of Canada's Information Session' (n 149) 7.

[172] Standards Council of Canada, 'Summary of the Standards Council of Canada's 2nd Information Session' (n 162) 5.

[173] Under the 2011 FDA/EMA programme, applications were submitted either to both agencies at the same time, resulting in a parallel evaluation, or to either the EMA or the FDA, in which case the agency doing the evaluation obtains consultative advice from the other agency.

as well as achieving procedural improvements in order to facilitate future parallel assessments.[174]

## D. Business Involvement

A distinctive feature of the 1998 EU-US MRA is the highly effective involvement of business leaders in the process of treaty negotiation, primarily through the Transatlantic Business Dialogue (TABD), which was a government-initiated organisation comprising the chief executive officers (CEOs) of European and US companies. Industry leaders were involved from the outset of trade talks, when the US Commerce Department approached a number of businesses seeking advice on how to proceed with the negotiations.[175]

The involvement of the industry leaders in the negotiations of the 1998 EU-US MRA did, however, raise certain challenges. Some have argued that the idea of business interacting directly with the European Commission, which was their point of contact rather than the Member States, was unusual. According to the lead EU negotiator, Karl Falkenberg, traditionally the CEOs of industries worked with national administrations, and the Commission was not used to working directly with individual enterprises and CEOs.[176] It has been suggested that the European business community, too, was much less connected to government initiatives than its US counterparts and was not used to active lobbying.[177] Overall, however, the TABD initiative has been, rather unanimously, considered as a catalyst that helped move the otherwise sluggish and troublesome negotiations forward. Its positive impact was most notable in the negotiations of the Pharmaceutical GMPs Annex, the most complex MRA among those part of the 1998 EU-US framework agreement.

According to the lead US negotiator Charles Ludolph, when in August 1996 negotiations hit a serious impasse due to the inability of the FDA and the European Commission to reach a common position on the pharmaceuticals sector, he turned to the TABD, asserting that 'These MRAs are going to die if I don't get direct help, participation and support from the pharmaceutical industry. And TABD has got to orchestrate that.'[178] Ludolph suggests that a number of industry leaders were very responsive, and 'The CEOs provided the strategic umbrella and overall focus.'[179]

---

[174] See European Medicines Agency, US Food and Drug Administration, 'EMA-FDA Pilot Program for Parallel Assessment of Quality-by-Design Applications: Lessons Learnt and Q&A Resulting From the First Parallel Assessment' (20 August 2013, EMA/430501/2013) available at www.ema.europa.eu/en/documents/other/european-medicines-agency-food-drug-administration-pilot-programme-parallel-assessment-quality_en.pdf, last accessed 15 May 2020.

[175] KSG Case Study (n 1) 6.

[176] ibid 16.

[177] ibid.

[178] ibid 22.

[179] ibid 23.

TABD's role as a trust-building instrument was also noted by Walter Batts, who was, at the time, an international director of international relations. According to Batts, US industry was crucial in helping to communicate the FDA's position to the European negotiators, by assisting them in understanding the FDAs statutory authority and the US Food, Drug and Cosmetics Act.[180]

The OECD says the TABD was a unique move, the strength of which consisted not only in the fact that CEOs were running the trade talk meetings but that they succeeded, time and again, in assuming common positions.[181] Due to its ability to provide impetus to negotiations by acting as an intermediary between the negotiating regulators, the TABD, which was intended to last only three months, became fully involved in the talks.

In conclusion, these and other techniques have proved effective in helping negotiators of MRAs achieve mutual trust, which is essential to MRA treaty-making. It is difficult, however, to evaluate whether it is these trust-building strategies or the fact that the new-wave MRAs have been built on past negotiation experience that differentiates the more troubled trade talks of the 1998 EU-US MRA from those of, say, CETA.

# VI. Conclusions

Mutual recognition agreements are an increasingly popular form of international economic cooperation. They facilitate trade without requiring regulatory harmonisation. There are a number of incentives to negotiate MRAs, including increasing trade flows and the elimination of TBTs in highly regulated economic sectors.

Nevertheless, past experience of MRA negotiations suggests that MRA treaty-making is complex and requires a high degree of mutual trust. Regulatory divergence and institutional differences may seriously impede the progress of trade talks, as was the case during the negotiations of the 1998 EU-US MRA.

There are, however, a number of techniques that help build trust between the parties. Inter-agency cooperation agreements and pilot projects assist in information-sharing, which helps achieve mutual trust. While the aim of MRAs of conformity assessment is to avoid alignment of product standards and safety requirements, regulatory flexibility is important in adapting the parties' regulatory regimes to accommodate mutual recognition. Business involvement, too, may serve as a strong catalyst for trade negotiations, by serving as an intermediary between the parties' regulators.

These past lessons from MRA treaty-making will be helpful in the negotiations of future MRAs, including a potential post-Brexit UK-EU arrangement. Negotiations between the latter will likely be particularly sensitive. On the one hand, the UK has been part of the EU's regulatory framework for 50 years,

---

[180] ibid.
[181] OECD Report 2016 (n 1) 28.

pointing to a possibility of negotiating an MRA based on the highest regulatory alignment to have ever been present between two MRA treaty partners. On the other hand, the UK's quest for regulatory divergence may put EU negotiators in the difficult position of dealing with a country that offers no guarantees, perhaps even the opposite, that its technical regulations will remain what they are. It is one thing to negotiate with a country that has different technical regulations; it is yet another thing to negotiate with a country whose regulations are likely to change. The future UK-EU negotiations are thus likely to offer new challenges and techniques for MRA treaty-making.

## PART III

# *Cassis de Dijon* in the Landscape of European Legal and Market Integration

# 11

## Big Decisions in European Legal and Economic Integration: What Have We Learned?

KAREN J ALTER

## I. Introduction

I am honoured to have been asked to write a concluding chapter for this exciting book. The European Court of Justice's (ECJ's) *Cassis de Dijon* case has a special place in my heart. The article 'Judicial Politics in the European Community: European Integration and the Path-Breaking *Cassis de Dijon* Decision' was Sophie Meunier's and my first piece of scholarship, our first conference presentation, our first effort to write about law and to combine law and political science, and our first publication.[1] It was also my first collaboration with anyone, and Sophie and I had such a great time that we have thrice repeated the collaboration. It is extremely gratifying that our analysis is still seen as relevant.

*Cassis de Dijon: 40 Years On* offers a re-examination and reconsideration of the impact of the ECJ landmark *Cassis de Dijon* ruling, which has been credited with catalysing the turn to mutual recognition as a strategy to construct a single European market. The enterprise of reconsidering a landmark ruling, with new questions that bring in new insights and access to historical materials that were unavailable to scholars writing at the time, provides an opportunity to reflect upon developments in European legal scholarship and what new historiography reveals about European legal integration. My contribution to this endeavour is partly a retrospective on the development of European legal scholarship, and partly a critical examination of what the book's chapters say and do not say.

Section II explores how European law scholarship has evolved since the *Cassis de Dijon* ruling, offering a different perspective on what the various authors

---

[1] KJ Alter and S Meunier-Aitsahalia, 'Judicial Politics in the European Community: European Integration and the Pathbreaking Cassis de Dijon decision' (1994) 24 *Comparative Political Studies* 535. I still cringe that throughout our 1994 article, we refer to the ECJ's ruling as a 'verdict'. I did not know better, and no one pointed out the problem until after the article was published.

expect to have found compared to what they then found. In our original article we focused on how the Commission amplified the *Cassis* ruling. This section argues that 'integration through law' activism more broadly amplified the *Cassis* ruling, and this amplification went beyond the launching of a conversation about mutual recognition. Section III discusses sensibilities that are still absent from the conversation, concluding with a set of challenges for scholars who want to revisit the history of European legal integration. This part of the chapter proposes that we need to approach the development of EU law over time from a global perspective, a perspective that critically reflects on the sui generis elements of EU law, and that openly explores and discusses how forces beyond Europe shaped European legal and economic integration.

## II.  Advances in Writing and Thinking About European Legal Integration

The chapters in this book could not have been written in 1980 when the *Cassis de Dijon* decision was the subject of much political discussion. They could not have been written in the 1990s, when Sophie Meunier and I were researching our article. They also could not have been written in the early 2000s, when I published my dissertation/book, *Establishing the Supremacy of European Law: The Making of a Rule of Law in Europe.* Neither the materials nor the sensibility of the times allowed for a consideration of the factors the authors of the chapters discuss. Yet at the same time, the chapters in this book leave so much unexplored. In particular, we are still lacking a critical reflection of the role of legal scholarship in creating myths and in seeing what was and is really happening.

### A.  Introduction: Situating the *Cassis* Decision in its Time

It is safe to say that when Sophie Meunier and I wrote our article, we had no idea what we were doing. We were in our third year of graduate school, which in the American system is when students shift focus from course work and comprehensive exams to exploring and developing a dissertation project. I was developing my PhD project on how the ECJ became a powerful political actor, which is why I decided to audit Joseph Weiler's European Community law short-course.[2] Sophie was studying European trade politics. I was not even a legal novice, but Sophie and I nonetheless decided to bring together the law and policy-making conversations we were both just embarking on.

---

[2] A shout out to Joseph Weiler, who was teaching at Harvard Law School. Technically, I was not allowed to audit his short course. But Professor Weiler generously allowed me full access to the course and the materials he had prepared for the course. Joseph helped me in so many ways as I journeyed into studying European law and becoming an academic. With this course, he was there at the very beginning of my career.

We were clueless because we were young and inexperienced, because we had no training in judicial politics, law and politics, or law more generally, but also because there was virtually no political science scholarship on European legal integration, and thus nothing that really addressed the questions in our minds.[3] Our cluelessness was an advantage in that we had no roadmap of what we were supposed to be doing. We were both conducting exploratory research for our dissertations, which brought me to Luxembourg and then Germany, and Sophie to Brussels in the summer and fall of 1992. We interviewed four key actors who created the *Cassis de Dijon* moment: Dr Gert Meier (the lawyer who brought the case), Judge Pierre Pescatore (the ECJ judge who wrote the *Cassis* decision), Dr Alfonso Mattera (the Commission official who amplified the ruling) and Professor Dr Martin Seidel (a legal advisor at the Commission). By the act of interviewing participants in the process, we took European legal scholarship in a new direction.

I need to return a moment to the time of the *Cassis* ruling to indicate how big a change our approach was. In 1980, one year after the ECJ's *Cassis de Dijon* ruling, Martin Shapiro wrote a comment on Ami Barav's article, 'The Judicial Power of the European Economic Community'. Shapiro lamented that European scholars mostly ignored 200 years of American constitutional experience, and 70 years of American legal scholarship, and he continued:

> Professor Barav presents the Community as a juristic idea; the written constitution (the treaty) as a sacred text; the professional commentary as a legal truth; the case law as the inevitable working out of the correct implications of the constitutional text; and the constitutional court (the ECJ) as the disembodied voice of right reason and constitutional teleology. If such an approach has proved fundamentally arid in the study of individual constitutions, this approach must also be fruitless in the comparative study of constitutions.[4]

Shapiro's description applied to the vast majority of European legal scholarship that I was consulting.[5] To keep the law as separate and sacred, one can only rely on the written text. Said differently, *no one* bothered to interview the participants in the legal process.[6]

---

[3] The three publications I knew of were A-M Burley and W Mattli, 'Europe before the Court' (1993) 47 *International Organization* 41; G Garrett, 'The European Community's Internal Market' (1992) 46 *International Organization* 533; M Volcansek, *Judicial Politics in Europe*, vol 7 (Bern, Peter Lang Publishers, 1986). Elsewhere I reconstruct why political scientists were so ill-equipped to think about law and politics. See KJ Alter, 'Visions of International Law: An Interdisciplinary Retrospective' (2020) *Leiden Journal of International Law*, https://doi.org/10.1017/S0922156520000485.

[4] M Shapiro, 'Comparative Law and Comparative Politics' (1980) 53 *Southern California Law Review* 537, 538. This article was published a year before Shapiro's seminal book took the study of judicial politics in a new direction. See M Shapiro, *Courts: A Comparative Political Analysis* (Chicago, IL, University of Chicago Press, 1981).

[5] The three exceptions to this rule passed through the Center for European Studies at Harvard as I was developing my research interest. Joseph Weiler presented his 'Transformation of Europe' article; Federico Mancini presented his chapter on how European judges helped to build a European Constitution; and Hjalte Rasmussen commented on Mancini's analysis. Kalypso Nicolaidis was also based at Harvard's Center for European Studies and working on mutual recognition as a market integration strategy. Her early engagement with us spurred us on. See at https://kalypsonicolaidis.com/managed-mutual-recognition/.

[6] Sophie shared this anecdote regarding her interview with Mattera, 'At the beginning of the interview, he was quite bored and disengaged. As the interview progressed, he grew more excited. At the

Already in 1980, Shapiro put his finger on why European legal scholarship was mostly arid and formalist. Shapiro questioned if the article he was critiquing was not the more politically astute form of scholarship. Think about what his answer to this question meant for European law scholars. Could they have done the kind of research and analysis that Sophie and I undertook? Shapiro reflected:

> It might well be argued that in the final analysis, mine is the politically naive analysis, and Professor Barav's the politically sophisticated one. For we must bear in mind that particularly in the European tradition, professional writing is simultaneously an act of scholarship and an act of law-making – that is to say an act of politics. In this light there is much to be said for Professor Barav's unspoken, but none the less emphatic, assertion of the autonomy of law and the teleological inevitability of the Community's legal system … [F]rom the point of view, not of comparative scholarship, but of European political action, is not what Professor Barav has done the best thing to do? … [I]t may be best to preserve the myth of the founding years, to deal with juristic developments as if they were autonomous, and to speak as little as possible about economic and political threats.[7]

Shapiro is pointing out that European scholarship was about 'preserving the myth'. What we called the 'court as a hero' narrative was part of this myth.[8]

Shapiro made these observations just before ideas about European legal integration were about to change. A key piece of this change was the European University Institute's (EUI) *Integration through Law* project, directed by Mauro Cappelletti, Monica Seccombe and Joseph Weiler. Brigitte Leucht's chapter (chapter 4) mentions that Commission members were inspired to use the ECJ's *Cassis de Dijon* ruling to build the internal market through their participation in this EUI project. The behind-the-scenes coordination of lawyers, judges, scholars and Commission officials in building integration-through-law began well before the EUI project.[9] In this respect, the EUI project was another step on a trodden path.[10]

In retrospect, it is clear that Sophie and I were part of an emerging scholarly shift in the study of European legal integration. Perhaps because we were political science graduate students, and surely because we were not based at the EUI, we

---

end, he told me that he had answered maybe 100 interviews about *Cassis* over the years, but I was the first person to ask him the political questions and he had been waiting for this moment for a long time.'
   [7] Shapiro, 'Comparative Law and Comparative Politics' (n 4) 540.
   [8] Sophie and I named the court as an integration hero narrative, which did exist, and gave more credit than deserved to the political science idea that states are inevitably the puppet-masters of law, judicial rulings and policy.
   [9] Eric Stein had suggested a very loose coordination of legal actors in his 1981 article on European legal integration, E Stein, 'Lawyers, Judges and the Making of a Transnational Constitution' (1981) 75 *American Journal of International Law* 1. Historians are discovering longer and deeper links between ECJ judges, Commission officials, members of national ministries of justices and members of the Federation International de Droit Européens. See M Rasmussen, 'The Origins of a Legal Revolution – the Early History of the European Court of Justice' (2008) 14 *Journal of European History* 77; M Rasmussen, 'From Costa v Enel to the Treaties of Rome: A Brief History of Legal Revolution' in MP Maduro and L Azoulai (eds), *The Past and Future of Eu Law: The Classics of Eu Law Revisited on the 50th Anniversary of the Rome Treaty* (Oxford, Hart Publishing, 2010); M Rasmussen, 'Establishing a Constitutional Practice of European Law: The History of the Legal Service of the European Executive' (2012) 21 *Contemporary European History* 375; M Rasmussen, 'Towards a New History of European Law' (2013) 21 *Contemporary European History* 305; M Rasmussen, 'From International Law to a

had no awareness of and very little contact with scholars who were starting to think about the ECJ in different ways. Our failure to see ourselves as part of a change or a movement gets to a larger point about what was happening in European law, and in European law scholarship. Twenty-twenty hindsight always looks clearer, and more connected. And maybe it *is* more coherent and connected than the participants themselves recognise.

Today it is clear that there were two separate time lines developing. The first time line involved changes occurring among the participants in legal integration. The close-knit community of Euro-law activists and the benign political neglect of what these activists were doing was actually starting to unravel in the 1980s. The *Integration through Law* project had nothing to do with this trend. Rather, politicians were engaging with European integration more deeply. According to French scholar Buffett-Tchakaloff, European governments were starting to wake up to the reality that ECJ rulings had consequences.[11]

Secondly, perhaps because the ECJ was now seen as important, European legal scholarship was expanding as well. By expanding, I mean that there was an influx of scholars who were not part of the European law myth-making project. That an American doctoral student of political science began to study the ECJ is evidence of this change. Both of these developments were unrelated to the *Cassis de Dijon* ruling, but they have an impact on how we should think about the *Cassis* ruling and the writings in this book.

## B. Developments in Legal Integration: Was the *Cassis* Decision Exceptional?

A standard trope of scholarship is to suggest that a finding is counterintuitive to an expectation. This scholarly device often involves constructing the 'common

Constitutionalist Dream? The History of European Law and the European Court of Justice, 1950–1993' in I de la Rasilla and JE Viñuales (eds), *Experiments in International Adjudication: Historical Accounts* (Cambridge, Cambridge University Press, 2019); A Vauchez, *L'Europe et Son 'Triangle Magique': Retour sur des Arrêts 'Foundateurs' (Van Gend en Loos et Costa C Enel)* (2007); A Vauchez, 'Judge-Made Law. Aux Origines du Modèle Politique Communautaire (Retour Sur Van Gend en Loos et Costa C Enel)' in O Costa and P Magnette (eds), *Une Europe Des Élites? Réflexions sur la Fracture Démocratique de l'union Européenne* (Brussels, Presses de l'Université libre de Bruxelles, 2007); A Vauchez, 'Integration through Law' Socio-History of EU Political Common Sense* (2008); A Vauchez, *Europe's First Trustees: Lawyers' Politics at the Outset of the European Communities (1950–1970)* (2007); A Vauchez, 'The Transnational Politics of Judicialization: Van Gend en Loos and the Making of EU Polity' (2010) 16 *European Law Journal* 1; A Cohen and M Rask Madsen, 'Cold War Law: Legal Entreprenuers and the Emergence of a European Legal Field (1946–1965)' in V Gessner and D Nelken (eds), *European Ways of Law* (Oxford, Hart Publishing, 2007).

[10] Moreover, according to Rebekka Byberg, European officials were as much a part of the creation of the EUI project as they were participants in it. See R Byberg, 'The History of the Integration through Law Project: Creating the Academic Expression of a Constitutional Legal Vision for Europe' (2017) 18 *German Law Journal* 1531.

[11] M-F Buffet-Tchakaloff, *La France Devant La Cour De Justice Des Communautés Européennes* (Aix-en-Provence, Presses Universitaires d'Aix-Marseille, 1984).

perception' that is intuitively persuasive, after which a scholar demonstrates how this common perception is oversimplified or inaccurate. Many of this book's chapters repeat this strategy, which Sophie and I also used. In different ways, the authors in this book stress how the roll-out of mutual recognition was not nearly as smooth or comprehensive as the 'ECJ-launching followed by Commission-inspired policy-making' narrative suggested. I do not think I actually suggested this narrative. Instead, we argued that judge-made law could never deliver mutual recognition, and that the Commission's follow-on actions (eg Mattera's 'interpretive communication' of the *Cassis* precedent) provoked a new policy precisely because Member States did not like the legal interpretation the Commission offered. In any event, I want to suggest that the expectation embedded in this 'false narrative' is actually the myth that legal analysis generates. We see this myth-making again in Oliver's chapter on 'Mutual Recognition: Addressing Some Outstanding Conundrums' (see chapter 9), which suggests that one can sum up the ECJ's doctrine on mutual recognition into a legally coherent whole.

What happened in the *Cassis* case – from beginning to end – was far from unique. Indeed the messiness of the *Cassis de Dijon* story *was* the process of European legal integration. Some of the chapters in *Cassis de Dijon: 40 Years On* take us back before the *Cassis* ruling to suggest that the common linear narrative from *Dassonville* to *Cassis* to mutual recognition was always false. Joseph Weiler had taught me the *Dassonville* to *Cassis* narrative, and I imagine that Pescatore also implied this narrative in the *Cassis* ruling, since this narrative suggests that the *Cassis de Dijon* ruling changed very little.

Schütze's revision – 'From *Dassonville* to *Cassis*: The Revolution that Did Not Take Place' (chapter 2) – questions the claim that the *Dassonville* ruling created a formula that the *Cassis de Dijon* decision then barely changed. Schütze argues instead that a series of ECJ decisions adapted GATT categories, so that there was no '*Dassonville* formula' that applied across cases. Given that pre-*Cassis de Dijon* ECJ doctrine was based on GATT law, Schütze argues that the real revolution was the *Cassis de Dijon* ruling, in that it abandoned the implicit link to GATT categories and law.

From a legal perspective, I am sure he is right. One wonders, however, if Schütze's analysis, framed in terms of debunking our understanding of the *Dassonville–Cassis* nexus, rather misses the point. The deep reliance on GATT ideas in the EU context is, for me, the most novel discovery, one that I will return to in this chapter's conclusion. Overall, I think that his analysis mostly shows that European judges were trying to have their cake and eat it. The unstated similarity with GATT principles made ECJ judges appear less radical, and the GATT principles were also more politically flexible, in that they allowed the 'national treatment' ideas to be applied in a variegated way. By dressing up these principles in European clothing – whether this happened via the '*Dassonville* formula' or a *Cassis* formula – the ECJ suggested that the doctrine European judges were developing was 'European'. In other words, ECJ judges, supported by legal analysis of the time, could claim that the legal steps were small and uniquely European.

Schütze does not unmask this legal subterfuge, and to me this subterfuge was the actual strategy. Burley and Mattli discuss this strategy in terms of the 'mask' of law, and the 'fiction' that the ECJ is merely interpreting the law.[12] Today we know even more about this fiction. We know that Pierre Pescatore had a larger agenda of building integration-through-law. Pescatore wrote perhaps the first book to address the human rights question in European law, as a counter to the German conversation he saw emerging.[13] Pescatore created the doctrine of '*effet utile*', wherein European texts should be interpreted in a goal-orientated way, to help realise the larger objectives of European integration.[14] European judges made a subtle but important shift from the *Van Gend en Loos* ruling, which discussed a 'new legal order of international law', towards the idea of 'community law'. According to Pescatore, the phrase 'new legal order of international law' never again appeared in an ECJ ruling. Pescatore and Robert Lecourt then wrote numerous articles to explain to national judges that they should not treat European law as normal international law.[15] My point is that Pescatore was not nearly as interested in careful legal applications and analysis as Schütze. Other participants may have cared, and thus Schütze may be right about the antecedent factors that fed into the *Cassis* ruling. But this is where the technique of talking to participants puts one on a different trajectory. Every point I just made about Pescatore – what he wrote, and why he wrote it – I learned about because I spoke with Pescatore about the *Cassis* ruling, and later about my dissertation research.

Of course, you cannot always trust interview subjects; legal scholars must base their analysis on the written law, not the spoken words of a judge. Also, Pescatore was subtler in explaining his strategy than I have just been. Pescatore was a modest person, so he would never take the credit that I have just given him. What he told me about the *Cassis de Dijon* decision (perhaps with a wink that I missed) was that he added as an afterthought the following throw-away line:

> There is therefore no valid reason why, provided that they have been lawfully produced and marketed in one of the Member States, alcoholic beverages should not be introduced into any other Member State.

---

[12] Burley and Mattli, 'Europe before the Court' (n 3).

[13] P Pescatore, 'Die Menschenrechte Und Die Europäische Integration' (1969) *Integration* 103.

[14] P Pescatore, 'The Doctrine of "Direct Effect": An Infant Disease of Community Law' (1983) 8 *EL Rev* 155.

[15] P Pescatore, 'Community Law and the National Judge' (January 1973) *The Law Guardian* 41; P Pescatore, 'L'attitude Des Juridictions Nationales à l'Égard du Problème des Effets Direct du Droit Communautaire' (1970)  2 *Revue trimestrielle de droit europeén* 296; P Pescatore, *References for Preliminary Rulings under Article 177 of the EEC Treaty and Cooperation between the Court and National Courts* (Luxembourg, European Court of Justice, 1986); P Pescatore, 'La Clarence du Législateur Communautaire et le Devoir du Juge', *Gedächtnisschrift für L-J Constantinesco* (Cologne, Carl Heymanns Verlag, 1983). Bill Davies explains this shift in much more detail. See B Davies, *Resisting the European Court of Justice: West Germany's Confrontation with European Law 1949–1979* (Cambridge, Cambridge University Press, 2012).

Sophie and I stressed that this sentence was provocative, but it 'carried no legal weight in the context of the rest of the decision'.[16] I do not think this sentence was an afterthought, and I think we dismissed it too readily.[17] But neither do I think Pescatore was implementing some master plan.

Here is where I depart a bit from many of the chapters. Progress only looks linear when we know the end of the story, which allow us to look for and connect earlier dots. But in real time, everything looks and feels contingent and uncertain, and the dots actually are scattered all over the place. Because I do not expect a master plan, I also do not expect that there will be coherence or linearity in the plan's execution. Yet it is the task of a legal scholar to find coherence, and thus to draw a clear thread across legal rulings, and to suggest that law – not politics – creates this thread. The linearity is the construct; for the disparate participants in the legal process – litigants, lawyers, diverse judges, legal interpreters, etc – the through-line is neither as clear, nor as solid.

Barnard's chapter – 'The Missing Ingredient in *Cassis de Dijon*: an Exercise in Legal Archaeology' (see chapter 3) – breaks from a legal narrative of path-dependent legal development. She asks why the ECJ picked this particular case as a vehicle to champion mutual recognition. Again her analysis is probably right, but why expect the ECJ to have picked this case? This expectation also suggests some master plan. More likely, I think, is that the ECJ did not really pick this case. What Sophie and I learned is that Meier picked up the legal issue that the Commission had settled in the earlier *Annisette* case – Meier created and framed the case, but the framing was passed on from the Commission.[18] Then Pescatore ended up as the Juge Rapporteur, and he added his pregnant throw-away line. Pescatore's addition, Ehlerman's participation in the *European through Law* project discussed in Brigitte Leucht's chapter (chapter 4) and the Commission memo may well have inspired actions in ways that the participants themselves neither anticipated nor named. So I am not saying that the participants' narrative is the whole truth, or that the archeological, legal exegesis and historical investigations provide no new insight. My larger point has to do with the expectation that there would be a through-line, either because law creates coherence or because actors were following some master strategy.

On the one hand, I think it is true that there was an implausibly ambitious strategy to build integration-through-law. Burley and Mattli, drawing on neo-functionalist theory, suggest that there was a set of actors that were mutually

---

[16] KJ Alter and S Meunier-Aitsahalia, 'Judicial Politics in the European Community: European Integration and the Pathbreaking *Cassis De Dijon* Decision' (1994) 24 *Comparative Political Studies* 535, 539.

[17] One should never blame the teacher for a student's mistake, but everything I knew about this decision I learned from Joseph Weiler. Meanwhile Schütze pinpoints Weiler as the propagator of the false '*Dassonville* to *Cassis*' claim, and he implies that Weiler was wrong when he said that the *Dassonville* ruling broke from GATT law.

[18] Alter and Meunier-Aitsahalia, 'Judicial Politics in the European Community' (n 16) 538. Meier was fed the case by the Commission, which settled a similar infringement suit. The Commission made a political compromise, and passed the information on to Meier that there was a winnable legal suit to pursue.

self-interested in this strategy. In their 1993 article, Burley and Mattli suggested that for ECJ judges, lower court national judges and legal scholars, the mutual interest was in personal empowerment, and for litigants the interest came from their narrow pursuit of economic interests.[19] Stone Sweet also endorses this idea of mutual interest driving the construction of integration-orientated legal governance.[20]

My argument has always been different. In the 1990s, I suggested that one needed a story that could explain why those actors who did not share an interest in European legal integration went along with the integration-through-law plan.[21] Later I argued that one also needs an explanation of why European judges were so audaciously and iconoclastically activist. For me, the answer to this second question lay in ideology, not a less political and uncoordinated pursuit of self-interest.[22]

A question to ask is why we scholars, myself included, did not talk about either the ideology or the integration-through-law strategy. I would suggest two reasons for our silence. First, as others have also noted, legal scholars were complicit supporters of the European law myth.[23] Not only did legal scholars avoid discussing motives and politics, they also did not 'out' the connections between the legal actors involved in the integration-through-law process. This complicit silence made it very hard for outsiders like me to connect all of the dots.

There was overt cause-lawyering occurring in the 1970s and 1980s. Harlow and Rawling were writing about this cause-lawyering in 1992, around the time that Sophie and I were researching the cause-lawyering in the *Cassis de Dijon* case.[24] The four of us separately, and without real-time knowledge of each other, wrote about these two dots, but there was no way for those of us writing in the 1990s to connect them into a larger whole. The silence of European legal scholars in this way facilitated the myth-making of ECJ judges and the very small activist legal community that supported them.[25]

---

[19] Burley and Mattli, 'Europe before the Court' (n 3).

[20] A Stone Sweet, 'Judicialization and the Construction of Governance' (1999) 32 *Comparative Political Studies* 147.

[21] KJ Alter, 'The European Court's Political Power' (1996) 19 *West European Politics* 458; KJ Alter, 'Who Are the Masters of the Treaty?: European Governments and the European Court of Justice' (1998) 52 *International Organization* 125.

[22] KJ Alter, 'Jurist Advocacy Movements in Europe: The Role of Euro-Law Associations in European Integration (1953–1975)' in KJ Alter (ed), *The European Court's Political Power* (Oxford, Oxford University Press, 2009).

[23] Burley and Mattli, 'Europe before the Court' (n 3) 70; H Rasmussen, *On Law and Policy in the European Court of Justice* (Dordrecht, Martinus Nijhoff Publishers, 1986).

[24] Harlow and Rawlings explain how an equal pay activist in 1967 openly wondered if the Treaty provisions requiring equal pay for equal work could be self-executing (see C Harlow and R Rawlings, *Pressure through Law* (London, Routledge, 1992) 283).

[25] Only later did I unite the different actors into what I called a 'jurist advocacy movement', which I defined as 'a group of legal actors (jurists) who organize collectively and deploy legal tools strategically to promote a shared cause. Jurist advocacy movements have specific policy and legal goals, whether they be the promotion of originalist interpretations of a constitution, abolition of the death penalty, advocacy of same- sex marriage, or the construction of a supranational legal order.' KJ Alter and LR Helfer, *Transplanting International Courts: The Law and Politics of the Andean Tribunal of Justice* (Oxford, Oxford University Press, 2017) 230.

So here is my bottom line about how legal integration was developing. I think that a relatively small group of integration-through-law enthusiasts were meeting throughout Europe from the 1950s through the 1980s, including at the EUI's *Integration through Law* project. These actors, whom I later labelled a 'jurist advocacy movement', were mutually inspiring each other. They were generating test cases, serving as the ECJ and the European Commission's 'kitchen cabinet' of like-minded friends debating strategy together. Together they were a community of iconoclasts, inspiring and emboldening each other.[26] This group would gather at various scholarly meetings, share ideas and then return home, after which they each picked up the ball and moved it forward in their small way. Meier constructed a test case to build the *Cassis de Dijon* precedent. Pescatore added the throw-away line in the *Cassis* decision. Ehlermann and Mattera worked within the Commission to advance the ball.

Legal scholars were part of this process too. Scholars wrote articles championing ECJ rulings so as to suggest that there was momentum and legal coherence behind the ECJ's doctrine, and later they constructed an *Integration through Law* project that compared European legal integration to the process of building federal law in the US system. Legal scholars were also doing what European legal scholars generally did; they ignored the activist social connections occurring behind the scenes, and down-played the relevance of general or GATT international law arguments while emphasising the revolutionary importance of Community-law arguments. Commission members facilitated these developments. They helped to create journals, sponsored positions teaching European law to law students, created the EUI and participated in the *Integration through Law* project. Supportive officials based in national judicial ministries calmed nerves and later became European legal officials (eg Claus-Dieter Ehlermann). Some civil servant and scholarly Euro-law activists became national judges or European judges, which expanded their capacity to promote European legal integration (eg Adolphe Touffait). This type of activity was a key driver of ECJ jurisprudence in the 1960s, 1970s and 1980s.[27] The *Cassis de Dijon* story is just one example of these legal politics.

The more scholars dig into the history, the more connections between participants in the Euro-law advocacy movement they discover. Leucht's contribution in this book, for example (see chapter 4), brings in the European Parliament and the EUI's *Integration through Law* part of this story. Yet even though this collusion is clear in retrospect, it probably still is too much to expect that these actors were crafting and then implementing some coherent master plan. Yes, ardent lawyers, judges and legal scholars were committed to European integration-through-law; they were debating each step in the process; and they were knowingly each doing their own part to advance the ball. But the set of actors willing to pick up and move

---

[26] ibid.
[27] Alter, 'Jurist Advocacy Movements in Europe' (n 22).

a ball were too few and far between for there to be much coherence and long-term envisioning across their efforts.

Why am I insisting that there was no master plan? There were back then, and still are today, many actors who are not inspired by the idea of integration-through-law.[28] Inge Govaere, in her chapter entitled "*Ceci n'est pas … Cassis De Dijon*": Some Reflections on its Triple Regulatory Impact' (chapter 5), examines the regulatory impact of the *Cassis* ruling and finds that mutual recognition did not end up being an all-encompassing practice. Instead, policy makers responded to different interests and incentives, so that the implementation of the mutual recognition policy at both the legal and political levels was rather messy and perhaps even incoherent. Stephen Weatherill, in his analysis 'Did *Cassis de Dijon* Make a Difference?' (chapter 6), suggests that as time went on, even the Commission became convinced that mutual recognition was too deregulatory an approach to market integration. So in practice, there was no implementable master plan. Various actors pushed the idea of mutual recognition as far as they could, and some legal scholars tried to suggest a coherent doctrine; but the interests and politics of the time could accept national treatment with caveats but not a pure-form mutual recognition.

In short, I am arguing that there was no master plan for at least two reasons: first, because the participants themselves knew of their piece of the story, yet they did not really understand the whole. In fact, every piece was so contingent that participants at the time would have been hard-pressed to even call it a whole. And, second, most of the participants in European legal and political integration *were not* Euro-law activists. Given that few lawyers, judges, scholars or policy-makers were open to the integration-through-law project, plans would inevitably have to change in response to the concerns and ideas of the larger set of actors who remained rather unconvinced that deep market integration, spearheaded by the European Community rather than firms, industry and civil society groups, and elected politicians, let alone promoted through case law, was desirable.

The idea that there was some linear narrative from *Dassonville* to *Cassis* to mutual recognition is the current false narrative that European legal scholars construct, after which historians and law-in-context scholars deconstruct. In this volume, one sees the whole spectrum, starting with the trope, followed by a disassembly of the trope, only to see European lawyers like Peter Oliver reconstruct the linearity and coherence in a slightly amended form.

---

[28] In 1990, Gert Meier was still lamenting the lack of activism within the larger legal community, complaining that politicians, judges and common folk were still expecting integration to come about on its own, via the zeitgeist of the times. He saw a constellation of political actors mobilised against European integration, and he complained that national judges were not doing enough to facilitate the penetration of European law into national legal orders. G Meier, 'Zur Mitverantwortung Deutscher Richter für die Vollendung des Europäischen Binnenmarktes' (1990) Heft 3 *Europäische Zeitschrift für Wirtschaft* 81. I wrote about the resistance of the non-Euro-law legal community in KJ Alter, *Establishing the Supremacy of European Law: The Making of an International Rule of Law in Europe* (Oxford, Oxford University Press, 2001). Bill Davies has greatly developed this argument (see Davies, *Resisting the European Court of Justice* (n 15)).

## C.  Developments in Legal Integration Scholarship

The 'judge as a hero' scholarship Shapiro wrote about in the 1980s, and which Sophie and I dismissed in the 1990s, started to undergo a transformation in the late 1980s and early 1990s. Meanwhile, *Cassis de Dijon: 40 Years On* is yet another transformation.

In the 1980s, Hjalte Rasmussen tore off the veil of legal consensus in his dissertation/book, *On Law and Policy in the European Court of Justice*. He was pilloried for doing so.[29] Rasmussen's book was a polemic, in that Rasmussen accused ECJ judges and European law lawyers of acting as political rather than legal actors. This accusation went too far for the lawyer-scholars of the time. Indeed the EUI *Integration through Law* project took a more nuanced approach, comparing what happened in the US to what was occurring in Europe. This comparison is in itself audacious (and also what Rasmussen was doing). The *Integration through Law* project could get away with more because Community officials and big-name legal scholars endorsed it, and the American contributors were able to act as independent scholars applying their legal realist sensibilities. In this way, American legal realism, and with it the idea that it is both acceptable and inevitable that judges will be policy-makers in robes, seeped into the European conversation.

I do not think it is at all an accident that outsiders were the original authors of a new more empirical and politically open approach to studying European legal integration. We outsiders could do what Rasmussen could not, and Shapiro predicted this development as well, speculating in 1980 that

> Perhaps comparative constitutional law can play a special role in resolving the tension between scholarly and political action. … Just as European scholars have shed light on a United States Constitution, in which they have no direct political stake, perhaps non-Europeans will be able to make some contribution to a more direct understanding of the evolving constitution of Europe precisely because they have no direct responsibility for that evolution.[30]

So let me return to the puzzle of why European law scholars did not see or write about the legal strategy as it was unfolding in front of them. Key participants were advertising what they were doing. The ultimate insiders – Pescatore, Robert Lecourt, Federico Mancini and others – would take off the veil of a legal scholar and a judge, writing articles, books, newspaper op-eds and more. Pescatore and Lecourt wrote to persuade European and national officials and judges, and they tied their arguments to the law. These ultimate insiders were telegraphing what they were doing, but European legal scholars in the 1970s, 1980s and 1990s mostly

---

[29] Rasmussen, *On Law and Policy in the European Court of Justice* (n 23). Rasmussen's 1986 book was subjected to a withering 34-page critique by Joseph Weiler in J Weiler, 'The Court of Justice on Trial: Hjalte Rasmussen: On Law and Policy in the European Court of Justice' (1987) 24 *CML Rev* 555. Would any one of us want Weiler's sharp mind focused on our own work for 34 pages?

[30] Shapiro, 'Comparative Law and Comparative Politics' (n 4) 542.

ignored it (in the Wizard of Oz sort of way, meaning as complicit actors who 'pay no attention to the man behind the curtain'). These legal scholars were – as Shapiro noted – analysing European law as, we saw before, 'a juristic idea; the written constitution (the treaty) as a sacred text; the professional commentary as a legal truth; the case law as the inevitable working out of the correct implications of the constitutional text; and the constitutional court (the ECJ) as the disembodied voice of right reason and constitutional teleology'.[31] To do otherwise might cost a scholar a position as a professor of European law.

What I am calling the 'outsider' approach sees lawyers, judges and legal scholars as political actors, and it takes the interests and incentives of a wider group of participants into account.[32] Of course Hjalte Rasmussen did this too, but he was an insider, so he could not get away with it. We outsiders did not have to worry about finding jobs in Europe, or publishing in important European journals.[33] We therefore had no qualms about examining legal decisions and scholarship not as truth, but as a set of contested ideas and perspectives.

But the literature we could draw on remained scarce, fragmented and incomplete. You could not find scholarship like Schütze's, who openly disagrees with Joseph Weiler and Pierre Pescatore, or Barnard's chapter, which discovers a 'missing ingredient' by considering the diverse pressures shaping the Commission, including what was going on in the alcohol sector more generally. Because the literature mostly hid the coordination, activism and social networking that was happening, there were simply not many dots to connect.

*Cassis de Dijon: 40 Years On* is a new chapter in historical, law-in-context and legal scholarship, revealing the extent to which the older borders and barriers have been removed. The lens of focus is expanded to a wide-angle that allows for more issues, actors and institutions to be part of the story. The chapters that revisit what was happening in the 1970s and 1980s reveal how the new European legal history has come of age.[34] European legal scholars are going to archives, looking beyond legal rulings, and considering legal interpretations within the larger political context in which they occurred and talking about the social connections. They are doing law-in-context analysis, and in doing so they are uncovering new histories. *Cassis de Dijon: 40 Years On* continues this trajectory by looking outside

---

[31] See n 5.

[32] The outsider authorship began with Stein, 'Lawyers, Judges and the Making of a Transnational Constitution' (n 9); followed by J Weiler, 'The Transformation of Europe' (1991) 100 *Yale Law Journal* 2403. Carol Harlow took this strategy in a far larger direction: C Harlow, 'Towards a Theory of Access of the European Court of Justice' (1992) 12 *Yearbook of European Law* 213; C Harlow, 'A Community of Interests? Making the Most of European Law' (1992) 55 *MLR* 331; Harlow and Rawlings, *Pressure through Law* (n 24).

[33] Sophie and I never actually submitted our *Cassis* article for peer review. Instead, we were invited to add it to an in-progress special issue of *Comparative Political Studies* on the new constitutional politics in Europe. Martin Shapiro and Alec Stone served as our editors and reviewers, which means that no European legal scholars reviewed it or weighed in (with the exception of Renaud Dehousse, our discussant at the ECSA conference where we presented a draft of the paper).

[34] Rasmussen, 'Towards a New History of European Law' (n 9).

of EU law. Schütze re-examines the so-called break with GATT law (see chapter 2). Emilija Leinarte and Catherine Barnard (in chapter 10) examine how the *Cassis* principle was – and was not – carried into mutual recognition agreements negotiated between European and non-European trading partners. Georges Baur (in chapter 9) considers how the mutual recognition principle is applied vis-à-vis EFTA countries, especially in the remarkable way in Switzerland.

## III.  The Next Step: Examining European Integration within its Larger Legal and Political Context

The previous section explained how European lawyers hid their integration-through-law strategy in plain sight, with legal scholars refusing to write and publish about what they knew. Outsiders started to write about what was going on, and later European historians connected even more dots and revealed the greater whole. Legal scholars also became more comfortable engaging in law-in-context analysis, and were less concerned with constructing and defending the European project.

Yet I also explained how many of today's legal scholars still want to suggest linear coherence, which then allows the contributors to *Cassis de Dijon: 40 Years On* to counter-intuitively find much less linear coherence than both legal scholars and historians imply. I want to take my final thoughts in two different directions. First I will stress how unique the European experience actually was. Then I will suggest how incomplete our stories about this experience remain.

### A.  The EU is Sui Generis: It is Time to Explain Why this is So

When I began researching the EU, it was commonplace to assert that the EU was sui generis. Quite honestly, I did not know what this claim meant. It was far from unique for international judges to interpret, apply, fill in and expand treaty law. Indeed there were many legal treaties that looked quite a bit like the Treaty of Rome, and there were scholars who suggested that the European experience was a template that was being followed.[35] Maybe the EU was more successful in comparison to other supranational projects, but it hardly looked more successful in the 1960s, when the legal revolution was launched, or the 1970s, when the ECJ was promoting case-law-induced market integration. If the EU was not unique in

---

[35] E Haas, *Beyond the Nation-State: Functionalism and International Organization* (Stanford, CA, Stanford University Press, 1964); E Haas, *The Uniting of Europe* (Stanford, CA, Stanford University Press 1958); E Haas, 'International Integration: The European, and the Universal Process' (1961) 13 *International Organization* 366. Today the EU process also look less unique, since there are European Community replicants in many parts of the world. See, eg, KJ Alter, 'The Global Spread of European Style International Courts' (2012) 35 *West European Politics* 135.

the 1960s and 1970s then its 'sui generis' nature could not explain what was happening at that time. And if scholars were unwilling to say that the ECJ was unusually activist, what exactly was sui generis? Because I was focused on a legal answer, I looked far and wide – and fruitlessly – for an explanation.[36]

The more I study other international legal systems, the more equipped I feel to answer the 'what was sui generis?' question. Neither the legal texts, nor the fact that these texts are interpreted and expanded upon by judges were unique, which is why my search for a legal answer to the 'sui generis' question was so fruitless. Looking from today, neither the fact of a preliminary ruling procedure, nor the direct effect and supremacy of community law are unique.[37] Instead, I have come to realise how unbelievably audacious the ECJ was in declaring the direct effect and supremacy of European law, despite the tenuous political climate in Europe in the 1960s.[38] In the 1960s the ECJ was overtly activist, and in the 1970s the ECJ continued this activism with the same support structure. The *Cassis de Dijon* ruling was part of this same story. Meanwhile, as mentioned, through the 1980s European legal scholars were maintaining the fiction that law in combination with the functional demands imposed by European integration, rather than judicial activism, explained the ECJ's audacious legal rulings.

Having studied legal integration projects that have been much less successful, what now appears sui generis is the legal strategy this chapter discusses; namely, the existence of a jurist advocacy movement encouraging and emboldening the integration-through-law strategy while staying complicitly silent about the behind-the-scenes efforts. The presence and relative wealth of this community, small as it was, and the infrastructure this community could build on, have yet to be replicated.[39] Also important is that the European Economic Community (EEC) had a diverse range of secondary legislation, which, following the Single European Act, became unparalleled in size and scope.[40] The detailed and extensive nature of this secondary legislation provides a lot of legal fodder for lawyers, litigants and judges.

I do not think these insights are the full story of how, let alone why, the EU was sui generis. It probably also mattered that European countries were relatively

---

[36] I admit that not being a lawyer, and thus not having a baseline expectation, perhaps made me rather obtuse. Stein had explained how the ECJ was building a constitution for Europe, but I did not know what to make of this claim. Was this constitution the sui generis part? Was direct effect the sui generis part (apparently not …). Meanwhile from today's vantage point, legal scholars are finding global constitutions in many places so, again, I was looking for a very clear statement as to what, exactly, was unusual.

[37] Alter, 'The Global Spread of European Style International Courts' (n 35).

[38] Why the ECJ was so audacious is something I try to address in Alter, 'Jurist Advocacy Movements in Europe' (n 22); K Alter and L Helfer, 'Nature or Nurture: Judicial Lawmaking in the European Court of Justice and the Andean Tribunal of Justice' (2010) 64 *International Organization* 563.

[39] Alter, 'Jurist Advocacy Movements in Europe' (n 22); Alter and Helfer, 'Nature or Nurture' (n 38).

[40] Helfer and I compare the subject matter of preliminary ruling references in the first 25 years of European and Andean economic integration, demonstrating the wide range of issues that were litigated in Europe. KJ Alter and LR Helfer, *Transplanting International Courts: The Law and Politics of the Andean Tribunal of Justice* (Oxford, Oxford University Press, 2017).

stable from 1950 on, a stability that the Cold War can probably help to explain. This stability meant that national constitutions, judiciaries and political climates did not radically shift, so judges and legal scholars could afford to take legally and politically iconoclastic positions that in more volatile contexts might have been too risky. Other factors may have also been at play.

What I can see is that the Andean community and the Organisation for the Harmonisation of Business Law in Africa (Organisation pour l'Harmonisation en Afrique du Droit des Affaires (OHADA)) have both tried to replicate the EU's experience of integration-through-law, with much less success. The Andean community has officials writing books and teaching Andean law courses. A handful of Andean officials have served as legal advisors who help construct test cases, and the Andean Tribunal of Justice (ATJ) has been handed cases to help it build Andean law. There is also an Andean version of the EUI.[41] Allow me to plug for a moment my recent book with Laurence Helfer, *Transplanting International Courts: The Law and Politics of the Andean Tribunal of Justice*.[42] While the book is first and foremost about the Andean Tribunal, a direct replica of the ECJ, throughout it we contrast what happened in the Andes with the European experience. There are, as noted, many parallels, including the direct effect and supremacy of Andean law, but the Andean Tribunal never turned into the ECJ. We began by trying to explain the absence of Andean activism, and ended by concluding that the choices made by Andean judges are probably the more representative and prudent approach that most international judges follow.[43]

A second comparison could also involve OHADA, a system of regional commercial law in Francophone Africa that is also inspired by the EU's legal system (even if it is structured differently).[44] OHADA has helped to create 'OHADA clubs' throughout OHADA Member States and in France, and there is a special Training College for Judges, Magistrates and Prosecutors to train OHADA judges.[45] OHADA is also one of the most active international courts in the world, but like the ATJ, its Community Court of Justice and Arbitration is active but not activist.

In other words, the integration-through-law activism that this volume, and EU law scholarship more generally, now takes for granted is what makes the EU *sui generis*. Neofunctionalist theory famously expected an interest-driven integrationist logic to propel regional integration around the world.[46] If this story were true

---

[41] It is called Universidad de Los Andes. See at https://udelosandes.edu.bo/, last accessed 24 June 2020.

[42] See n 40.

[43] Alter and Helfer, *Transplanting International Courts* (n 40). Ch 4 examines the divergent law-building strategies, and the book's conclusion (esp at 272–74) considers why the Andean strategy was so different.

[44] I chose to ignore the Andean system and instead focus on OHADA and ECOWAS in Alter, 'The Global Spread of European Style International Courts' (n 35) 146.

[45] It is called the L'Ecole Régionale Supérieure de la Magistrature. See at https://www.ohada.org/index.php/fr/ecole-regionale-superieure-de-magistrature-ersuma/ersuma-en-bref, last visited June 24, 2020.

[46] Haas, 'International Integration' (n 35).

then the numerous copies of the ECJ would be more successful. These neofunctionalist expectations were thoroughly rejected by political scientists around the world, including Ernst Haas,[47] but then resurrected by legal scholars writing about Europe and the market-driven dynamics of legal integration.[48] Yet nowhere else in the world have I found international judges writing op-eds and articles in major papers to exhort their domestic counterparts (especially while judges are still in office) to act as community judges at home; they are not adding pregnant sentences to legal rulings that are then picked up and pushed by supranational officials; and there is much less of a mobilised and coordinated community of legal enablers. Because of this difference, a proper account of what occurred in Europe is going to need to explain why the various participants played their parts in the integration-through-law story, and exactly how 'typical' or 'unusual' these roles were. Current socio-legal accounts provide biographical histories of European individuals, but we are still missing the individual and institutional comparisons that might help us understand the social and cultural context that led European participants in the EEC project to conceive of their roles in larger terms, and that allowed so many actors to pick up and advance the legal integration ball in their own ways.[49]

## B. The International Institutional Complex in Europe

*Cassis de Dijon: 40 Years On* takes the study of mutual recognition beyond a focus on European market integration. As I noted, Schütze finds that GATT law rather than a *Dassonville* formula shaped the ECJ's jurisprudence before the *Cassis* ruling. Albors-Llorens considers how the doctrine established in the *Cassis* ruling migrated into competition law, not mutual recognition but the shift from a focus on form to effects, and the use of public interest objectives as a justification. Leinarte and Barnard consider mutual recognition agreements as tools of trade policy, and Baur explores how mutual recognition is applied in the EFTA context. Yet for the most part, EU law scholars still remain focused on European integration dynamics and how these dynamics radiate out beyond European borders. In other words, the study of European integration remains stubbornly EU-centric.

Part of the integration-through-law project was to create this EU-centrism through the myth of a separate and unique entity called 'community law'. If EU

---

[47] E Haas, *The Obsolescence of Regional Integration Theory* (Berkeley, CA, University of California Press, 1975); J Caporaso and J Keeler, 'The European Union and Regional Integration Theory' in C Rhodes and S Mazey (eds), *The State of the European Union*, vol 3 (Boulder, CO, Lynne Rienner/ Longmann, 1995).

[48] Burley and Mattli, 'Europe before the Court' (n 3); Stone Sweet, 'Judicialization and the Construction of Governance' (n 20); A Stone Sweet and T Brunell, 'Constructing a Supranational Constitution: Dispute Resolution and Governance in the European Community' (1998) 92 *American Political Science Review* 63; A Stone Sweet, *The Evolution of International Arbitration: Judicialization, Governance, Legitimacy*, 1st edn (Oxford, Oxford University Press, 2017).

[49] Early hints of an answer can be found in M Rask Madsen and A Vauchez, 'European Constitutionalism at the Cradle. Law and Lawyers in the Construction of a European Political Order (1920–1960)' in

law is its own entity, and a 'self-contained' system of law, then it only makes sense to study this law within its bubble. But if the idea of 'self-contained' law is itself a myth,[50] we need to examine the European legal strategy within the larger institutional complex it sits in.

The European integration process was part of a larger historical moment, and part of a number of international institutions. As a new crop of historians are documenting, the architects of the European integration project were people whose reputations were not tarnished by fascism and World War II. The group of elites who remained untarnished were in short supply, so their energies were deployed in many different directions. Many lawyers who became important in European legal integration were also involved in prosecuting war crimes following World War II. They were also involved in drafting the post-war international agreements and in working in post-war international institutions. And they were involved in the Council of Europe.[51] Historians are also documenting how ideas external to the EU were shaping what was done in the EU.[52] Schütze's chapter in this volume (chapter 2) provides one example, but there are many more.

When one thinks more about it, it is rather surprising how little scholarship on the EU says about the synergies and tensions between European integration, the GATT and the Council of Europe's human rights project. The literatures remain divided, and the pieces connecting these projects remain passing comments, if mentioned at all. In this sense, the new historiography is hewing too closely to, and

A Jettinghoff and H Schepel (eds), *In Lawyers' Circles Lawyers and European Legal Integration* (The Hague, Elzevir Reed, 2005); G Sacriste and A Vauchez, 'The Force of International Law: Lawyer's Diplomacy on the International Scene in the 1920s' (2007) 32 *Law & Social Inquiry* 83; P Lindseth, 'The Contradictions of Supranationalism: Administrative Governance and Constitutionalization in European Integration Since the 1950s' (2003) 37 *Loyola-Los Angeles Law Review* 363; A Boerger-De Smedt, 'La Court De Justice dans les Négociationis du Traité de Paris Instituant la Ceca' (2008) 14 *Journal of European History* 7; A Boerger-De Smedt, 'Negotiating the Foundations of European Law, 1950–1957: The Legal History of the Treaties of Paris and Rome' (2012) 21 *Contemporary European History* 339. I think there is more to find in connections to wartime and lustration experiences. There is also a growing role of the state that made judges uncomfortable. This growing role is discussed in A Shonfield, *Modern Capitalism* (Oxford, Oxford University Press, 1969); M Cappelletti, *The Judicial Process in Comparative Perspective* (Oxford, Claredon Press, 1989); P Lindseth, 'Always Embedded Administration: The Historical Evolution of Administrative Justice as an Aspect of Modern Governance in the Economy as Polity' in BSC Joerges, and P Wagner (eds), *The Economy as Polity* (London, UCL Press (Routledge-Cavendish), 2005); PL Lindseth, *Power and Legitimacy: Reconciling Europe and the Nation-State* (Oxford, Oxford University Press, 2010).

[50] The idea of a self-contained system is that a system of rules is a *lex specialis* that is both autonomous and exempt from larger (international) legal practices. The idea that any international legal regime is 'self-contained' is contested. See B Simma and D Pulkowski, 'Of Planets and the Universe: Self-Contained Regimes in International Law' (2006) 17 *European Journal of International Law* 483.

[51] See n 49's references to the work of Madsen, Vauchez, Boerger and Cohen, who write about these connections.

[52] Cf, eg, B Leucht and M Marquis, 'American influences on EEC competition law: Two paths, how much dependence?' in K Patel and H Schweitzer (eds), *The Historical Foundations of EU Competition Law* (Oxford, Oxford University Press, 2013) 125; K Patel and W Kaiser (eds), *Multiple Connections in European Cooperation: International Organizations, Policy Ideas, Practices and Transfers 1967–1992* (London, Routledge, 2018).

thereby reifying, the narratives of European legal integration that the proponents of these narratives created and to this day maintain.

What I am suggesting is that we start to think about how the EU was sui generis, and about how being embedded in a larger regime complex was itself shaping of EU policy and politics.[53] Historiographies will only find what the authors are looking for. My guess is that the connections between World War II and European integration will help to explain the ideologically driven legal activism; connections between European and the GATT law – following Schütze – will reveal much about the ECJ's early trade law jurisprudence; connections between European integration, the Cold War and NATO will help us understand the relative stability in Western Europe as a background condition facilitating European legal integration; and connections between the Cold War and the Council of Europe will be a more present part of the European integration story regarding human rights. Moreover, I suspect that European integration moves were intentionally designed with a chessboard-like understanding of how any European move impacted on and needed to be differentiated from these other projects.

I think it is time to move beyond a European particularist history. To be sure, there are pieces of European legal history that we still need to add, and *Cassis de Dijon: 40 Years On* is an example of what we can learn when we dig deeper into European history. What we learn is that the story is more complicated, and maybe even more contingent. But I am looking for a true global history of Europe, one that considers the importance of forces beyond Europe. Perhaps when we consider the Treaty of Rome at 75, or the *Cassis de Dijon* ruling at 50, scholars will search both within and without for insight into how the larger regional and international context shaped what European actors imagined, tried or strategised about.

---

[53] Sophie and I went on to focus on regime complexes, and the literature has since grown. See KJ Alter and S Meunier, 'The Politics of International Regime Complexity' (2009) 7 *Perspective on Politics* 13; KJ Alter and K Raustiala, 'The Rise of International Regime Complexity' (2018) 14 *The Annual Review of Law and Social Science* 329.

# INDEX

Milton Keynes UK
Ingram Content Group UK Ltd.
UKHW021439220823
427203UK00006B/160